TAKING SIDES

Clashing Views in

Crime and Criminology

SEVENTH EDITION

Selected, Edited, and with Introductions by

Thomas J. Hickey
University of Tampa

Mc Graw Hill **Contemporary Learning Series**

A Division of The McGraw-Hill Companies

*This book is dedicated to my wife Nancy; my son, Michael;
and my daughter, Megan. I love you.*

Photo Acknowledgment
Cover image: Corbis/Royalty Free

Cover Acknowledgment
Maggie Lytle

Manufactured in the United States of America

Seventh Edition

Library of Congress Cataloging-in-Publication Data
Main entry under title:
Taking sides: clashing views on controversial issues in crime and criminology/selected, edited, and
with introductions by Thomas J. Hickey.—7th ed.
Includes bibliographical references and index.
1. Crime and criminals. I. Hickey, Thomas J., *comp.*
364

0-07-319490-5
ISSN: 1098-5379

Printed on Recycled Paper

Clashing Views in

Crime and Criminology

SEVENTH EDITION

Thomas J. Hickey
University of Tampa

Advisory Board

Sue Titus Reid
Florida State University

Rolando v. del Carmen
Sam Houston State University

W. Wesley Johnson
Sam Houston State University

Richard Ayre
University of Maine, Presque Isle

Robert H. Whorf
Barry University School of Law

Barbara Sims
Penn State Harrisburg

Staff

Larry Loeppke
Managing Editor

Jill Peter
Senior Developmental Editor

Nichole Altman
Developmental Editor

Beth Kundert
Production Manager

Jane Mohr
Project Manager

Tara McDermott
Design Coordinator

Bonnie Coakley
Editorial Assistant

Lori Church
Permissions Coordinator

Luke David
eContent Coordinator

Preface

> But the peculiar evil of silencing the expression of an opinion is that it is robbing the human race, posterity as well as the existing generation—those who dissent from the opinion, still more than those who hold it. If the opinion is right, they are deprived of the opportunity of exchanging error for truth; if wrong, they lose, what is almost as great a benefit, the clearer perception and livelier impression of truth produced by its collision with error.
>
> —John Stuart Mill, *On Liberty*, 1859

Discussion and debate are essential components of the learning process. To have confidence in our viewpoints, we must expose them to others and learn from their ideas in a constant process of reformulation and refinement. As J.S. Mill teaches, only rarely does any point of view present a complete version of the truth; however, we move closer to the truth when we are willing to exchange our opinions with others, defend our positions, and refine our ideas by what we learn from an intellectual opponent.

This book presents students and teachers with an opportunity to exchange viewpoints by focusing on a series of controversial issues in crime and criminology. Few issues in modern society generate more substantial disagreement in our morning newspapers or around the dinner table. The topics in this book focus on an important aspect of modern life and were selected in an effort to engage students. Hopefully, they will also generate classroom discussion and debate and provide a vehicle for interactive learning.

Many of the topics presented in this volume are hotly contested. Few reflective people will find themselves adopting truly neutral positions on these issues, and there may be a tendency to embrace one side of a debate without fully considering the opposing arguments. As you read these materials, try to resist that temptation and keep an open mind. For example, if you are a death penalty advocate, think about how you would develop an argument against capital punishment. Even though such an exercise may not change your views, it will provide you with greater insight into the capital punishment debate.

Organization of the book This book considers 19 issues in crime and criminology and includes 38 articles presented in a pro and con format. The *Introduction* to each issue presents a synopsis and sets the stage for the *Yes* and *No* debate between the authors. All issues conclude with a *Postscript* that considers some of the more important points in the debate and includes up-to-date suggestions for further reading on the topics. In addition, the *On the Internet* page that accompanies each issue provides a list of Internet site addresses (URLs) that should prove informative. At the back of the book is a list of the *contributors to this volume*, which provides a short biographical sketch of each contributing author.

Changes to this edition   This edition of *Taking Sides* continues the tradition of providing a detailed analysis of contemporary issues in crime and criminology. Because this field changes so rapidly, however, it is important to reevaluate prior editions to determine if there are issues that have taken on a greater importance. Thus, considerable changes have been made to this edition. There are five new issues: "Is Criminal Behavior Biologically Determined?" (Issue 2); "Is Racial Profiling an Acceptable Law Enforcement Strategy?" (Issue 6); "Should Serious Sex Offenders Be Castrated?" (Issue 7); "Should Marijuana Be Legalized?" (Issue 16); and "Should Behavior Modification Techniques Be Used to Brainwash Criminals?" (Issue 19).

A word to the instructor   An *Instructor's Manual With Test Questions* (multiple-choice and essay) is available from the publisher for instructors using *Taking Sides* in their courses. A guidebook, *Using Taking Sides in the Classroom*, which considers methods and techniques for integrating the pro-con format into a classroom setting, is available as well. An online version of *Using Taking Sides in the Classroom* and a correspondence service for adopters can be found at `http://www.mhcls.com/usingts/`.

Acknowledgments   I would like to thank several of my friends and colleagues for their help and support: Jeff Klepfer, Steve Kucera, Dick Ayre, Joe O'Neill, Tony LaRose, Chris Capsambelis, Alisa Smith, Jim Beckman, Connie Rynder, and Steven Hekkanen. My research assistant, Kim Richardson, as always did a fine job.

Thomas J. Hickey
University of Tampa

Contents In Brief

Contents

Professor of management and public policy James Q. Wilson and the late psychologist Richard J. Herrnstein argue that crime studies should focus on street criminals. Philosophy professor Jeffrey Reiman contends that pollution, medical malpractice, and dangerous working conditions that go uncorrected are for more serious than street crime.

Janell D. Schmidt, supervisor of the Milwaukee County Child Protective Services, and criminology professor Lawrence W. Sherman argue that arresting batterers in many cases does more harm than good. Associate professor of public administration and social work Evan Stark contends that arresting batterers is a vital step for female empowerment and for women achieving full citizenship status.

Jared Taylor, president of the New Century Foundation, and the late psychology and neuroscience professor Glayde Whitney argue that the disparity in crimes committed by members of different races justifies racial profiling by the police. Professor Michael J. Lynch, however, argues that a proper analysis of the crime data does not support Taylor and Whitney's conclusions. He finds racial profiling to be objectionable from a legal and moral perspective as well.

Penny A. Robinette, an administrator at Presbyterian Child Welfare Services in Richmond, Kentucky, contends that mandatory testing and segregation of HIV-positive inmates is justified. Assistant professor of criminal justice Billy Long argues that mandatory testing and segregation of inmates will have more negative than positive consequences.

Assistant professor of criminal justice Jill Gordon identifies and defends several humanitarian and practical reasons for allowing family visitations in adult prisons. Associate professor of criminal justice Elizabeth H. McConnell maintains that there is little empirical support that conjugal visits are useful for either inmates or their families.

Professor of psychiatry Frank M. Ochberg argues that some violent offenders are incurable and should be confined for life to mental hospitals. Professor of psychiatry and law Howard Zonana contends that doctors have no business becoming jailers for those who are perceived as dangerous by legal authorities.

PART 4   CRIMINAL JUSTICE RESEARCH, EVALUATION, AND POLICY ANALYSIS   243

David Von Drehle, a writer and the arts editor for *The Washington Post,* examines specific capital punishment cases and data and concludes that capital punishment is a bad social policy. Ernest van den Haag, a professor of jurisprudence and public policy (now retired), maintains that the death penalty is just retribution for heinous crime.

John R. Lott, Jr., the John M. Olin Visiting Law and Economics Fellow at the University of Chicago Law School, contends that rather than increasing crime, gun ownership actually reduces it for several reasons. Franklin E. Zimring and Gordon Hawkins, director and senior fellow, respectively, of the Earl Warren Legal Institute, assert that possession and use of handguns causes the vastly disproportionate number of homicides in the United States.

George L. Kelling, a professor in the School of Criminal Justice at Rutgers University, and William J. Bratton, former New York City Police Department commissioner, strongly defend Kelling's formulation of zero tolerance/ broken windows theory and Bratton's implementation of Kelling's ideas. Judith A. Greene, senior fellow of the Institute on Criminal Justice of the University of Minnesota Law School, compares New York's policing style with San Diego's community policing model and argues that the latter is as effective and less costly.

PART 5   FUTURE TRENDS IN CRIMINOLOGY AND CRIMINAL JUSTICE   323

Ethan A. Nadelmann, the founder and director of the Drug Policy Alliance, contends that contemporary marijuana laws are unique among American criminal laws because no other law is both enforced so widely and yet deemed unnecessary by such a substantial portion of the public. Enforcing marijuana laws also wastes tens of billions of taxpayer dollars annually. John P. Walters, director of the Office of National Drug Control Policy, argues that marijuana does the most social harm of any illegal drug. Moreover, Walters asserts that the ultimate goal of those who advocate marijuana legalization is tolerated addiction.

Eugene H. Methvin, senior editor for *Reader's Digest,* contends that a very small number of juveniles and adults commit the majority of serious crimes. The main solution to the crime problem, then, is to identify them as early as possible and increase the punishments each time they offend, eventually incarcerating the repeat offenders. Professor of criminal justice David Shichor argues that "three strikes" laws are costly, inefficient, unfair, and do little to reduce crime.

Paul Butler, an associate professor at the George Washington University Law School, argues that black jurors should acquit black defendants of certain crimes to make up for inequities in the criminal justice system. Randall Kennedy, a professor at the Harvard Law School, finds it tragic that black jurors would pronounce a murderer "not guilty" just to send a message to white people.

The late University of Michigan psychologist James V. McConnell argues that society has the technology to brainwash criminals and turn them into productive citizens. Celebrated author the late Jessica Mitford contends, however, that sensory deprivation and other forms of behavior modification are immoral and constitute the legally sanctioned use of torture.

Introduction

The study of human behavior is a fascinating and complex enterprise. Throughout recorded history, people have speculated about the origins and causes of behavior. Early explanations focused on metaphysical forces, such as evil spirits or the devil, which were believed to somehow compel people to act. Later, the philosophers of the Enlightenment, including Jeremy Bentham and Jean Jacques Rosseau, who emphasized the rational nature of human behavior, believed that one's actions were freely chosen.

Based on this important idea, the early classical theorists maintained that crime could be controlled by making punishments associated with criminal behavior more painful than the pleasure that could be derived from the acts. Later, with the emergence of positivism, biological theories of human behavior became popular. Early biological positivists believed that a person's propensity for criminal behavior could be determined with simple measurements of physical features. For example, in the late nineteenth century, Cesare Lombroso, regarded by many to the father of modern criminology, believed that the length of a person's arms and the size of his teeth could indicate a criminal predisposition.

During the 1930s, sociological theories of criminal behavior became prominent in the United States. Theorists of the Chicago School of Sociology emphasized urban social conditions as the primary determinant of criminal behavior. The social policies that emerged from these theories became the driving force behind modern efforts to eradicate poverty, provide children with better educational opportunities, build stronger communities, and create better employment prospects for the poor. In fact, many of the crime-control strategies that emerged from the Chicago School have become cornerstones of American social policy in the twenty-first century. For example, even politically conservative social programs with attractive slogans such as "No child left behind" proceed directly from the assumption that adverse social conditions, such as those produced by bad schools, broken homes, single-parent families, a lack of parental attachment, and drug abuse lead directly to antisocial behavior.

While many U.S. social programs continued to assume a deterministic relationship between adverse social conditions and criminal behavior, a more conservative political climate began to emerge in the early 1970s. One influential criminologist, Robert Martinson, who had evaluated prison rehabilitation programs throughout the United States, concluded that they were largely ineffective. In the aftermath of these findings, as well as the realization that official measures of reported crime rates had increased during this period, conservative criminologists began to embrace a "new," more punitive approach to criminals and a return to the classical approach. This time, classical criminology was repackaged as rational choice theory.

James Q. Wilson, a UCLA political scientist, became one of the primary crusaders for the new classical movement. Wilson believes that regardless of the causes of criminal behavior, society must recognize the fact that "[w]icked people exist." Thus, the only solution is "to set them apart from innocent people."[1] The revised edition of his now-classic 1975 work, *Thinking About Crime,* outlined the foundations of the new classical philosophy:

[T]he rate of crime is influenced by its costs. It is possible to lower the crime rate by increasing the certainty of sanctions . . . the wisest course of action for society is to try simultaneously to increase both the benefits of non-crime and the costs of crime. . . .[2]

Other prominent criminologists also embraced the new conservative approach to crime prevention. Economist Andrew Von Hirsh developed a model of punishment termed "just deserts," which emphasizes that criminals should be punished simply because they have earned it. Moreover, Von Hirsh believes that punishing criminals can have a utilitarian effect: It helps to return society to a condition of equilibrium that is disrupted by crime. In addition, imitating the philosophies of Cesare Beccaria and Jeremy Bentham of the late eighteenth century, Von Hirsh asserts that principles of social justice require that all criminals who commit a particular offense should be punished in the same way.

Rational Choices, Irrational Policies?

Has rational choice theory produced irrational social policies? After three decades, the weight of the evidence suggests that it may have. According to some criminologists, the ideas of the new rational choice advocates were converted into draconian and regressive social policies by politicians eager to find reductionist, "sound bite" solutions to criminal behavior. The problem is that some of these policies have had disastrous consequences for the U.S. justice system. For example, during the early part of his presidency, Ronald Reagan, who had embraced James Q. Wilson's new classical criminology, declared a "war on drugs." Since it began, this initiative has emphasized stringent law enforcement, interdiction efforts, and increasing sanctions for drug law violations, including mandatory minimum sentencing policies. The results of these initiatives have been striking: From 1980 to 1997, the number of persons incarcerated for drug offenses has risen by approximately 1040 percent, an elevenfold increase.[3]

Recently, even very conservative social critics such as William F. Buckley, Jr., have questioned the wisdom of this so-called war on drugs. Stated Buckley:

What are the relative costs, on the one hand, of medical and psychological treatment for addicts and, on the other incarceration for drug offenses? [T]reatment is seven times more cost-effective. By this is meant that one dollar spent on the treatment of an addict reduces the probability of continued addiction seven times more than one dollar spent on incarceration. . . . [T]he cost of the drug war is many times more painful, in all its manifestations, than would be the licensing of drugs combined with intensive education of non-users and intensive education designed to warn those who experiment with drugs. . . . [I]t is outrageous to live in a society whose laws tolerate sending young people to life in prison because they grew, or distributed, a dozen ounces of marijuana.[4]

Data from a wide variety of sources, including the U.S. Department of Justice, appear to support Buckley's position. According to the Bureau of Justice Statistics, in 2000, 64.4 percent of the inmates confined in U.S. federal prisons and approximately 20.7 percent of those in state prisons were confined for drug law violations.[5] The costs of confining these individuals are a fiscal time bomb. At an average rate of $21,837.95 per inmate, per year in the federal prison system, the annual cost to confine the 72,764 incarcerated drug offenders is approximately $1.6 billion.[6] At an average cost of $20,261.15, the price tag to the states for confining drug offenders exceeds $50 billion annually.[7]

A related policy trend has been the passage of "three strikes" sentencing laws, which generally provide that an offender will receive a mandatory life prison sentence upon conviction of a third felony. Such laws are rapidly turning U.S. prisons into expensive retirement homes for an aging inmate population. One study has projected that in 2010, U.S. prisons will confine approximately 200,000 elderly inmates, who will require special treatment and advanced medical care.[8] At an average cost of $75,000 for each elderly inmate, that amounts to a price tag in the neighborhood of $15 billion annually.[9]

Furthermore, the Bureau of Justice Statistics has found that in 2000, persons 45 years of age or more, who comprise approximately 33 percent of the U.S. population, accounted for less than 10 percent of the serious crime arrests.[10] This finding is consistent with virtually all of the credible research that points to a very strong inverse relationship between age and crime. Thus, it makes very little sense to confine elderly inmates in U.S. prisons. In view of these policies, perhaps the new mantra for U.S. corrections will become: "Three strikes, we're out of money."

Moreover, the preceding discussion considered only the direct costs of imprisoning large numbers of nonviolent offenders. The indirect costs of confining these individuals may be substantially greater still. According to criminologist Todd Clear, "The removal of offenders who pose no risk to society can deplete valued resources, a particularly costly outcome for already disadvantaged neighborhoods." One must also question the wisdom of non-violent offender confinement policies that produce single-parent households, financial instability, and social disorganization in many of our nation's poorest neighborhoods. As one of my students has cogently observed, "It's hard to coach your kid's basketball team from the inside of a prison."

Several important questions emerge logically from the preceding analysis: Are we utilizing justice system policies that simply don't work? Are governmental budgets so flush with cash that we can afford to fill our prisons with nonviolent inmates who present little genuine threat to society? Are we wasting our money on failed crime-control policies when we could better spend it providing shelter for homeless families, affordable health care for the poor, or a better education for our children? Are we as a society being sold a "bill of goods" by persons masquerading as experts who have a vested interest in keeping the current system the way it is?

Answers to the preceding questions must emerge from the systematic scientific study of crime and human behavior. Moreover, although there is much that we still have to learn, substantial progress has already been made.

Rational Justice System Policies that Work

Our thinking about crime has often been preoccupied with the idea of "causation." Voluminous research into crime and criminality demonstrates conclusively, however, that social scientists are on much more solid footing when they identify factors that correlate with higher crime rates. For example, while it would be inaccurate to state that "drinking alcohol causes crime" (because not all people who drink alcohol commit crimes), it would be quite accurate to suggest that alcohol consumption correlates with higher crime rates. Moreover, a great deal of solid research suggests that the relationship is a compelling one.

There are other things we know about crime as well, although once again, the relationships are best described as correlations, rather than causes. While far from exhaustive, the following list of factors that appear to correlate with higher crime rates is instructive:

- Broken homes produce more criminals than two-parent families.
- People learn to commit crime; therefore, many children who are abused by their parents are more likely to become abusive adults.
- Children need a structured home environment in order to develop their full human potential.
- The ingestion of lead paint by children is strongly related to low intelligence and failure in school.
- Substance abuse (including alcohol and illegal drugs) is related to criminal behavior.
- Deteriorated urban areas have higher crime rates.
- African-Americans and members of other minority groups are more often arrested and processed in our justice system.
- Women commit less crime than men, but the rate of female offending is increasing.
- Older people commit less crime than young persons.
- People tend to drift in and out of conventional and criminal behavior.
- Areas that have developed a sense of "community" have lower crime rates.
- Some human behavior may have a biological/genetic basis. Punishing such behaviors may be a waste of time and resources.

What we do know about crime and criminality should be used to develop effective social policies. For example, if poor nutrition is related to deficient school performance, policies that provide children from low-income homes with an adequate breakfast make a great deal of sense.

While spending on prisons has skyrocketed under the current Bush administration, nutritional programs have been gutted. It may be that such "liberal" policies are inconsistent with a conservative ideology stressing "just deserts" and social Darwinism. In the long run, however, providing children with a nutritious breakfast, better schools, and a stronger sense of community affiliation may be far cheaper than incarcerating them in prison for the rest of their lives.

Circularity in Our Study of Crime and Justice—Old Becomes New Once Again

To paraphrase George Santayana, "Those who cannot remember the lessons of history are condemned to repeat it." It is hard to study the history of crime and criminality and fail to notice a striking circularity in criminological theory. To illustrate, the Classical approach, which originated in the late eighteenth century, emphasized free will and a utilitarian approach to punishment. The early classicists also urged the elimination of judicial sentencing discretion, adoption of determinate sentencing laws, and the use of imprisonment as a form of punishment. Rational choice proponents also emphasize free will and a utilitarian approach to punishing criminals. Furthermore, the determinate sentencing laws that have been adopted by many states and the federal government virtually eliminate judicial sentencing discretion.

Just as classical criminology reemerged during the 1970s, biological positivism has reappeared more recently. Although the theories of the nineteenth and twentieth century positivists were interesting and novel in their time, their technical ability to measure and quantify their findings in a scientifically accurate way was very limited. As we begin the new millennium, we may be witnessing the development of a new biological positivism in criminology, one that emphasizes the interaction of genetic and environmental forces to produce human behavior. This time, however, our scientific measurement capabilities may actually have evolved to the point we will be able to draw meaningful conclusions about how biological factors interact with environmental forces to produce human behavior. In fact, we may be at the cutting edge of the emergence of a truly "new criminology," which emphasizes a synthesis of biological and social forces that produce human behavior.

In any case, it is an exciting time to be engaged in the study of criminal behavior. Criminology in the twenty-first century may provide us with the opportunity to learn to creatively manage human behavior in a way that is more consistent with human value and dignity. In the years ahead, criminologists will be called upon to provide honest answers to important policy questions that will have a substantial impact on the quality of life in the United States. We can only hope that those entrusted to develop enlightened social policies based on the answers we provide will learn history's lessons and resist the temptation to embrace politically expedient solutions that will eventually be exposed as expensive policy failures.

References

1. James Q. Wilson, *Thinking About Crime*, rev. ed. (New York: Vintage Books, 1983), p. 128.
2. Ibid., p. 143.
3. Center on Juvenile and Criminal Justice Executive Summary, "Poor Prescription: The Costs of Imprisoning Drug Offenders in the United States," (San Francisco: July 2000).
4. William F. Buckley, Jr., "The War on Drugs Is Lost," *The National Review* (February 12, 1996).
5. Bureau of Justice Statistics, *Sourcebook of Criminal Justice Statistics 2001* (Washington, D.C.: U.S. Department of Justice, 2002).
6. George M. Camp and Camille Graham Camp, *The Corrections Yearbook, 1998* (Middletown, CT: Criminal Justice Institute, 1999).
7. Ibid.
8. Herbert J. Hoelter, "Proceedings: Technologies for Successful Aging: Institutional Issues," *Journal of Rehabilitation Research and Development* (Washington, D.C.: Vol. 38, issue 1, pg. S38, 2001).
9. Ibid.
10. Ibid., note 5, at 345.

On the Internet . . .

The Critical Criminology Division of the ASC

This site of the American Society of Criminology links to basic criminology sources and to resources developed within a critical sociology framework.

http://sun.soci.niu.edu/~critcrim/

National Crime Victims Research and Treatment Center

This site, sponsored by the National Crime Victims Research and Treatment Center of the Medical University of South Carolina, describes the work of the center and provides an excellent list of related resources.

http://www.musc.edu/cvc/

Criminal Justice Sources

This site features an extensive list of criminal justice links compiled by Dr. Matthew Robinson of Appalachian State University. Categories include crime data, criminal law, criminological theory, and law enforcement.

http://www.acs.appstate.edu/dept/ps-cj/
cj-sour.html

PART 1

Definitions and Explanations of Crime

*E*xactly what is crime, who commits crime, and why, where, when, and how crimes are committed remain core questions for the public, criminal justice practitioners, and scholars alike. It would seem that defining crime, as well as explaining crime, is a straightforward matter. In reality, definitions, explanations, and even assessments of the harm that criminals do is problematic. Some experts, for instance, contend that crime is necessary and functional in all societies. Others say that society is concerned about the wrong kinds of crime. These questions are important for criminologists and policymakers.

- Is Crime Always Functional?

- Is Criminal Behavior Biologically Determined?

- Does IQ Significantly Contribute to Crime?

- Is Street Crime More Serious Than White-Collar Crime?

ISSUE 1

Is Crime Always Functional?

YES: Emile Durkheim, from *The Rules of Sociological Method* (Free Press, 1938)

NO: Daniel Patrick Moynihan, from "Defining Deviancy Down," *The American Scholar* (Winter 1993)

ISSUE SUMMARY

YES: Classic sociologist Emile Durkheim (1858–1917) theorizes that crime exists in all societies because it reaffirms moral boundaries and at times assists needed social changes.

NO: Former U.S. Senator Daniel Patrick Moynihan (D-NY) worries that Durkheim's thinking omits the possibility of "too much crime," especially violent crime, so that deviancy as a serious societal problem is not addressed.

What is crime? Who commits it? And why? The importance given to these questions, and their answers, varies among different categories of people, although there is little certainty that any one group's meanings and interpretations are superior to those of another.

For example, younger and older people have different perceptions of crime (older people are more likely to fear crime, even though younger people are far more likely to be victims of crime). Public officials also disagree about crime. During election years many politicians have inflated the number of crimes committed and have attributed crime to forces and influences that only the politicians, if elected, can combat.

Criminological and criminal justice scholars, although generally slightly less shrill and self-serving than politicians in their definitions and explanations of crime, are also very likely to disagree among themselves about what crime is and what its causes are. Unlike politicians, they do not follow four-year cycles in their crime conceptualizations, but they do reflect trends. For example, 20 years ago most criminologists probably reflected a liberal ideology in their crime explanations and suggested treatments. Today some are more likely to reflect an ideologically conservative scholarly bias. Radical or Marxist criminologists continue to have a marginal position within the discipline.

The seminal essay by Emile Durkheim, excerpted in the first of the following selections, argues that deviancy, including crime, is functional and exists in all societies because it is needed to establish moral boundaries and to distinguish between those who obey and those who disobey society's rules. Although it was written almost 100 years ago, Durkheim's original structural or sociological approach continues to be relied on by criminological and criminal justice scholars.

There are, of course, many variants of the sociological approach to crime, its definitions, and its causes. However, Durkheim's approach is central for many criminologists and especially *structural functionalists*. Structural functionalists attempt to determine what patterns of interaction or structures exist in various groups. They investigate what these patterns contribute to the maintenance of a group and of the society to which the group belongs. In the United States, for example, dating patterns and their relation to marriage are studied. Marriage patterns and their relation to the economy, to religion, and so on are traced. In addition, structural functionalists want to know about the consequences of patterns of behavior for groups, for members of groups, and for society as a whole. Such consequences can be both positive and negative, intentional and unintentional.

Durkheim selects a pattern of behavior, in this case deviant acts, and attempts to determine what it contributes to the maintenance of society and what its consequences might be, including intended and unintended ones. Durkheim asserts that crime is functional (not necessarily good and certainly not to be encouraged) and helps to establish moral boundaries. Deviant acts also provide a sense of propriety and a feeling of righteousness for those who do not commit crimes, as they share sentiments of moral indignation about those who do violate society's norms. Durkheim says that crime also allows for a social change. It prevents a society from having too much rigidity and from becoming too slavish in its obedience to norms.

In the second selection, politician and sociologist Daniel Patrick Moynihan acknowledges his debt to Durkheim and to sociologist Kai T. Erikson, a follower of some of Durkheim's ideas. But he questions the soundness of Durkheim's contention that crime is functional for societies, especially in the context of violence-ridden 1990s America. Moynihan argues that on the one hand, certain classes of relatively harmless behavior are nowadays being defined as deviant, if not criminal (dysfunctional contraction of moral boundaries). On the other hand, and far more serious to Moynihan, moral boundaries are becoming too elastic as society expands its tolerance for serious crime. He asks, How can deviancy be said to be functional if citizens are no longer shocked by outrageous violence?

As you read the selections by Durkheim and Moynihan, consider examples from your life in which a type of deviancy might be functional or an act that might have been viewed as criminal a generation ago but that is no longer viewed that way. In addition, what types of acts do you tolerate today that would have been morally outrageous to your grandparents? Have society's legal and ethical boundaries become "too elastic"?

The Normal and the Pathological

Crime is present not only in the majority of societies of one particular species but in all societies of all types. There is no society that is not confronted with the problem of criminality. Its form changes; the acts thus characterized are not the same everywhere; but, everywhere and always, there have been men who have behaved in such a way as to draw upon themselves penal repression. If, in proportion as societies pass from the lower to the higher types, the rate of criminality, i.e., the relation between the yearly number of crimes and the population, tended to decline, it might be believed that crime, while still normal, is tending to lose this character of normality. But we have no reason to believe that such a regression is substantiated. Many facts would seem rather to indicate a movement in the opposite direction. From the beginning of the [nineteenth] century, statistics enable us to follow the course of criminality. It has everywhere increased. In France the increase is nearly 300 percent. There is, then, no phenomenon that presents more indisputably all the symptoms of normality, since it appears closely connected with the conditions of all collective life. To make of crime a form of social morbidity would be to admit that morbidity is not something accidental, but, on the contrary, that in certain cases it grows out of the fundamental constitution of the living organism; it would result in wiping out all distinction between the physiological and the pathological. No doubt it is possible that crime itself will have abnormal forms, as, for example, when its rate is unusually high. This excess is, indeed, undoubtedly morbid in nature. What is normal, simply, is the existence of criminality, provided that it attains and does not exceed, for each social type, a certain level, which it is perhaps not impossible to fix in conformity with the preceding rules.[1]

Here we are, then, in the presence of a conclusion in appearance quite paradoxical. Let us make no mistake. To classify crime among the phenomena of normal sociology is not to say merely that it is an inevitable, although regrettable phenomenon, due to the incorrigible wickedness of men; it is to affirm that it is a factor in public health, an integral part of all healthy societies. This result is, at first glance, surprising enough to have puzzled even ourselves for a long time. Once this first surprise has been overcome, however, it is not difficult to find reasons explaining this normality and at the same time confirming it.

In the first place crime is normal because a society exempt from it is utterly impossible. Crime, we have shown elsewhere, consists of an act that offends certain very strong collective sentiments. In a society in which criminal acts are no longer committed, the sentiments they offend would have to be found without exception in all individual consciousnesses, and they must be found to exist with the same degree as sentiments contrary to them. Assuming that this condition could actually be realized, crime would not thereby disappear; it would only change its form, for the very cause which would thus dry up the sources of criminality would immediately open up new ones.

Indeed, for the collective sentiments which are protected by the penal law of a people at a specified moment of its history to take possession of the public conscience or for them to acquire a stronger hold where they have an insufficient grip, they must acquire an intensity greater than that which they had hitherto had. The community as a whole must experience them more vividly, for it can acquire from no other source the greater force necessary to control these individuals who formerly were the most refractory. For murderers to disappear, the horror of bloodshed must become greater in those social strata from which murderers are recruited; but, first it must become greater throughout the entire society. Moreover, the very absence of crime would directly contribute to produce this horror; because any sentiment seems much more respectable when it is always and uniformly respected.

One easily overlooks the consideration that these strong states of the common consciousness cannot be thus reinforced without reinforcing at the same time the more feeble states, whose violation previously gave birth to mere infraction of convention—since the weaker ones are only the prolongation, the attenuated form, of the stronger. Thus robbery and simple bad taste injure the same single altruistic sentiment, the respect for that which is another's. However, this same sentiment is less grievously offended by bad taste than by robbery; and since, in addition, the average consciousness had not sufficient intensity to react keenly to the bad taste, it is treated with greater tolerance. That is why the person guilty of bad taste is merely blamed, whereas the thief is punished. But, if this sentiment grows stronger, to the point of silencing in all consciousnesses the inclination which disposes man to steal, he will become more sensitive to the offenses which, until then, touched him but lightly. He will react against them, then, with more energy; they will be the object of greater opprobrium, which will transform certain of them from the simple moral faults that they were and give them the quality of crimes. For example, improper contracts, or contracts improperly executed, which only incur public blame or civil damages, will become offenses in law.

Imagine a society of saints, a perfect cloister of exemplary individuals. Crimes, properly so called, will there be unknown; but faults which appear venial to the layman will create there the same scandal that the ordinary offense does in ordinary consciousnesses. If, then, this society has the power to judge and punish, it will define these acts as criminal and will treat them as such. For the same reason, the perfect and upright man judges his smallest failings with a severity that the majority reserve for acts more truly in the nature of an offense. Formerly, acts of violence against persons were more frequent than they are today, because respect for individual dignity was less strong. As this has increased, these crimes have become more rare; and also, many acts violating this sentiment have been introduced into the penal law which were not included there in primitive times.[2]

In order to exhaust all the hypotheses logically possible, it will perhaps be asked why this unanimity does not extend to all collective sentiments without exception. Why should not even the most feeble sentiment gather enough energy to prevent all dissent? The moral consciousness of the society would be present in its entirety in all the individuals, with a vitality sufficient to prevent all acts offending it—the purely conventional faults as well as the crimes. But a uniformity so universal and absolute is utterly impossible; for the immediate physical milieu in which each one of us is placed, the hereditary antecedents, and the social influences vary from one individual to the next, and consequently diversify consciousnesses. It is impossible for all to be alike, if only because each one has his own organism and that these organisms occupy different areas in space. That is why, even among the lower peoples, where individual originality is very little developed, it nevertheless does exist.

Thus, since there cannot be a society in which the individuals do not differ more or less from the collective type, it is also inevitable that, among these divergences, there are some with a criminal character. What confers this character upon them is not the intrinsic quality of a given act but that definition which the collective conscience lends them. If the collective conscience is stronger, if it has enough authority practically to suppress these divergences, it will also be more sensitive, more exacting; and, reacting against the slightest deviations with the energy it otherwise displays only against more considerable infractions, it will attribute to them the same gravity as formerly to crimes. In other words, it will designate them as criminal.

Crime is, then, necessary; it is bound up with fundamental conditions of all social life, and by that very fact it is useful, because these conditions of which it is a part are themselves indispensable to the normal evolution of morality and law.

Indeed, it is no longer possible today to dispute the fact that law and morality vary from one social type to the next, nor that they change within the same type if the conditions of life are modified. But, in order that these transformations may be possible, the collective sentiments at the basis of morality must not be hostile to change, and consequently must have but moderate energy. If they were too strong, they would no longer be plastic. Every pattern is an obstacle to new patterns, to the extent that the first pattern is inflexible. The better a structure is articulated, the more it offers a healthy resistance to all modification; and this is equally true of functional, as of anatomical, organization. If there were no crimes, this condition could not have been fulfilled; for such a hypothesis presupposes that collective sentiments have arrived at a degree of intensity unexampled in history. Nothing is good indefinitely and to an unlimited extent. The authority which the moral conscience enjoys must not be excessive; otherwise no one would dare criticize it, and it would too easily congeal into an immutable form. To make progress, individual originality must be able to express itself. In order that the originality of the idealist whose dreams transcend this century may find expression, it is necessary that the originality of the criminal, who is below the level of his time, shall also be possible. One does not occur without the other.

Nor is this all. Aside from this indirect utility, it happens that crime itself plays a useful role in this evolution. Crime implies not only that the way remains open to necessary changes but that in certain cases it directly prepares these changes. Where crime exists, collective sentiments are sufficiently flexible to take on a new form, and crime sometimes helps to determine the form they will take. How many times, indeed, it is only an anticipation of future morality—a step toward what will be! According to Athenian law, Socrates was a criminal, and his condemnation was no more than just. However, his crime, namely, the independence of this thought, rendered a service not only to humanity but to his country. It served to prepare a new morality and faith which the Athenians needed, since the traditions by which they had lived until then were no longer in harmony with the current conditions of life. Nor is the case of Socrates unique; it is reproduced periodically in history. It would never have been possible to establish the freedom of thought we now enjoy if the regulations prohibiting it had not been violated before being solemnly abrogated. At that time, however, the violation was a crime, since it was an offense against sentiments still very keen in the average conscience. And yet this crime was useful as a prelude to reforms which daily become more necessary. Liberal philosophy had as its precursors the heretics of all kinds who were justly punished by secular authorities during the entire course of the Middle Ages and until the eve of modern times.

From this point of view the fundamental facts of criminality present themselves to us in an entirely new light. Contrary to current ideas, the criminal no longer seems a totally unsociable being, a sort of parasitic element, a strange and unassimilable body, introduced into the midst of society.[3] On the contrary, he plays a definite role in social life. Crime, for its part, must no longer be conceived as an evil that cannot be too much suppressed. There is no occasion for self-congratulation when the crime rate drops noticeably below the average level, for we may be certain that this apparent progress is associated with some social disorder. Thus, the number of assault cases never falls so low as in times of want.[4] With the drop in the crime rate, and as a reaction to it, comes a revision, or the need of a revision in the theory of punishment. If, indeed, crime is a disease, its punishment is its remedy and cannot be otherwise conceived; thus, all the discussions it arouses bear on the point of determining what the punishment must be in order to fulfil this role of remedy. If crime is not pathological at all, the object of punishment cannot be to cure it, and its true function must be sought elsewhere.

Notes

1. From the fact that crime is a phenomenon of normal sociology, it does not follow that the criminal is an individual normally constituted from the biological and psychological points of view. The two questions are independent of each other. This independence will be better understood when we have shown, later on, the difference between psychological and sociological facts.

2. Calumny, insults, slander, fraud, etc.

3. We have ourselves committed the error of speaking thus of the criminal, because of a failure to apply our rule (*Division du travail social*, pp. 395–96).

4. Although crime is a fact of normal sociology, it does not follow that we must not abhor it. Pain itself has nothing desirable about it; the individual dislikes it as society does crime, and yet it is a function of normal physiology. Not only is it necessarily derived from the very constitution of every living organism, but it plays a useful role in life, for which reason it cannot be replaced. It would, then, be a singular distortion of our thought to present it as an apology for crime. We would not even think of protesting against such an interpretation, did we not know to what strange accusations and misunderstandings one exposes oneself when one undertakes to study moral facts objectively and to speak of them in a different language from that of the layman.

NO

Daniel Patrick Moynihan

Defining Deviancy Down

In one of the founding texts of sociology, *The Rules of Sociological Method* (1895), Emile Durkheim set it down that "crime is normal." "It is," he wrote, "completely impossible for any society entirely free of it to exist." By defining what is deviant, we are enabled to know what is not, and hence to live by shared standards. . . . Durkheim writes:

> From this viewpoint the fundamental facts of criminology appear to us in an entirely new light. . . . [T]he criminal no longer appears as an utterly unsociable creature, a sort of parasitic element, a foreign, inassimilable body introduced into the bosom of society. He plays a normal role in social life. For its part, crime must no longer be conceived of as an evil which cannot be circumscribed closely enough. Far from there being cause for congratulation when it drops too noticeably below the normal level, this apparent progress assuredly coincides with and is linked to some social disturbance.

Durkheim suggests, for example, that "in times of scarcity" crimes of assault drop off. He does not imply that we ought to approve of crime—"[p]ain has likewise nothing desirable about it"—but we need to understand its function. He saw religion, in the sociologist Randall Collins's terms, as "fundamentally a set of ceremonial actions, assembling the group, heightening its emotions, and focusing its members on symbols of their common belongingness." In this context "a punishment ceremony creates social solidarity."

The matter was pretty much left at that until seventy years later when, in 1965, Kai T. Erikson published *Wayward Puritans*, a study of "crime rates" in the Massachusetts Bay Colony. The plan behind the book, as Erikson put it, was "to test [Durkheim's] notion that the number of deviant offenders a community can afford to recognize is likely to remain stable over time." The notion proved out very well indeed. Despite occasional crime waves, as when itinerant Quakers refused to take off their hats in the presence of magistrates, the amount of deviance in this corner of seventeenth-century New England fitted nicely with the supply of stocks and shipping posts. Erikson remarks:

> It is one of the arguments of the . . . study that the amount of deviation a community encounters is apt to remain fairly constant over time. To start

From Daniel Patrick Moynihan, "Defining Deviancy Down," *The American Scholar*, vol. 62, no. 1 (Winter 1993). Copyright © 1992 by Daniel Patrick Moynihan. Reprinted by permission of *The American Scholar*.

at the beginning, it is a simple logistic fact that the number of deviancies which come to a community's attention are limited by the kinds of equipment it uses to detect and handle them, and to that extent the rate of deviation found in a community is at least in part a function of the size and complexity of its social control apparatus. A community's capacity for handling deviance, let us say, can be roughly estimated by counting its prison cells and hospital beds, its policemen and psychiatrists, its courts and clinics. Most communities, it would seem, operate with the expectation that a relatively constant number of control agents is necessary to cope with a relatively constant number of offenders. The amount of men, money, and material assigned by society to "do something" about deviant behavior does not vary appreciably over time, and the implicit logic which governs the community's efforts to man a police force or maintain suitable facilities for the mentally ill seems to be that there is a fairly stable quota of trouble which should be anticipated.

In this sense, the agencies of control often seem to define their job as that of keeping deviance within bounds rather than that of obliterating it altogether. Many judges, for example, assume that severe punishments are a greater deterrent to crime than moderate ones, and so it is important to note that many of them are apt to impose harder penalties when crime seems to be on the increase and more lenient ones when it does not, almost as if the power of the bench were being used to keep the crime rate from getting out of hand.

Erikson was taking issue with what he described as "a dominant strain in sociological thinking" that took for granted that a well-structured society "is somehow designed to prevent deviant behavior from occurring." In both authors, Durkheim and Erikson, there is an undertone that suggests that, with deviancy, as with most social goods, there is the continuing problem of demand exceeding supply. Durkheim invites us to

imagine a society of saints, a perfect cloister of exemplary individuals. Crimes, properly so called, will there be unknown; but faults which appear venial to the layman will create there the same scandal that the ordinary offense does in ordinary consciousness. If, then, this society has the power to judge and punish, it will define these acts as criminal and will treat them as such.

Recall Durkheim's comment that there need be no cause for congratulations should the amount of crime drop "too noticeably below the normal level." It would not appear that Durkheim anywhere contemplates the possibility of too much crime. Clearly his theory would have required him to deplore such a development, but the possibility seems never to have occurred to him.

Erikson, writing much later in the twentieth century, contemplates both possibilities. "Deviant persons can be said to supply needed services to society." There is no doubt a tendency for the supply of any needed thing to run short. But he is consistent. There can, he believes, be *too much* of a good thing. Hence "the number of deviant offenders a community can *afford* to recognize is likely to remain stable over time." [My emphasis]

Social scientists are said to be on the lookout for poor fellows getting a bum rap. But here is a theory that clearly implies that there are circumstances in which society will choose *not* to notice behavior that would be otherwise controlled, or disapproved, or even punished.

It appears to me that this is in fact what we in the United States have been doing of late. I proffer the thesis that, over the past generation, since the time Erikson wrote, the amount of deviant behavior in American society has increased beyond the levels the community can "afford to recognize" and that, accordingly, we have been re-defining deviancy so as to exempt much conduct previously stigmatized, and also quietly raising the "normal" level in categories where behavior is now abnormal by any earlier standard. This redefining has evoked fierce resistance from defenders of "old" standards, and accounts for much of the present "cultural war" such as proclaimed by many at the 1992 Republican National Convention.

Let me, then, offer three categories of redefinition in these regards: the *altruistic*, the *opportunistic*, and the *normalizing*.

The first category, the *altruistic*, may be illustrated by the deinstitutionalization movement within the mental health profession that appeared in the 1950s. The second category, the *opportunistic*, seen in the interest group rewards derived from the acceptance of "alternative" family structures. The third category, the *normalizing*, is to be observed in the growing acceptance of unprecedented levels of violent crime. . . .

Our *normalizing* category most directly corresponds to Erikson's proposition that "the number of deviant offenders a community can afford to recognize is likely to remain stable over time." Here we are dealing with the popular psychological notion of "denial." In 1965, having reached the conclusion that there would be a dramatic increase in single-parent families, I reached the further conclusion that this would in turn lead to a dramatic increase in crime. In an article in *America*, I wrote:

> From the wild Irish slums of the 19th century Eastern seaboard to the riot-torn suburbs of Los Angeles, there is one unmistakable lesson in American history: a community that allows a large number of young men to grow up in broken families, dominated by women, never acquiring any stable relationship to male authority, never acquiring any set of rational expectations about the future—that community asks for and gets chaos. Crime, violence, unrest, unrestrained lashing out at the whole social structure—that is not only to be expected; it is very near to inevitable.

The inevitable, as we now know, has come to pass, but here again our response is curiously passive. Crime is a more or less continuous subject of political pronouncement, and from time to time it will be at or near the top of opinion polls as a matter of public concern. But it never gets much further than that. In the words spoken from the bench, Judge Edwin Torres of the New York State Supreme Court, Twelfth Judicial District, described how "the slaughter of the innocent marches unabated: subway riders, bodega owners, can drivers, babies; in laundromats, at cash machines, on elevators, in hallways." In personal communication, he writes: "This numbness, this near narcoleptic state can diminish the human condition to the level of combat infantrymen, who, in protracted campaigns, can eat their battlefield rations seated on the bodies of the fallen, friend and foe alike. A society that loses its sense of outrage is doomed to extinction." There is no expectation that this will change, nor any efficacious public insistence that it do so. The crime level has been *normalized.*

Consider the St. Valentine's Day Massacre. In 1929 in Chicago during Prohibition, four gangsters killed seven gangsters on February 14. The nation was shocked. The event became legend. It merits not one but two entries in the *World Book Encyclopedia.* I leave it to others to judge, but it would appear that the society in the 1920s was simply not willing to put up with this degree of deviancy. In the end, the Constitution was amended, and Prohibition, which lay behind so much gangster violence, ended.

In recent years, again in the context of illegal traffic in controlled substances, this form of murder has returned. But it has done so at a level that induces denial. James Q. Wilson comments that Los Angeles has the equivalent of a St. Valentine's Day Massacre every weekend. Even the most ghastly re-enactments of such human slaughter produce only moderate responses. On the morning after the close of the Democratic National Convention in New York City in July, there was such an account in the second section of the *New York Times.* It was not a big story; bottom of the page, but with a headline that got your attention. "3 Slain in Bronx Apartment, but a Baby is Saved." A subhead continued: "A mother's last act was to hide her little girl under the bed." The article described a drug execution; the now-routine blindfolds made from duct tape; a man and a woman and a teenager involved. "Each had been shot once in the head." The police had found them a day later. They also found, under a bed, a three-month-old baby, dehydrated but alive. A lieutenant remarked of the mother, "In her last dying act she protected her baby. She probably knew she was going to die, so she stuffed the baby where she knew it would be safe." But the matter was left there. The police would do their best. But the event passed quickly; forgotten by the next day, it will never make *World Book.*

Nor is it likely that any great heed will be paid to an uncanny reenactment of the Prohibition drama a few months later, also in the Bronx. The *Times* story, page B3, reported:

9 Men Posing as Police
Are Indicted in 3 Murders
Drug Dealers Were Kidnapped for Ransom

The *Daily News* story, same day, page 17, made it *four* murders, adding nice details about torture techniques. The gang members posed as federal Drug Enforcement Administration agents, real badges and all. The victims were drug dealers, whose families were uneasy about calling the police. Ransom seems generally to have been set in the $650,000 range. Some paid. Some got it in the back of the head. So it goes.

Yet, violent killings, often random, go on unabated. Peaks continue to attract some notice. But these are peaks above "average" levels that thirty years ago would have been thought epidemic.

LOS ANGELES, AUG. 24. (Reuters) Twenty-two people were killed in Los Angeles over the weekend, the worst period of violence in the city since it was ravaged by riots earlier this year, the police said today.

Twenty-four others were wounded by gunfire or stabbings, including a 19-year old woman in a wheelchair who was shot in the back when she failed to respond to a motorist who asked for directions in south Los Angeles.

["The guy stuck a gun out of the window and just fired at her," said a police spokesman, Lieut. David Rock. The woman was later described as being in stable condition.

Among those who died was an off-duty officer, shot while investigating reports of a prowler in a neighbor's yard, and a Little League baseball coach who had argued with the father of a boy he was coaching.]

The police said at least nine of the deaths were gang-related, including that of a 14-year old girl killed in a fight between rival gangs.

Fifty-one people were killed in three days of rioting that started April 29 after the acquittal of four police officers in the beating of Rodney G. King.

Los Angeles usually has above-average violence during August, but the police were at a loss to explain the sudden rise. On an average weekend in August, 14 fatalities occur.

Not to be outdone, two days later the poor Bronx came up with a near record, as reported in *New York Newsday*:

Armed with 9-mm. pistols, shotguns and M-16 rifles, a group of masked men and women poured out of two vehicles in the South Bronx early yesterday and sprayed a stretch of Longwood Avenue with a fustillade of bullets, injuring 12 people.

A Kai Erikson of the future will surely need to know that the Department of Justice in 1990 found that Americans reported only about 38 percent of all crimes and 48 percent of violent crimes. This, too, can be seen as a means of *normalizing* crime. In much the same way, the vocabulary of crime reporting can be seen to move toward the normal-seeming. A teacher is shot on her way to class. The *Times* subhead reads: "Struck in the Shoulder in the Year's First Shooting Inside a School." First of the season.

It is too early, however, to know how to regard the arrival of the doctors on the scene declaring crime a "public health emergency." The June 10, 1992, issue of the *Journal of the American Medical Association* was devoted entirely to papers on the subject of violence, principally violence associated with firearms. An editorial in the issue signed by former Surgeon General C. Everett Koop and Dr. George D. Lundberg is entitled: "Violence in America: A Public Health Emergency." Their proposition is admirably succinct.

Regarding violence in our society as purely a sociological matter, or one of law enforcement, has led to unmitigated failure. It is time to test further whether violence can be amenable to medical/public health interventions.

We believe violence in America to be a public health emergency, largely unresponsive to methods thus far used in its control. The solutions are very complex, but possible.

The authors cited the relative success of epidemiologists in gaining some jurisdiction in the area of motor vehicle casualties by re-defining what had been seen as a law enforcement issue into a public health issue. Again, this process began during the Harriman administration in New York in the 1950s. In the 1960s the morbidity and mortality associated with automobile crashes was, it could be argued, a major public health problem; the public health strategy, it could also be argued, brought the problem under a measure of control. Not in "the 1970s and 1980s," as the *Journal of the American Medical Association* would have us think: the federal legislation involved was signed in 1965. Such a strategy would surely produce insights into the control of violence that elude law enforcement professionals, but whether it would change anything is another question.

For some years now I have had legislation in the Senate that would prohibit the manufacture of .25 and .32 caliber bullets. These are the two calibers most typically used with the guns known as Saturday Night Specials. "Guns don't kill people," I argue, "bullets do."

Moreover, we have a two-century supply of handguns but only a four-year supply of ammunition. A public health official would immediately see the logic of trying to control the supply of bullets rather than of guns.

Even so, now that the doctor has come, it is important that criminal violence not be defined down by epidemiologists. Doctors Koop and Lundberg note that in 1990 in the state of Texas "deaths from firearms, for the first time in many decades, surpassed deaths from motor vehicles, by 3,443 to 3,309." A good comparison. And yet keep in mind that the number of motor vehicle deaths, having leveled off since the 1960s, in now pretty well accepted as normal at somewhat less then 50,000 a year, which is somewhat less than the level of the 1960s—the "carnage," as it once was thought to be, is now accepted as normal. This is the price we pay for high-speed transportation: there is a benefit associated with it. But there is no benefit associated with homicide, and no good in getting used to it. Epidemiologists have powerful insights that can contribute to lessening the medical trauma, but they must be wary of normalizing the social pathology that leads to such trauma.

The hope—if there be such—of this essay has been twofold. It is, first, to suggest that the Durkheim constant, as I put it, is maintained by a dynamic process which adjusts upwards and *downwards*. Liberals have traditionally been alert for upward redefining that does injustice to individuals. Conservatives have been correspondingly sensitive to downward redefining that weakens societal standards. Might it not help if we could all agree that there is a dynamic at work here? It is not revealed truth, nor yet a scientifically derived formula. It is simply a pattern we observe in ourselves. Nor is it rigid. There may once have been an unchanging supply of jail cells which more or less determined the number of prisoners. No longer. We are building new prisons at a prodigious rate. Similarly, the executioner is back. There is something of a competition in Congress to think up new offenses for which the death penalty is seemed the only available deterrent. Possibly also modes of execution, as in "fry the kingpins." Even so, we are getting used to a lot of behavior that is not good for us.

As noted earlier, Durkheim states that there is "nothing desirable" about pain. Surely what he meant was that there is nothing pleasurable. Pain, even so, is an indispensable warning signal. But societies under stress, much like individuals, will turn to pain killers of various kinds that end up concealing real damage. There is surely nothing desirable about *this*. If our analysis wins general acceptance, if, for example, more of us came to share Judge Torres's genuine alarm at "the trivialization of the lunatic crime rate" in his city (and mine), we might surprise ourselves how well we respond to the manifest decline of the American civic order. Might.

POSTSCRIPT

Is Crime Always Functional?

One of the first American sociologists to attempt to use the insights of Durkheim was Robert Merton in his classic article "Social Structure and Anomie," *American Sociological Review* (1938). Merton attempted to show the bearing that culturally established goals and legitimate means for achieving them or their absence has upon criminogenic behavior. A significant revision of Durkheim's and Merton's thinking is *Crime and the American Dream*, 2d ed., by S. Messner and R. Rosenfeld (Wadsworth, 1997). Also helpful is F. Hearn, *Moral Order and Social Disorder* (Aldine de Gruyter, 1998), especially chapters 3 and 4 on anomie and Durkheim's sociology of morality. An analysis of communities' responses to crime in a culture outside of America is *Banana Justice: Field Notes on Philippine Crime and Customs* by W. T. Austin (Greenwood, 1999).

Note that Moynihan argues roughly from the same theoretic tradition as Durkheim: structural functionalism. Their disagreement centers around when deviancy becomes dysfunctional. A third argument would be that of some Marxists who see crime, including violent crime, as *functional* but only for the *elite* because it deflects society's concerns away from their own corporate crimes. For an outstanding presentation of this view, see J. Reiman's *The Rich Get Richer and the Poor Get Prison: Ideology, Class, and Criminal Justice*, 5th ed. (Allyn & Bacon, 1998). M. Lynch et al. identify linkages between economic cycles and criminal justice in "A Further Look at Long Cycles, Legislation and Crime," *Justice Quarterly* (June 1999).

Partial support of Moynihan's thinking can be found in *To Establish Justice, to Insure Domestic Tranquility* (Milton S. Eisenhower Foundation, 1999), a 30-year update of the 1969 violence report by the National Commission on the Causes and Prevention of Violence. A recent work by Moynihan is *Miles to Go: A Personal History of Social Policy* (Harvard University Press, 1997), and a discussion of Moynihan's ideas can be found in R. A. Katzmann, *Daniel Patrick Moynihan: The Intellectual in Public Life* (Johns Hopkins University Press, 1998).

There are many current analyses of crime and justice in terms of gender, including *Working With Women in the Criminal Justice System* by K. S. van Wormer and C. Bartollas (Allyn & Bacon, 1999) and part 1 of Sally Simpson, ed., *Of Crime and Criminality: The Use of Theory in Everyday Life* (Pine Forge Press, 2000). The neglected theoretical and research contributions of black criminologists are delineated by S. L. Gabbidon in "W. E. B. Du Bois on Crime," *The Criminologist* (January/February 1999). An interesting study on how U.S. scholars currently view crime is "Criminologists' Opinions About Causes and Theories of Crime," by L. Ellis and A. Walsh, *The Criminologist* (July/August 1999).

ISSUE 2

Is Criminal Behavior Biologically Determined?

YES: Adrian Raine, from "The Biological Basis of Crime," in James Q. Wilson and Joan Petersilia, eds., *Crime: Public Policies for Crime Control* (ICS Press, 2002)

NO: Robert K. Merton, from "Social Structure and Anomie," *American Sociological Review* (volume 3, 1938)

ISSUE SUMMARY

YES: Professor Adrian Raine argues that one of the reasons why we have been so unsuccessful in preventing adult crime is because crime-control policies have systematically ignored the biological side of human behavior.

NO: In a now-classic article, the late eminent sociologist Robert K. Merton, asserts that social conditions produce deviations from accepted norms of human conduct.

Is human behavior a product of our biological makeup, or is it socially determined? This question has confronted those who have studied human behavior throughout history. It is an extremely important question, however, because the answer determines everything from the types of social policies used to control deviant behavior, to philosophical questions including the nature of human morality.

The classical legal reform movement, a product of the Enlightenment, originated during the late eighteenth century in Europe. In reaction to the idea that metaphysical forces controlled all aspects of human existence, classical theorists, including Cesare Beccaria and Jeremy Bentham, believed that people were motivated by hedonism—the pursuit of pleasure and avoidance of pain. They also embraced the notion of rationality and free will as guiding principles in human affairs. The classicists believed that people, as rational beings, would choose to obey the law if punishments were slightly more severe than the pleasure they would derive from committing unlawful acts. In addition, they embraced the doctrine of utilitarianism, a principle that holds that the guiding principle of all social policy, including criminal punishment, must be "the greatest good for the greatest number."

Modern Western legal systems are predicated on these ideals. For example, criminal responsibility is based on the principle that a criminal has the capacity to formulate mens rea, or criminal intent based on an evil mind. Thus, at common law, children under the age of 7 years were presumed incapable of committing a crime because they were unable to foster criminal intent. Likewise, those who are proved to be mentally insane at the time they committed a crime are not held responsible for their actions.

Contemporary ideas about punishing criminals are largely based on classical principles as well. Our legal system assumes that punishment is justified because a criminal has freely chosen to violate the law and embraces the proposition that it serves a utilitarian purpose and will deter others from committing similar offenses.

What would happen to these assumptions, however, if internal biological forces were shown to compel people to act? Would it then be morally acceptable for society to "punish" criminals for committing antisocial acts? What if criminologists were able to completely eradicate an offender's desire to commit crime? Would such a treatment also eliminate the moral aspect of human conduct? Anthony Burgess, in the introduction to his classic work, *A Clockwork Orange,* considered this dilemma. Stated Burgess:

> [B]y definition, a human being is endowed with free will. He can use this to choose between good and evil. If he can only perform good or only perform evil, then he is a clockwork orange—meaning that he has the appearance of an organism lovely with colour and juice but is in fact only a clockwork toy to be wound up by God or the Devil or (since this is increasingly replacing both) the Almighty State.

The issues contemplated in this passage may have important consequences for the study of criminology as well as justice system policy in the twenty-first century. Professor Raine details many compelling examples of the emerging vitality of the biological approach to the study of human behavior. His extensive review of twin studies, human cortical arousal, and brain abnormalities in criminals presents compelling evidence of a biological component of human behavior.

Robert K. Merton, however, asserts that social factors generate circumstances in which violation of the law becomes a "normal" response and that society sometimes exerts a pressure on people to engage in deviant behavior. Merton believes that U.S. society is characterized by culture goals, which emphasize the attainment of wealth, and institutional means to attain the goals, such as hard work and getting a good education. When there is a disjunction between these forces, persons feel "strain" and are pressured by the social structure to commit crimes designed to produce wealth and power.

What are the arguments on both sides of the "nature or nurture" controversy? Perhaps criminal behavior is a complex combination of both types of factors. Do you think criminality is equally split between biological and social factors? Or, is it more skewed toward one side of the equation or the other? When you read these articles, try to develop your own sense of whether criminality is primarily determined by biological or social forces as well as the implications of this controversy for our notions of criminal responsibility and justice system policy.

YES

Adrian Raine

The Biological Basis of Crime

Recognition is increasing that biological processes are at some level implicated in the development of criminal behavior. There is certainly debate about the precise contribution of such factors to crime outcome, and there is considerable debate about the precise mechanisms that these biological factors reflect. Yet few serious scientists in psychology and psychiatry would deny that biological factors are relevant to understanding crime, and public interest in and understanding of this perspective are increasing. The discipline of criminology, on the other hand, has been reluctant to embrace this new body of knowledge. Part of the reason may be interdisciplinary rivalries, part may simply be a lack of understanding, and part may be due to deep-seated historical and moral suspicions of a biological approach to crime causation. For whatever reason, these data have been largely ignored by criminologists and sociologists. . . .

Genetics

Twin Studies

The twin method for ascertaining whether a given trait is to any extent heritable makes use of the fact that monozygotic (MZ) or "identical" twins are genetically identical, having 100 percent of their genes in common with one another. Conversely, dizygotic (DZ) or "fraternal" twins are less genetically alike than MZ twins, and are in fact no more alike genetically than non-twin siblings. . . .

Are identical twins more concordant for criminality than fraternal twins? The answer from many reviews conducted on this expanding field is undoubtedly yes. As one example, a review of all the twin studies of crime conducted up to 1993 showed that although twin studies vary widely in terms of the age, sex, country of origin, sample size, determination of zygosity, and definition of crime, nevertheless all thirteen studies of crime show greater concordance rates for criminality in MZ as opposed to DZ twins. If one averages concordance rates across all studies (weighting for sample sizes), these thirteen studies result in concordances of 51.5 percent of MZ twins and 20.6 percent for DZ twins. Furthermore, the twin studies that have been conducted since 1993 have confirmed the hypothesis that there is greater concordance for antisocial and aggressive behavior in MZ relative to DZ twins. . . .

Adoption Studies

Adoption studies also overcome the problem with twin studies because they more cleanly separate out genetic and environmental influences. We can examine offspring who have been separated from their criminal, biological parents early in life and sent out to other families. If these offspring grow up to become criminal at greater rates than foster children whose biological parents were not criminal, this would indicate a genetic influence with its origin in the subject's biological parents. . . .

[A] review of fifteen other adoption studies conducted in Denmark, Sweden, and the United States shows that all but one find a genetic basis to criminal behavior. Importantly, evidence for this genetic predisposition has been found by several independent research groups in several different countries. . . .

Psychophysiology

Since the 1940s an extensive body of research has been built up on the psychophysiological basis of antisocial, delinquent, criminal, and psychopathic behavior. For example, there have been at least 150 studies on electrodermal (sweat rate) and cardiovascular (heart rate) activity in such populations, and in electroencephalographic (EEG) research alone there have been hundreds of studies on delinquency and crime. . . .

Definitions of psychophysiology vary, but one useful perspective outlined by Dawson is that it is "concerned with understanding the relationships between psychological states and processes on the one hand and physiological measures on the other hand." Psychophysiology is uniquely placed to provide important insights into criminal behavior because it rests at the interface between clinical science, cognitive science, and neuroscience. . . .

There are many psychophysiological correlates of antisocial, criminal, and psychopathic behavior. The focus here will lie with one particular psychophysiological construct, low arousal, because—as will become clear—it is the strongest psychophysiological finding in the field of antisocial and criminal behavior.

EEG Underarousal

One influential psychophysiological theory of antisocial behavior is that antisocial individuals are chronically underaroused. Traditional psychophysiological measures of arousal include heart rate, skin conductance activity, and electroencephalogram (EEG) measured during a "resting" state. Low heart rate and skin conductance activity, and more excessive slow-wave EEG . . . indicate underarousal, that is, less than average levels of physiological arousal. Most studies tend to employ single measures of arousal, although studies that employ multiple measures are in a stronger position to test an arousal theory of antisocial behavior.

EEG is recorded from scalp electrodes that measure the electrical activity of the brain. Literally hundreds of studies assessing EEG in criminals, delinquents, psychopaths, and violent offenders have been done over the past sixty years, and it is clear that a large number of them implicate EEG abnormalities in violent recidivistic offending. . . . Murderers have more recently been shown to have more EEG deficits in the right than the left hemisphere of the brain, with multiple abnormalities being especially present in the right temporal cortex. On the other hand, Pillmann et al. showed greater abnormalities in the *left* temporal region of repeat violent offenders.

Generally speaking, the prevalence of EEG abnormalities in violent individuals in this large literature ranges from 25 percent to 50 percent, with the rate of abnormalities in normals estimated as ranging from 5 percent to 20 percent. The bulk of this research implicated the more frontal regions of the brain, areas that regulate executive functions such as planning and decision making. . . .

Cardiovascular Underarousal

Data on resting heart rate provides striking support for underarousal in antisocial. Indeed, the findings for heart rate level (HRL) on non-institutionalized antisocials are believed to represent the strongest and best replicated biological correlate of antisocial behavior.

A low resting heart rate is the best-replicated biological marker of antisocial and aggressive behavior in childhood and adolescent community samples. Resting HRL was measured in a wide variety of ways, including polygraphs, pulse meters, and stopwatches. A wide number of definitions of antisocial behavior are used, ranging from legal criminality and delinquency to teacher ratings of antisocial behavior in school, self-report socialization measures, diagnostic criteria for conduct disorder, and genetically inferred law breaking (i.e. offspring of criminals). Subjects were also assessed in a wide variety of settings, including medical interview, study office, school, university laboratory, and hospital. In the light of such variability, it is surprising that consistency in findings have been obtained, attesting to the robustness of the observed effects. Importantly, there has also been good cross-laboratory replication of the finding, and it has also been found in six different countries—England, Germany, New Zealand, the United States, Mauritius, and Canada—illustrating invariance to cultural context.

The link between low heart rate and crime is not the result of such things as height, weight, body bulk, physical development, and muscle tone; scholastic ability and IQ; excess motor activity and inattention; drug and alcohol use; engagement in physical exercise and sports; or low social class, divorce, family size, teenage pregnancy, and other psychosocial adversity. Intriguingly, an unusual and important feature of the relationship is its diagnostic specificity. No other psychiatric condition has been linked to low resting heart rate. Other psychiatric conditions, including alcoholism, depression, schizophrenia, and anxiety disorder, have, if anything, been linked to *higher* (not lower) resting heart rate.

Low heart rate has been found to be an independent predictor of violence. . . . Indeed, low heart rate was more strongly related to both self-report and teacher measures of violence than having a criminal parent. These findings led Farrington to conclude that low heart rate may be one of the most important explanatory factors for violence. . . . Low heart rate characterizes female as well as male antisocial individuals. Several studies, including two that are prospective, have now established that, *within* females, low heart rate is linked to antisocial behavior. . . .

Interpretations of Low Arousal: Fearlessness and Stimulation-Seeking Theories

Why should low arousal and low heart rate predispose to antisocial and criminal behavior? There are two main theoretical interpretations. Fearlessness theory indicates that low levels of arousal are markers of low levels of fear. For example, particularly fearless individuals such as bomb disposal experts who have been decorated for their bravery have particularly low HRLs and reactivity, as do British paratroopers decorated in the Falklands War. A fearlessness interpretation of low arousal levels assumes that subjects are not actually at "rest," but that instead the rest periods of psychophysiological testing represent a mildly stressful paradigm and that low arousal during this period indicates lack of anxiety and fear. Lack of fear would predispose to antisocial and violent behavior because such behavior (for example, fights and assaults) requires a degree of fearlessness to execute, while lack of fear, especially in childhood, would help explain poor socialization since low fear of punishment would reduce the effectiveness of conditioning. Fearlessness theory receives support from the fact that autonomic underarousal also provides the underpinning for a fearless or uninhibited temperament in infancy and childhood.

A second theory explaining reduced arousal is stimulation-seeking theory. This theory argues that low arousal represents an unpleasant physiological state; antisocials seek stimulation in order to increase their arousal levels back to an optimal or normal level: Antisocial behavior is thus viewed as a form of stimulation-seeking, in that committing a burglary, assault, or robbery could be stimulating for some individuals. . . .

Psychophysiological Protective Factors against Crime Development

Until recently, there had been no research on biological factors that *protect* against crime development, but that is changing. We are discovering that *higher* autonomic activity during adolescence may act as a protective factor against crime development. . . . Findings suggest that boys who are antisocial during adolescence but who do not go on to adult criminal offending may be protected from such an outcome by their high arousal levels.

Overall, the initial profile that is being built up on the psychophysiological characteristics of the Desistor is one of heightened information processing (better orienting), greater responsivity to environmental stimuli in general (fast recovery), greater sensitivity to cues predicting punishment in particular (better classical conditioning), and higher fearfulness (high HRLs). The importance of research on psychophysiological protective factors such as these is that they offer suggestions for possible intervention and prevention strategies.

Brain Imaging

Advances in brain imaging techniques in the past fifteen years have provided the opportunity to gain dramatic new insights into the brain mechanisms that may be dysfunctional in violent, psychopathic offenders. In the past, the idea of peering into the mind of a murderer to gain insights into his or her acts was the province of pulp fiction or space-age movies. Yet now we can literally look at, and into, the brains of murderers using functional and structural imaging techniques that are currently revolutionizing our understanding of the causes of clinical disorders.

Brain imaging studies of violent and psychopathic populations . . . concur in indicating that violent offenders have structural and functional deficits to the frontal lobe (behind the forehead) and the temporal lobe (near the ears). . . . Despite some discrepancies, the first generation of brain imaging studies supports earlier contentions from animal and neurological studies implicating the frontal (and to some extent temporal) brain regions in the regulation and expression of aggression.

Prefrontal Dysfunction in Murderers

In the first published brain imaging study of murderers, we scanned the brains of twenty-two murderers pleading not guilty by reason of insanity (or otherwise found incompetent to stand trial) and compared them to the brains of twenty-two normal controls who were matched with the murderers on sex and age. The technique we used was positron emission tomography (PET), which allowed us to measure the metabolic activity of many different regions of the brain including the prefrontal cortex, the frontalmost part of the brain. We had subjects perform a task that required them to maintain focused attention and be vigilant for a continuous period of time, and it is the prefrontal region of the brain that in part subserves this vigilance function.

The key finding was that the murderers showed significantly poorer functioning of the prefrontal cortex, that part of the brain lying above the eyes and behind the forehead. . . . Prefrontal damage also encourages risk-taking, irresponsibility, rule breaking, emotional and aggressive outbursts, and argumentative behavior that can also predispose to violent criminal acts. Loss of self-control, immaturity, lack of tact, inability to modify and inhibit behavior appropriately, and poor social judgment could predispose to violence as well. This loss of intellectual flexibility and problem-solving skills, and reduced ability to use information provided by verbal cues can impair social skills essential for formulating nonaggressive solutions to fractious encounters. Poor reasoning ability and divergent thinking that results from prefrontal damage can lead to school failure, unemployment, and economic deprivation, thereby predisposing to a criminal and violent way of life. . . .

Other Biological Processes: Birth Complications, Minor Physical Anomalies, Nutrition, and Neurochemistry

Birth Complications

Several studies have shown that babies who suffer birth complications are more likely to develop conduct disorder, delinquency, and impulsive crime and violence in adulthood. Birth complications such as anoxia (getting too little oxygen), forceps delivery, and preeclampsia (hypertension leading to anoxia) are thought to contribute to brain damage, and this damage in turn may predispose to antisocial and criminal behavior. On the other hand, birth complications may not by themselves predispose to crime, but may require the presence of negative environmental circumstance to trigger later adult crime and violence.

One example of this "biosocial interaction" is a study of birth complications and maternal rejection in all 4,269 live male births that took place in one hospital in Copenhagen, Denmark. A highly significant interaction was found between birth complications and maternal rejection. Babies who only suffered birth complications or who only suffered maternal rejection were no more likely than normal controls to become violent in adulthood. On the other hand, those who had both risk factors were much more likely to become violent. . . .

Nutrition

Although deficiency in nutrition itself has been rarely studied in relation to childhood aggression, several studies have demonstrated the effects of related processes including food additives, hypoglycemia, and more recently cholesterol on human behavior. In addition, some studies have shown associations between overaggressive behavior and vitamin and mineral deficiency. Furthermore, one study claimed that nearly a third of a population of juvenile delinquents (mostly males) showed evidence of iron deficiency. Nevertheless, these findings remain both conflicting and controversial.

One intriguing study illustrates the potentially causal role of malnutrition as early as pregnancy in predisposing to antisocial behavior. Toward the end of World War II when Germany was withdrawing from Holland, they placed a food blockade on the country that led to major food shortages and near starvation in the cities and towns for several months. Women who were pregnant at this time were exposed to severe malnutrition at different stages of pregnancy. The male offspring of these women were followed up into adulthood to ascertain rates of Antisocial Personality Disorder and were compared to controls who were not exposed to malnutrition. Pregnant women starved during the blockade had 2.5 times the rates of Antisocial Personality Disorder in their adult offspring compared to controls.

Initial evidence also shows relationships between both protein and zinc deficiency and aggression in animals. Recent studies of humans support these animal findings. Protein and zinc deficiency may lead to aggression by negatively impacting brain functioning. . . . In humans, zinc deficiency in pregnancy has been linked to impaired DNA, RNA, and protein synthesis during brain development, and congenital brain abnormalities. . . . The amygdala, which also shows abnormal functioning in PET imaging of violent offenders, is densely innervated by zinc-containing neurons, and males with a history of assaultive behavior were found to have lower zinc relative to copper ratios in their blood compared to nonassaultive controls. Consequently, protein and zinc deficiency may contribute to the brain impairments shown in violent offenders which in turn are thought to predispose to violence.

Environmental Pollutants and Neurotoxicity

It has long been suspected that exposure to pollutants, particularly heavy metals that have neurotoxic effects, can lead to mild degrees of brain impairment which in turn predisposes to antisocial and aggressive behavior. One of the best studies to date is that of Needleman et al. who assessed lead levels in the bones of 301 eleven-year-old schoolboys. Boys with higher lead levels were found to have significantly higher teacher ratings of delinquent and aggressive behavior, higher parent ratings of delinquent and aggressive behavior, and higher self-report delinquency scores. These findings do not occur in isolation: Similar links between lead levels and antisocial, delinquent behavior and aggression have been found in at least six other studies in several different countries. . . .

Less strong to date, but nevertheless provocative, are findings with respect to manganese. At high levels, manganese has toxic effects on the brain and can damage the brain so much that it can even lead to Parkinson-like symptoms. Furthermore, it reduces levels of serotonin and dopamine, neurotransmitters that play a key role in brain communication. . . .

Hormones

Testosterone. Excellent reviews and discussions of the potential role played by testosterone in both animals and man can be found in Olweus, Brain, Archer, and Susman and Ponirakis. Animal research suggests that the steroid hormone testosterone plays an important role in the genesis and maintenance of some forms of aggressive behavior in rodents, and early exposure to testosterone had been found to increase aggression in a wide range of animal species. . . .

The critical question in this literature concerns whether testosterone-violence relationships are causal. Little doubt exists that castration decreases aggression in animals and administration of testosterone increases aggression. Few experimental studies have been conducted in humans, but there is nevertheless evidence of a causal relationship. Olweus et al. assessed their finding of higher testosterone in male adolescents with high levels of self-report aggression using path analysis and concluded that testosterone had causal effects on both provoked and unprovoked aggressive behavior. One study that comes close to such an ideal experiment is that of Wille and Beier, who showed that ninety-nine castrated German sex offenders had a significantly lower recidivism rate eleven years postrelease (3 percent) compared to thirty-five noncastrated sex offenders (46 percent). . . .

Clearly, links between testosterone and aggression are complex, and simplistic explanations of this link are probably incorrect. By the same token, it would be equally erroneous to discount the evidence for the role of hormones in influencing aggression merely because hormones are influenced by the environment. . . .

Policy Implications

One of the biggest and widely held myths in criminology research is that biology is destiny. Instead, the reality is that the biological bases of crime and violence are amenable to change through benign interventions. In the past fifty years, intervention programs have not been as successful in reducing crime and violence as had been hoped, and it is possible that part of their failure has been due to the fact that they have systematically ignored the biological component of the biosocial equation.

Brain damage and poor brain functioning have been shown to predispose to violence, and one possible source of this brain damage could be birth complications. The implication is that providing better pre- and postbirth health care to poor mothers may help reduce birth complications and thus reduce violence. . . .

Another source of brain damage could be poor nutrition; and as has been seen earlier, there is evidence for a link between poor nutrition during pregnancy and later crime. Furthermore, cigarette and alcohol usage during pregnancy have been linked to later antisocial behavior. . . . These studies provide more support to the notion that nutrition plays a causal role in the development of childhood aggression, but future prevention trials that focus explicitly on the specific role of nutrition are required to further support the specific role of malnutrition.

It has been shown that low physiological arousal is the best-replicated biological correlate of antisocial behavior in child and adolescent samples. An important question from a prevention perspective concerns whether low arousal is amenable to change using noninvasive procedures. Recent findings from Mauritius suggest that it is. A nutritional, physical exercise, and educational enrichment from ages three to five resulted in increased psychophysiological arousal and orienting at age eleven compared to a matched control group. . . .

The policy implications of biological research on crime also extend to the criminal justice system. One question raised by these and other studies is whether any of us have freedom of will in the strict sense of the term. If brain deficits make it more likely that a person will commit violence, and if the cause of the brain deficits was not under the control of the individual, then the question becomes whether or not that person should be held fully responsible for the crimes. Of course we have to protect society, and unless we can treat this brain dysfunction, we may need to keep violent offenders in secure conditions for the rest of their lives; but do they deserve to be executed given the early constraints on their free will? It could be argued that if an individual possesses risk factors that make him disproportionately more likely to commit violence, then he has to take responsibility for these predispositions. Just like an alcoholic who knows he suffers from the disease of alcoholism, the person at risk for violence needs to recognize his risk factors and take preventive steps to ensure that he does not harm others. These persons have risk factors, but they still have responsibility and they have free will. . . .

Biological research is beginning to give us new insights into what makes a violent criminal offender. It is hoped that these early findings may lead us to rethink our approach to violence and goad us into obtaining new answers to the causes and cures of crime while we continue to protect society.

Robert K. Merton

 **NO**

Social Structure and Anomie

There persists a notable tendency in sociological theory to attribute the malfunctioning of social structure primarily to those of man's imperious biological drives which are not adequately restrained by social control. In this view, the social order is solely a device for "impulse management" and the "social processing" of tensions. These impulses which break through social control, be it noted, are held to be biologically derived. Nonconformity is assumed to be rooted in original nature.[1] Conformity is by implication the result of an utilitarian calculus or unreasoned conditioning. This point of view, whatever its other deficiences, clearly begs one question. It provides no basis for determining the nonbiological conditions which induce deviations from prescribed patterns of conduct. In this paper, it will be suggested that certain phases of social structure generate the circumstances in which infringement of social codes constitutes a "normal" response.[2]

The conceptual scheme to be outlined is designed to provide a coherent, systematic approach to the study of socio-cultural sources of deviate behavior. Our primary aim lies in discovering how some social structures *exert a definite pressure* upon certain persons in the society to engage in nonconformist rather than conformist conduct. The many ramifications of the scheme cannot all be discussed; the problems mentioned outnumber those explicitly treated.

Among the elements of social and cultural structure, two are important for our purposes. These are analytically separable although they merge imperceptibly in concrete situations. The first consists of culturally defined goals, purposes, and interests. It comprises a frame of aspirational reference. These goals are more or less integrated and involve varying degrees of prestige and sentiment. They constitute a basic, but not the exclusive, component of what Linton aptly has called "designs for group living." Some of these cultural aspirations are related to the original drives of man, but they are not determined by them. The second phase of the social structure defines, regulates, and controls the acceptable modes of achieving these goals. Every social group invariably couples its scale of desired ends with moral or institutional regulation of permissible and required procedures for attaining these ends. These regulatory norms and moral imperatives do not necessarily coincide with technical or efficiency norms. Many procedures which from the standpoint of *particular*

From *American Sociological Review*, vol. 3, no. 5, 1938, pp. 672–679. Copyright © 1938 by American Sociological Association.

individuals would be most efficient in securing desired values, e.g., illicit oil-stock schemes, theft, fraud, are ruled out of the institutional area of permitted conduct. The choice of expedients is limited by the institutional norms.

To say that these two elements, culture goals and institutional norms, operate jointly is not to say that the ranges of alternative behaviors and aims bear some constant relation to one another. The emphasis upon certain goals may vary independently of the degree of emphasis upon institutional means. There may develop a disproportionate, at times, a virtually exclusive, stress upon the value of specific goals, involving relatively slight concern with the institutionally appropriate modes of attaining these goals. The limiting case in this direction is reached when the range of alternative procedures is limited only by technical rather than institutional considerations. Any and all devices which promise attainment of the all important goal would be permitted in this hypothetical polar case.[3] This constitutes one type of cultural malintegration. A second polar type is found in groups where activities originally conceived as instrumental are transmuted into ends in themselves. The original purposes are forgotten and ritualistic adherence to institutionally prescribed conduct becomes virtually obsessive.[4] Stability is largely ensured while change is flouted. The range of alternative behaviors is severely limited. There develops a tradition-bound, sacred society characterized by neophobia. The occupational psychosis of the bureaucrat may be cited as a case in point. Finally, there are the intermediate types of groups where a balance between culture goals and institutional means is maintained. These are the significantly integrated and relatively stable, though changing, groups.

An effective equilibrium between the two phases of the social structure is maintained as long as satisfactions accrue to individuals who conform to both constraints, viz., satisfactions from the achievement of the goals and satisfactions emerging directly from the institutionally canalized modes of striving to attain these ends. Success, in such equilibrated cases, is twofold. Success is reckoned in terms of the product and in terms of the process, in terms of the outcome and in terms of activities. Continuing satisfactions must derive from sheer *participation* in a competitive order as well as from eclipsing one's competitors if the order itself is to be sustained. The occasional sacrifices involved in institutionalized conduct must be compensated by socialized rewards. The distribution of statuses and roles through competition must be so organized that positive incentives for conformity to roles and adherence to status obligations are provided *for every position* within the distributive order. Aberrant conduct, therefore, may be viewed as a symptom of dissociation between culturally defined aspirations and socially structured means.

Of the types of groups which result from the independent variation of the two phases of the social structure, we shall be primarily concerned with the first, namely, that involving a disproportionate accent on goals. This statement must be recast in a proper perspective. In no group is there an absence of regulatory codes governing conduct, yet groups do vary in the degree to which these folkways, mores, and institutional controls are effectively integrated with the more diffuse goals which are part of the culture matrix. Emotional convictions may cluster about the complex of socially acclaimed ends, meanwhile shifting their support from the culturally defined implementation of these ends. As we shall see, certain aspects of the social structure may generate countermores and antisocial behavior precisely because of differential emphases on goals and regulations. In the extreme case, the latter may be so vitiated by the goal-emphasis that the range of behavior is limited only by considerations of technical expediency. The sole significant question then becomes, which available means is most efficient in netting the socially approved value?[5] The technically most feasible procedure, whether legitimate or not, is preferred to the institutionally prescribed conduct. As this process continues, the integration of the society becomes tenuous and anomie ensues.

Thus, in competitive athletics, when the aim of victory is shorn of its institutional trappings and success in contests becomes construed as "winning the game" rather than "winning through circumscribed modes of activity," a premium is implicitly set upon the use of illegitimate but technically efficient means. The star of the opposing football team is surreptitiously slugged; the wrestler furtively incapacitates his opponent through ingenious but illicit techniques; university alumni covertly subsidize "students" whose talents are largely confined to the athletic field. The emphasis on the goal has so attenuated the satisfactions deriving from sheer participation in the competitive activity that these satisfactions are virtually confined to a successful outcome. Through the same process, tension generated by the desire to win in a poker game is relieved by successfully dealing oneself four aces, or, when the cult of success has become completely dominant, by sagaciously shuffling the cards in a game of solitaire. The faint twinge of uneasiness in the last instance and the surreptious nature of public delicts indicate clearly that the institutional rules of the game *are known* to those who evade them, but that the emotional supports of these rules are largely vitiated by cultural exaggeration of the success–goal.[6] They are microcosmic images of the social macrocosm.

Of course, this process is not restricted to the realm of sport. The process whereby exaltation of the end generates a *literal demoralization,* i.e., a deinstitutionalization, of the means is one which characterizes many[7] groups in which the two phases of the social structure are not highly integrated. The extreme emphasis upon the accumulation of wealth as a symbol of success[8] in our own society militates against the completely effective control of institutionally regulated modes of acquiring a fortune.[9] Fraud, corruption, vice, crime, in short, the entire catalogue of proscribed behavior, becomes increasingly common when the emphasis on the *culturally induced* success-goal becomes divorced from a coordinated institutional emphasis. This observation is of crucial theoretical importance in examining the doctrine that antisocial behavior most frequently derives from biological drives breaking through the restraints imposed by society. The difference is one between a strictly utilitarian interpretation which conceives man's ends as random and an analysis which finds these ends deriving from the basic values of the culture.[10]

Our analysis can scarcely stop at this juncture. We must turn to other aspects of the social structure if we are to deal with the social genesis of the varying rates and types of deviate behavior characteristic of different societies. Thus far, we have sketched three ideal types of social orders constituted by distinctive patterns of relations between culture ends and means. Turning from these types of *culture patterning,* we find five logically possible, alternative modes of adjustment or adaptation *by individuals* within the culture-bearing society or group.[11] These are schematically presented in the following table, where (+) signifies "acceptance," (–) signifies "elimination" and (±) signifies "rejection and substitution of new goals and standards."

	Culture Goals	Institutionalized Means
I. Conformity	+	+
II. Innovation	+	–
III. Ritualism	–	+
IV. Retreatism	–	–
V. Rebellion[12]	±	±

Our discussion of the relation between these alternative responses and other phases of the social structure must be prefaced by the observation that persons may shift from one alternative to another as they engage in different social activities. These categories refer to role adjustments in specific situations, not to personality *in toto.* To treat the development of this process in various spheres of conduct would introduce a complexity unmanageable within the confines of this paper. For this reason, we shall be concerned primarily with economic activity in the broad sense, "the production, exchange, distribution and consumption of goods and services" in our competitive society, wherein wealth has taken on a highly symbolic cast. Our task is to search out some of the factors which exert pressure upon individuals to engage in certain of these logically possible alternative responses. This choice, as we shall see, is far from random.

In every society, Adaptation I (conformity to both culture goals and means) is the most common and widely diffused. Were this not so, the stability and continuity of the society could not be maintained. The mesh of expectancies which constitutes every social order is sustained by the modal behavior of its members falling within the first category. Conventional role behavior oriented toward the basic values of the group is the rule rather than the exception. It is this fact alone which permits us to speak of a human aggregate as comprising a group or society.

Conversely, Adaptation IV (rejection of goals and means) is the least common. Persons who "adjust" (or maladjust) in this fashion are, strictly speaking, *in* the society but not *of* it. Sociologically, these constitute the true "aliens." Not sharing the common frame of orientation, they can be included within the societal population merely in a fictional sense. In this category are *some* of the activities of psychotics, psychoneurotics, chronic autists, pariahs, outcasts, vagrants, vagabonds, tramps, chronic drunkards and drug addicts.[13] These have relinquished, in certain spheres of activity, the culturally defined goals, involving complete aim-inhibition in the polar case, and their adjustments are not in accord with institutional norms. This is not to say that in some cases the source of their behavioral adjustments is not in part the very social structure which they have in effect repudiated nor that their very existence within a social area does not constitute a problem for the socialized population.

This mode of "adjustment" occurs, as far as structural sources are concerned, when both the culture goals and institutionalized procedures have been assimilated thoroughly by the individual and imbued with affect and high positive value, but where those institutionalized procedures which promise a measure of successful attainment of the goals are not available to the individual. In such instances, there results a twofold mental conflict insofar as the moral obligation for adopting institutional means conflicts with the pressure to resort to illegitimate means (which may attain the goal) and inasmuch as the individual is shut off from means which are both legitimate *and* effective. The competitive order is maintained, but the frustrated and handicapped individual who cannot cope with this order drops out. Defeatism, quietism and resignation are manifested in escape mechanisms which ultimately lead the individual to "escape" from the requirements of the society. It is an expedient which arises from continued failure to attain the goal by legitimate measures and from an inability to adopt the illegitimate route because of internalized prohibitions and institutionalized compulsives, *during which process the supreme value of the success-goal has as yet not been renounced.* The conflict is resolved by eliminating *both* precipitating elements, the goals and means. The escape is complete, the conflict is eliminated and the individual is a socialized.

Be it noted that where frustration derives from the inaccessibility of effective institutional means for attaining economic or any other type of highly valued "success," that Adaptations II, III and V (innovation, ritualism and rebellion) are also possible. The result will be determined by the particular personality, and thus, the *particular* cultural background, involved. Inadequate socialization will result in the innovation response whereby the conflict and frustration are eliminated by relinquishing the institutional means and retaining the success-aspiration; an extreme assimilation of institutional demands will lead to ritualism wherein the goal is dropped as beyond one's reach but conformity to the mores persists; and rebellion occurs when emancipation from the reigning standards, due to frustration or to marginalist perspectives, leads to the attempt to introduce a "new social order."

Our major concern is with the illegitimacy adjustment. This involves the use of conventionally proscribed but frequently effective means of attaining at least the simulacrum of culturally defined success,—wealth, power, and the like. As we have seen, this adjustment occurs when the individual has assimilated the cultural emphasis on success without equally internalizing the morally prescribed norms governing means for its attainment. The question arises, Which phases of our social structure predispose toward this mode of adjustment? We may examine a concrete instance, effectively analyzed by Lohman,[14] which provides a clue to the answer. Lohman has shown that specialized areas of vice in the near north side of Chicago constitute a "normal" response to a situation where the cultural emphasis upon pecuniary success has been absorbed, but where there is little access to conventional and legitimate means for attaining such success. The conventional occupational opportunities of persons in this area are almost completely limited to manual labor. Given our cultural stigmatization of manual labor, and its correlate, the prestige of white collar work, it is clear that the result is a strain toward innovational practices. The limitation of opportunity to unskilled labor and the resultant low income can not compete *in terms of conventional standards of achievement* with the high income from organized vice.

For our purposes, this situation involves two important features. First, such antisocial behavior is in a sense "called forth" by certain conventional values of the culture *and* by the class structure involving differential access to the approved opportunities for legitimate, prestige-bearing pursuit of the culture goals. The lack of high integration between the means-and-end elements of the cultural pattern and the particular class structure combine to favor a heightened frequency of antisocial conduct in such groups. The second consideration is of equal significance. Recourse to the first of the alternative responses, legitimate effort, is limited by the fact that actual advance toward desired success-symbols through conventional channels is, despite our persisting open-class ideology,[15] relatively rare and difficult for those handicapped by little formal education and few economic resources. The dominant pressure of group standards of success is, therefore, on the gradual attenuation of legitimate, but by and large ineffective, strivings and the increasing use of illegitimate, but more or less effective, expedients of vice and crime. The cultural demands made on persons in this situation are incompatible. On the one hand, they are asked to orient their conduct toward the prospect of accumulating wealth and on the other, they are largely denied effective opportunities to do so institutionally. The consequences of such structural inconsistency are psychopathological personality, and/or antisocial conduct, and/or revolutionary activities. The equilibrium between culturally designated means and ends becomes highly unstable with the progressive emphasis on attaining the prestige-laden ends by any means whatsoever. Within this context, Capone represents the triumph of amoral intelligence over morally prescribed "failure," when the channels of vertical mobility are closed or narrowed[16] *in a society which places a high premium on economic affluence and social ascent for all its members.*[17]

This last qualification is of primary importance. It suggests that other phases of the social structure besides the extreme emphasis on pecuniary success, must be considered if we are to understand the social sources of antisocial behavior. A high frequency of deviate behavior is not generated simply by "lack of opportunity" or by this exaggerated pecuniary emphasis. A comparatively rigidified class structure, a feudalistic or caste order, may limit such opportunities far beyond the point which obtains in our society today. It is only when a system of cultural values extols, virtually above all else, certain *common* symbols of success *for the population at large* while its social structure rigorously restricts or completely eliminates access to approved modes of acquiring these symbols *for a considerable part of the same population,* that antisocial behavior ensues on a considerable scale. In other words, our egalitarian ideology denies by implication the existence of non-competing groups and individuals in the pursuit of pecuniary success. The same body of success-symbols is held to be desirable for all. These goals are held to *transcend class lines*, not to be bounded by them, yet the actual social organization is such that there exist class differentials in the accessibility of these *common* success-symbols. Frustration and thwarted aspiration lead to the search for avenues of escape from a culturally induced intolerable situation; or unrelieved ambition may eventuate in illicit attempts to acquire the dominant values.[18] The American stress on pecuniary success and ambitiousness for all thus invites exaggerated anxieties, hostilities, neuroses and antisocial behavior.

This theoretical analysis may go far toward explaining the varying correlations between crime and poverty.[19] Poverty is not an isolated variable. It is one in a complex of interdependent social and cultural variables. When viewed in such a context, it represents quite different states of affairs. Poverty as such, and consequent limitation of opportunity, are not sufficient to induce a conspicuously high rate of criminal behavior. Even the often mentioned "poverty in the midst of plenty" will not necessarily lead to this result. Only insofar as poverty and associated disadvantages in competition for the culture values approved for *all* members of the society is linked with the assimilation of a cultural emphasis on monetary accumulation as a symbol of success is antisocial conduct a "normal" outcome. Thus, poverty is less highly correlated with crime in southeastern Europe than in the United States. The possibilities of vertical mobility in these European areas would seem to be fewer than in this country, so that neither poverty *per se* nor its association with limited opportunity is sufficient to account for the varying correlations. It is only when the full configuration is considered, poverty, limited opportunity and a commonly shared system of success symbols, that we can explain the higher association between poverty and crime in our society than in others where rigidified class structure is coupled with *differential class symbols of achievement*.

In societies such as our own, then, the pressure of prestige-bearing success tends to eliminate the effective social constraint over means employed to this end. "The-end-justifies-the-means" doctrine becomes a guiding tenet for action when the cultural structure unduly exalts the end and the social organization unduly limits possible recourse to approved means. Otherwise put, this notion and associated behavior reflect a lack of cultural coordination. In international relations, the effects of this lack of integration are notoriously apparent. An emphasis upon national power is not readily coordinated with an inept organization of legitimate, i.e., internationally defined and accepted, means for attaining this goal. The result is a tendency toward the abrogation of international law, treaties become scraps of paper, "undeclared warefare" serves as a technical evasion, the bombing of civilian populations is rationalized,[20] just as the same societal situation induces the same sway of illegitimacy among individuals.

The social order we have described necessarily produces this "strain toward dissolution." The pressure of such an order is upon outdoing one's competitors. The choice of means within the ambit of institutional control will persist as long as the sentiments supporting a competitive system, i.e., deriving from the possibility of outranking competitors and hence enjoying the favorable response of others, are distributed throughout the entire system of activities and are not confined merely to the final result. A stable social structure demands a balanced distribution of affect among its various segments. When there occurs a shift of emphasis from the satisfactions deriving from competition itself to almost exclusive concern with successful competition, the resultant stress leads to the breakdown of the regulatory structure.[21] With the resulting attenuation of the institutional imperatives, there occurs an approximation of the situation erroneously held by utilitarians to be typical of society generally wherein calculations of advantage and fear of punishment are the sole regulating agencies. In such situations, as Hobbes observed, force and fraud come to constitute the sole virtues in view of their relative efficiency in attaining goals,—which were for him, of course, not culturally derived.

It should be apparent that the foregoing discussion is not pitched on a moralistic plane. Whatever the sentiments of the writer or reader concerning the ethical desirability of coordinating the means-and-goals phases of the social structure, one must agree that lack of such coordination leads to anomie. Insofar as one of the most general functions of social organization is to provide a basis for calculability and regularity of behavior, it is increasingly limited in effectiveness as these elements of the structure become dissociated. At the extreme, predictability virtually disappears and what may be properly termed cultural chaos or anomie intervenes.

This statement, being brief, is also incomplete. It has not included an exhaustive treatment of the various structural elements which predispose toward one rather than another of the alternative responses open to individuals; it has neglected, but not defined the relevance of, the factors determining the specific incidence of these responses; it has not enumerated the various concrete responses which are constituted by combinations of specific values of the analytical variables; it has omitted, or included only by implication, any consideration of the social functions performed by illicit responses; it has not tested the full explanatory power of the analytical scheme by examining a large number of group variations in the frequency of deviate and conformist behavior; it has not adequately dealt with rebellious conduct which seeks to refashion the social framework radically; it has not examined the relevance of cultural conflict for an analysis of culture-goal and institutional-means malintegration. It is suggested that these and related problems may be profitably analyzed by this scheme.

Notes

1. E.g., Ernest Jones, *Social Aspects of Psychoanalysis*, 28, London, 1924. If the Freudian notion is a variety of the "original sin" dogma, then the interpretation advanced in this paper may be called the doctrine of "socially derived sin."
2. "Normal" in the sense of a culturally oriented, if not approved, response. This statement does not deny the relevance of biological and personality differences which may be significantly involved in the *incidence* of deviate conduct. Our focus of interest is the social and cultural matrix; hence we abstract from other factors. It is in this sense, I take it, that James S. Plant speaks of the

"normal reaction of normal people to abnormal conditions." See his *Personality and the Cultural Pattern,* 248, New York, 1937.

3. Contemporary American culture has been said to tend in this direction. See André Siegfried, *America Comes of Age,* 26–37, New York, 1927. The alleged extreme(?) emphasis on the goals of monetary success and material prosperity leads to dominant concern with technological and social instruments designed to produce the desired result, inasmuch as institutional controls become of secondary importance. In such a situation, innovation flourishes as the *range of means* employed is broadened. In a sense, then, there occurs the paradoxical emergence of "materialists" from an "idealistic" orientation. Cf. Durkheim's analysis of the cultural conditions which predispose toward crime and innovation, both of which are aimed toward efficiency, not moral norms. Durkheim was one of the first to see that "contrairement aux idées courantes le criminel n'apparait plus comme up être radicalement insociable, comme une sorte d'elément parasitaire, de corps étranger et inassimilable, introduit au sein de la société; c'est un agent régulier de la vie sociale." See *Les Règles de la Méthode Sociologique,* 86–89, Paris, 1927.

4. Such ritualism may be associated with a mythology which rationalizes these actions so that they appear to retain their status as means, but the dominant pressure is in the direction of strict ritualistic conformity, irrespective of such rationalizations. In this sense, ritual has proceeded farthest when such rationalizations are not even called forth.

5. In this connection, one may see the relevance of Elton Mayo's paraphrase of the title of Tawney's well known book. "Actually the problem *is not that of the sickness of an acquisitive society; it is that of the acquisitioness of a sick society." Human Problems of an Industrial Civilization,* 153, New York, 1933. Mayo deals with the process through which wealth comes to be a symbol of social achievement. He sees this as arising from a state of anomie. We are considering the unintegrated monetary-success goal as an element in producing anomie. A complete analysis would involve both phases of this system of interdependent variables.

6. It is unlikely that interiorized norms are completely eliminated. Whatever residuum persists will induce personality tensions and conflict. The process involves a certain degree of ambivalence. A manifest rejection of the institutional norms is coupled with some latent retention of their emotional correlates. "Guilt feelings," "sense of sin," "pangs of conscience" are obvious manifestations of this unrelieved tension; symbolic adherence to the nominally repudiated values or rationalizations constitute a more subtle variety of tensional release.

7. "Many," and not all, unintegrated groups, for the reason already mentioned. In groups where the primary emphasis shifts to institutional means, i.e., when the range of alternatives is very limited, the outcome is a type of ritualism rather than anomie.

8. Money has several peculiarities which render it particularly apt to become a symbol of prestige divorced from institutional controls. As Simmel emphasized, money is highly abstract and impersonal. However acquired, through fraud or institutionally, it can be used to purchase the same goods and services. The anonymity of metropolitan culture, in conjunction with this peculiarity of money, permits wealth, the sources of which may be unknown to the community in which the plutocrat lives, to serve as a symbol of status.

9. The emphasis upon wealth as a success-symbol is possibly reflected in the use of the term "fortune" to refer to a stock of accumulated wealth. This meaning becomes common in the late sixteenth century (Spenser and Shakespeare). A similar usage of the Latin *fortuna* comes into prominence during the first century B.C. Both these periods were marked by the rise to prestige and power of the "bourgeoisie."

10. See Kingsley Davis, "Mental Hygiene and the Class Structure," *Psychiatry*, 1928, I, esp. 62–63; Talcott Parsons, *The Structure of Social Action*, 59–60, New York, 1937.

11. This is a level intermediate between the two planes distinguished by Edward Sapir; namely, culture patterns and personal habit systems. See his "Contribution of Psychiatry to an Understanding of Behavior in Society," *Amer. J. Sociol.*, 1937, 42:862–70.

12. This fifth alternative is on a plane clearly different from that of the others. It represents a *transitional* response which seeks to *institutionalize* new procedures oriented toward revamped cultural goals shared by the members of the society. It thus involves efforts to *change* the existing structure rather than to perform accommodative actions *within* this structure, and introduces additional problems with which we are not at the moment concerned.

13. Obviously, this is an elliptical statement. These individuals may maintain some orientation to the values of their particular differentiated groupings within the larger society or, in part, of the conventional society itself. Insofar as they do so, their conduct cannot be classified in the "passive rejection" category (IV). Nels Anderson's description of the behavior and attitudes of the bum, for example, can readily be recast in terms of our analytical scheme. See *The Hobo*, 93–98, *et passim*, Chicago, 1923.

14. Joseph D. Lohman, "The Participant Observer in Community Studies," *Amer. Sociol. Rev.*, 1937, 2:890–98.

15. The shifting historical role of this ideology is a profitable subject for exploration. The "office-boy-to-president" stereotype was once in approximate accord with the facts. Such vertical mobility was probably more common then than now, when the class structure is more rigid. (See the following note.) The ideology largely persists, however, possibly because it still performs a useful function for maintaining the *status quo*. For insofar as it is accepted by the "masses," it constitutes a useful sop for those who might rebel against the entire structure, were this consoling hope removed. This ideology now serves to lessen the probability of Adaptation V. In short, the role of this notion has changed from that of an approximately valid empirical theorem to that of an ideology, in Mannheim's sense.

16. There is a growing body of evidence, though none of it is clearly conclusive, to the effect that our class structure is becoming regidified and that vertical mobility is declining. Taussig and Joslyn found that American business leaders are being *increasingly* recruited from the upper ranks of our society. The Lynds have also found a "diminished chance to get ahead" for the working classes in Middletown. Manifestly, these objective changes are not alone significant; the individual's subjective evaluation of the situation is a major determinant of the response. The extent to which this change in opportunity for social mobility has been recognized by the least advantaged classes is still conjectural, although the Lynds present some suggestive materials. The writer suggests that a case in point is the increasing frequency of cartoons which observe in a tragi-comic vein that "my old man says everybody can't be President. He says if ya can get three days a week steady on W.P.A. work ya ain't doin' so bad either." See F. W. Taussig and C. S. Joslyn, *American Business Leaders*, New York, 1932; R. S. and H. M. Lynd, *Middletown in Transition*, 67 ff., chap. 12, New York, 1937.

17. The role of the Negro in this respect is of considerable theoretical interest. Certain elements of the Negro population have assimilated the dominant caste's values of pecuniary success and social advancement, but they also recognize that social ascent is at present restricted to their own caste almost exclusively. The pressures upon the Negro which would otherwise derive from the structural inconsistencies we have noticed are hence not identical with those upon lower class whites. See Kingsley Davis, *op. cit.*, 63; John

Dollard, *Caste and Class in a Southern Town*, 66 ff., New Haven, 1936; Donald Young, *American Minority Peoples*, 581, New York, 1932.

18. The psychical coordinates of these processes have been partly established by the experimental evidence concerning *Anspruchsniveaus* and levels of performance. See Kurt Lewin, *Vorsatz, Wille und Bedurfnis*, Berlin, 1926; N. F. Hoppe, "Erfolg und Misserfolg," *Psychol. Forschung*, 1930, 14: 1–63; Jerome D. Frank, "Individual Differences in Certain Aspects of the Level of Aspiration," *Amer. J. Psychol.*, 1935, 47: 119–28.

19. Standard criminology texts summarize the data in this field. Our scheme of analysis may serve to resolve some of the theoretical contradictions which P. A. Sorokin indicates. For example, "not everywhere nor always do the poor show a greater proportion of crime . . . many poorer countries have had less crime than the richer countries . . . The [economic] improvement in the second half of the nineteenth century, and the beginning of the twentieth, has not been followed by a decrease of crime." See his *Contemporary Sociological Theories*, 560–61, New York, 1928. The crucial point is, however, that poverty has varying social significance in different social structures, as we shall see. Hence, one would not expect a linear correlation between crime and poverty.

20. See M. W. Royse, *Aerial Bombardment and the International Regulation of War*, New York, 1928.

21. Since our primary concern is with the socio-cultural aspects of this problem, the psychological correlates have been only implicitly considered. See Karen Horney, *The Neurotic Personality of Our Time*, New York, 1937, for a psychological discussion of this process.

POSTSCRIPT

Is Criminal Behavior Biologically Determined?

For much of the twentieth century, the biological perspective in criminology was regarded as an anachronism that conjured images of Cesare Lombroso slicing open cadavers and the early phrenologists measuring the contours of criminals' heads. As Adrian Raine demonstrates, however, the biological approach to the study of criminal behavior is making a strong comeback. For example, it is difficult for modern criminologists to ignore identical twin studies, which indicate a significant amount of behavioral concordance, even when the individuals are separated shortly after birth and raised apart. In fact, as technology advances and our ability to identify the biological correlates of human behavior further improves, we may reach a point where behavioral scientists are more prepared to assign hard percentages to the nature/nurture controversy.

On the other hand, as Robert K. Merton demonstrates, there is also a significant social component to human behavior. People are social beings. Just examine the interaction dynamics in your classroom and think about how we influence the behavior of others in virtually every social situation.

Moreover, Merton's theory has a great deal of intuitive appeal. Most people would agree that U.S. society values conspicuous consumption and maximization of wealth. People in the lower classes value these things every bit as much as wealthy people. Is it really surprising that members of the lower class would seek to attain wealth by using alternative methods, such as selling drugs?

It appears likely that the definitive answer to the mystery of human behavior may eventually determine that both biological factors and social forces combine in a complex interactive web. Thus, for future behavioral scientists, it is quite possible that the "nature *or* nurture" controversy will become the "nature *and* nurture" issue.

Fortunately, there are many outstanding resources that shed additional light on the issues presented in this section. For example, an excellent article that discusses potential strategies to reduce violent crime that considers environmental and biological correlates of human behavior is Robert M. Sade's "Introduction: Evolution, Prevention, and Responses to Aggressive Behavior and Violence," *The Journal of Law, Medicine & Ethics* (Spring 2004). Insightful discussions of the interplay among conscious choice, environmental factors, and basic human biology are presented as well by Michael Edmund O'Neill in "Stalking the Mark of Cain," *Harvard Journal of Law and Public Policy* (Fall 2001); Gene E. Robinson, "Beyond Nature and Nurture," *Science* (April 16, 2004); and Christiane Charlemaine, "What Might MZ Twin Research Teach Us about Race, Gender & Class Issues," *Race, Gender & Class* (October 31, 2002). Julie Horney considers the relationship between menstruation and crime in "Menstrual Cycles and Criminal Responsibility," *Law and Human Nature* (vol. 2, 1978).

Additional resources that consider the role of genetic and environmental factors in human behavior include: Edmund O. Wilson, *Sociobiology* (Harvard University Press, 1975); Lee Ellis, *Theories of Rape* (Hemisphere Publications, 1989); and Deborah Denno, *Biology, Crime and Violence* (Cambridge University Press, 1989).

ISSUE 3

Does IQ Significantly Contribute to Crime?

YES: Richard J. Herrnstein and Charles Murray, from *The Bell Curve: Intelligence and Class Structure in American Life* (Free Press, 1994)

NO: Francis T. Cullen et al., from "Crime and the Bell Curve: Lessons from Intelligent Criminology," *Crime and Delinquency* (October 1997)

ISSUE SUMMARY

YES: The late psychologist and criminologist Richard J. Herrnstein and Charles Murray, a fellow of the American Enterprise Institute, argue that a significant cause of crime is low IQ. Indeed, criminological theories and policies ignore this at great peril, they contend.

NO: Criminologists Francis T. Cullen, Paul Gendreau, G. Roger Jarjoura, and John Paul Wright concede that IQ at times may have a minor role in crime commission and that rational penal policies ought to take that into account. However, they assert that Herrnstein and Murray utilize faulty data, ignore the many significant environmental factors related to both crime and intelligence, and derive mean-spirited and repressive policy conclusions.

Two things should be noted about this controversy. First, while the issue goes directly to Richard J. Herrnstein and Charles Murray's theory of crime causation—low IQ, or being "cognitively disadvantaged"—the authors also work out an implicit treatment modality from their theory. All criminological and criminal justice theories contain concomitant treatment modalities that are logically derived from the theory. For example, if the theory is that crime results from poverty or blocked opportunities, then the implicit solution is to provide funds and jobs. If crime results from unfair, discriminatory laws or selective enforcement, then change the legal system. If crime results from a lack of proper adult role models or from delinquent peer pressure, then provide mentors or alternative friends for juveniles, or provide delinquent peers with socially acceptable activities, such as organized basketball games or job training.

Each theory's treatment modality can become the basis of policies to respond to and prevent crimes. As you read the following debate, you will notice that Francis T. Cullen et al. reject any theory of crime that gives low IQ centrality, especially the theory of Herrnstein and Murray. They also challenge the alleged benevolence of Herrnstein and Murray's policy conclusions, maintaining that the scholars are simply bootlegging their conservative agenda.

Theories of crime based on race, genes, or biology have been shunned since the 1930s. From a sociology of knowledge perspective, the idea that traits (including IQ) are passed on through genes instead of through cultural transmission (learned behavior) is considered by most people to be empirically absurd and politically incorrect. Hence, the enormous amount of controversy generated by the publication of *The Bell Curve*, the book in which Herrnstein and Murray delineate their theory of crime as based on low IQ.

As various groups representing the knowledge industry square off against *The Bell Curve* because of political, social, and personal reasons (it *is* a genuine threat to traditional social scientific conceptions of reality), others' attacks reflect philosophy of science concerns. There is simply no such thing as "IQ," some claim. Moreover, it is argued, all IQ tests are biased in favor of middle-class students and against poor or ethnic test takers, who frequently have abilities drawn from their social class or ethnic groups that are utterly ignored in most tests. The idea that entire groups on the average have lower IQs smacks of racism, critics say.

Criminological critics point out that crime rates vary dramatically between and even within the same generation. Therefore, since IQs are not likely to increase or decrease in such a short span of time, what possible bearing could they have on crime? These critics insist that we must look elsewhere for explanations, such as to traditional theories linking environmental factors (culture, socioeconomic status, neighborhood, peers) with crime and delinquency. But Herrnstein and Murray maintain that, although traditional factors may be contributors, when explanatory models are reduced to the single most important variables, then IQ is often the best predictor. Indeed, they argue that IQ explains most structural or sociological variables, such as income of parents, neighborhoods, amount of education, and so on.

Cullen et al. (and others) argue that *The Bell Curve's* test of IQ and crime and many of its own tables actually refute its argument. Intellectually disadvantaged people are not more likely to commit crimes, they say. Moreover, within criminological theory, efforts to link IQ, race, biology, or genes to crime functioned as what some philosophers of science refer to as a "negative heuristic." That is, explanations based on those variables were thought to have been discredited long ago, with most, if not all, "acceptable" criminological theories constituting a refutation of Herrnstein and Murray's theory.

As you read the following selections, note how crucial concepts are operationalized (measured) and defined. What is the structure of Herrnstein and Murray's theory? What is Cullen et al.'s theoretical perspective? What are the protagonists' policy solutions? What seems to be the scope of their respective theories (e.g., which crimes are included, excluded, or ignored in their explanations)? Is there any hope of a synthesis of the tow positions?

YES

Richard J. Herrnstein and Charles Murray

Crime

Among the most firmly established facts about criminal offenders is that their distribution of IQ scores differs from that of the population at large. Taking the scientific literature as a whole, criminal offenders have average IQs of about 92, eight points below the mean. More serious or chronic offenders generally have lower scores than more casual offenders. The relationship of IQ to criminality is especially pronounced in the small fraction of the population, primarily young men, who constitute the chronic criminals that account for a disproportionate amount of crime. Offenders who have been caught do not score much lower, if at all, than those who are getting away with their crimes. Holding socioeconomic status constant does little to explain away the relationship between crime and cognitive ability.

High intelligence also provides some protection against lapsing into criminality for people who otherwise are at risk. Those who have grown up in turbulent homes, have parents who were themselves criminal, or who have exhibited the childhood traits that presage crime are less likely to become criminals as adults if they have high IQ.

These findings from an extensive research literature are supported by the evidence from white males in the NLSY [National Longitudinal Survey of Youth]. Low IQ was a risk factor for criminal behavior, whether criminality was measured by incarceration or by self-acknowledged crimes. The socioeconomic background of the NLSY's white males was a negligible risk factor once their cognitive ability was taken into account.

Crime can tear a free society apart, because free societies depend so crucially on faith that the other person will behave decently. As one grows, society must substitute coercion for cooperation. The first penalty is not just freedom but the bonds that make community life attractive. Yes, it is always possible to buy better locks, stay off the streets after dark, regard every stranger suspiciously, post security guards everywhere, but these are poor substitutes for living in a peaceful and safe neighborhood.

Most Americans think that crime has gotten far too high. But in the ruminations about how the nation has reached this state and what might be done, too little attention has been given to one of the best-documented relationships in the study of crime: As a group, criminals are below average in intelligence.

. . . [T]hings were not always so bad. Good crime statistics do not go back very far in the United States, but we do not need statistics to remind Americans alive in the 1990s of times when they felt secure walking late at night, alone, even in poor neighborhoods and even in the nation's largest cities. In the mid-1960s, crime took a conspicuous turn for the worse. . . .

[C]rime that worries most people most viscerally: violent crime, which consists of robbery, murder, aggravated assault, and rape. From 1950 through 1963, the rate for violent crime was almost flat, followed by an extremely rapid rise from 1964 to 1971, followed by continued increases until the 1980s. The early 1980s saw an interlude in which violent crime decreased noticeably. But the trend-line for 1985–1992 is even steeper than the one for 1963–1980, making it look as if the lull was just that—a brief respite from an increase in violent crime that is now thirty years old. . . .

Depraved or Deprived?

The juvenile delinquents in Leonard Bernstein's *West Side Story* tell Officer Krupke that they are "depraved on account of we're deprived," showing an astute grasp of the poles in criminological theory: the psychological and the sociological. Are criminals psychologically distinct? Or are they ordinary people responding to social and economic circumstances?

Theories of criminal behavior were mostly near the sociological pole from the 1950s through the 1970s. Its leading scholars saw criminals as much like the rest of us, except that society earmarks them for a life of criminality. Some of these scholars went further, seeing criminals as free of personal blame, evening up the score with a society that has victimized them. The most radical theorists from the sociological pole argued that the definition of crime was in itself ideological, creating "criminals" of people who were doing nothing more than behaving in ways that the power structure chose to define as deviant. In their more moderate forms, sociological explanations continue to dominate public discourse. Many people take it for granted, for example, that poverty and unemployment cause crime—classic sociological arguments that are distinguished more by their popularity than by evidence.

Theories nearer the psychological pole were more common earlier in the history of criminology and have lately regained acceptance among experts. Here, the emphasis shifts to the characteristics of the offender rather than to his circumstances. The idea is that criminals are distinctive in psychological (perhaps even biological) ways. They are deficient, depending on the particular theory, in conscience or in self-restraint. They lack normal attachment to the mores of their culture, or they are peculiarly indifferent to the feelings or the good opinion of others. They are overendowed with restless energy or with a hunger for adventure or danger. . . .

We are at neither of these theoretical poles. Like almost all other students of crime, we expect to find explanations from both sociology and psychology. The reason for calling attention to the contrast between the theories is that public discussion has lagged; it remains more nearly stuck at the sociological pole in public discourse than it is among experts. . . . [W]e are interested in the role that cognitive ability pays in creating criminal offenders. This by no means requires us to deny that sociology, economics, and public policy might play an important part in sharing crime rates. . . .

Among the arguments often made against the claim that criminals are psychologically distinctive, two are arguments in principle rather than in fact. . . .

Argument 1: Crime rates have changed in recent times more than people's cognitive ability or personalities could have. We must therefore find the reason for the rising crime rates in people's changing circumstances.

. . . [P]ersonal characteristics need not change everywhere in society for crime's aggregate level in society to change. Consider age, for example, since crime is mainly the business of young people between 15 and 24. When the age distribution of the population shifts toward more people in their peak years for crime, the average level of crime may be expected to rise. Or crime may rise disproportionately if a large bulge in the youthful sector of the population fosters a youth culture that relishes unconventionality over traditional adult values. The exploding crime rate of the 1960s is, for example, partly explained by the baby boomers' reaching adolescence. Or suppose that a style of child rearing sweeps the country, and it turns out that this style of child rearing leads to less control over the behavior of rebellious adolescents. The change in style of child rearing may predictably be followed, fifteen or so years later, by a change in crime rates. If, in short, circumstances tip toward crime, the change will show up most among those with the strongest tendencies to break laws (or the weakest tendencies to obey them). Understanding those tendencies is the business of theories at the psychological pole.

Argument 2: Behavior is criminal only because society says so. There cannot be psychological tendencies to engage in behavior defined so arbitrarily.

This argument, made frequently during the 1960s and 1970s and always most popular among intellectuals than with the general public, is heard most often opposing any suggestion that criminal behavior has biological roots. How can something so arbitrary, say, as not paying one's taxes or driving above a 55 mph speed limit be inherited? the critics ask. Behavior regarding taxes and speed limits certainly cannot be coded in our DNA; perhaps even more elemental behaviors such as robbery and murder cannot either.

Our counterargument goes like this: Instead of crime, consider behavior that is less controversial and even more arbitrary, like playing the violin. A violin is a cultural artifact, no less arbitrary than any other man-made object, and so is the musical scale. Yet few people would argue that the first violinists in the nation's great orchestra are a random sample of the population. The interests, talents, self-discipline, and dedication that it takes to reach their level of accomplishment have roots in individual psychology—quite possibly even in biology. The variation across people in *any* behavior, however arbitrary, will have such roots. . . .

But even if crime is admitted to be a psychological phenomenon, why should intelligence be important? What is the logic that might lead us to expect low intelligence to be more frequently linked with criminal tendencies than high intelligence is?

One chain of reasoning starts from the observation that low intelligence often translates into failure and frustration in school and in the job market. If, for example, people of intelligence have a hard time finding a job, they might have more reason to commit crimes as a way of making a living. If people of low intelligence have a hard time acquiring status through the ordinary ways, crime might seem like a good alternative route. At the least, their failures in school and at work may foster resentment toward society and its laws.

Perhaps the link between crime and low IQ is even more direct. A lack of foresight, which is often associated with low IQ, raises the attractions of the immediate gains from crime and lowers the strength of the deterrents, which come later (if they come at all). To a person of low intelligence, the threats of apprehension and prison may fade to meaninglessness. They are too abstract, too far in the future, too uncertain.

Low IQ may be part of a broader complex of factors. An appetite for danger, a stronger-than-average hunger for the things that you can get only by stealing if you cannot buy them, an antipathy toward conventionality, an insensitivity to pain or to social ostracism, and a host of derangements of various sorts, combined with low IQ, may set the stage for a criminal career.

Finally, there are moral considerations. Perhaps the ethical principles for not committing crimes are less accessible (or less persuasive) to people of low intelligence. They find it harder to understand why robbing someone is wrong, find it harder to appreciate the values of civil and cooperative social life, and are accordingly less inhibited from acting in ways that are hurtful to other people and to the community at large. . . .

The Link Between Cognitive Ability and Criminal Behavior: An Overview

The statistical association between crime and cognitive ability has been known since intelligence testing began in earnest. The British physician Charles Goring mentioned a lack of intelligence as one of the distinguishing traits of the prison population that he described in a landmark contribution to modern criminology early in the century. In 1914, H. H. Goddard, an early leader in both modern criminology and the use of intelligence tests, concluded that a large fraction of convicts were intellectually subnormal.

The subsequent history of the study of the link between IQ and crime replays the larger story of intelligence testing, with the main difference being that the attack on the IQ/crime link began earlier than the broader attempt to discredit IQ tests. Even in the 1920s, the link was called into question, for example, by psychologist Carl Murchison, who produced data showing that the prisoners of Leavenworth had a higher mean IQ than that of enlisted men in World War I. Then in 1931, Edwin Sutherland, America's most prominent criminologist, wrote "Mental Deficiency and Crime," an article that effectively put an end to the study of IQ and crime for half a century. Observing (accurately) that the ostensible IQ differences between criminals and the general population were diminishing as testing procedures improved, Sutherland leaped to the conclusion that the remaining differences would disappear altogether as the state of the art improved.

The difference, in fact, did not disappear, but that did not stop criminology from denying the importance of IQ as a predictor of criminal behavior. For decades, criminologists who followed Sutherland argued that the IQ numbers said nothing about a real difference in intelligence between offenders and nonoffenders. They were skeptical about whether the convicts in prisons were truly representative of offenders in general, and they disparaged the tests' validity. Weren't tests just measuring socioeconomic status by other means, and weren't they biased against the people from the lower socioeconomic classes or the minority groups who were most likely to break the law for other reasons? they asked. By the 1960s, the association between intelligence and crime was altogether dismissed in criminology textbooks, and so it remained until recently. . . .

It took two of the leading criminologists of another generation, Travis Hirschi and Michael Hindelang, to resurrect the study of IQ and criminality that Sutherland had buried. In their 1977 article, "Intelligence and Delinquency: A Revisionist View," they reviewed many studies that included IQ measures, took into account the potential artifacts, and concluded that juvenile delinquents were in fact characterized by substantially below-average levels of tested intelligence. Hirschi and Hindelang's work took a while to percolate through the academy, . . . but by the end of the 1980s, most criminologists accepted not just that an IQ gap separates offenders and nonoffenders, but that the gap is genuinely a difference in average intellectual level. . . .

The Size of the IQ Gap

How big is the difference between criminals and the rest of us? Taking the literature as a whole, incarcerated offenders average an IQ of about 92, 8 points below the mean. The population of nonoffenders averages more than 100 points; an informed guess puts the gap between offenders and nonoffenders at about 10 points. More serious or more chronic offenders generally have lower scores than more casual offenders. The eventual relationship between IQ and repeat offending is already presaged in IQ scores taken when the children are 4 years old.

Not only is there a gap in IQ between offenders and nonoffenders, but a disproportionately large fraction of all crime is committed by people toward the low end of the scale of intelligence. . . .

Do the Unintelligent Ones Commit More Crimes—or Just Get Caught More Often?

Some critics continue to argue that offenders whose IQs we know are unrepresentative of the true criminal population; the smart ones presumably slipped through the net. Surely this is correct to some degree. . . . Is there a population of uncaught offenders with high IQs committing large numbers of crimes? The answer seems to be no. . . .

[T]he IQs of uncaught offenders are not measurably different from the ones who get caught. Among those who have criminal records, there is still a significant negative correlation between IQ and frequency of offending. Both of these kinds of evidence imply that differential arrests of people with varying IQs, assuming they exist, are a minor factor in the aggregate data.

Intelligence As a Preventative

Looking at the opposite side of the picture, those who do not commit crimes, it appears that high cognitive ability protects a person from becoming a criminal even if the other precursors are present. One study followed a sample of almost 1,500 boys born in Copenhagen, Denmark, between 1936 and 1938. Sons whose fathers had a prison record were almost six times as likely to have a prison record themselves (by the age of 34–36) as the sons of men who had no police record of any sort. Among these high-risk sons, the ones who had no police record at all had IQ scores on standard deviation higher than the sons who had a police record.

The protective power of elevated intelligence also shows up in a New Zealand study. . . .

Children growing up in troubled circumstances on Kauai in the Hawaiian chain confirm the pattern. . . .

The Link Between Cognitive Ability and Criminal Behavior: White Men in the NLSY

In the United States, where crime and race have become so intertwined in the public mind, it is especially instructive to focus on just whites. To simplify matters, we also limit the NLSY sample to males. Crime is still overwhelmingly a man's vice. Among whites in the sample, 83 percent of all persons who admitted to a criminal conviction were male.

Interpreting Self-Report Data

In the 1980 interview wave, the members of the NLSY sample were asked detailed questions about their criminal activity and their involvement with the criminal justice system. These data are known as self-report data, meaning that we have to go on what the respondent says. One obvious advantage of self-reports is that they presumably include information about the crimes of offenders whether or not they have been caught. Another is that they circumvent any biases in the criminal justice system, which, some people argue, contaminate official criminal statistics. . . . [W]e will concentrate in this analysis on events that are on the public record (and the respondent knows are on the public record): being stopped by the police, formal charges, and convictions. In doing so, we are following a broad finding in crime research that official contacts with the law enforcement and criminal justice system are usefully accurate reflections of the underlying level of criminal activity. . . .

IQ and Types of Criminal Involvement

The typical finding has been that between a third and a half of all juveniles are stopped by police at some time or another (a proportion that has grown over the last few decades) but that 5 to 7 percent of the population account for about half the total number of arrests. . . .

Something similar applies as we move up the ladder of criminal severity. Only 18 percent of white males had ever formally been charged with an offense, and a little less than 3 percent of them accounted for half the charges. Only 13 percent of white males had ever been convicted of anything, and 2 percent accounted for half of the convictions. . . .

Like studies using all races, the NLSY results for white males show a regular relationship between IQ and criminality. . . . Those who reported they had never even been stopped by the police (for anything other than a minor traffic violation) were above average in intelligence, with a mean IQ of 106, and things went downhill from there. Close to a standard deviation separated those who had never been stopped by the police from those who went to prison [IQ = 93]. . . .

In addition to self-reports, the NLSY provides data on criminal behavior by noting where the person was interviewed. In all the interviews from 1979 to 1990, was the young man ever interviewed in a correctional facility? The odds . . . that a white male had ever been interviewed in jail were fourteen times greater for Class V [bottom five percent] than for white males anywhere in the top quartile of IQ.

. . . The NLSY sample of white males echoes the scientific literature in general in showing a sizable IQ gap between offenders and nonoffenders at each level of involvement with the criminal justice system.

The Role of Socioeconomic Background

We will use both self-reports and whether the interviewee was incarcerated at the time of the interview as measures of criminal behavior. . . . Our definition of criminality here is that the man's description of his own behavior put him in the top decile of frequency of self-reported criminal activity. The other measure is whether the man was ever interviewed while being confined in a correctional facility between 1979 and 1990. . . .

For both measures, after controlling for IQ, the men's socioeconomic background had little or nothing to do with crime. In the case of the self-report data, higher socioeconomic status was associated with *higher* reported crime after controlling for IQ. In the case of incarceration, the role of socioeconomic background was close to nil after controlling for IQ, and statistically insignificant. By either measure of crime, a low IQ was a significant risk factor.

The Role of a Broken Home

When people think about the causes of crime, they usually think not only of the role of juvenile delinquent's age and socioeconomic background but also of what used to be called "broken homes." It is now an inadequate phrase, because many families do not even begin with a married husband and wife, and many broken homes are reconstituted (in some sense) through remarriage. But whatever the specific way in which a home is not intact, the children of such families are usually more likely to get in trouble with the law than children from intact families. . . .

Although family setting had an impact on crime, it did not explain away the predictive power of IQ. For example, a young man from a broken family and an average IQ and socioeconomic background had a 4 percent chance of having been interviewed in jail. Switch his IQ to the 2d centile, and the odds rise to 22 percent. . . .

The Role of Education

Scholars have been arguing about the relationship of education to crime and delinquency for many years without settling the issue. The case of the NLSY white males is a classic example. Of those who were ever interviewed in jail, 74 percent had not gotten a high school diploma. None had a college degree. Clearly something about getting seriously involved in crime competes with staying in school. Low IQ is part of that "something" in many cases, but the relationship is so strong that other factors are probably involved—for example, the same youngster who is willing to burglarize a house probably is not the most obedient of pupils; the youngster who commits assaults on the street probably gets in fights on the school grounds; . . . and so forth. . . .

Crime, Cognitive Ability, and Conscience

By now, you will already be anticipating the usual caution: Despite the relationship of low IQ to criminality, the great majority of people with low cognitive ability are law abiding. We will also take this opportunity to reiterate that the increase in crime over the last thirty years (like the increases in illegitimacy and welfare) cannot be attributed to changes in intelligence but rather must be blamed on other factors, which may have put people of low cognitive ability at greater risk than before.

The caveats should not obscure the importance of the relationship of cognitive ability to crime, however. Many people tend to think of criminals as coming from the wrong side of the tracks. They are correct, insofar as that is where people of low cognitive ability disproportionately live. They are also correct insofar as people who live on the right side of the tracks—whether they are rich or just steadily employed working-class people—seldom show up in the nation's prisons. But the assumption that too glibly follows from these observations is that the economic and social disadvantage is in itself the cause of criminal behavior. That is not what the data say, however. In trying to understand how to deal with the crime problem, much of the attention now given to problems of poverty and unemployment should be shifted to another question altogether: coping with cognitive disadvantage. . . .

Making It Easier to Live a Virtuous Life

. . . Human beings in general are capable of deciding between right and wrong. This does not mean, however, that everyone is capable of deciding between right and wrong with the same sophistication and nuances. The difference between people of low cognitive ability and the rest of society may be put in terms of a metaphor: Everyone has a moral compass, but some of those compasses are more susceptible to magnetic storms than others. . . .

Imagine living in a society where the rules about crime are simple and the consequences are equally simple. "Crime" consists of a few obviously wrong acts: assault, rape, murder, robbery, theft, trespass, destruction of another's property, fraud. Someone who commits a crime is probably caught—and almost certainly punished. The punishment almost certainly hurts (it is meaningful). Punishment follows arrest quickly. . . .

Now imagine that all the rules are made more complicated. The number of acts defined as crimes has multiplied, so that many things that are crimes are not nearly as obviously "wrong" as something like robbery or assault. The link between moral transgression and committing crime is made harder to understand. Fewer crimes lead to an arrest. Fewer arrests lead to prosecution. . . . When people are convicted, the consequences have no apparent connection to how much harm they have done. These events are typically spread out over months and sometimes years. To top it all off, even the "wrongness" of the basic crimes is called into question. In the society at large (and translated onto the television and movie screens), it is commonly argued that robbery, for example, if not always wrong if it is in a good cause (stealing medicine to save a dying wife) or if it is in response to some external condition (exploitation, racism, etc.). . . .

The two worlds we have described are not far removed from the contrast between the criminal justice system in the United States as recently as the 1950s and that system as of the 1990s. We are arguing that a person with comparatively low intelligence, whose time horizon is short and ability to balance many competing and complex incentives is low, has much more difficulty following a moral compass in the 1990s than he would have in the 1950s. . . . People of limited intelligence can lead moral lives in a society that is run on the basis of "Thou shalt not steal." They find it much harder to lead moral lives in a society that is run on the basis of "Thou shalt not steal unless there is a really good reason to."

The policy prescription is that the criminal justice system should be made *simpler*. The meaning of criminal offenses used to be clear and objective, and so were the consequences. It is worthy trying to make them so again.

Francis T. Cullen et al.

NO

Crime and the Bell Curve

In their best-selling book, *The Bell Curve*, [Richard J.] Herrnstein and [Charles] Murray argue that IQ is a powerful predictor of a range of social ills including crime. They use this "scientific reality" to oppose social welfare policies and, in particular, to justify the punishment of offenders. By reanalyzing the data used in *The Bell Curve* and by reviewing existing meta-analyses assessing the relative importance of criminogenic risk factors, the present authors show empirically that Herrnstein and Murray's claims regarding IQ and crime are misleading. The authors conclude that Herrnstein and Murray's crime control agenda is based on ideology, not on intelligent criminology.

In the aftermath of the publication of the *The Bell Curve: Intelligence and Class Structure in American Life*, Charles Murray has remained remarkably calm amid a storm of criticism that has accused him of being stupid about intelligence and, still worse, of giving solace to racists. . . . Murray repeatedly informs interviewers that he simply is being a good social scientist who is conveying unpleasant truths that can be ignored only at the nation's long-term peril.

At least with regard to crime, we claim otherwise; Murray's social science is misleading, and his message is erroneous. He needs a boost in his criminological intelligence. The apparent persuasiveness of *The Bell Curve*, which Murray coauthored with the late Richard Herrnstein, is that it purports to show that IQ has *powerful* and largely *immutable* effects across a range of behaviors. If "cognitively disadvantaged," a person is going to commit crimes, fail at school, be unemployed, end up on welfare, produce illegitimate kids, and be a lousy citizen. But if these effects do not in fact exist, or if these effects are in fact amenable to reversal, then the foundation on which Herrnstein and Murray's thesis is built crumbles.

We evaluate *The Bell Curve* only with regard to claims made about crime and, in turn, about crime-related policies. If Herrnstein and Murray are wrong about crime, then their science elsewhere in the book may be equally suspect—a fact other social scientists have attempted to demonstrate. . . .

We also should note that the initial wave of reviews of *The Bell Curve* primarily criticized Herrnstein and Murray for employing a narrow, outdated conceptualization of "intelligence," for claiming that IQ is difficult to boost, and for implying that African Americans are intellectually inferior. . . .

Toward this end, we reanalyze the data on crime reported in *The Bell Curve* and show that the effects of IQ on criminal involvement are, at best, modest. We then supplement this reanalysis by summarizing previous meta-analyses and studies of the predictors of crime. We show, again, that IQ is a weak to modest risk factor in offending and that its criminogenic effects are dwarfed by a range of factors, many of which are amenable to change.

. . . [W]e contend that Herrnstein and Murray's policies to control crime, especially among the cognitively disadvantaged, have virtually no empirical support and, on their face, are certainly preposterous. . . . We consider these policy proposals as dangerous not so much because they may be implemented but because they reinforce—persuasively, we must admit—a way of thinking about crime that is seductive, simplistic, and punitive. . . . We believe that it is important to use "intelligent criminology" to deconstruct [their] "science" and to unmask the ideology underlying *The Bell Curve*.

. . . [W]e contend that cognitive differences among offenders should not be ignored but rather taken into account when dispensing treatments—a far different perspective from that of Herrnstein and Murray, who dismiss a treatment agenda. We also suggest that criminologists should remain attentive to efforts within psychology to reconceptualize IQ, which in turn may lead to even more constructive methods of delivering effective services to offenders.

Crime and The Bell Curve: A Reassessment

Analysis in The Bell Curve

In *The Bell Curve*, Herrnstein and Murray use data from the National Longitudinal Survey of Youth (NLSY). The NLSY, initiated in 1979, surveyed 12,686 respondents ages 14 to 22 years. The study oversampled minorities and low-income groups; however, with weighted scores, the data provide nationally representative estimates. In 1980, the NLSY added a measure of cognitive ability, the Armed Forces Qualification Test (AFQT). Herrnstein and Murray claim that the AFQT is a psychometrically valid and reliable test that correlates well with standard IQ tests and measures general intelligence (the so-called "*g* factor"). . . .

The NLSY contains several measures of crime. In 1980, the respondents were asked to complete a standard 20-item self-report delinquency scale. The sample members also self-reported the extent of their "penetration" into the criminal justice system, that is, whether they had been "stopped by the police but not booked, booked but not convicted, convicted but not incarcerated, [or] sentenced to a correctional facility" (Herrnstein and Murray). The NLSY also can determine whether respondents ever were interviewed in jail when the annual NLSY survey was conducted between 1979 and 1990.

Herrnstein and Murray devote a full chapter of *The Bull Curve* to crime. Their general strategy is to show the salience of IQ in crime causation. In using the NLSY data, they first establish that those with lower AFQT scores have higher odds of penetrating the criminal justice system. They then show that even with SES [socioeconomic status] controlled, the IQ-crime relationship holds both for self-reported crime and for being interviewed while in jail; in fact, SES effects are minimal and, if anything, are positive. They also report that being from a "broken home" increases the risk of crime, but it too does not eliminate IQ's criminogenic influence. They offer a convoluted discussion of the "role of education" in which they show that poor educational performance is associated with being interviewed in jail. Strangely, however, how IQ is implicated in the school-crime relationship is not pursued empirically or theoretically. . . .

Reanalysis of the NLSY Data

We attempt to show below that Herrnstein and Murray's analysis of the NLSY data misleads about the relationship between IQ and crime. In investigating these data, we are prepared, for the sake of argument, to accept their much-contested assumption that general intelligence exists and can be measured through a single IQ score. Furthermore, we are prepared to ignore white-collar crime, a domain of lawlessness peculiarly suited to the cognitive elite. Instead, our goal is to demonstrated that even on their own terms, Herrnstein and Murray's claims about crime are based on questionable science and . . . furnish a "shaky bridge to policy."

Explained Variation

The existing research suggests that intelligence is *a* risk factor in juvenile and adult crime. The key issue, however, is whether the *magnitude* of IQ's effects on criminal behavior is small or large. Small effects would discourage making intelligence a major determinant of social policy, whereas large effects would suggest that crime control policies, should be reformulated to focus directly on cognitive disadvantage—which, of course, is Herrnstein and Murray's position.

A common way in which to assess the importance of a theoretical variable (in this case, IQ) is to see how much variation the variable can explain in type dependent variable (in this case, crime). As readers familiar with statistics know, the term R^2 typically is used to measure the amount of explained variation. Herrnstein and Murray do not report the R^2s for their analyses in the text of *The Bell Curve* but instead confine them to an appendix. As several critics note, the amount of variance that IQ explains across many outcomes is weak to modest. Crime is no exception to this pattern.

. . . [T]he authors provide the logistic regression analyses for only two measures of crime: being in the top decile on the self-report crime scale and having been interviewed in a correctional facility between 1979 and 1990. With the AFQT score, age, and SES in the equation, the analysis explains 1.5% of the variation in self-reported crime and 9.6% of the variation in being interviewed in jail.

We are interested in assessing the amount of explained variation in the different measures of crime that could be attributed solely to the AFQT. Therefore, we reestimate the Herrnstein and Murray models after removing SES. . . . The results are reported based on both the 1980 and 1990 sample weights.

. . . [F]or the three measures of self-reported crime, less than 1% of the variation is explained. Regardless of whether the 1980 or 1990 sample weights are used, the R^2 climbs at most to 2.6% for ever interviewed in jail and to 3.4% for penetration into the criminal justice system (i.e., none to being sentenced to a correctional facility). Again, we would not dismiss these findings on IQ as being unimportant. We question, however, whether explaining less than 4% of the variation in crime warrants an 845-page book whose underlying goal ostensibly is to use science to justify dismantling social welfare approaches to crime and other societal problems.

Misspecified Models

As noted, Herrnstein and Murray seek to establish the causal significance of IQ by showing how AFQT scores are related more strongly to crime than to social class with age controlled in the analysis. Other factors—family structure and education—are considered haphazardly. This methodological approach, which characterizes much of *The Bell Curve*, obviously is flawed. . . .

In a normal scientific approach, Herrnstein and Murray would have first identified the known predictors of crime and then sought to demonstrate that IQ could explain variation above and beyond these criminogenic risk factors. . . . By limiting their analysis primarily to three factors—IQ, SES, and age—they risk misspecifying their model and inflating the effects of IQ. . . .

The NLSY data set is not ideal for studying crime causation because it was not designed to operationalize the major psychological or sociological theories of criminality. For illustrative purposes, however, we more fully specified Herrnstein and Murray's model by including urban-rural residence, family structure (living with mother and father at age 14), frequency of religious participation, internal locus of control (youth reports having little influence over things that happen to him), and a range of items that might be seen as indicators of conventional bonds and attitudes (youth would shoplift if unable to support family, would choose to work if he could live comfortably without working, and expects to be working in five years; highest grade youth would like to complete). Like Herrnstein and Murray, we use logistic analysis to assess two crime measures: being in the top decile of self-reported crime and being interviewed in a correctional facility at least once between 1979 and 1990.

. . . [T]he Herrnstein and Murray three-variable model suggests that IQ is significantly related to self-reported crime. In the more fully specified model, however, IQ no longer retains statistical significance. By contrast, a number of social variables have a significant impact on crime. Thus, being in the top decile on the 20-item self-report scale is positively related to urban residence and social class and is negatively related to living with one's father at age 14, frequency of religious participation, commitment to a work ethic, and academic aspirations.

. . . [I]n the fully specified model, IQ's effects on being interviewed in a correctional facility are reduced but not eliminated. Even so, the crime measure is related negatively to living with one's father at age 14, religious participation, expectations of being able to work, and academic aspirations.

These analyses are not simply an exercise in statistical gymnastics but rather make a telling point: The effects of the sociological variables are not eliminated by IQ and, in fact, outweigh the causal importance of intelligence. . . . [T]heir analysis pits IQ against a sociological variable, SES, long known to be a weak predictor of crime. On this basis, they dismiss social welfare interventions and urge that social policy be driven by the overriding reality that people differ in their cognitive abilities.

In their own data, however, the potential importance of social factors could easily have been demonstrated. But to do so would have raised two disturbing—to Herrnstein and Murray—policy implications. First, IQ is merely one of many predictors of crime and, thus, is hardly in a position to dictate the future of crime control policy. Second, because factors such as religious participation, attitudes, conventional bonds, or even living at home with one's father are not immutable, the NLSY data provide a basis for designing programs that target criminogenic risk factors for change.

Crime or Detection?

In both Herrnstein and Murray's and our analysis of the NLSY data, IQ is weakly related or unrelated to self-reported crime but is more strongly related, albeit modestly, to measures of crime that depend on a respondent being processed by the criminal justice system such as being in jail or penetrating into the system (we refer to these as "system measures of crime"). Herrnstein and Murray's explanation for this finding, of course, is that the cognitively disadvantaged are more involved in crime. An alternative explanation, however, is that individuals' levels of intelligence affect not their criminality but rather the likelihood that, if they break the law, they will be caught and processed by the justice system; in short, smarter criminals are better at avoiding detection. The research on this topic is limited, but previous studies tend to suggest that such a detection effect does not exist or that, if it does exist, it is not substantively meaningful. This conclusion usually is made on the grounds that IQ is related to both self-report and official measures of crime in roughly similar magnitudes.

We hasten to point out that this is *not* the case in the NLSY data, a fact that Herrnstein and Murray ignore. As seen in the more fully specified equations, IQ is not statistically related to self-reported crime but is related to being interviewed in a correctional facility. Furthermore, IQ explains different amounts of variation in self-report and system measures of crime. . . .

The Relative Importance of IQ As a Criminogenic Risk Factor

In addition to analyzing NLSY data, Herrnstein and Murray provide a selective review of previous empirical studies that illustrate the negative relationship of IQ to crime. Their review of this research is not so much wrong as it is misleading; although they discuss the IQ-crime link, they remain silent on how powerfully IQ is associated with criminal behavior versus other potential risk factors. Remember, the critical issue is not whether IQ is related to crime but rather whether it is, as Herrnstein and Murray claim, the *overriding* factor. Resolving this criminological question is critical because it is the basis for evaluating Herrnstein and Murray's policy claims. Only if IQ is a powerful risk factor in crime should cognitive differences be allowed to play a salient role in formulating crime control and related social policies.

Perhaps the best method to assess the relative importance of causal variables is through a quantitative research synthesis or meta-analysis, a technique that dates back more than 50 years and that has gained increasing use in medicine and in the social sciences, including criminology, over the past two decades. Meta-analytic techniques are especially useful in providing a relatively precise quantitative assessment of how strongly two variables are associated when their relationship is calculated across a number of studies in which the two variables appear.

Fortuitously, there recently have been four meta-analyses on the predictors of recidivism for various types of adult male offenders and one on male and female juvenile offenders. Taken together, these meta-analyses encompass almost 500 studies and 4,000 effect sizes or correlations between predictors and crime. From these, we abstracted 86 effect sizes or correlations between IQ and recidivism based on studies that assess a total of 42,831 offenders. . . .

Two major conclusions can be drawn. First, the effect size or correlation between IQ and crime is weak to modest in magnitude with no effect size in the meta-analyses for adults exceeding .10. For juveniles, the correlation climbs upward but only to a high of .17. Second, in the relative ranking of predictors, IQ generally is among the weakest of the risk factors assessed in the meta-analyses. For example, across all the meta-analyses, IQ is in the top half of the predictors only once. On average, approximately 80% of the competing risk factors rank as more powerful predictors than intelligence when examining the unweighted effect sizes; the comparable mean score across the weighted effect sizes is about 70%. It appears, therefore, that IQ is hardly the preeminent determinant of crime that Herrnstein and Murray claim it to be.

. . . [A]mong the most powerful predictors is a class of risk factors that Andrews and Bonta call "criminogenic needs": attitudes, values, beliefs, and behaviors (e.g., having delinquent associates) that support an antisocial lifestyle. . . . [C]riminogenic needs usually have larger effect sizes than even the best results in favor of IQ. . . .

Criminogenic need factors not only are robust predictors of crime but also are "dynamic" in nature; that is, they can change and, thus, are amenable to correctional treatment. This reality contravenes the bell curve paradigm put forth by Herrnstein and Murray, which sees crime as rooted in the supposedly immutable trait of low IQ. An approach that stresses criminogenic needs leads to a progressive correctional agenda based on intervention and offender rehabilitation. . . . Herrnstein and Murray, by embracing the bell curve paradigm and ignoring the scientific evidence on criminogenic needs and rehabilitation, ultimately draw the "logical" but misguided conclusion that punishing the cognitively disadvantaged is the best means of achieving a safer society.

The Bell Curve and Crime Control Policy

By itself, Herrnstein and Murray's discussion of IQ and crime might be seen as provocative and as a useful, albeit exaggerated, corrective to those who dismiss out of hand the idea that criminal behavior could be linked to cognitive ability. In the end, however, the agenda of *The Bell Curve* is not science but rather social policy. . . .

The Dangers of Bell Curve Thinking

. . . As supposed friends of the cognitively disadvantaged, Herrnstein and Murray warn that American society increasingly is being socially and physically segregated by intelligence. They offer the dire prediction that unless this trend is reversed, we will head toward a "custodial state" in which the cognitively advantaged will use their brains, affluence, and political power to have the state isolate, monitor, coercively punish, and generally neglect the well-being of stupid Americans. In Herrnstein and Murray's scenario, fed up with the dangerous and profligate behaviors of low-IQ citizens, the cognitive elite will use their influence to create "a high tech and more lavish version of the Indian reservation for some substantial minority of the nation's population, while the rest of America tries to go about its business."

How might we reverse "the way we are headed"? Herrnstein and Murray's solution is to recreate a society, much like small towns used to be in the 1950s, in which "everyone has a valued place" in local communities and in which life is governed by "simple rules" uncomplicated by unnecessary government interference. And how, then, might this approach solve America's enduring crime problem? In the kinder and gentler society that Herrnstein and Murray envision, steps would be taken to "make it easier to live a virtuous life." Thus, the rules about violating the law would be made "simpler" and highlighted with a bold magic marker so that even the cognitively disadvantaged would understand them. . . .

[T]hese simple crime rules become clear and morally vivid only if violating them has consequences. Legal transgressions would have to trigger unambiguously administered *punishments* that give short shrift to personal excuses or social circumstances. This is the way it once was, Herrnstein and Murray claim, back in the 1950s when the United States was morally uncomplicated and crime was commensurately lower. . . .

One might have expected that in advancing this policy proposal, Herrnstein and Murray would have made some attempt to show that it was based on scientific evidence rather than on pure speculation. For example, they might have tried to show that because the United States was "simpler" in the 1950s, the relationship of IQ to crime was much lower in that era than it is in today's complex society where victim ideology and the "abuse excuse" supposedly make moral messages weak and unclear. Or, they might have marshaled cross-cultural data showing that in "simpler" or more communal societies—say, New Zealand—IQ does not predict crime. If they had undertaken these comparative analyses, however, then they would have learned that the data do not support these suppositions.

They also might have tried to cite data showing that maximally effective punishment-based strategies work better with dull people or dull criminals than with smart ones. Again, there are not data to support this idea either in the experimental or the clinical punishment literature. . . .

The danger is not that legislators will rush off to write simpler laws but rather that *The Bell Curve*—and other works like it—will help to legitimize a way of thinking about crime that will both be ineffective and contribute to what Clear (1994) calls the "penal harm movement." This mind-set typically combines three features. First, it reduces the complex phenomenon of crime and its control to a simple equation. . . . Second, offenders are seen to have some immutable trait, in this case low intelligence. Third, although this trait cannot be changed through the delivery of social services, offenders still can be induced to conform through punishment, that is, by seeing that bad acts have "consequences." Therefore, logic dictates that the solution to crime is to inflict pain on offenders. Indeed, whether in the "custodial state" or in the "virtuous society," Herrnstein and Murray see stupid people who break the law as ending up in jail.

The scientific poverty of this thinking is readily apparent. IQ is at best a modest predictor of crime; many other factors, which are amenable to change, are much stronger criminogenic risk factors; and deterrence-based interventions generally have been shown to be ineffective in reducing, if not positively related to, offender recidivism. In light of this scientific knowledge base, to propose formulating simple rules backed up by punishment as the main solution to crime control strains credulity. Such a proposal could come only from those who are criminologically challenged or intellectually duplicitous. . . .

The Responsible Use of IQ

Although we are highly critical of Herrnstein and Murray's slanted analysis of IQ and crime, we believe that criminologists should not "throw the baby out with the bathwater" and ignore the role of intelligence in crime and corrections. Both the NLSY data and the meta-analyses reveal that IQ is a criminogenic risk factor and, thus, is an individual difference that must be included in theories of crime causation. . . .

Herrnstein and Murray favor an approach to IQ that stresses the immutability of cognitive ability and the ineffectiveness of government-run interventions aimed at improving people's lives (other than, of course, building a "simpler" society). By contrast, we see IQ as information that can be used to design and deliver more effective treatment interventions. In the end, when people violate the law, Herrnstein and Murray's policy agenda offers punishment and incapacitation. Our agenda offers the hope, rooted in scientific criminology, that positive behavioral change is possible and can be made more likely when treatment interventions take into account people's individual differences including their intellectual competencies.

Conclusion: Intelligent Criminology

Close scrutiny of *The Bell Curve* reveals both the lack of and the important role to be played by intelligent criminology. We argue that Herrnstein and Murray are "cognitively challenged" criminologists. Their analysis exaggerates the causal importance of intelligence in criminal behavior and ignores an enormous body of research on competing predictors of crime. Their failure to consider alternative criminogenic risk factors is inexcusable not only because the research documenting their salience is readily available but also because doing so leads them to justify ill-conceived, repressive crime policies. By portraying offenders as driven into crime predominantly by cognitive disadvantage, Herrnstein and Murray mask the reality that stronger risk factors not only exist but also are amenable to effective correctional intervention.

We hope, however, that we have illuminated how positivist criminology can be valuable in deconstructing bell curve "science" and in revealing its ideological base. In this instance, we tried to move beyond the type of broad, ideologically inspired condemnation found in many reviews of Herrnstein and Murray's work. Instead, our goal was to show that the best way in which to fashion an intelligent criminological response to *The Bell Curve* was to draw on the discipline's empirical knowledge base. To the extent that we have achieved this goal, we trust that we have provided a more general lesson in the power of a scientific approach to criminology to combat mean-spirited ideology and to justify confronting crime with a more progressive policy agenda.

References

Glass, Gene V., Barry McGaw, and Mary Lee Smith. 1981. *Meta-Analysis in Social Research*. Beverly Hills, CA: Sage.

Harland, Alan T., ed. 1996. *Choosing Correctional Options That Work: Defining the Demand and Evaluating the Supply*. Thousand Oaks, CA: Sage.

Hauser, Robert M. 1995. "Symposium: *The Bell Curve*." *Contemporary Sociology* 24: 149–153.

Hunt, Morton. 1997. *How Science Takes Stock: The Story of Meta-Analysis*. New York: Russell Sage.

Ward, David A. and Charles R. Tittle. 1994. "IQ and Delinquency: A Test of Two Competing Explanations." *Journal of Quantitative Criminology* 10: 189–212.

POSTSCRIPT

Does IQ Significantly Contribute to Crime?

In the parlance of philosophy of science, a "paradigmatic shift" may be occurring, at least if Herrnstein and Murray are to be believed (Cullen et al.'s acknowledgment of the limited role of IQ actually lends some support to this thesis). Since the time of criminologist Edwin Sutherland, biological factors as causes of crime were viewed as a negative heuristic. Following the horrors of the Nazi genocide program in the 1940s, genetic links to crime were even more vehemently rejected as terrible, dangerous criminology, if not evil.

Yet there have always been at least some distinguished scholars, including within criminology and psychology, who long for a reconsideration of biological influences. Today, unlike 20 or 30 years ago, virtually all standard texts dealing with causes of crime examine biological variants. These often are no longer treated exclusively as historical relics (e.g., discussions of highly selected aspects of pioneer criminologist Cesare Lombroso and other nineteenth-century writings). Does this mean that a paradigmatic shift is occurring within criminology and criminal justice? Will criminology students now be trained in biology, physiology, and genetics, instead of sociology, political science, and traditional psychology? Will structural theories of crime (environmental, sociocultural explanations) be abandoned?

Probably not. As Cullen et al. make clear, the task of sound theory is to explain variations in behavior. They argue that IQ explains relatively little about variations in crime, while traditional independent variables (causes) such as socioeconomic status, neighborhood, peers, and so on explain far more.

A related issue is that genetic explanations are only one variant of biological ones. For instance, diet, presence of lead in the home, neurological disorders, toxic poisoning, and many other biological factors could contribute to crime (and other forms of behavior). These generally have little direct relation to genetics (such correlations are unlikely to be passed on or be disproportionately in one group of people if these factors are removed). While these factors still explain a relatively small percentage of variations in crime rates, they are far more palpable empirically, theoretically, and ethically to most criminologists. From a sociology of knowledge perspective, it is intriguing to theorize about why genetic-biological theories are currently emerging in abundance (Cullen et al., like many others, simply link it with the conservative political mood America is currently in).

Part of the reason why *The Bell Curve* has been so vehemently attacked by traditional scholars may be that they perceive a hidden racist agenda in efforts to link IQ with negative behavior such as crime. Although the studies drawn from in the excerpt by Herrnstein and Murray deal with white subjects, much of the thrust of their book seems to be developing the argument that blacks, on average, have lower IQs and, hence, cannot compete as well in a rapidly changing technological society. For many, the political and moral implications of the *Bell Curve* theory are extremely harmful. For example, neither side considers the logical, if hideous, treatment modality implicit in the IQ-crime theory: sterilization or extermination of "biologically unfit" people. For the first third of the twentieth century, at least 16 states had sterilization laws. In *Buck v. Bell* (1927) Chief Justice Oliver Wendell Holmes proclaimed, "Three generations of imbeciles are enough," allowing Virginia to forceably sterilize a woman. And many sociology textbooks before World War II devoted several pages to favorable discussions of eugenics.

If IQ does influence criminal behavior, then there are many additional issues to address. Luckily, there is a growing literature dealing with this controversy. Among the best works looking at IQ testing from both the sociology of knowledge and the philosophy of science perspectives are S. Gould, *The Mismeasure of Man* (W. W. Norton, 1996); L. Kamin, "Behind the Curve," *Scientific American* (February 1995); and C. Fischer et al., *Inequality by Design* (Princeton University Press, 1996). Special issues devoted to *The Bell Curve* include *Current Anthropology* (February 1996) and *The Black Scholar* (Winter 1995). Anthologies include R. Jacoby and N. Glauberman, eds., *The Bell Curve Debate: History, Documents, Opinions* (Times Books, 1995) and *Measured Lies: The Bell Curve Examined* edited by J. L. Kincheles, S. R. Steinberg, and A. D. Gresson III (St. Martin's Press, 1996).

Broader discussions dealing with genetic influences on behavior can be found in the October 1997 issue of *Discover*. A good book on problems with genetics and criminology is *Genetics and Criminality: The Potential Misuse of Scientific Information in Court* edited by J. Botkin, W. M. McMahon, and L. P. Francis (American Psychological Association, 1999). A study that supports Herrnstein and Murray is *Race, Evolution and Behavior: A Life History Perspective* by J. Rushton (Transaction, 1995). A more neutral overview is "Gene-Based Evolutionary Theories in Criminology," by L. Ellis and A. Walsh, *Criminology* (May 1997).

Recent research that calls into question IQ testing includes N. Lemann's *The Big Test: The Secret History of the American Meritocracy* (Farrar, Straus & Giroux, 1999); "The Big Score," by D. McGinn, *Newsweek* (September 6, 1999); and D. Goleman, *Working With Emotional Intelligence* (Bantam Books, 1998). An account of top biologists at Harvard University battling over the issue is "Oh My Darwin: Who's the Fittest Evolutionary Thinker of Them All?" by J. Schwartz, *Lingua Franca* (November 1999). A more balanced position can be found in J. R. Harris's *The Nurture Assumption: Why Children Turn Out the Way They Do* (Free Press, 1998). An interesting though highly controversial look at black athletic achievement is *Taboo: Why Black Athletes Dominate Sports and Why We Are Afraid to Talk About It* by J. Entine (Public Affairs, 2000). Finally, a report that looks at the high regard in which Americans hold IQ is "Infertile Couples Shop in Ivy League: Seek Eggs from Women With High IQs," *The Washington Times* (January 4, 1999).

ISSUE 4

Is Street Crime More Serious Than White-Collar Crime?

YES: James Q. Wilson and Richard J. Herrnstein, from *Crime and Human Nature* (Simon & Schuster, 1985)

NO: Jeffrey Reiman, from *The Rich Get Richer and the Poor Get Prison: Ideology, Class, and Criminal Justice*, 5th ed. (Allyn & Bacon, 1998)

ISSUE SUMMARY

YES: Professor of management and public policy James Q. Wilson and the late psychologist Richard J. Herrnstein argue that the focus of crime study ought to be on people who "hit, rape, murder, steal, and threaten."

NO: Professor of philosophy Jeffrey Reiman contends that a focus on street crimes is little more than a cover-up for more serious crimes such as pollution, medical malpractice, and dangerous working conditions that go uncorrected.

$\mathbf{S}$cholars and the general public differ intellectually, ideologically, and politically in their definitions of crime as well as with regard to why it exists. Liberal, conservative, and radical ideologies are likely to generate different definitions and explanations of crime.

One aspect of American society is its extremely heavy emphasis on economic success. Apparently, for many who desire the material benefits that "the haves" seem to take for granted but who are thwarted by lack of training or skills or by discrimination, one recourse is to engage in predatory street crimes. Others are able to succeed financially because they are taught how to and are fully allowed to participate: they can attend good schools, join a solid corporation, and work their way up the ladder. Probably very few business executive types would dream of holding up someone, breaking into a house, or attacking someone in a rage.

Yet in certain companies, the pressure to succeed, to keep corporate profits up, and to fulfill the expectations of managers and administrators drives many to commit white-collar crimes. No one knows for sure how many street crimes occur each day (many are not reported). Nor do we know how many white-collar crimes occur each day. The latter are much more likely to be carefully hidden and their consequences delayed for months or even years. Moreover, white-collar crimes are far more likely to be dismissed as "just another shrewd business practice by an ambitious executive in order to keep ahead of competitors." Most of us never directly see the results of white-collar crimes, nor do we know many people who are visibly harmed by them. By contrast, many of us have been victims of street crimes or know such victims. The results of a direct physical assault or the fear of discovering a burglarized home or a stolen car are relatively easy to observe in a victim of these crimes.

But how should we view those who shiver in the cold because their utility bills were hiked illegally, forcing them to keep their thermostats under 60 degrees? Or those robbed of health because of lung infections contracted while they worked in unsafe mines or around unsafe chemicals? Are they usually thought of as the victims of criminals? Are people who are killed in traffic accidents because their automobiles left the factory in unsafe condition—with the factory's full knowledge and approval—thought of as murder victims?

Frequently, both the general public and criminologists concentrate on street crimes, their perpetrators and victims, while ignoring white-collar crimes. But beginning with the seminal work of Edwin Sutherland, *White Collar Crime* (1949), some criminologists have demonstrated concern with this form of violation.

In spite of the fact that, in general, white-collar crime receives less attention and less serious attention than street crime, several white-collar criminals have in recent years been the focus of extensive media coverage. Yet in almost each case, the criminals have been viewed as isolated deviants who just happened to engage in wrongdoing. Neither the organizations for which they worked nor the broader corporate system and the values it promotes came under much scrutiny by the public.

Although many large corporations have been ordered to pay out huge monetary awards for extensive harms, most have not been subject to criminal charges, and none have been convicted of any crime. For example, tobacco companies will be paying out $246 billion over 25 years in a settlement with the U.S. states. In addition, American Home Products agreed to pay a total of $3.75 billion to thousands of consumers who claim to have been injured by the company's diet pill program, and three Japanese corporations have been fined $137 million for fixing the prices of vitamins sold in the United States. Meanwhile, huge awards for damages are being won against lead paint manufacturers, asbestos companies, and so on. However, none of these cases raised incarceration as a contingency, even those that involved fraud or criminal negligence.

As you study the position of James Q. Wilson and Richard J. Herrnstein and that of Jeffrey Reiman, notice that it remains problematic as to not only what crime is and what its most adequate scientific explanations are but also which crimes are the most harmful and dangerous to members of society.

YES

James Q. Wilson and
Richard J. Herrnstein

Crime and Human Nature

Crime and Its Explanation

Predatory street crimes are most commonly committed by young males. Violent crimes are more common in big cities than in small ones. High rates of criminality tend to run in families. The persons who frequently commit the most serious crimes typically begin their criminal careers at a quite young age. Persons who turn out to be criminals usually do not do very well in school. Young men who drive recklessly and have many accidents tend to be similar to those who commit crimes. Programs designed to rehabilitate high-rate offenders have not been shown to have much success, and those programs that do manage to reduce criminality among certain kinds of offenders often increase it among others.

These facts about crime—some well known, some not so well known—are not merely statements about traits that happen occasionally, or in some places but not others, to describe criminals. They are statements that, insofar as we can tell, are pretty much true everywhere. They are statements, in short, about human nature as much as about crime.

All serious political and moral philosophy, and thus any serious social inquiry, must begin with an understanding of human nature. Though society and its institutions shape man, man's nature sets limits on the kinds of societies we can have. Cicero said that the nature of law must be founded on the nature of man (*a natura hominis discenda est natura juris*). . . . We could have chosen to understand human nature by studying work, or sexuality, or political activity; we chose instead to approach it through the study of crime, in part out of curiosity and in part because crime, more dramatically than other forms of behavior, exposes the connection between individual dispositions and the social order.

The problem of social order is fundamental: How can mankind live together in reasonable order? Every society has, by definition, solved that problem to some degree, but not all have done so with equal success or without paying a high cost in other things—such as liberty—that we also value. If we believe that man is naturally good, we will expect that the problem of order can be rather easily managed; if we believe him to be naturally wicked, we will expect the provision of order to require extraordinary measures; if we believe his nature to be infinitely plastic, we will think the problem of order can be solved entirely by plan and that we may pick and choose freely among all possible plans. Since every known society has experienced crime, no society has ever entirely solved the problem of order. The fact that crime is universal may suggest that man's nature is not infinitely malleable, though some people never cease searching for an anvil and hammer sufficient to bend it to their will.

Some societies seem better able than others to sustain order without making unacceptable sacrifices in personal freedom, and in every society the level of order is greater at some times than at others. These systematic and oft-remarked differences in the level of crime across time and place suggest that there is something worth explaining. But to find that explanation, one cannot begin with the society as a whole or its historical context, for what needs explanation is not the behavior of "society" but the behavior of individuals making up a society. Our intention is to offer as comprehensive an explanation as we can manage of why some individuals are more likely than others to commit crimes.

The Problem of Explanation

That intention is not easily realized, for at least three reasons. First, crime is neither easily observed nor readily measured. . . . [T]here is no way of knowing the true crime rate of a society or even of a given individual. Any explanation of why individuals differ in their law-abidingness may well founder on measurement errors. If we show that Tom, who we think has committed a crime, differs in certain interesting ways from Dick, who we think has not, when in fact both Tom and Dick have committed a crime, then the "explanation" is meaningless.

Second, crime is very common, especially among males. Using interviews and questionnaires, scholars have discovered that the majority of all young males have broken the law at least once by a relatively early age. By examining the police records of boys of a given age living in one place, criminologists have learned that a surprisingly large fraction of all males will be arrested at least once in their lives for something more serious than a traffic infraction. Marvin Wolfgang found that 35 percent of all the males born in Philadelphia in 1945 and living there between the ages of ten and eighteen had been arrested at least once by their eighteenth birthday.[1] Nor is this a peculiarly American phenomenon. Various surveys have found that the proportion of British males who had been convicted in court before their twenty-first birthday ranged from 15 percent in the nation as a whole to 31 percent for a group of boys raised in London. David Farrington estimates that 44 percent of all the males in "law-abiding" Britain will be arrested sometime in their lives.[2] If committing a crime at least once is so commonplace, then it is quite likely that there will be few, if any, large differences between those who never break the law and those who break it at least once—even if we had certain knowledge of which was which. Chance events as much as or more than individual predispositions will determine who commits a crime.

Third, the word "crime" can be applied to such varied behavior that it is not clear that it is a meaningful category of analysis. Stealing a comic book, punching a friend, cheating on a tax return, murdering a wife, robbing a bank, bribing a politician, hijacking an airplane—these and countless other acts are all crimes. Crime is as broad a category as disease, and perhaps as useless. To explain why one person has ever committed a crime and another has not may be as pointless as explaining why one person has ever gotten sick and another has not. We are not convinced that "crime" is so broad a category as to be absolutely meaningless—surely it is not irrelevant that crime is that form of behavior that is against the law—but we do acknowledge that it is difficult to provide a true and interesting explanation for actions that differ so much in their legal and subjective meanings.

To deal with these three difficulties, we propose to confine ourselves, for the most part, to explaining why some persons commit serious crimes at a high rate and others do not. By looking mainly at serious crimes, we escape the problem of comparing persons who park by a fire hydrant to persons who rob banks. By focusing on high-rate offenders, we do not need to distinguish between those who never break the law and those who (for perhaps chance reasons) break it only once or twice. And if we assume (as we do) that our criminal statistics are usually good enough to identify persons who commit a lot of crimes even if these data are poor at identifying accurately those who commit only one or two, then we can be less concerned with measurement errors.

The Meaning of Crime

A crime is any act committed in violation of a law that prohibits it and authorizes punishment for its commission. If we propose to confine our attention chiefly to persons who commit serious crimes at high rates, then we must specify what we mean by "serious." The arguments we shall make and the evidence we shall cite . . . will chiefly refer to aggressive, violent, or larcenous behavior; they will be, for the most part, about persons who hit, rape, murder, steal, and threaten.

In part, this limited focus is an unfortunate accident: We report only what others have studied, and by and large they have studied the causes of what we call predatory street crime. We would like to draw on research into a wider variety of law-violating behavior—embezzlement, sexual deviance, bribery, extortion, fraud—but very little such research exists.

But there is an advantage to this emphasis on predatory crime. Such behavior, except when justified by particular, well-understood circumstances (such as war), is condemned, in all societies and in all historical periods, by ancient tradition, moral sentiments, and formal law. Graeme Newman . . . interviewed people in six nations (India, Indonesia, Iran, Italy, the United States, and Yugoslavia) about their attitudes toward a variety of behaviors and concluded that there is a high—indeed, virtually universal—agreement that certain of these behaviors were wrong and should be prohibited by law.[3] Robbery, stealing, incest, and factory pollution were condemned by overwhelming majorities in every society; by contrast, abortion and homo-sexuality, among other acts, were thought to be crimes in some places but not in others. Interestingly, the characteristics of the individual respondents in these countries—their age, sex, education, social class—did not make much difference in what they thought should be treated as crimes. Newman's finding merely reinforces a fact long understood by anthropologists: Certain acts are regarded as wrong by every society, preliterate as well as literate; that among these "universal crimes" are murder, theft robbery, and incest.[4]

Moreover, people in different societies rate the seriousness of offenses, especially the universal crimes, in about the same way. Thorsten Sellin and Marvin E. Wolfgang developed a scale to measure the relative gravity of 141 separate offenses. This scale has been found to be remarkably stable, producing similar rankings among both American citizens and prison inmates,[5] as well as among Canadians,[6] Puerto Ricans,[7] Taiwanese,[8] and Belgian Congolese.[9]

By drawing on empirical studies of behaviors that are universally regarded as wrong and similarly ranked as to gravity, we can be confident that we are in fact theorizing about *crime* and human nature and not about actions that people may or may not think are wrong. If the studies to which we refer were to include commercial price-fixing, political corruption, or industrial monopolization, we would have to deal with the fact that in many countries these actions are not regarded as criminal at all. If an American business executive were to bring all of the nation's chemical industries under his control, he would be indicted for having formed a monopoly; a British business executive who did the same thing might be elevated to the peerage for having created a valuable industrial empire. Similarly, by omitting studies of sexual deviance (except forcible rape), we avoid modifying our theory to take into account changing social standards as to the wrongness of these acts and the legal culpability of their perpetrators. In short, we seek . . . to explain why some persons are more likely than others to do things that all societies condemn and punish.

To state the same thing a bit differently, we will be concerned more with criminality than with crime. Travis Hirschi and Michael Gottfredson have explained this important distinction as follows. *Crimes* are short-term, circumscribed events that result from the (perhaps fortuitous) coming together of an individual having certain characteristics and an opportunity having certain (immediate and deferred) costs and benefits. . . . *Criminality* refers to "stable differences across individuals in the propensity to commit criminal (or equivalent) acts."[10] The "equivalent" acts will be those that satisfy, perhaps in entirely legal ways, the same traits and predispositions that lead, in other circumstances, to crime. For example, a male who is very impulsive and so cannot resist temptation may, depending on circumstances, take toys from his playmates, money from his mother, billfolds from strangers, stamps from the office, liquor in the morning, extra chocolate cake at dinner time, and a nap whenever he feels like it. Some of these actions break the law, some do not.

The Categories of Explanation

Because we state that we intend to emphasize individual differences in behavior or predisposition, some readers may feel that we are shaping the argument in an improper manner. These critics believe that one can explain crime only by beginning with the society in which it is found. Emile Durkheim wrote: "We must, then, seek the explanation of social life in the nature of society itself."[11] Or, put another way, the whole is more than the sum of its parts. We do not deny that social arrangements and institutions, and the ancient customs that result from living and working together, affect behavior, often profoundly. But no explanation of social life explains anything until it explains individual behavior. Whatever significance we attach to ethnicity, social class, national character, the opinions of peers, or the messages of the mass media, the only test of their explanatory power is their ability to account for differences in how individuals, or groups of individuals, behave.

Explaining individual differences is an enterprise much resisted by some scholars. To them, this activity implies reducing everything to psychology, often referred to as "mere psychology." David J. Bordua, a sociologist, has pointed out the bias that can result from an excessive preference for social explanations over psychological ones.[12] Many criminologists, he comments, will observe a boy who becomes delinquent after being humiliated by his teacher or fired by his employer, and will conclude that his delinquency is explained by his "social class." But if the boy becomes delinquent after having been humiliated by his father or spurned by his girl friend, these scholars will deny that these events are explanations because they are "psychological." Teachers and employers are agents of the class structure, fathers and girl friends are not; therefore, the behavior of teachers and employers must be more important.

We believe that one can supply an explanation of criminality—and more important, of law-abidingness—that begins with the individual in, or even before, infancy and that takes into account the impact on him of subsequent experiences in the family, the school, the neighborhood, the labor market, the criminal justice system, and society at large. Yet even readers who accept this plan of inquiry as reasonable may still doubt its importance. To some, explaining crime is unnecessary because they think the explanation is already known; to others, it is impossible, since they think it unknowable.

Having taught a course on the causes of crime, and having spoken to many friends about our research, we have become acutely aware that there is scarcely any topic—except, perhaps, what is wrong with the Boston Red Sox or the Chicago Cubs—on which people have more confident opinions. Crime is caused, we are told, by the baby boom, permissive parents, brutal parents, incompetent schools, racial discrimination, lenient judges, the decline of organized religion, televised violence, drug addiction, ghetto unemployment, or the capitalist system. We note certain patterns in the proffered explanations. Our tough-minded friends blame crime on the failings of the criminal justice system; our tender-minded ones blame it on the failings of society.

We have no *a priori* quarrel with any of these explanations, but we wonder whether all can be true, or true to the same degree. The baby boom may help explain why crime rose in the 1960s and 1970s, but it cannot explain why some members of that boom became criminals and others did not. It is hard to imagine that both permissive and brutal parents produce the same kind of criminals, though it is conceivable that each may contribute to a different kind of criminality. Many children may attend bad schools, but only a small minority become serious criminals. And in any case, there is no agreement as to what constitutes an incompetent school. Is it an overly strict one that "labels" mischievous children as delinquents, or is it an overly lax one that allows normal mischief to degenerate into true delinquency? Does broadcast violence include a football or hockey game, or only a detective story in which somebody shoots somebody else? Economic conditions may affect crime, but since crime rates were lower in the Great Depression than during the prosperous years of the 1960s, the effect is, at best, not obvious or simple. The sentences given by judges may affect the crime rate, but we are struck by the fact that the most serious criminals begin offending at a very early age, long before they encounter, or probably even hear of, judges, whereas those who do not commit their first crime until they are adults (when, presumably, they have some knowledge of law and the courts) are the least likely to have a long or active criminal career. Racism and capitalism may contribute to crime, but the connection must be rather complicated, since crime has risen in the United States (and other nations) most rapidly during recent times, when we have surely become less racist and (given the growth of governmental controls on business) less capitalist. In any event, high crime rates can be found in socialist as well as capitalist nations, and some capitalist nations, such as Japan and Switzerland, have very little crime. In view of all this, some sorting out of these explanations might be useful.

But when we discuss our aims with scholars who study crime, we hear something quite different. There is no well-accepted theory of the causes of crime, we are told, and it is unlikely that one can be constructed. Many explanations have been advanced, but all have been criticized. What is most needed is more research, not better theories. Any theory specific enough to be testable will not explain very much, whereas any theory broad enough to explain a great deal will not be testable. It is only because they are friends that some of our colleagues refrain from muttering about fools rushing in where wise men, if not angels, fear to tread. . . .

But there is one version of the claim that explaining crime is impossible to which we wish to take immediate exception. That is the view, heard most frequently from those involved with criminals on a case-by-case basis (probation officers and therapists, for example), that the causes of crime are unique to the individual criminal. Thus, one cannot generalize about crime because each criminal is different. Now, in one sense that argument is true—no two offenders are exactly alike. But we are struck by the fact that there are certain obvious patterns to criminality, suggesting that something more than random individual differences is at work. We think these obvious patterns, if nothing else, can be explained.

Patterns in Criminality

Crime is an activity disproportionately carried out by young men living in large cities. There are old criminals, and female ones, and rural and small-town ones, but, to a much greater degree than would be expected by chance, criminals are young urban males. This is true, insofar as we can tell, in every society that keeps any reasonable criminal statistics.[13] These facts are obvious to all, but sometimes their significance is overlooked. Much time and effort may be expended in trying to discover whether children from broken homes are more likely to be criminals than those from intact ones, or whether children who watch television a lot are more likely to be aggressive than those who watch it less. These are interesting questions, and we shall have something to say about them, but even if they are answered satisfactorily, we will have explained rather little about the major differences in criminality. Most children raised in broken homes do not become serious offenders; roughly half of such children are girls, and . . . females are often only one-tenth as likely as males to commit crimes. Crime existed abundantly long before the advent of television and would continue long after any hint of violence was expunged from TV programs. Any worthwhile explanation of crime must account for the major, persistent differences in criminality.

The fact that these regularities exist suggests that it is not impossible, in principle, to provide a coherent explanation of crime. It is not like trying to explain why some people prefer vanilla ice cream and others chocolate. And as we shall see . . . there are other regularities in criminality beyond those associated with age, sex, and place. There is mounting evidence that, on the average, offenders differ from nonoffenders in physique, intelligence, and personality. Some of these differences may not themselves be a cause of crime but only a visible indicator of some other factor that does contribute to crime. . . . [W]e shall suggest that a certain physique is related to criminality, not because it causes people to break the law, but because a particular body type is associated with temperamental traits that predispose people to offending. Other individual differences, such as in personality, may directly contribute to criminality.

There are two apparent patterns in criminality that we have yet to mention, though they are no doubt uppermost in the minds of many readers—class and race. To many people, it is obvious that differences in social class, however defined, are strongly associated with lawbreaking. The poor, the unemployed, or the "underclass" are more likely than the well-to-do, the employed, or the "respectable poor" to commit certain kinds of crimes. We are reluctant, however, at least at the outset, to use class as a major category of explanations of differences in criminality for two reasons.

First, scholars who readily agree on the importance of age, sex, and place as factors related to crime disagree vigorously as to whether social class, however defined, is associated with crime. Their dispute may strike readers who have worked hard to move out of slums and into middle-class suburbs as rather bizarre; can anyone seriously doubt that better-off neighborhoods are safer than poorer ones? As John Braithwaite has remarked, "It is hardly plausible that one can totally explain away the higher risks of being mugged and raped in lower class areas as a consequence of the activities of middle class people who come into the area to perpetrate such acts."[14]

We have much sympathy with his view, but we must recognize that there are arguments against it. When Charles R. Tittle, Wayne J. Villemez, and Douglas A. Smith reviewed thirty-five studies of the relationship between crime rates and social class, they found only a slight association between the two variables.[15] When crime was measured using official (e.g., police) reports, the connection with social class was stronger than when it was measured using self-reports (the crimes admitted to by individuals filling out a questionnaire or responding to an interview). This conclusion has been challenged by other scholars who find, on the basis of more extensive self-report data than any previously used, that crime, especially serious crime, is much more prevalent among lower-class youth.[16] Michael J. Hindelang, Travis Hirschi, and Joseph G. Weis have shown that self-report studies tend to measure the prevalence of trivial offenses, including many things that would not be considered a crime at all (e.g., skipping school, defying parents, or having unmarried sex).[17] Even when true crimes are reported, they are often so minor (e.g., shoplifting a pack of gum) that it is a mistake—but, alas, a frequently made mistake—to lump such behavior together with burglary and robbery as measures of criminality. We agree with Hindelang et al., as well as with many others,[18] who agrue that when crime is properly measured, the relationship between it and social class is strong—lower-class persons are much more likely to have committed a serious "street" crime than upper-status ones. But we recognize that this argument continues to be controversial, and so it seems inappropriate to begin an explanation of criminality by assuming that it is based on class.

Our second reason for not starting with class as a major social factor is, to us, more important. Unlike sex, age, and place, class is an ambiguous concept. A "lower-class" person can be one who has a low income, but that definition lumps together graduate students, old-age pensioners, welfare mothers, and unemployed steelworkers—individuals who would appear to have, as far as crime is concerned, little in common. Many self-report studies of crime use class categories so broad as to obscure whatever connection may exist between class and criminality.[19] And studies of delinquency typically describe a boy as belonging to the class of his father, even if the boy in his own right, in school or in the labor force, is doing much better or much worse than his father.[20] By lower class one could also mean having a low-prestige occupation, but it is not clear to us why the prestige ranking of one's occupation should have any influence on one's criminality.

Class may, of course, be defined in terms of wealth or income, but using the concept in this way to explain crime, without further clarification, is ambiguous as to cause and effect. One's wealth, income, status, or relationship to the means of production could cause certain behavior (e.g., "poor people must steal to eat"), or they could themselves be caused by other factors (impulsive persons with low verbal skills tend to be poor and to steal). By contrast, one's criminality cannot be the cause of, say, one's age or sex. . . .

Race is also a controversial and ambiguous concept in criminological research. Every study of crime using official data shows that blacks are heavily overrepresented among persons arrested, convicted, and imprisoned.[21] Some people, however, suspect that official reports are contaminated by the racial bias of those who compile them. Self-report studies, by contrast, tend to show fewer racial differences in criminality, but these studies have the same defect with respect to race as they do with regard to class—they overcount trivial offenses, in which the races do not differ, and undercount the more serious offenses, in which they do differ.[22] Moreover, surveys of the victims of crimes reveal that of the offenders whose racial identity could be discerned by their victims, about half were black; for the most serious offenses, two-thirds were black.[23] Though there may well be some racial bias in arrests, prosecutions, and sentences, there is no evidence . . . that it is so great as to account for the disproportionate involvement of blacks in serious crime, as revealed by both police and victimization data and by interviews with prison inmates.[24]

Our reason for not regarding, at least at the outset, race as a source of individual differences in criminality is not that we doubt that blacks are over-represented in crime. Rather, there are two other considerations. First, racial differences exist in some societies and not others, yet all societies have crime. Though racial factors may affect the crime rate, the fundamental explanation for individual differences in criminality ought to be based—indeed, must be based, if it is to be a general explanation—on factors that are common to all societies.

Second, we find the concept of race to be ambiguous, but in a different way from the ambiguity of class. There is no reason to believe that the genes determining one's skin pigmentation also affect criminality. At one time in this nation's history, persons of Irish descent were heavily overrepresented among those who had committed some crime, but it would have been fool-ish then to postulate a trait called "Irishness" as an explanation. If racial or ethnic identity affects the likelihood of committing a crime, it must be because that identity co-varies with other characteristics and experiences that affect criminality. The proper line of inquiry, then, is first to examine those other characteristics and experiences to see how and to what extent they pre-dispose an individual toward crime, and then to consider what, if anything, is left unexplained in the observed connection between crime and racial identity. After examining constitutional, familial, educational, economic, neighborhood, and historical factors, there may or may not be anything left to say on the subject of race. . . .

Are There Types of Criminals?

We are concerned mainly with explaining criminality—why some people are more likely than others to commit, at a high rate, one or more of the universal crimes. But even if the behaviors with which we are concerned are alike in being universally regarded as serious crimes, are not the *motives* for these crimes so various that they cannot all be explained by one theory? Possibly. But this objection assumes that what we want to know are the motives of lawbreakers. It is by no means clear that the most interesting or useful way to look at crime is by trying to discover the motives of individual criminals—why some offenders like to steal cash, others like stolen cash plus a chance to beat up on its owner, and still others like violent sex—any more than it is obvious that the best way to understand the economy is by discovering why some persons keep their money in the bank, others use it to buy tickets to boxing matches, and still others use it to buy the favors of a prostitute. The motives of criminal (and of human) behavior are as varied as the behavior itself; we come to an understanding of the general processes shaping crime only when we abstract from particular motives and circumstances to examine the factors that lead people to run greater or lesser risks in choosing a course of action.

To us, offenders differ not so much in what kind of crimes they commit, but in the rate as which they commit them. In this sense, the one-time wife murderer is different from the persistent burglar or the organized drug trafficker—the first man breaks the law but once, the latter two do it every week or every day. . . . [T]he evidence suggests that persons who frequently break universal laws do not, in fact, specialize very much. A high-rate offender is likely to commit a burglary today and a robbery tomorrow, and sell drugs in between.

Explaining why some persons have a very high rate and others a low one is preferable, we think, to the major alternative to this approach: trying to sort offenders and offenses into certain categories or types. Creating—and arguing about—typologies is a major preoccupation of many students of crime because, having decided that motives are what count and having discovered that there are almost as many motives as there are people, the only way to bring any order to this variety is by reducing all the motives to a few categories, often described as personality types.

For example, a common distinction in criminology is between the "subcultural" offender and the "unsocialized" or "psychopathic" one. The first is a normal person who finds crime rewarding (perhaps because he has learned to commit crimes from friends he admires) and who discounts heavily the risks of being punished. The second is abnormal: He commits crimes because he has a weak conscience and cares little about the opinions of friends. Now, as even the authors of such distinctions acknowledge, these categories overlap (some subcultural thieves, for example, may also take pleasure in beating up on their victims), and not all offenders fit into either category. But to us, the chief difficulty with such typologies is that they direct attention away from individual differences and toward idealized—and abstract—categories.

Crime is correlated, as we have seen, with age, sex, and place of residence, and it is associated . . . with other stable characteristics of individuals. Understanding those associations is the first task of criminological theory. Our approach is not to ask which persons belong to what category of delinquents but rather to ask whether differences in the frequency with which persons break the law are associated with differences in the rewards of crime, the risks of being punished for a crime, the strength of internalized inhibitions against crime, and the willingness to defer gratifications, and then to ask what biological, developmental, situational, and adaptive processes give rise to these individual characteristics.

Notes

1. Wolfgang, 1973.
2. Farrington, 1979c, 9_{25}, 1981.
3. Newman, G., 1976.
4. Hoebel, 1954.
5. Sellin and Wolfgang, 1964; Figlio, 1972.
6. Akman and Normandeau, 1968.
7. Valez-Diaz and Megargee, 1971.
8. Hsu, cited in Wellford, 1975.
9. DeBoeck and Houschou, cited in Wellford, 1975.
10. Hirschi and Gottfredson, 1984.
11. Durkheim, 1964, p. 102.
12. Bordua, 1962.
13. Radzinowicz and King, 1977; Archer, Gartner, Akert, and Lockwood, 1978.
14. Braithwaite, 1981.
15. Tittle, Villemez, and Smith, 1978.
16. Elliott and Ageton, 1980; Elliott and Huizinga, 1983.
17. Hindelang, Hirschi, and Weis, 1979, 1981.
18. For example, Kleck, 1982.
19. Johnson, R. E., 1979.
20. Braithwaite, 1981.
21. For example, Wolfgang, Figlio, and Sellin, 1972.
22. Hindelang, Hirschi, and Weis, 1979, 1981; Berger and Simon, 1982.
23. Hindelang, Hirschi, and Weis, 1979, p. 1002; Hindelang, 1978.
24. Blumstein, 1982; Petersilia, 1983.

A Crime by Any Other Name . . .

If one individual inflicts a bodily injury upon another which leads to the death of the person attacked we call it manslaughter; on the other hand, if the attacker knows beforehand that the blow will be fatal we call it murder. Murder has also been committed if society places hundreds of workers in such a position that they inevitably come to premature and unnatural ends. Their death is as violent as if they had been stabbed or shot. . . . Murder has been committed if society knows perfectly well that thousands of workers cannot avoid being sacrificed so long as these conditions are allowed to continue. Murder of this sort is just as culpable as the murder committed by an individual.

—Frederick Engels
The Condition of the Working Class in England

What's In a Name?

If it takes you an hour to read this chapter, by the time you reach the last page, three of your fellow citizens will have been murdered. *During that same time, at least four Americans will die as a result of unhealthy or unsafe conditions in the workplace!* Although these work-related deaths could have been prevented, they are not called murders. Why not? Doesn't crime by any other name still cause misery and suffering? What's in a name?

The fact is that the label "crime" is not used in America to name all or the worst of the actions that cause misery and suffering to Americans. It is primarily reserved for the dangerous actions of the poor.

In the February 21, 1993, edition of the *New York Times*, an article appears with the headline: "Company in Mine Deaths Set to Pay Big Fine." It describes an agreement by the owners of a Kentucky mine to pay a fine for safety misconduct that may have led to "the worst American mining accident in nearly a decade." Ten workers died in a methane explosion, and the company pleaded guilty to "a pattern of safety misconduct" that included falsifying reports of methane levels and requiring miners to work under unsupported roofs. The company was fined $3.75 million. The acting foreman at the mine was the only individual charged by the federal government, and for his cooperation with the investigation, prosecutors were recommending that he receive the minimum sentence: probation to six months in prison.

The company's president expressed regret for the tragedy that occurred. And the U.S. attorney said he hoped the case "sent a clear message that violations of Federal safety and health regulations that endanger the lives of our citizens will not be tolerated."

Compare this with the story of Colin Ferguson, who prompted an editorial in the *New York Times* of December 10, 1993, with the headline: "Mass Murder on the 5:33." A few days earlier, Colin had boarded a commuter train in Garden City, Long Island, and methodically shot passengers with a 9-millimeter pistol, killing 5 and wounding 18. Colin Ferguson was surely a murderer, maybe a mass murderer. My question is, Why wasn't the death of the miners also murder? Why weren't those responsible for subjecting ten miners to deadly conditions also "mass murderers"?

Why do ten dead miners amount to an "accident," a "tragedy," and five dead commuters a "mass murder"? "Murder" suggests a murderer, whereas "accident" and "tragedy" suggest the work of impersonal forces. But the charge against the company that owned the mine said that they "repeatedly exposed the mine's work crews to danger and that such conditions were frequently concealed from Federal inspectors responsible for enforcing the mine safety act." And the acting foreman admitted to falsifying records of methane levels only two months before the fatal blast. Someone was responsible for the conditions that led to the death of ten miners. Is that person not a murderer, perhaps even a *mass murderer*?

These questions are at this point rhetorical. My aim is not to discuss this case but rather to point to the blinders we wear when we look at such an "accident." There was an investigation. One person, the acting foreman, was held responsible for falsifying records. He is to be sentenced to six months in prison (at most). The company was fined. But no one will be tried for *murder*. No one will be thought of as a murderer. *Why not?. . .*

Didn't those miners have a right to protection from the violence that took their lives? *And if not, why not?*

Once we are ready to ask this question seriously, we are in a position to see that the reality of crime—that is, the acts we label crime, the acts we think of as crime, the actors and actions we treat as criminal—is *created*: It is an image shaped by decisions as to *what* will be called crime and *who* will be treated as a criminal.

The Carnival Mirror

It is sometimes coyly observed that the quickest and cheapest way to eliminate crime would be to throw out all the criminal laws. There is a sliver of truth to this view. Without criminal laws, there would indeed be no "crimes." There would, however, still be dangerous acts. This is why we cannot really solve our crime problem quite so simply. The criminal law *labels* some acts "crimes." In doing this, it identifies those acts as so dangerous that we must use the extreme methods of criminal justice to protect ourselves against them. This does not mean the criminal law *creates* crime—it simply "mirrors" real dangers that threaten us. What is true of the criminal law is true of the whole justice system. If police did not arrest or prosecutors charge or juries convict, there would be no "criminals." This does not mean that police or prosecutors or juries create criminals any more than legislators do. They *react* to real dangers in society. The criminal justice system—from lawmakers to law enforcers—is just a mirror of the real dangers that lurk in our midst. *Or so we are told.*

How accurate is this mirror? We need to answer this in order to know whether or how well the criminal justice system is protecting us against the real threats to our well-being. The more accurate a mirror is, the more the image it shows is created by the reality it reflects. The more misshapen a mirror is, the more the distorted image it shows is created by the mirror, not by the reality reflected. It is in this sense that I will argue that the image of crime is created: The American criminal justice system is a mirror that shows a distorted image of the dangers that threaten us—an image created more by the shape of the mirror than by the reality reflected. What do we see when we look in the criminal justice mirror?

On the morning of September 16, 1975, the *Washington Post* carried an article in its local news section headlined "Arrest Data Reveal Profile of a Suspect." The article reported the results of a study of crime in Prince George's County, a suburb of Washington, D.C. It read in part as follows:

> The typical suspect in serious crime in Prince George's County is a black male, aged 14 to 19. . . .

This report is hardly a surprise. The portrait it paints of "the typical suspect in serious crime" is probably a pretty good rendering of the image lurking in the back of the minds of most people who fear crime. . . . [T]he portrait generally fits the national picture presented in the FBI's *Uniform Crime Reports* for the same year, 1974. In Prince George's County, "youths between the ages of 15 and 19 were accused of committing nearly half [45.5 percent] of all 1974 crimes.". . .

That was 1974. But little has changed since. In his 1993 book, *How to Stop Crime*, retired police chief Anthony Bouza writes: "Street crime is mostly a black and poor young man's game." And listen to the sad words of the Reverend Jesse Jackson: "There is nothing more painful to me at this stage of my life than to walk down the street and hear footsteps and start thinking about robbery—and then look around and see someone white and feel relieved."

This, then, is the Typical Criminal, the one whose portrait President Reagan described as "that of a stark, staring face, a face that belongs to a frightening reality of our time—the face of a human predator, the face of the habitual criminal. Nothing in nature is more cruel and more dangerous." This is the face that Ronald Reagan saw in the criminal justice mirror, more than a decade ago. Let us look more closely at the face in today's criminal justice mirror, and we shall see much the same Typical Criminal:

He is, first of all, a *he*. Out of 2,012,906 persons arrested for FBI Index crimes [which are criminal homicide, forcible rape, robbery, aggravated assault, burglary, larceny, and motor vehicle theft] in 1991, 1,572,591, or 78 percent, were males. Second, he is a *youth*. . . . Third, he is predominantly *urban*. . . . Fourth, he is disproportionately *black*—blacks are arrested for Index crimes at a rate three times that of their percentage in the national population. . . . Finally, he is *poor:* Among state prisoners in 1991, 33 percent were unemployed prior to being arrested—a rate nearly four times that of males in the general population. . . .

This is the Typical Criminal feared by most law-abiding Americans. Poor, young, urban, (disproportionately) black males make up the core of the enemy forces in the war against crime. They are the heart of a vicious, unorganized guerrilla army, threatening the lives, limbs, and possessions of the law-abiding members of society—necessitating recourse to the ultimate weapons of force and detention in our common defense.

But how do we know who the criminals are who so seriously endanger us that we must stop them with force and lock them in prisons?

. . . "Arrest records" reflect decisions about which crimes to investigate and which suspects to take into custody. All these decisions rest on the most fundamental of all *decisions:* the decisions of legislators as to which acts shall be labeled "crimes" in the first place.

The reality of crime as the target of our criminal justice system and as perceived by the general populace is not a simple objective threat to which the system reacts: *It is a reality that takes shape as it is filtered through a series of human decisions running the full gamut of the criminal justice system*—from the lawmakers who determine what behavior shall be in the province of criminal justice to the law enforcers who decide which individuals will be brought within that province.

Note that by emphasizing the role of "human decisions," I do not mean to suggest that the reality of crime is voluntarily and intentionally "created" by individual "decision makers." Their decisions are themselves shaped by the social system, much as a child's decision to become an engineer rather than a samurai warrior is shaped by the social system in which he or she grows up. Thus, to have a full explanation of how the reality of crime is created, we have to understand how our society is structured in a way that leads people to make the decisions they do. In other words, these decisions are part of the social phenomena to be explained—they are not the explanation.

. . . Where the reality of crime does not correspond to the real dangers, we can say that it is a reality *created* by those decisions. And then we can investigate the role played by the social system in encouraging, reinforcing, and otherwise shaping those decisions.

It is to capture this way of looking at the relation between the reality of crime and the real dangers "out there" in society that I refer to the criminal justice system as a "mirror." Whom and what we see in this mirror is a function of the decisions about who and what are criminal, and so on. Our poor, young, urban, black male, who is so well represented in arrest records and prison populations, appears not simply because of the undeniable threat he poses to the rest of society. As dangerous as he may be, he would not appear in the criminal justice mirror *if* it had not been decided that the acts he performs should be labeled "crimes," *if* it had not been decided that he should be arrested for those crimes, *if* he had access to a lawyer who could persuade a jury to acquit him and perhaps a judge to expunge his arrest record, and *if* it had not been decided that he is the type of individual and his the type of crime that warrants imprisonment. *The shape of the reality we see in the criminal justice mirror is created by all these decisions.* We want to know how accurately the reality we see in this mirror reflects the real dangers that threaten us in society.

. . . The acts of the Typical Criminal are not the only acts that endanger us, nor are they the acts that endanger us the most. As I shall show . . . , we have as great or sometimes even a greater chance of being killed or disabled by an occupational injury or disease, by unnecessary surgery, or by shoddy emergency medical services than by aggravated assault or even homicide! Yet even though these threats to our well-being are graver than those posed by our poor young criminals, they do not show up in the FBI's Index of serious crimes. The individuals responsible for them do not turn up in arrest records or prison statistics. *They never become part of the reality reflected in the criminal justice mirror, although the danger they pose is at least as great and often greater than the danger posed by those who do!*

Similarly, the general public loses more money *by for* . . . from price-fixing and monopolistic practices and from consumer deception and embezzlement than from all the property crimes in the FBI's Index combined. Yet these far more costly acts are either not criminal, or if technically criminal, not prosecuted, or if prosecuted, not punished, or if punished, only mildly . . . *Their faces rarely appear in the criminal justice mirror, although the danger they pose is at least as great and often greater than that of those who do. . . .*

The criminal justice system is like a mirror in which society can see the face of the evil in its midst. Because the system deals with some evil and not with others, because it treats some evils as the gravest and treats some of the gravest evils as minor, the image it throws back is distorted like the image in a carnival mirror. Thus, the image cast back is false not because it is invented out of thin air but because the proportions of the real are distorted. . . .

If criminal justice really gives us a carnival-mirror of "crime," we are doubly deceived. First, we are led to believe that the criminal justice system is protecting us against the gravest threats to our well-being when, in fact, the system is protecting us against only some threats and not necessarily the gravest ones. We are deceived about how much protection we are receiving and thus left vulnerable. The second deception is just the other side of this one. If people believe that the carnival mirror is a true mirror—that is, if they believe the criminal justice system simply *reacts* to the gravest threats to their well-being—they come to believe that whatever is the target of the criminal justice system must be the greatest threat to their well-being. . . .

A Crime by Any Other Name . . .

Think of a crime, any crime. Picture the first "crime" that comes into your mind. What do you see? The odds are you are not imagining a mining company executive sitting at his desk, calculating the costs of proper safety precautions and deciding not to invest in them. Probably what you do see with your mind's eye is one person physically attacking another or robbing something from another via the threat of physical attack. Look more closely. What does the attacker look like? It's a safe bet he (and it is a *he*, of course) is not wearing a suit and tie. In fact, my hunch is that you—like me, like almost anyone else in America—picture a young, tough lower-class male when the thought of crime first pops into your head. You (we) picture someone like the Typical Criminal described above. The crime itself is one in which the Typical Criminal sets out to attack or rob some specific person.

This last point is important. It indicates that we have a mental image not only of the Typical Criminal but also of the Typical Crime. If the Typical Criminal is a young, lower-class male, the Typical Crime is *one-on-one harm*—where harm means either physical injury or loss of something valuable or both. If you have any doubts that this is the Typical Crime, look at any random sample of police or private eye shows on television. How often do you see the cops on "NYPD Blue" investigate consumer fraud or failure to remove occupational hazards? And when Jessica Fletcher (on "Murder, She Wrote") tracks down well-heeled criminals, it is almost always for garden-variety violent crimes like murder. . . . [C]riminals portrayed on television are on the average both older and wealthier than the real criminals who figure in the FBI *Uniform Crime Reports*, "TV crimes are almost 12 times as likely to be violent as crimes committed in the real world." TV crime shows broadcast the double-edged message that the one-on-one crimes of the poor are the typical crimes of all and thus not uniquely caused by the pressures of poverty; *and* that the criminal justice system pursues rich and poor alike—thus, when the criminal justice system happens mainly to pounce on the poor in real life, it is not out of any class bias.

In addition to the steady diet of fictionalized TV violence and crime, there has been an increase in the graphic display of crime on many TV news programs. Crimes reported on TV news are also far more frequently violent than real crimes are. . . . [A] new breed of nonfictional "tabloid" TV show has appeared in which viewers are shown films of actual violent crimes—blood, screams, and all—or reenactments of actual violent crimes, sometimes using the actual victims playing themselves! Among these are "COPS," "Real Stories of the Highway Patrol," "America's Most Wanted," and "Unsolved Mysteries." Here, too, the focus is on crimes of one-on-one violence, rather than, say, corporate pollution. The *Wall Street Journal*, reporting on the phenomenon of tabloid TV, informs us that "Television has gone tabloid. The seamy underside of life is being bared in a new rash of true-crime series and contrived-confrontation talk shows." Is there any surprise that a survey by *McCall's* indicates that its readers have grown more afraid of crime in the mid-1980s—even though victimization studies show a stable level of crime for most of this period?

It is important to identify this model of the Typical Crime because it functions like a set of blinders. It keeps us from calling a mine disaster a mass murder even if ten men are killed, even if someone is responsible for the unsafe conditions in which they worked and died. I contend that this particular piece of mental furniture so blocks our view that it keeps us from using the criminal justice system to protect ourselves from the greatest threats to our persons and possessions.

What keeps a mine disaster from being a mass murder in our eyes is that it is not a one-on-one harm. What is important in one-on-one harm is not the numbers but the *desire of someone (or ones) to harm someone (or ones) else*. An attack by a gang on one or more persons or an attack by one individual on several fits the model of one-on-one harm; that is, for each person harmed there is at least one individual who wanted to harm that person. Once he selects his victim, the rapist, the mugger, the murderer all want this person they have selected to suffer. A mine executive, on the other hand, does not want his employees to be harmed. He would truly prefer that there be no accident, no injured or dead miners. What he does want is something legitimate. It is what he has been hired to get: maximum profits at minimum costs. If he cuts corners to save a buck, he is just doing his job. If ten men die because he cut corners on safety, we may think him crude or callous but not a murderer. He is, at most, responsible for an *indirect harm,* not a one-on-one harm. For this, he may even be criminally indictable for violating safety regulations—but not for murder. The ten men are dead as an unwanted consequence of his (perhaps overzealous or undercautious) pursuit of a legitimate goal. So, unlike the Typical Criminal, he has not committed the Typical Crime—or so we generally believe. As a result, ten men are dead who might be alive now if cutting corners of the kind that leads to loss of life, whether suffering is specifically aimed at or not, were treated as murder.

This is my point. Because we accept the belief . . . that the model for crime is one person specifically trying to harm another, we accept a legal system that leaves us unprotected against much greater dangers to our lives and well-being than those threatened by the Typical Criminal. . . .

According to the FBI's *Uniform Crime Reports,* in 1991, there were 24,703 murders and nonnegligent manslaughters, and 1,092,739 aggravated assaults. In 1992, there were 23,760 murders and nonnegligent manslaughters, and 1,126,970 aggravated assaults. . . . Thus, as a measure of the physical harm done by crime in the beginning of the 1990s, we can say that reported crimes lead to roughly 24,000 deaths and 1,000,000 instances of serious bodily injury short of death a year. As a measure of monetary loss due to property crime, we can use $15.1 billion—the total estimated dollar losses due to property crime in 1992 according to the UCR. Whatever the shortcomings of these reported crime statistics, they are the statistics upon which public policy has traditionally been based. Thus, I will consider any actions that lead to loss of life, physical harm, and property loss comparable to the figures in the UCR as actions that pose grave dangers to the community comparable to the threats posed by crimes. . . .

Work May Be Dangerous to Your Health

Since the publication of *The President's Report on Occupational Safety and Health* in 1972, numerous studies have documented the astounding incidence of disease, injury, and death due to hazards in the workplace *and* the fact that much or most of this carnage is the consequence of the refusal of management to pay for safety measures and of government to enforce safety standards—and sometimes of willful defiance of existing law.

In that 1972 report, the government estimated the number of job-related illnesses at 390,000 per year and the number of annual deaths from industrial disease at 100,000. For 1990, the Bureau of Labor Statistics (BLS) of the U.S. Department of Labor estimates 330,800 job-related illnesses and 2,900 work-related deaths. Note that the latter figure applies only to private-sector work environments with 11 or more employees. And it is not limited to death from occupational disease but includes all work-related deaths, including those resulting from accidents on the job.

Before we celebrate what appears to be a dramatic drop in work-related mortality, we should point out that the BLS itself "believes that the annual survey significantly understates the number of work-related fatalities." And there is wide agreement that occupational diseases are seriously underreported. . . .

For these reasons, plus the fact that BLS's figures on work-related deaths are only for private workplaces with 11 or more employees, we must supplement the BLS figures with other estimates. In 1982, then U.S. Secretary of Health and Human Services Richard Schweiker stated that "current estimates for overall workplace-associated cancer mortality vary within a range of five to fifteen percent. With annual cancer deaths currently running at about 500,000, that translates into about 25,000 to 75,000 job-related cancer deaths per year. More recently, Edward Sondik, of the National Cancer Institute, states that the best estimate of cancer deaths attributable to occupational exposure is 4 percent of the total, with the range of acceptable estimates running between 2 and 8 percent. That translates into a best estimate of 20,000 job-related cancer deaths a year, within a range of acceptable estimates between 10,000 and 40,000.

Death from cancer is only part of the picture of death-dealing occupational disease. In testimony before the Senate Committee on Labor and Human Resources, Dr. Philip Landrigan, director of the Division of Environmental and Occupational Medicine at the Mount Sinai School of Medicine in New York City, stated that

> Recent data indicate that occupationally related exposures are responsible each year in New York State for 5,000 to 7,000 deaths and for 35,000 new cases of illness (not including work-related injuries). These deaths due to occupational disease include 3,700 deaths from cancer. . . .
>
> [I]t may be calculated that occupational disease is responsible each year in the United States for 50,000 to 70,000 deaths, and for approximately 350,000 new cases of illness.

. . . The BLS estimate of 330,000 job-related illnesses for 1990 roughly matches Dr. Landrigan's estimates. For 1991, BLS estimates 368,000 job-related illnesses. These illnesses are of varying severity. . . . Because I want to compare these occupational harms with those resulting from aggravated assault, I shall stay on the conservative side here too, as with deaths from occupational diseases, and say that there are annually in the United States approximately 150,000 job-related serious illnesses. Taken together with 25,000 deaths from occupational diseases, how does this compare with the threat posed by crime?

Before jumping to any conclusions, note that the risk of occupational disease and death falls only on members of the labor force, whereas the risk of crime falls on the whole population, from infants to the elderly. Because the labor force is about half the total population (124,810,000 in 1990, out of a total population of 249,900,000), to get a true picture of the *relative* threat posed by occupational diseases compared with that posed by crimes, we should *halve* the crime statistics when comparing them with the figures for industrial disease and death. Using the crime figures for the first years of the 1990s, . . . we note that the *comparable* figures would be

	Occupational Hazard	Crime (halved)
Death	25,000	12,000
Other physical harm	150,000	500,000

. . . Note . . . that the estimates in the last chart are *only* for occupational *diseases* and deaths from those diseases. They do not include death and disability from work-related injuries. Here, too, the statistics are gruesome. The National Safety Council reported that in 1991, work-related accidents caused 9,600 deaths and 1.7 million disabling work injuries, a total cost to the economy of $63.3 billion. This brings the number of occupation-related deaths to 34,600 a year and other physical harms to 1,850,000. If, on the basis of these additional figures, we recalculated our chart comparing occupational harms from both disease and accident with criminal harms, it would look like this:

	Occupational Hazard	Crime (halved)
Death	34,600	12,000
Other physical harm	1,850,000	500,000

Can there be any doubt that workers are more likely to stay alive and healthy in the face of the danger from the underworld than in the work-world? If any doubt lingers, consider this: Lest we falter in the struggle against crime, the FBI includes in its annual *Uniform Crime Reports* a table of "crime clocks," which graphically illustrates the extent of the criminal menace. For 1992, the crime clock shows a murder occurring every 22 minutes. If a similar clock were constructed for occupational deaths—using the conservative estimate of 34,600 cited above and remembering that this clock ticks only for that half of the population that is in the labor force—this clock would show an occupational death about every 15 minutes! In other words, in the time it takes for three murders on the crime clock, four workers have died *just from trying to make a living.*

To say that some of these workers died from accidents due to their own carelessness is about as helpful as saying that some of those who died at the hands of murderers asked for it. It overlooks the fact that where workers are careless, it is not because they love to live dangerously. They have production quotas to meet, quotas that they themselves do not set. If quotas were set with an eye to keeping work at a safe pace rather than to keeping the production-to-wages ratio as high as possible, it might be more reasonable to expect workers to take the time to be careful. Beyond this, we should bear in mind that the vast majority of occupational deaths result from disease, not accident, and disease is generally a function of conditions outside a worker's control. Examples of such conditions are the level of coal dust in the air ("260,000 miners receive benefits for [black lung] disease, and perhaps as many as 4,000 retired miners die from the illness or its complications each year"; about 10,000 currently working miners "have X-ray evidence of the beginnings of the crippling and often fatal disease") or textile dust . . . or asbestos fibers . . . or coal tars . . .; (coke oven workers develop cancer of the scrotum at a rate five times that of the general population). Also, some 800,000 people suffer from occupationally related skin disease each year. . . .

To blame the workers for occupational disease and deaths is to ignore the history of governmental attempts to compel industrial firms to meet safety standards that would keep dangers (such as chemicals or fibers or dust particles in the air) that are outside the worker's control down to a safe level. This has been a continual struggle, with firms using everything from their own "independent" research institutes to more direct and often questionable forms of political pressure to influence government in the direction of loose standards and lax enforcement. So far, industry has been winning because OSHA [Occupational Safety and Health Administration] has been given neither the personnel nor the mandate to fulfill its purpose. It is so understaffed that, in 1973, when 1,500 federal sky marshals guarded the nation's airplanes from hijackers, only 500 OSHA inspectors toured the nation's workplaces. By 1980, OSHA employed 1,581 compliance safety and health officers, but this still enabled inspection of only roughly 2 percent of the 2.5 million establishments covered by OSHA. The *New York Times* reports that in 1987 the number of OSHA inspectors was down to 1,044. As might be expected, the agency performs fewer inspections that it did a dozen years ago. . . .

According to a report issued by the AFL-CIO [American Federation of Labor and Congress of Industrial Organizations] in 1992, "The median penalty paid by an employer during the years 1972–1990 following an incident resulting in death or serious injury of a worker was just $480." The same report claims that the federal government spends $1.1 billion a year to protect fish and wildlife and only $300 million a year to protect workers from health and safety hazards on the job. . . .

Is a person who kills another in a bar brawl a greater threat to society than a business executive who refuses to cut into his profits to make his plant a safe place to work? By any measure of death and suffering the latter is by far a greater danger than the former. Because he wishes his workers no harm, because he is only indirectly responsible for death and disability while pursuing legitimate economic goals, his acts are not called "crimes." Once we free our imagination from the blinders of the one-on-one model of crime, can there be any doubt that the criminal justice system does *not* protect us from the gravest threats to life and limb? It seeks to protect us when danger comes from a young, lower-class male in the inner city. When a threat comes from an upper-class business executive in an office, the criminal justice system looks the other way. This is in the face of growing evidence that for every three American citizens murdered by thugs, at least four American workers are killed by the recklessness of their bosses and the indifference of their government.

Health Care May Be Dangerous to Your Health

. . . On July 15, 1975, Dr. Sidney Wolfe of Ralph Nader's Public Interest Health Research Group testified before the House Commerce Oversight and Investigations Subcommittee that there "were 3.2 million cases of unnecessary surgery performed each year in the United States." These unneeded operations, Wolfe added, "cost close to $5 billion a year and kill as many as 16,000 Americans.". . .

In an article on an experimental program by Blue Cross and Blue Shield aimed at curbing unnecessary surgery, *Newsweek* reports that

> a Congressional committee earlier this year [1976] estimated that more than 2 million of the elective operations performed in 1974 were not only unnecessary—but also killed about 12,000 patients and cost nearly $4 billion.

Because the number of surgical operations performed in the United States rose from 16.7 million in 1975 to 22.4 million in 1991, there is reason to believe that at least somewhere between . . . 12,000 and . . . 16,000 people a year still die from unnecessary surgery. In 1991, the FBI reported that 3,405 murders were committed by a "cutting or stabbing instrument." Obviously, the FBI does not include the scalpel as a cutting or stabbing instrument. If they did, they would have had to report that between 15,405 and 19,405 persons were killed by "cutting or stabbing" in 1991. . . . No matter how you slice it, the scalpel may be more dangerous than the switchblade. . . .

Waging Chemical Warfare Against America

One in 4 Americans can expect to contract cancer during their lifetimes. The American Cancer Society estimated that 420,000 Americans would die of cancer in 1981. The National Cancer Institute's estimate for 1993 is 526,000 deaths from cancer. "A 1978 report issued by the President's Council on Environmental Quality (CEQ) unequivocally states that 'most researchers agree that 70 to 90 percent of cancers are caused by environmental influences and are hence theoretically preventable.'" This means that a concerted national effort could result in saving 350,000 or more lives a year and reducing each individual's chances of getting cancer in his or her lifetime from 1 in 4 to 1 in 12 or fewer. If you think this would require a massive effort in terms of money and personnel, you are right. How much of an effort, though, would the nation make to stop a foreign invader who was killing a thousand people and bent on capturing one-quarter of the present population?

In face of this "invasion" that is already under way, the U.S. government has allocated $1.9 billion to the National Cancer Institute (NCI) for fiscal year 1992, and NCI has allocated $219 million to the study of the physical and chemical (i.e., environmental) causes of cancer. Compare this with the (at least) $45 billion spent to fight the Persian Gulf War. The simple truth is that the government that strove so mightily to protect the borders of a small, undemocratic nation 7,000 miles away is doing next to nothing to protect us against the chemical war in our midst. This war is being waged against us on three fronts:

- Pollution
- Cigarette smoking
- Food additives

. . . The evidence linking *air pollution* and cancer, as well as other serious and often fatal diseases, has been rapidly accumulating in recent years. In 1993, the *Journal of the American Medical Association* reported on research that found "'robust' associations between premature mortality and air pollution levels." They estimate that pollutants cause about 2 percent of all cancer deaths (at least 10,000 a year). . . .

A . . . recent study . . . concluded that air pollution at 1988 levels was responsible for 60,000 deaths a year. The Natural Resources Defense Council sued the EPA [Environmental Protection Agency] for its foot-dragging in implementation of the Clean Air Act, charging that "One hundred million people live in areas of unhealthy air."

This chemical war is not limited to the air. The National Cancer Institute has identified as carcinogens or suspected carcinogens 23 of the chemicals commonly found in our drinking water. Moreover, according to one observer, we are now facing a "new plague—toxic exposure.". . .

The evidence linking *cigarette smoking* and cancer is overwhelming and need not be repeated here. The Centers for Disease Control estimates that cigarettes cause 87 percent of lung cancers—approximately 146,000 in 1992. Tobacco continues to kill an estimated 400,000 Americans a year. Cigarettes are widely estimated to cause 30 percent of all cancer deaths. . . .

This is enough to expose the hypocrisy of running a full-scale war against heroin (which produces no degenerative disease) while allowing cigarette sales and advertising to flourish. It also should be enough to underscore the point that once again there are threats to our lives much greater than criminal homicide. The legal order does not protect us against them. Indeed, not only does our government fail to protect us against this threat, it promotes it! . . .

If you think that tobacco harms only people who knowingly decide to take the risk, consider the following: Documents recently made public suggest that, by the mid-1950's, Liggett & Myers, the makers of Chesterfield and L&M cigarettes, had evidence that smoking is addictive and cancer-causing, and that they were virtually certain of it by 1963—but they never told the public and "actively misled" the U.S. surgeon general. Moreover, the cigarette industry intentionally targets young people—who are not always capable of assessing the consequences of their choices—with its ads, and it is successful. Some 2.6 million youngsters between the ages of 12 and 18 are smokers.

In addition, the Environmental Protection Agency has released data on the dangers of "secondhand" tobacco smoke (which nonsmokers breathe when smoking is going on around them). They report that each year secondhand smoke causes 3,000 lung-cancer deaths, contributes to 150,000 to 300,000 respiratory infections in babies, exacerbates the asthmatic symptoms of 400,000 to 1,000,000 children with the disease, and triggers 8,000 to 26,000 new cases of asthma in children who don't yet have the disease. A 1993 issue of the *Journal of the American Medical Association* reports that tobacco contributes to 10 percent of infant deaths.

The average American consumes *one pound* of chemical *food additives* per year. . . . A hard look at the chemicals we eat and at the federal agency empowered to protect us against eating dangerous chemicals reveals the recklessness with which we are being "medicated against our will.". . .

Based on the knowledge we have, there can be no doubt that air pollution, tobacco, and food additives amount to a chemical war that makes the crime wave look like a football scrimmage. Even with the most conservative estimates, it is clear that *the death toll in this war is far higher than the number of people killed by criminal homicide!*

Poverty Kills

. . . We are prone to think that the consequences of poverty are fairly straight-foward: less money means fewer things. So poor people have fewer clothes or cars or appliances, go to the theater less often, and live in smaller homes with less or cheaper furniture. This is true and sad, but perhaps not intolerable. However, in addition, one of the things poor people have less of is *good health.* Less money means less nutritious food, less heat in winter, less fresh air in summer, less distance from other sick people or from unhealthy work or dumping sites, less knowledge about illness or medicine, fewer doctor visits, fewer dental visits, less preventive health care, and (in the United States at least) less first-quality medical attention when all these other deprivations take their toll and a poor person finds himself or herself seriously ill. The result is that the poor suffer more from poor health and die earlier than do those who are well off. Poverty robs them of their days while they are alive and kills them before their time. A prosperous society that allows poverty in its midst is a party to murder.

A review of more than 30 historical and contemporary studies of the relationship of economic class and life expectancy affirms the obvious conclusion that "class influences one's chances of staying alive. Almost without exception, the evidence shows that classes differ on mortality rates." An article in the November 10, 1993 issue of the *Journal of the American Medical Association* confirms the continued existence of this cost of poverty:

> People who are poor have higher mortality rates for heart disease, diabetes mellitus, high blood pressure, lung cancer, neural tube defects, injuries, and low birth weight, as well as lower survival rates from breast cancer and heart attacks.

. . . In short, *poverty hurts, injuries, and kills—just like crime.* A society that could remedy its poverty but does not is an accomplice in crime.

Summary

Once again, our investigations lead to the same result. The criminal justice system does not protect us against the gravest threats to life, limb, or possessions. Its definitions of crime are not simply a reflection of the objective dangers that threaten us. The workplace, the medical profession, the air we breathe, and the poverty we refuse to rectify lead to far more human suffering, far more death and disability, and take far more dollars from our pockets than the murders, aggravated assaults, and thefts reported annually by the FBI. What is more, this human suffering is preventable. A government really intent on protecting our well-being could enforce work safety regulations, police the medical profession, require that clean air standards be met, and funnel sufficient money to the poor to alleviate the major disabilities of poverty—but it does not. Instead we hear a lot of cant about law and order and a lot of rant about crime in the streets. It is as if our leaders were not only refusing to protect us from the major threats to our well-being but trying to cover up this refusal by diverting our attention to crime—as if this were the only real threat.

As we have seen, the criminal justice system is a carnival mirror that presents a distorted image of what threatens us. The distortions do not end with the definitions of crime. . . . All the mechanisms by which the criminal justice system comes down more frequently and more harshly on the poor criminal than on the well-off criminal take place *after* most of the dangerous acts of the well-to-do have been excluded from the definition of crime itself. The bias against the poor within the criminal justice system is all the more striking when we recognize that the door to that system is shaped in a way that excludes in advance the most dangerous acts of the well-to-do.

POSTSCRIPT

Is Street Crime More Serious Than White-Collar Crime?

American society is currently in the throes of disdain, if not out-and-out hatred, for street crimes and the people who commit them. Yet according to Reiman and others, street thugs are not nearly as dangerous or harmful to life and limb as corporate criminals are. Ironically, as a growing number of corporations are being heavily fined for breaking affirmative action laws (as well as for a variety of other violations), there are currently more young, black males incarcerated than at any other time in U.S. history. Relatively few white-collar criminals are incarcerated, and when they are, they often face relatively short sentences. The subjective emphasis regardless of the objective harm remains on cracking down on street crime.

Among the more recent works by Wilson is *Moral Judgment: Does the Abuse Excuse Threaten Our Legal System?* (Basic Books, 1997). A current book by Reiman is *Critical Moral Liberalism: Theory and Practice* (Rowman & Littlefield, 1997).

This debate is an old one. Paul Tappan, in "Who Is the Criminal?" *American Sociological Review* (February 1947), arguing along the same lines as Wilson and Herrnstein, insisted that criminology's emphasis should be on familiar criminals (such as robbers), not on people who engage in questionable business practices. Among the many current works that largely parallel Reiman's thinking are *The Politics of Injustice: Crime and Punishment in America* by K. Beckett and T. Sasson (Pine Forge, 2000) and *Power, Politics and Crime* by W.J. Chambliss (Westview Press, 1999).

The journals *Critical Criminologist* and *Social Justice* often feature articles attacking Wilson's ideas. Two articles that are somewhat supportive of Wilson and Herrnstein and that reflect an international perspective are J. M. Chaiken's "Crunching Numbers: Crime and Incarceration at the End of the Millennium," and J. Van Dijk and K. Kangaspunta's "Piecing Together the Cross-National Crime Puzzle," both in *National Institute of Justice Journal* (January 2000). Two works that debate the pervasive issue of environmental justice are *Toxic Capitalism: Corporate Crime and the Chemical Industry* by F. Pearce and S. Tombs (Ashgate, 1998) and *The Promise and Peril of Environmental Justice* by C. H. Foreman, Jr. (Brookings Institution, 1998).

Books on errors—some would say crimes—of criminal justice agencies are J. H. Henderson and D. R. Simon, *Crimes of the Criminal Justice System* (Anderson, 1994); A. V. Merlo and P. J. Benekos, *What's Wrong With the Criminal Justice System: Ideology, Politics, and the Media* (Anderson, 2000); and J. Wiener, *Gimme Some Truth: The John Lennon FBI Files* (University of California Press, 1999).

Allyn & Bacon Sociology Links: Criminal Justice System

This page provides dozens of links to sites related to the criminal justice system. Subcategories of links include victims, general law enforcement sites, forensics, community corrections, federal agencies, and prisons.

http://www.abacon.com/sociology/soclinks/cj.html

American Society of Criminology

An excellent starting point for a study of all aspects of criminology and criminal justice, this page provides links to sites on criminal justice in general, international criminal justice, juvenile justice, courts, the police, and the government.

http://www.bsos.umd.edu/asc/four.htm

Basics of Juvenile Justice

A list of similarities and differences between juvenile and adult justice systems is available at this site. Also listed are changes in the philosophy of juvenile justice by time periods.

http://www.uaa.alaska.edu/just/just110/intro2.html

National Institute of Justice

The National Institute of Justice (NIJ) sponsors projects and conveys research to practitioners in the field. From the institute's home page, you can link to NIJ programs, publications, and related sites.

http://www.ojp.usdoj.gov/nij/

Office for Victims of Crime

The Office for Victims of Crime (OVC) was established by the 1984 Victims of Crime Act to oversee diverse programs that benefit victims of crime. From this Web site of the OVC, you can download a great deal of pertinent information.

http://www.ojp.usdoj.gov/ovc/

Partnerships Against Violence Network

The Partnerships Against Violence Network is a virtual library of information about violence and at-risk youth, representing data from seven different federal agencies.

http://www.pavnet.org

PART 2

Justice Issues and Contemporary Public Policy

*U*nderstanding society's reactions to crime—such as investigating, arresting, and incarcerating criminals, as well as providing alternatives to incarceration—is often complicated. Scholars and practitioners also have to reckon with the unanticipated negative outcomes of that system. The criminal justice system has been accused of ignoring crimes and injustices committed against women, racial and ethnic minorities, and children. Some say that policies and procedures adopted in fighting the war on crime may very well be more harmful than helpful. In addition, people have questioned efforts to protect children against predators, both on the streets and on the Internet; the effects of the war on drugs on the black, inner-city community; and whether or not juvenile courts should be abolished. These issues are explored in this section.

- Does Arresting Spousal Batterers Do More Harm Than Good?

- Is Racial Profiling an Acceptable Law Enforcement Strategy?

- Should Serious Sex Offenders Be Castrated?

- Should Juvenile Courts Be Abolished?

- Are the Dangers of Internet Child Pornography Exaggerated?

ISSUE 5

Does Arresting Spousal Batterers Do More Harm Than Good?

YES: Janell D. Schmidt and Lawrence W. Sherman, from "Does Arrest Deter Domestic Violence?" in Eve S. Buzawa and Carl G. Buzawa, *Do Arrests and Restraining Orders Work?* (Sage Publications, 1996)

NO: Evan Stark, from "Mandatory Arrest for Batterers: A Reply to Its Critics," in Eve S. Buzawa and Carl G. Buzawa, *Do Arrests and Restraining Orders Work?* (Sage Publications, 1996)

ISSUE SUMMARY

YES: Janell D. Schmidt, supervisor of the Milwaukee County Child Protective Services, and professor of criminology Lawrence W. Sherman argue that arresting batterers in many cases does more harm than good, and they advocate alternatives to mandatory arrest.

NO: Associate professor of public administration and social work Evan Stark contends that those who argue against arresting batterers completely misunderstand the depth of women's exploitation by the legal system. He contends that arresting batterers is a vital step for female empowerment and for women achieving full citizenship status.

D omestic violence. It is not known if spouse, lover, wife, or child abuse has actually increased significantly in the past several years or if such abuse has simply been discovered because the current political and social climate validates worrying about it, researching it, and demanding that something be done about it.

While there is little doubt that sexual, psychological, and physical assaults occur within all domestic arrangements regardless of race, socioeconomic status, religion, ethnic origin, and so on, solid information on the rate, intensity, and types of assault is not available. In the past, the received wisdom among police agencies was that cops should avoid intervening in domestic abuse cases. If intervention could not be avoided, however, then couples were to be counseled, but no arrests were to be made. But ways of thinking about and studying domestic violence changed dramatically in 1984 when Lawrence W. Sherman and Richard Berk published the results of their research on domestic violence in Minneapolis, Minnesota. They found that when the police arrested males involved in misdemeanor domestic assaults, the arrested males were less likely to assault in the future than those who were not arrested.

Sherman and Berk pointed out that their findings were tentative and that policies should *not* be based on a single study. Yet four months later the U.S. attorney general recommended that arrests be made in domestic assault cases. Within five years approximately 84 percent of urban police agencies had preferred or mandatory arrest policies for misdemeanor domestic assault cases. Sherman has insisted that the reversal of policy was largely a function of the presence of powerful vested interest groups, in addition to the fact that the time was ripe for a "get tough" approach toward men who assault their wives or girlfriends.

Shortly after the political and legal fallout from Sherman and Berk's 1984 study resulted in policies advocating arresting assaulters, a number of studies were done. Several of them, summarized in the following selection by Sherman and Janell D. Schmidt, found that arrest did *not* deter domestic assault in many cases. In fact, the charge was made that for poor, black, female victims, arresting the male only aggravated the situation.

Surprisingly, Sherman encouraged scholarly competitors to present alternative findings. From a philosophy of science perspective, one of the sharpest criticisms of the social sciences, including criminology, is that little room is allowed for scientific advances via rejection of one's own initial conclusions.

Then, as Evan Stark points out in the second selection, Sherman publicly recants, stating that the new studies indicate that his original theory that arresting batterers is probably helpful in most cases is simply wrong. Policies that call for mandatory arrests, Sherman seems to say, are clearly wrong. This is indeed a rare about-face.

Stark argues that Sherman should have stuck with his original interpretation: that arrest is helpful. However, Stark contends, even though his initial analysis is correct in terms of its policy implications, Sherman's work has been clouded by an overdependence on a narrow variant of positivistic science. That is, Sherman et al. never really looked at the big picture. Instead, they concentrated on the narrow, relatively easy-to-research issue of arrest and the subsequent behavior of batterers. Stark insists that Sherman et al. neglect the cultural-historical fact that women are far less powerful than men. For example, even when documentable physical abuse occurs, when male police show up, the female victim is under enormous pressure to not press charges, and the general lack of options available to women, especially those with children, prevent anything close to a fair legal or moral playing field. Mandatory arrests change this, at least somewhat, Stark contends.

As you read the following selections, notice the differences in how the issue itself is framed by each side. What bearing does that have on the authors' conclusions? Which side seems to have a better understanding of the problem? Which side offers more rational policy recommendations?

Janell D. Schmidt and
Lawrence W. Sherman

 **YES**

Does Arrest Deter Domestic Violence?

During the mid-1980s, widespread concern about the incidence and prevalence of domestic violence led many big-city police departments to change radically the way they policed a crime that affects millions of women each year. The often-maligned "arrest as a last resort" tradition was replaced with written policies and state laws requiring arrest as the sole police recourse. Nationally, this enthusiastic shift generated, from 1984 to 1989, a 70% increase in arrests for minor assaults, including domestic. Yet, the movement to arrest batterers may be doing more harm than good. Research in six cities testing the "arrest works best" premise in deterring future assaults has produced complex and conflicting results. Police and policymakers are now faced with the dilemma that arrest may help some victims at the expense of others and that arrest may assist the victim in the short term but facilitate further violence in the long term.

The revolution in policing misdemeanor cases of domestic violence can be attributed, in part, to the 1984 publication of the Minneapolis Domestic Violence Experiment, the first controlled, randomized test of the effectiveness of arrest for any offense. Results from this endeavor were that arresting abusers cut in half the risk of future assaults against the same victim during a 6-month follow-up period. Alternative police responses tested were the traditional "send the suspect away for 8 hours" and "advise the couple to get help for their problems." The efficacy of each treatment was measured by interviews with victims and official records tracking the offense and arrest history of each suspect. Because arrest worked better than separating or advising couples, the authors recommended that states change laws prohibiting police from making warrantless arrests in misdemeanor domestic violence cases. They also advocated that replication studies be conducted to test the generalizability of the results in other cities with varying economic conditions and demographic complexions. But absent further research results, their recommendation to law enforcement was "to adopt arrest as the preferred policy for dealing with such cases, unless there were clearly stated reasons to do something else" (Sherman, Schmidt, & Rogan, 1992, p. 3).

From Janell D. Schmidt and Lawrence W. Sherman, "Does Arrest Deter Domestic Violence?" in Eve S. Buzawa and Carl G. Buzawa, *Do Arrests and Restraining Orders Work?* (Sage Publications, 1996). Copyright © 1996 by Sage Publications, Inc. Reprinted by permission.

Although the study authors opposed mandating arrest until further studies were completed, within 8 years legislatures in 15 states (including 1 in which a replication was being conducted) and the District of Columbia moved to enact laws requiring police to arrest in all probable cause incidents of domestic violence. This dramatic expansion of arrest practices has also been attributed to successful litigation against police departments who failed to arrest, to the recommendations of the 1984 Attorney General's Task Force on Domestic Violence, and to political pressure applied by women's advocacy groups.

It is not clear, however, how well these policies and laws have been followed or whether they have controlled repetitive acts of domestic assault. Observations of compliance of the Phoenix, Minneapolis, and Milwaukee police departments found that only Milwaukee officers consistently adhered to the policy. More important, the lack of labeling cases as domestic prior to policy changes renders attempts at before/after measures difficult. Further complicating evaluation or comparison efforts is the variable threshold for probable cause to arrest in incidents of domestic assault. In Wisconsin, only a complaint of pain is needed for police to effect an arrest; in Nebraska, visible injuries are required. Until 4 years ago, Florida law required the parties to be married or formerly married in order for the incident to be considered domestic.

What is known about the impact of police arrest policies relative to domestic assault is that the vast bulk of cases brought to police attention involve lower-income and minority-group households. One reason may be a higher rate of domestic disputes among these groups; another reason may be a lack of alternatives short of police intervention that offer immediate relief. Although arresting thousands of unemployed minority males each year may assist the goals of victim advocates and provide a brief respite for the victims, the skepticism of many police and criminologists relative to the deterrent power of arrest still remains. The key question of whether other police alternatives could prove more powerful or whether the police could be effective at all led the National Institute of Justice (NIJ) to fund replication studies in six major urban cities.

Beginning in 1986 and early 1987, police in Omaha (Nebraska), Milwaukee (Wisconsin), Charlotte (North Carolina), Metro-Dade County (Miami, Florida), Colorado Springs (Colorado), and Atlanta (Georgia) began controlled experiments to replicate the Minneapolis findings. Each site was afforded leeway to improve the methodology of the Minneapolis study and to design alternative nonarrest treatments to build on its theoretical foundation. Researchers in all the cities sought to obtain a sample size larger than the 314 cases analyzed in Minneapolis in order to test for interaction effects among the various treatments. In Metro-Dade, for example, a sample of 907 cases was obtained so that researchers could compare arrest to no arrest, both with and without follow-up counseling by a specially trained police unit. In Colorado Springs, more than 1,600 cases were used to contrast arrest and nonarrest with immediate professional counseling at police headquarters or the issuance of an emergency protection order. In Milwaukee, police provided 1,200 cases for the researchers to test the length of time in custody—a short 2-hour arrest versus arrest with an overnight stay in jail, compared to no arrest. The experimental team in Charlotte included a citation response along with arrest, mediation, or separation treatments in its 686-case sample. Only Omaha followed the Minneapolis design with 330 cases but added an offender-absent window of cases to test the effect of having police pursue an arrest warrant.

The results from five of these six later studies (results from Atlanta are not forthcoming) have clouded the issue for police and policymakers, although some victim advocates remain strident in their view that arrest works best. Perhaps most striking is that none of the innovative treatments—namely, counseling or protective orders—produced any improvement over arrest versus no arrest. The citation used to notify offenders to appear at a future court date in Charlotte caused more violence than an arrest. Only Omaha broke ground and found an effective innovation in its offender-absent experiment. Offenders who left the scene before police arrived and whose cases were randomly assigned to the warrant group produced less repeat violence than did similarly absent offenders assigned to the nonwarrant group. The issuance of a warrant may have acted as a "sword of Damocles" hanging over an offender's head.

In short, the new experiments reported both deterrent and backfiring effects of arrest. Arrest cured some abusers but made others worse; arrest eased the pain for victims of employed abusers but increased it for those intimate with unemployed partners; arrest assisted white and Hispanic victims but fell short of deterring further violence among black victims. To understand these diverse findings and move toward a policy resolution, it is necessary first to focus on the effects of arrest compared to nonarrest, because that is the central issue for police and policymakers concerned with determining the most effective or appropriate police response (see Table 1).

One central finding is that arrest increased domestic violence recidivism among suspects in Omaha, Charlotte, and Milwaukee. Although these three cities produced some evidence of a deterrent effect of arrest within the first 30 days, victims found that this protective shield quickly evaporated and that they suffered an escalation of violence over a longer period of time. None of the follow-up measures produced the 6-month deterrent effect reported in Minneapolis. Some measures showed no difference in the recidivism of offenders arrested, compared with those whom police did not arrest.

Researchers in Colorado Springs and Metro-Dade found some support for the Minneapolis findings but only with limited measures. A narrow window of victim interview data (a 58% response rate in Colorado and 42% in Metro-Dade) confirms the deterrent power of arrest. But the less than ideal response rate might mean that victims who were interviewed were different from those who were not interviewed. Official records tracking recidivism in Colorado Springs did not uncover a deterrent effect of arrest, as some records did in Metro-Dade. Confounding the interpretation of the Colorado results was the fact that the vast majority of experimental cases (58%) were based on the offender's nonviolent harassing or menacing behavior toward the victim, perhaps distinct from the physical attack required to arrest for battery in the other cities.

Table 1

Summary of Results of Six Arrest Experiments for
Repeat Violence Against the Same Victim

Finding	Minneapolis	Omaha	Charlotte	Milwaukee	Colorado Springs	Miami
6-month deterrence, official measures	Yes	No	No	No	No	1 of 2
6-month deterrence, victim interviews	Yes	Border	No	No	Yes	Yes
6- to 12-month escala-tion, official measures	No	Yes	Yes	Yes	No	No
6- to 12-month escala-tion, victim interviews	*	No	No	No	No	No
30- to 60-day deter-rence, official measures (any or same victim)	Yes	No	Border	Yes	No	1 of 2
Escalation effect for unemployed	*	Yes	*	Yes	Yes	*
Deterrence for employed	*	Yes	*	Yes	Yes	*

Note: * = relationship not reported
Source: From Sherman, Schmidt, and Rogan, 1992, p. 129.

The different results from different measures in these cities suggests, then, that arrest has a different effect on suspects from different kinds of households. This finding is best summarized by the following statement:

> Evidence that the effects of arrest vary by suspect comes from Milwaukee, Colorado Springs, and Omaha. In each of those cities, nonexperimental analyses of the official records data suggest that unemployed suspects become more violent if arrested, but that employed suspects do not. This consistent pattern supports a hypothesis that the effects of criminal pun-ishment depend upon the suspect's "stakes in conformity," or how much he has to lose from the social consequences of arrest. Similar effects were found in Milwaukee for unmarried versus married suspects; unemployed, unmarried suspects experienced the greatest escalation of violence after arrest. The unemployment result is the single most consistent finding from the domestic violence experiments, and has not been contradicted in any of the analyses reported to date. (Sherman et al., 1992, p. 17)

Could other factors explain this varying effect of arrest on different sus-pects in different cities? A comparison of the data on prosecution rates, level of victim injury, number of married couples, unemployment rate, and ages of the suspects across all studies showed no consistent variation between the two groups of cities finding a deterrent or escalating effect of arrest. The only major difference was that a larger proportion of black suspects was found in the "arrest backfires" cities (Omaha, Charlotte, and Milwaukee), compared to the "arrest deters" cities (Colorado Springs, Minneapolis, and Metro-Dade). But this pattern is not consistent: One deterrent city (Metro-Dade) shared a similar rate of black suspects with a backfiring city (Omaha)—42% and 43%, respectively.

How carefully should policymakers and advocates tread through this maze of diverse findings? Applying these results to crime control strategies is complicated by the dilemmas and choices they present. Urban legislators and police chiefs in at least 35 states can choose between continuing the status quo and not mandating arrest, a choice that will continue to harm some victims. They can also legislate arrest, a choice that may harm victims currently served by a lack of policy. Choosing between the lesser of two evils is best guided by the following summary of the facts and dilemmas gleaned from the domestic violence research published to date (see Sherman et al., 1992, pp.19–20):

1. *Arrest reduces domestic violence in some cities but increases it in others.* It is not clear from current research how officials in any city can know which effect arrest is likely to have in their city. Cities that do not adopt an arrest policy may pass up an opportunity to help victims of domestic violence. But cities that do adopt arrest policies—or have them imposed by state law—may catalyze more domestic violence than would otherwise occur. Either choice entails a possible moral wrong.
2. *Arrest reduces domestic violence among employed people but increases it among unemployed people.* Mandatory arrest policies may thus protect working-class women but cause greater harm to those who are poor. Conversely, not making arrests may hurt working women but reduce violence against economically poor women. Similar trade-offs may exist on the basis of race, marriage, education, and neighborhood. Thus, even in cities where arrest reduces domestic violence overall, as an unintended side effect it may increase violence against the poorest victims.
3. *Arrest reduces domestic violence in the short run but may increase it in the long run.* Three-hour arrests in Milwaukee reduced the 7% chance that a victim would be battered as soon as the police left to a 2% chance of being battered when the spouse returned from jail. But over the course of 1 year, those arrest doubled the rate of violence by the same suspects. No arrest means more danger to the victim now, whereas making an arrest may mean more danger of violence later for the same victim or for someone else.
4. *Police can predict which couples are most likely to suffer future violence, but our society values privacy too highly to encourage preventive action.* Largely because of the value our society attaches to privacy, especially marital and sexual privacy, no one has developed a recognized method, or even advice, for police to use in preventing domestic violence. A small group of chronically violent couples and incidents reported in apartment buildings produce most of the cases of domestic violence that police learn about, but the only policies now available react to the *incidents,* rather than to the *patterns.* Ignoring those patterns allows violence to continue; addressing them requires methods that many Americans would call invasions of family privacy.

Concomitant with these dilemmas is an even tougher question for officials charged with implementing effective policing strategies: Just how much research is enough to inform policy? The authors of the Minneapolis results were the target of much second-guessing and criticism from their colleagues over the reported findings and influence that the study enjoyed. Criminologists sought a more rigorous testing of the initial conclusions, perhaps foreseeing the risk of policy changes later proving to be unwise. Advocates, whose beliefs were validated by the results, and police policymakers, at least in Milwaukee, used the study to adopt arrest as the mandatory police response. In 1988, the Wisconsin legislature, perhaps less cautious than criminologists and motivated by ideological or politically pragmatic grounds, passed a law mandating arrest as the statewide response. This action occurred despite their awareness of the ongoing replication in Milwaukee testing the specific deterrent power of arrest. If a little medicine was good, a lot was even better.

The dilemma between limited research results and the need to do something about today's problems is also clearly illustrated by the Omaha offender-absent experiment. These findings may be far more compelling and relevant than the Minneapolis results because the offender is gone by the time police arrive in about half the cases brought to police attention. Yet, the study has had no observable influence on policy since its publication in an obscure journal. Modestly presented as a pilot study, no replications are being planned. Thus, there is little risk that the findings will inform policy and later be contradicted. In the meantime, assaults on thousands of victims could conceivably be thwarted if prosecutors heeded the policy implications.

Sherman et al. (1992) posited that

> the replication dilemma thus also poses a choice between two wrongs. Both using and burying research results entail risks of harm. But as Americans become more sophisticated about the scientific process, they may come to expect revisions of policy based on new scientific evidence in this realm of knowledge as in others. Americans are accustomed to constant revisions of findings about diet and disease. Cholesterol, sugar, caffeine, alcohol, jogging . . . the "latest" evidence about their relations to health and longevity has changed significantly and repeatedly over the last twenty years, and many people and businesses have changed their behavior in response. (p. 21)

To some the choice between two wrongs invokes despair and inaction. Yet, policing domestic violence may not be hopeless. Careful review of the policy implications, combined with the freedom to test alternative policies, can lead to more effective solutions. Use of the best information that Sherman et al. (1992, pp. 23–24) have to date guides the following five policy recommendations:

1. *Repeal mandatory arrest laws.* The most compelling implication of these findings is to challenge the wisdom of mandatory arrest. States and cities that have enacted such laws should repeal them, especially if they have substantial ghetto poverty populations with high unemployment rates. These are the settings in which mandatory arrest policies are most likely to backfire. It remains possible but unlikely that mandatory arrest creates a general deterrent effect among the wider public not arrested. Even if it does, however, increased violence

among unemployed persons who are arrested in a serious moral stain on the benefits of general deterrence. The argument that arrest expresses the moral outrage of the state also appears weak if the price of that outrage is increased violence against some victims.

2. *Substitute structured police discretion.* Instead of mandating arrest in cases of misdemeanor domestic violence, state legislatures should mandate that each police agency develop its own list of approved options to be exercised at the discretion of the officer. Legislatures might also mandate 1 day of training each year to ensure that discretion is fully informed by the latest research available. The options could include allowing victims to decide whether their assailants should be arrested, transporting victims to shelters, or taking the suspects to an alcohol detoxification center.

3. *Allow warrantless arrests.* Whereas mandatory arrest has become the major issue in some states, warrantless arrest remains an issue in others. Sixteen jurisdictions have adopted mandatory arrest laws, but at last report 9 others have still not given officers full arrest powers in misdemeanor domestic violence cases that they did not witness: Alabama, California, Michigan, Mississippi, Montana, Nebraska, New York, Vermont, and West Virginia. The success of arrest in some cities suggests that every state should add this option to the police tool kit. Deciding when to use it can then become a matter of police policy based on continuing research and clinical experience, rather than on the massive effort required to change state law.

4. *Encourage issuance of arrest warrants for absent offenders.* The landmark Omaha experiment suggests that more domestic violence could be prevented by this policy than by any offender-present policy. The kinds of people who flee the scene might be more deterrable than those who stay. A prosecutor willing to issue warrants and a police agency willing to serve them can capitalize on that greater deterrability. If the Omaha warrant experiment can be replicated in other cities—a very big if—then the warrant policy might actually deter more violence than do arrests of suspects who are still present. Because it will likely be years before more research on the question is done, such policies should be adopted now. They can easily be discarded later if they are found to be harmful or ineffective.

5. *Special units and policies should focus on chronically violent couples.* Because a limited number of couples produce most of the domestic violence incidents in any city, it makes little sense for police to treat all violent couples alike. It makes even less sense to frame the whole policy debate around responses to *incidents* when most of the problem is those chronic *couples*. The challenge is to develop procedures for violent couples that do not invade family privacy. Trial and error through research and development is required for any major breakthroughs. But an effective policy for dealing with chronic couples would have more impact than any other breakthrough. It deserves the highest priority in policing domestic violence.

The opposition to mandatory arrest laws presented here may frustrate or even anger many tireless advocates who have relentlessly grasped arrest as the preferred police response to incidents of domestic violence. To them, the suggestion that other institutions, such as shelters for battered women, treatment programs for victims and offenders, schools, and welfare agencies, may better serve victims is perhaps blasphemy. But they need not become too alarmed. However sensible that approach may be, the climate in many communities today is for law enforcement officials to get tough on crime. Regardless of the results of any scientific studies, the police will remain the primary institution coping with domestic violence among the poor and unemployed. This country's current fiscal crisis dooms any substantial investment in developing new programs in both the law enforcement and social services fields. The troublesome fact remains, however, that the punishment sought by advocates and community policymakers may encourage more crime.

Reference

Sherman, L. W., Schmidt, J. D., & Rogan, D. P. (1992). *Policing domestic violence: Experiments and dilemmas.* New York: Free Press.

Evan Stark

Mandatory Arrest for Batterers: A Reply to Its Critics

The Context and the Players

As a long-time activist in the battered women's movement, I welcome the debate about mandatory arrest.

There is a certain irony in defending the police powers of the state against critics who helped lay the basis for the proarrest policy in the first place. Larry Sherman's conversion is the most remarkable. Relying on recent evidence that certain men become more violent after arrest, Sherman has replaced his erstwhile ardor for arrest with an equally passionate belief that mandatory arrest laws should be immediately repealed, especially in cities "with substantial ghetto poverty populations with high unemployment rates." . . . [T]here are profound methodological flaws in both [Larry] Sherman and [Richard] Berk's original Minneapolis Domestic Violence Experiment and the replication studies that are the basis for Sherman's current position. . . .

Sherman's picture is constructed from a bygone devotion to positivist criminology. His is a world defined by the technological optimism of the pre-1960s, yet to be polluted by culture, politics, gender, and history. . . . In Sherman's [world], causality is singular, universal, and undirectional, and social science research guides professional/government intervention to right injustice. In the post-Law Enforcement Assistance Administration (LEAA) era, this neo-Keynesian belief in state intervention appears as naive as an early Doris Day film. Still, there is something seductive about a "preventive conceit" . . . that envisions modifying such complex behaviors as violence with minor adjustments in the criminal justice response (arrest vs. no arrest). Would it were so.

. . . Sherman's faith in the instrumentality of professional intervention—including the instrumentality of his own research—supports his belief that arrest increases violence. Hence, [the idea that] eliminating mandatory arrest will reduce the violent response [is] almost certainly wrong . . . because the paradigms from which they arise . . . discredit the role of social initiative—in this case, the role of the community-based women's movement—in shaping the outcome of policy change.

From Evan Stark, "Mandatory Arrest for Batterers: A Reply to Its Critics," in Eve S. Buzawa and Carl G. Buzawa, *Do Arrests and Restraining Orders Work?* (Sage Publications, 1996). Copyright © 1996 by Sage Publications, Inc. Reprinted by permission. Notes and some references omitted.

. . . I suspect that most people view policing as a body of available resources, like schooling or health care, say—a sort of lottery that circumstances periodically force us to enter. Given the complex political realities that shape crime (as well as, e.g., health, welfare, learning) and mediate how police and the public interact, it is hard to predict whether one's welfare will be helped or hindered in any given encounter or, more globally, what determines how a given set of actors (offenders, patients, students, police) will respond to a specific class of interventions (e.g., mandatory arrest). If people "play" nonetheless (call police, attend school, go to the emergency room), it is not because they believe they *will* win, but because this is one of the few shows in town at which they *can* win and because winning—in this case, having police resources at your disposal—is a highly desirable outcome in the long run.

. . . [O]ne can think of the proarrest strategy as a "basket of goods" that may include everything from a mere warning, handcuffing, or an arrest warrant through a weekend in jail, mandated treatment, a stalker's law, the community intervention programs, . . . real prison time, the provision of court-based advocates, and so forth. . . . Sherman . . . [is] recommending that this keystone to reform be removed from the basket because it fails to fulfill an important policy objective—the reduction of violence. Sherman's implication . . . [is] that the criminal justice system should no longer be the focal point of society's response to woman battering.

Even before we can ask whether the replication experiments are sufficiently robust to justify abandoning mandatory arrest, we need to question their fundamental premise: that the wisdom of arrest should be assessed solely in terms of its effects on violent behavior, *whatever they are*. To do this, we need to conceptualize the presumed object of the arrest policy—woman battering—and unpack the "demand" that arrest is designed to satisfy. . . .

Battering: The Social Phenomenon

Feminists have hardly been unambivalent about the wisdom of a proarrest strategy. Who is more aware that depending on protective intervention by a male institution is a two-edged sword? As the concern with "wife torture" emerged from the movements in the 1870s to protect animals and children, British feminist Frances Power Cobbe addressed the same questions we are debating today, and she did so, incidentally, with the same sort of evidence.

Cobbe (1878) believed that battering was rooted in women's status as men's property and that the only effective response was full economic and political independence. Women's subordinate position in the public sphere and their private vulnerability were inextricable, each a precondition for the other. Cobbe supported the arrest and prosecution of batterers as means to reduce women's political isolation. . . . Noninterference when women were assaulted constituted active support for male dominance. . . .

[A]fter studying arrest and court statistics, she concluded that the courts were focusing only on the most extreme cases of violence. As a result, she believed, criminal justice was effectively establishing a permissible level of harm: By punishing only "severe" injury, the court response actually caused the minimum levels of domestic violence to rise. . . .

I share Cobbe's fundamental conviction that violence against women is a political fact. This means that everything about it—when, how, why, and where it is used, whom it affects, the nature of intervention, and most important, the consequences of intervention for all involved—reflects the relative power of men over women and the struggles by particular men to assert and women to escape this power. Whether this violence is expressed through child sexual abuse, harassment, rape, or battering, the key is the selection of females as victims on the basis of their gender. Because of its roots in sexual inequality, whatever occasions violence in a given encounter, the ultimate cause of "battering" (as well as its consequence) is the denial of women's *civil rights*. . . .

In trying to conceptualize battering, we need to picture ongoing forms of control that are at once both personal and social, including economic exploitation, isolation from family and friends, intimidation, and a host of rules governing everyday activities. Ann Jones and Susan Schecter use the term *coercive control* to describe the systemic fusion of social and individual dominance that undermines the physical, psychological, or political autonomy of even the strongest, most aggressive and capable women. . . .

The term *entrapment* describes the cumulative effects of having one's political, social, and psychological identity subordinated to the will of a more powerful other who controls resources that are vital to one's survival.

Battering: The Crime

. . . [A]lthough safety and the reduction of fear remain important goals, their realization depends on making women's "empowerment" the ultimate standard against which the efficacy of various interventions is judged.

. . . *[B]attering, the social phenomenon,* occurs at three levels simultaneously: the political level of female subordination, the level of interpersonal assault, and the level of coercive control at which women's social vulnerability is exploited for personal gain. *Battering, the experience,* arises from the particular ways in which these three levels interrelate in a given relationship over time. The challenge is for criminal justice to recontextualize the sorts of disembodied acts of assault recorded by medicine, such as "punched with fist." . . . [I]n terms of entrapment and control, Sherman recognizes that this episodic focus also governs police work. The same could be said of the calculus of harms that guides criminal proceedings in the courts. Lacking a conceptual frame to understand the historical nature of battering, police, judges, physicians, and other professionals fall back on kitsch psychology or on cultural stereotypes to explain the patterns they observe among individuals, families, or entire groups who appear "violence prone." Absent a theory of coercive control, the traumatic effects of battering seem to be derived from victim psychology. . . .

Because the element of control is what links the assaultive dimensions of abuse to the political fact of female inequality, there can be no hope of preventing battering simply by regulating the degree of violence. This is why we call for "zero tolerance" of force in interpersonal relationships and oppose basing police intervention on a calculus of physical harm. . . .

Reframing *battering, the crime,* in terms of inequality, coercive control, and entrapment allows us to think in new ways about mandatory arrest. The critics make three powerful points:

1. *Mandatory arrest does not work.* Although arrest might reduce violence in some instances, it may actually increase it in others. Only in allowing police to exercise informed discretion—what Sherman termed *structured discretion*—can we meet the objectives of deterrence. . . .
2. *Mandatory arrest is inhumane.* Arrest does little for the victim and less for the offender. Worse, it jeopardizes the fundamental integrity of family life. It is far better to limit arrest to the most dangerous cases, use treatment for batterers, and offer a range of compassionate family supports. . . .
3. *The very people we are trying to protect do not want it.* It appears contradictory for us to value a woman's claim to liberty as a fully endowed citizen and then to devalue her assessment of a policy carried out in her name, such as mandatory arrest. Allowing women—and police—the discretion to decide whether arrests should occur satisfies the consumer interest of the former and sustains the morale of the latter.

Does Mandatory Arrest Work?

In one of the more dramatic self-critiques in the history of criminal justice research, Larry Sherman, an architect of the Minneapolis Domestic Violence Experiment, now argues that mandatory arrest does not deter domestic violence, except among very select groups (e.g., married, employed men). If the replication experiments failed to show the deterrent value of arrest, they did show, Sherman claims, that arrest actually *increases* violence in the long run, particularly among unemployed, unmarried, and minority males. Although Sherman bemoans the rush to implement the earlier research findings, on the basis of current finding he argues that as a general practice mandatory arrest should be ended immediately, particularly in cities with large ghetto populations. In place of mandatory arrest, he favors "structured police discretion," presumably so that alternatives can be used in cases in which arrest has been shown to increase risk. Because one logical outcome of this position is clearly absurd—namely, to arrest only white, married, employed batterers—in effect, Sherman's argument would virtually end arrest in domestic violence cases, at least in all major urban centers, except in the most severe cases.

No mea culpas are required from Sherman because the results of his Minneapolis Domestic Violence Experiment were misinterpreted. . . .

[T]he major importance of the Minneapolis Domestic Violence Experiment was to give women's advocates (who already favored arrest) a powerful weapon to use with lawmakers who viewed domestic violence, like child abuse, as a social welfare rather than a criminal justice problem. . . . [T]he Minneapolis results were accepted so uncritically because, as a management strategy, police discretion in domestic violence cases had already become *politically* untenable.

But what did the battered women's movement hope to accomplish through arrest? After all, having established an unprecedented woman-run, community-based alternative service movement, why risk losing our identity by placing so much emphasis on a male-run system that . . . we located on the far right of the political spectrum in terms of community participation, access to influence, attitudes toward women, and bureaucratic isolation?

The first reason for mandating arrest was to control police behavior. . . . The fact is that, in disregarding battering, minimizing its consequences, and blaming the victims of abuse, police were no different from other professional groups. . . . [T]here can be little question that police behavior has changed significantly with mandatory arrest. Whereas street-level resistance by police remains widespread, arrests for assault had risen 70% between 1984 and 1989, largely because of domestic violence laws.

However individual officers responded to calls for help, the absence of a standard for police practice increased women's sense of powerlessness and thus posed a major obstacle to their empowerment. . . .

The interest in controlling the police response had as much to do with accountability to shelters as to women generally. The legal mandate that expands the package of services that shelters can offer, including services to police, increases the safe mobility of shelter residents and advocates, provides a rationale for a regular shelter presence in the courts, and lays an empirical basis that shelters can exploit for custodial orders, orders of protection, and expanded services. These functions, in turn, provide the substantive basis for ongoing negotiations among shelters, the criminal justice system, and family and children's services, negotiations that have been formalized in many cities through coordinating councils, networks, or other forums that assume quasi-official oversight responsibility for the law. Because shelters often secure temporary restraining orders (TROs), their power has been greatly enhanced in places where police liability for failing to arrest has been extended to failure to enforce orders of restraint and protection. Liability is a particularly important source of redress. . . .

The second reason for mandatory arrest involved immediate protection from current violence. Arrest provides a meaningful opportunity for battered women to consider their options and gives those women ready to end the relationship time to go elsewhere or to obtain a protective order. The amount of time the batterer is physically out of the picture is crucial. In Milwaukee, for example, a woman was three times as likely to be assaulted if police left without an arrest than if the batterer was arrested and then released. . . .

Third in importance was the desire to reduce the overall incidence of domestic violence both directly, because arrest might deter recidivism, and by sending a clear message that battering was unacceptable. Whereas the replication studies clearly do not support the Minneapolis findings, other studies do. In Lincoln, Nebraska, for example, implementing a mandatory arrest law reduced recidivism dramatically—from 83% to 53%. . . .

According to deterrence theory, the function of mandatory arrest is to convey the criminal nature of battering. Although arrests have risen for domestic violence, because prosecution and sentencing patterns in domestic assault cases have changed very little since battering was criminalized, it is unclear what the NIJ [National Institute of Justice] experiments were actually measuring. The results could just as readily be interpreted to mean that arrest is ineffective in isolation from other sanctions. Indeed, just as violence may increase where orders of protection are unenforced, so too is it likely that arrest without serious follow-up is interpreted by some as a license to abuse. . . . The policy of mandatory arrest also has the indirect function of setting a standard of zero tolerance for battering that other institutions can emulate.

Fourth, making battering the only crime in which police discretion is removed acknowledges a special social interest in redressing the legacy of discriminatory treatment of women by law enforcement. It also forces the law to juxtapose the subjective experience of women and its traditional accommodation to the interests of propertied (male) strata. Setting the crime of battering apart in this way also helps distinguish battering from the two sets of crimes with which it is commonly confused: *familial* abuse, in which the victim is a minor or a frail elderly dependent, and assaults or muggings by strangers. Mandating arrest communicates how seriously we take the crime of battering and may have an effect on subsequent violence that is independent of arrest as such. . . . Mandating equal protection in this way also helps counter the general reluctance of courts to extend to women the civil rights protection granted to racial minorities.

A final reason for supporting mandatory arrest was what might be termed its "redistributive" function: the perception that police service is a resource that had heretofore been hoarded by others and now should be made available to women on a more egalitarian basis. . . .

The same historical and political context in which the proarrest strategy originated explains its uneven implementation. Differences in community response to mandated arrest reflect differences in this context. . . . Pennsylvania provides an interesting test case for the political hypothesis: There, despite the absence of a mandatory arrest law and the relative backwardness of the state's judiciary, powerful oversight of police practice by the battered women's coalition has made arrest of batterers routine.

The Minneapolis Domestic Violence Experiment also reflected this; . . . no area more supportive of battered women could have been chosen to prove the efficacy of arrest: But . . . the fact remains that the researchers, the Police Foundation, the NIJ, and those who supported and attacked the findings from Minneapolis failed to set their evidence in a historical, structural, or political context that could have made the contingent nature of deterrence intelligible to local policymakers. Whatever the replication experiments may or may not say about arrest, they speak eloquently to our failure to learn from our mistakes because they, like the original experiment, do not consider the political chain that might help us understand why arrest works in one setting but not in another. At a time when community support for police efforts is widely recognized as the single most important factor in police effectiveness, it is surprising that the NIJ gave no consideration to the political context that set the tone for enforcement either in selecting the research sites to replicate Minneapolis or in evaluating the findings. Shifting the blame to policymakers for implementing arrest prematurely simply makes it easier to curtail arrest now—a right hard-won by the battered women's movement—amid broad cuts in other services to women.

What are we to make of Sherman's conclusion that arrest works mainly with men who are employed and married and that recidivist violence after arrest in certain cities appears highest among minorities and the unemployed? Obvious structural factors are at work here. The correlation between crimes of violence (including assault) and the business cycle has been well known in criminology for some time. Because the replication experiments were conducted when the economy was entering the worst recession in three decades, with the most dramatic effects on minorities and the working poor, the most appropriate baseline is not prearrest levels of violence, but rather rates of violence in similar cities where no change was made in police policy. . . .

[A]lthough the employed, white, middle-class husband may be less violent following arrest, he is also more able than his unemployed, black counterpart to leverage resources other than physical force to continue subjugating his wife. Open warfare may be temporarily over in his household, but the control and coercion go on undisturbed. Has arrest worked in this situation?

This point raises the larger issue of what the replication experiments mean *even if we accept the evidence as Sherman presents it.* Our assumptions about the three levels of battering give us no hint what a change in postarrest violence signifies in terms of coercive control, entrapment, and/or inequality. . . . [V]iolence may cease because, following arrest, threats of repeat violence may be sufficient to maintain a power advantage over a spouse, as in the case of the employed middle-class husband described above. Conversely, violence may increase because women are empowered by arrest and/or threaten to leave or to have the man arrested again. On the basis of evidence that abuse escalates when males perceive their control threatened, as during separation and divorce, we would predict that postarrest violence would be greatest—as Sherman's data show it is—among those who are least integrated into the job market or other structures from which men garner their authority—namely, the poor, black, or unemployed. Again, violence may increase in this group because arrest works to empower women and undermine male control. . . .

Evidence suggests that even men who become angry following arrest may be no more violent as a result and that men who are violent after arrest are not necessarily angrier than others about arrest itself. Even if we assume that arrest provokes greater violence among a substantial number of men, Sherman's proposal that we respond by eliminating mandatory arrest appears perverse (to say the least). A far more humane and rational response would be to expand protection for the most vulnerable female populations—namely, single, minority, and low-income women—as well as to better integrate batterers into opportunity structures *without diminishing women's access to resources.* The bottom line, however, is that assault is merely one among many means available to men in battering relationships and that its absence, even for some extended period, may signify greater equality or greater dominance.

Let's assume that violence increases following arrest among certain groups and that little can be done to inhibit it. Even this worst case scenario barely affects the most important rationales for mandatory arrest—namely, controlling police behavior, setting a public standard for police response, offering immediate protection, embodying women's civil rights claims, and affording women access to a new "package of resources." . . .

[O]ther data sets . . . indicate that mandatory arrest may meet a number of our more important objectives. With respect to protection and control, for instance, recent Supreme Court and appellate court decisions suggest that battered women in states with mandatory arrest laws have far stronger claims to police protection than do battered women in states without such statutes. Furthermore, states with broad mandatory arrest laws are far more likely to allow liability of police officers than might states without such laws, such as New York.

Minority women deserve particular attention because they are most likely to use the service system (including police) and to suffer powerlessness as a result of institutional discrimination. . . . [T]he replication experiments indicate that minority women bear the major brunt of postarrest violence. As a result, argues Sherman, minority women would be the major beneficiaries if mandatory arrest is eliminated.

That arrest poses a series of unique dilemmas to minority women goes without question. But if police were reluctant to intervene generally in domestic violence cases prior to legal reform, they provided virtually no protection to blacks. . . . [M]any police conceive of blacks as what sociologist Darnel Hawkins terms "normal primitives" and only intervene in "domestics" when violence overflows into the public arena. This is one reason why violence—almost always by a spouse or a lover—is the major cause of death among black women under 44 years of age. That such attitudes are self-fulfilling is suggested by Sherman's observation that police can "predict" which couples (and which apartment buildings!) are chronically violent. Eliminating mandatory arrest, then, would do little more than reestablish a brutal status quo. . . .

Criminalization As Social Control

[Here is] a final argument against mandatory arrest: that it reflects a trend to criminalize behaviors and, as such, is a conservative effort to extend "social control.". . . Echoes of the social control argument can . . . be found in Sherman's . . . warnings against interference in "family privacy."

. . . That such intervention may . . . become a vehicle for imposing other systemic biases (e.g., race or class prejudice) highlights the problems with enforcement but is not an inevitable consequence of society's legitimate interest in limiting unacceptable behavior. Nor is the control function of the law a reason to abandon women's larger justice claims for the equitable distribution of criminal sanctions.

Like legal control, criminalization may or may not advance personal liberty and social justice. . . .

With respect to both control and criminalization, . . . there is simply no way to avoid the difficult process of making political decisions about where scarce resources will be distributed and on whose behalf. If we think of justice as a good in itself, not merely as a means to an end, we can ask whether the mandatory arrest of batterers represents a more or less equitable distribution of this good.

There is little question in my view that the mandatory arrest of batterers represents a progressive redistribution of justice on behalf of women. One measure of this is a growing suspicion among social scientists and policymakers that, in intervening to counteract the illegitimate coercive power of particular men, the law is being used "politically" to further the larger goals of sexual equality. Would it were so.

Reference

Cobbe, F. P. (1878). Wife torture in England. *Contemporary Review, 32*, 55–87.

POSTSCRIPT

Does Arresting Spousal Batterers Do More Harm Than Good?

Domestic violence is a multifaceted issue. It includes violence of parents against their children, of husband against wife, of wife against husband, and of adult child against an elderly parent. The causes are usually obscure and complex. In short, as in many areas of human behavior, *why* anyone assaults another is problematic, as are the "cures" for such assaults. There likely is no single panacea.

Moreover, as Stark argues, attempting to isolate a single factor, such as arrests, then making policy recommendations based on some quasi-experimental design comparing that factor with others is dubious. However, even if it is conceded that arrest is *not* a deterrent in many cases, can we say that its symbolic function justifies making arrests mandatory anyway? If careful research shows, as Schmidt and Sherman contend, that arrests have limited value and often make matters worse, should such research be ignored in order to send the signal that society will no longer tolerate this form of brutality? In addition to more counseling programs and shelters for women, other proposals are being formulated for battered women (e.g., quick and easy divorce for battered victims). Should such steps be carefully researched before a policy like mandatory arrest, which may have serious unanticipated negative consequences for many victims, is embraced?

A recent work that looks at family violence and other abuses is P. M. Tobolowsky, ed., *Understanding Victimology: Selected Readings* (Anderson, 2000). A broad look at causes of abuse is M. Harway and J. O'Neil, eds., *What Causes Men's Violence Against Women?* (Sage Publications, 1999). And a useful manual for abuse victims, scholars, and criminal justice personnel is *The Domestic Violence Survival Guide* by C. Mariani (Looseleaf Law Publications, 1996).

A legal discussion can be found in "Battered Woman's Defense Raises Public, Prosecutors' Consciousness," by G. Cox, *Criminal Justice Weekly* (January 11, 2000). A look at spousal abuse in nonurban areas is *Rural Woman Battering and the Justice System: An Ethnography* by N. Websdale (Sage Publications, 1998), and a more global look at domestic violence can be found in S. Kawewe and R. Dibie, "United Nations and the Problem of Women and Children Abuse in Third World Nations," *Social Justice* (Spring 1999). A recent study of same-sex abuse is S. Lundy and B. Leventhal, eds., *Same-Sex Domestic Violence: Strategies for Change,* Sage Series on Violence Against Women vol. 1 (Sage Publications, 1999). Finally, two helpful journals on domestic violence are *Domestic Violence Report* and *Trauma, Violence, and Abuse.*

ISSUE 6

Is Racial Profiling an Acceptable Law Enforcement Strategy?

YES: Jared Taylor and Glayde Whitney, from "Racial Profiling: Is There an Empirical Basis?" *Mankind Quarterly* (Spring 2002)

NO: Michael J. Lynch, from "Misleading 'Evidence' and the Misguided Attempt to Generate Racial Profiles of Criminals; Correcting Fallacies and Calculations Concerning Race and Crime in Taylor and Whitney's Analysis of Racial Profiling," *Mankind Quarterly* (Spring 2002)

ISSUE SUMMARY

YES: Jared Taylor, president of the New Century Foundation, and Glayde Whitney argue that the disparity in crimes committed by members of different races justifies racial profiling by the police.

NO: Professor Michael J. Lynch, however, argues that a proper analysis of the crime data does not support Taylor and Whitney's conclusions. He finds racial profiling to be objectionable from a legal and moral perspective as well.

One of the more controversial issues in American society is race relations. It has now been more than 50 years since U.S. Supreme Court's seminal decision in *Brown v. Board of Education*, 347 U.S. 483 (1954), which ended the doctrine of "separate but equal" treatment of the races. This decision was grounded on the principle that separate treatment based on race can never truly be equal. Stated Chief Justice Earl Warren:

> To separate [school children] from others of similar age and qualifications solely because of their race generates a feeling of inferiority as to their status in the community that may affect their hearts and minds in a way unlikely ever to be undone. . . (494).

Feelings of inferiority as to one's status in the community could be caused by many different things. Most of us have been stopped by the police for a traffic violation at one time or another. How did it make you feel? Did your heart rate increase? Did you begin to perspire slightly? Were you nervous, or did you become tongue-tied when you began to talk with the officer? Now, put yourself in the place of a 21-year-old African-American male who is stopped by the police. Would the experience be any different? Would you be suspicious that the only reason you were stopped was because of your race? If you were a young Hispanic-American male driving in an upscale neighborhood and were stopped by the police and were told "you don't belong here," would it produce the same feelings of inferiority Chief Justice Warren had described in *Brown v. Board of Education?*

In contrast, suppose that criminologists could show statistically that a disproportionate number of young minority group members were responsible for committing crimes such as burglary in the upscale neighborhood. Would the police be justified in questioning any young minority group member found in the area? Likewise, suppose it could be demonstrated that the individuals who carried out the September 11 bombings of the World Trade Center buildings were exclusively young males of Middle-eastern descent. Would TSA officials at our nation's airports be justified in targeting such individuals for intensive pre-flight searches?

Jared Taylor and Glayde Whitney assert that the police are justified in using racial profiling strategies based on their analysis of macro-level crime data. These authors contend that African-Americans commit violent crimes at four to eight times the white rate. Hispanics, they believe, commit violent crimes at approximately three times the white rate, and Asians at one-half to three-quarters of the white rate. Taylor and Whitney assert that criminologists, in a spirit of political correctness, have succumbed to media and political pressure to avoid acknowledgment of the differences and their implications for public policy.

Criminologist Michael J. Lynch maintains that Taylor and Whitney have made errors in their analysis that produce misleading conclusions about racial profiling. While he agrees that African-Americans are overrepresented in the crime data, he contends that this may be a measure of a bias that selects them more often for official processing within the justice system. Moreover, Lynch believes that Taylor and Whitney's views on the propriety of racial profiling by law enforcement officials either are purposely misleading or are completely naïve analyses of crime and victimization data.

Suppose you accept Taylor and Whitney's view that the members of racial minorities do commit more crime in the United States. Does that mean that racial profiling by law enforcement officials is justified? Or, might there be a moral component to this debate, which says that it is wrong to target persons based on their race, no matter how effective the practice may potentially be? When you read these articles try to develop your own sense of whether racial profiling is a legitimate law enforcement practice as well as its implications in a pluralistic nation.

Jared Taylor and
Glayde Whitney

 **YES**

Racial Profiling: Is There an Empirical Basis?

The disparity between public sensibilities and empirical data has become so extreme that certain topics can no longer be investigated without bringing down cries of "racism". Nevertheless, blacks commit violent crimes at four to eight times the white rate. Hispanics commit violent crimes at about three times the white rate, and Asians at one half to three quarters the white rate. Blacks are as much more criminally violent than whites, as men are more violent than women. Therefore, just as police stop and question men more often than women, they should stop blacks more often than whites. Of the approximately 1,700,000 interracial crimes of violence involving blacks and whites, 90 percent are committed by blacks against whites. Blacks are 50 times more likely than whites to commit individual acts of interracial violence. They are up to 250 times more likely than whites to engage in multiple-offender or group interracial violence. There is more black-on-white than black-on-black violent crime. Fifty-six percent of violent crimes committed by blacks have white victims. Only two to three percent of violent crimes committed by whites have black victims. Violent crime and interracial violence are important, agonizing concerns in this country, and we cannot begin to formulate solutions until we understand the problems.

One of the strangest phenomena in contemporary criminology is the treatment of race and ethnicity. On the one hand there is a long history of academic attention to differences among racial and ethnic groups in involvement in various sorts of criminality (Hooton, 1939; Wilson & Herrnstein, 1985). On the other hand there appears to be media and political pressure to avoid acknowledgement of the differences and possible consequences of the differences. Recently the New Jersey State Police Superintendent Col. Carl Williams was fired by Gov. Christie Whitman after he said in an interview that some minority groups were more likely to be involved in certain crimes (AP, 1999). The Governor is quoted as having said that Williams' comments were "inconsistent with our efforts to enhance public confidence in the State Police." The same article reports that Williams said he did not condone racial profiling, and has never condoned racial profiling, but at the same time he said "it is naive to think race is not an issue" in some sorts of crime

From *Mankind Quarterly*, vol. 42, issue 3, Spring 2002, pp. 285–312. Copyright © 2002 by Council for Social and Economic Studies. Reprinted by permission.

(AP, 1999). While Col. Williams claims not to condone racial profiling, the American Civil Liberties Union (ACLU) reported in June, 1999, that it was a widespread practice: "Citing police statistics, case studies from 23 states and media reports, the organization asserts that law-enforcement agencies have systematically targeted minority travelers for search . . . based on the belief that they are more likely than whites to commit crimes." (Drummond, 1999).

Although reports such as that of the ACLU which criticize the practice of racial profiling and criticize the "belief" that there may be race differences in criminality get wide media coverage, even being featured in national news magazines such as Time, (Drummond, 1999), other reports that deal with the actual incidence of crimes as related to race get short shrift. The nationally syndicated columnist Samuel Francis recently wrote:

> Black Americans commit 90 percent of the 1.7 million interracial crimes that occur in the United States every year and are more than 50 times more likely to commit violent crimes against whites than whites are against blacks. These facts were the main findings of a study released earlier this month by the New Century Foundation, but they're not the really big news.
>
> The big news is that the report, despite having been made available to virtually all newspapers and news outlets in the United States as well as to most major columnists and opinion writers, has been almost totally ignored by the national news media. The study was released on June 2 of this year. To date, all of one single news story about it has appeared. (Francis, 1999).

It does indeed seem strange for there to be a great disparity between media reports and the subsequent public apperception, and the actual data concerning one of the more important issues in criminology today.

The inconsistency between media reports and criminological data concerning race is not a new phenomenon. About a decade ago we reviewed the literature dealing with race differences in criminal behavior. Taylor (1992) largely reviewed media reports, while Whitney (1990) reviewed the scientific literature. A main finding of the review of media accounts of race and crime was the existence of a double standard with regard to reports of crime that mentioned race of perpetrator or race of victim, with white victimization of blacks receiving considerably more prominent coverage than black victimization of whites (Taylor, 1992). The review of scientific literature was remarkable for both the quantity and consistency of prior literature (Whitney, 1990). Furthermore, the racial differences were accentuated when one considered more serious offenses and offenses that were variously described as victimful or predatory crimes. In a major review Ellis (1988) had reported that for serious victimful crimes, whenever comparisons had been made, blacks had always had higher rates than whites. Whenever blacks or whites had been compared with Orientals in roughly the same geographical areas, Orientals had always had the lowest serious victimful crime rates. The results were much less consistent for minor and/or victimless offenses. Overall, and order of blacks > whites >

Orientals prevailed, with racial differences being larger the more serious and clearly victimful the offenses (Whitney, 1990).

In their classic *Crime and Human Nature*, Wilson and Herrnstein (1985:461) reviewed some literature on race and crime. They mentioned that blacks then constituted about oneeighth of the population of the United States and about one-half of arrestees for murder, rape, and robbery, and from one-fourth to one-third of arrestees for burglary, larceny, auto theft, and aggravated assault. Even with adjustments for other demographic variables, such as age and urban residence, in comparison to whites, blacks were overrepresented about four to one with regard to violent crimes and about three to one with regard to property crimes. Rushton (1985) pointed out that experience in England was consistent with that in the United States: blacks then constituted about 13 percent of the population of London and accounted for 50 percent of the crime. Indeed, violent crime by blacks had been mentioned as a factor contributing to the rearming of London's Metropolitan Police (Could & Waldren, 1986). Blacks were similarly overrepresented with regard to white-collar crimes such as fraud and embezzlement. Blacks were underrepresented only with regard to offenses, such as securities violations, that usually required access to high-status occupations in which they were at that time underrepresented (Wilson & Herrnstein, 1985:462).

Whitney (1990) analyzed the race-specific arrest rates for various offenses that had been compiled for the years 1965 to 1986 (UCRP, 1988). For 19 categories listed in each of 22 years (418 comparisons), the rate for nonwhites always exceeded the rate for whites in the same year, typically by a factor of four to ten. For example, averaged across years, the nonwhite murder rate was nine times the white rate. Considerations of rate of crime combine prevalence (individuals who participate in crime) and incidence (recidivism, number of crimes by individuals who participate). Prevalence has been estimated through accumulation of first arrests across age (Blumstein & Graddy, 1981-1982; Blumstein & Cohen, 1987). Blumstein's results suggest that incidence is not strongly different among participants of different races. Rather, the race differences in crime rates are largely attributable to differences in the proportion of individuals of various races that participate in crime (Blumstein & Cohen, 1987). Among urban males the probability that by age 55 a black had been arrested for an FBI index crime was about 0.51; for whites it was 0.14 (Blumstein & Graddy, 1981-1982). Comparable age accumulated participation rates are not available for Orientals due primarily to their very low overall participation rates. Conversion of percentages to areas under a normal curve can be useful for comparing populations. These individual participation rates suggest about a one-standard-deviation difference between male urban blacks and whites for criminal liability (Whitney, 1990). The apologist argument that arrest data are inappropriate for documentation of race differences in crime rates due to bias in arrests was thoroughly considered, and essentially debunked in Wilbank's 1987 book *The Myth of a Racist Criminal Justice System*. More recently Dilulio (1996) has also presented data concerning crime disparities among races, and the suggestion that the disparities are real in that they do not reflect differential law enforcement.

For regions within the United States, Whitney (1995) pointed out that the best predictor of local murder rate was simply the percent of the population that was black. Across all of the 170 cities in the United States that had a 1980 population of at least 100,000, the correlation between murder rate and percent of the population that was black was r = +0.69. With data from 1980 aggregated for the 50 states of the United States, the simple correlation between murder rate and percent of the population that was black was r = +0.77. More recently Hama (1999) used data from 1995 to calculate the correlation across the 50 states between percent of the population that is black and violent crime rate, where violent crime rate was an aggregate of murder, non-negligent manslaughter, rape, robbery, and aggravated assault. Hama (1999) reported the correlation to be r = +0.76.

Clearly the existing data briefly reviewed above are quite consistent. They are also somewhat limited in scope. There are two areas of criminality related to race that are not considered above, but which have become of interest in recent years. One is the question of hate crime categorization, and the other is that of interracial crime. In crimes where the perpetrator and the victim are of different races, are there any patterns in incidence, and what amount of interracial crime gets included in hate crime statistics? The analyses reported in the present paper were conducted to obtain information concerning the questions of interracial crime and hate crimes, as well as to update the investigation of incidence of crime as related to race in the United States.

Sources and Methods

The primary sources of data for consideration were governmental compilations of statistical information having to do with crime. The major sources are described here. One of the most important sources is the National Crime Victimization Survey (NCVS). Every year since 1972, the U.S. Department of Justice has carried out what is called the NCVS to ascertain the frequency of certain kinds of crimes. The NCVS sample is large, upwards of 80,000 people from about 50,000 households, and carefully stratified on the basis of census data to be representative of the nation as a whole. The NCVS is unique as a record of criminal victimization as reported directly by Americans, not filtered through police reports. It is the only significant nationwide measure of interracial crime. The NCVS is carried out annually, but the Department of Justice does not issue full reports every year; 1994 is the most recent year for complete data.

Ever since passage of the Hate Crime Statistics act of 1990, the FBI has been charged with collecting national statistics on criminal acts "motivated, in whole or in part, by bias." The law does not compel local law enforcement agencies to supply the FBI with this information, but many do. In 1997, the most recent year for which data are available, the FBI received hate crime information from 11,211 local agencies serving more than 83 percent of the United States population.

Uniform Crime Reports (UCR), published annually by the FBI, is the standard reference work for crime and crime rates in the United States. The UCR is a nationwide compilation of criminal offenses and arrest data, reported voluntarily by local law enforcement agencies. In the most recent UCR, which covers 1997, the FBI included reports from 17,000 law enforcement agencies, covering 95 percent of the country's population. The UCR is unquestionably the most comprehensive and authoritative report on crimes brought to the attention of the police. News stories about rising or falling crime rates are almost always based on the UCR.

Our primary methodology throughout this study is to calculate rates of various offenses as a function of victim and offender characteristics. Such calculations are straightforward, but can appear arcane to investigators experienced with other analytical approaches. Therefore we here provide a detailed example.

The most recent complete NCVS data are for the year 1994 (USDJ, 1997). In that report Table 42 lists categories of single-offender interracial violent crimes. The various numbers at the top of the table represent totals calculated for single-offender violent crimes reported for that year. They are extrapolated from the actual crimes reported by the survey sample. We find that in 1994 6,830,360 whites were victims of violent crimes, and that 16.7 percent (1,140,670) reported that the perpetrator was black. Blacks were victims of 1,100,490 violent crimes, of which 12.3 percent (135,360) were committed by whites. Summing these figures for interracial crime (1,140,670 plus 135,360) we get a total of 1,276,030 interracial crimes, of which 1,140,670 or 89 percent were committed by blacks.

To get the rates at which blacks and whites commit interracial crime we divide the number of crimes by the population to get crimes per 100,000 population. The Census Bureau reports that the 1994 white and black populations were 216,413,000 and 32,653,000 respectively. Whites therefore committed acts of interracial violence at a rate of 62.55 per 100,000 while the black rate was 3,493.63 per 100,000, a figure that is 55.85 times the white rate. Put in the most straightforward terms, the average black was 56 times more likely to commit criminal violence against a white than was a white to commit criminal violence against a black. The multiple of 56 does not mean that blacks commit 56 times as much interracial violence as whites. What it means is that if whites commit interracial violence at a rate of 10 crimes per 100,000 whites, the rate for blacks is 560 per 100,000, or 56 times the white rate. This is the kind of calculation that is represented in most of the analyses in this report.

Results and Discussion

Calculations from the NCVS similar to those detailed above indicate that the black rate for interracial robbery, or "mugging", was 103 times the white rate. . . .

Again using the NCVS (USDJ, 1997), we calculate the total number of crimes committed by perpetrators of each race, and the percentage that is committed against the other race. The 1,140,670 acts of violence committed by blacks against whites constitute 56.3 percent of all violent crimes committed by blacks. That is to say that when blacks commit violent crimes they target whites more than half the time or, put differently, there is more black-on-white crime than black-on-black crime. Similar calculations for whites show that of the 5,114,696 acts of criminal violence committed by whites, only 2.6 percent were directed at blacks. Although homicide is a violent crime, the NCVS does not include it because victims cannot be interviewed. The number of interracial homicides is rather small and does not substantially affect the percentages and ratios presented here.

It may be suggested that blacks commit violence against whites because whites are more likely to have money and are therefore more promising robbery targets. However, of the 1,140,670 black-on-white acts of single-perpetrator violence reported in 1994, only 173,374 were robberies. The remaining 84.8 percent were aggravated assaults, rapes, and simple assaults, which presumably were not motivated by profit. Rape, in particular, has nothing to do with the presumed wealth of the victim. More than 30,000 white women were raped by black men in 1994, while about 5,400 black women were raped by white men. The black interracial rape rate was thus 38 times the white rate.

The NCVS (USDJ, 1997) Table 48 contains interracial crime data for acts of violence committed by multiple offenders. By doing calculations as before, we determine how much group or "gang" violence (not in the sense of organized gangs) is interracial and how much is committed by blacks and by whites. Of the total of 490,266 acts of multiple-offender interracial violence, no fewer than 93.9 percent were committed by blacks against whites. Robbery, for which there is a monetary motive, accounted for fewer than one third of these crimes. The rest were gang assaults, including rapes, presumably for motives other than profit.

Rates of group violence for each race can be calculated as before, and the difference between the races is stark. The black rate of overall interracial gang violence is 101.75 times the white rate; for robbery it is 277.31 times the white rate. . . .

Race and Crime

Different racial groups in the United States commit crimes at different rates. Most Americans have a sense that non-white neighborhoods are more dangerous than white neighborhoods—and they are correct. However, it is very unusual to find reliable information on just how much more dangerous some groups are than others.

The Uniform Crime Reports (UCR) from the FBI is the standard reference for crime and crime rates in the United States. In trying to determine crime rates for different racial groups, it is important to be aware of the differences between the UCR and the NCVS referenced above. The NCVS contains only one kind of information: crimes Americans say they have suffered. The UCR includes two different kinds of data: crimes reported to the police and arrests of perpetrators. Even for the same year and for the same crime, these three sets of numbers are different. The largest numbers are in the NCVS, because they include crimes not reported to the police. Somewhat smaller are the UCR figures on offenses reported to authorities, and smaller still are arrest figures, which represent offenses for which a suspect is arrested.

For example, in the 1997 NCVS Americans say they suffered a total of 1,883,000 cases of aggravated assault (USDJ, 1998a), but according to the UCR, only 1,022,000 were reported to the police. During that same year, there were only 535,000 arrests for aggravated assault (UCR, 1998). Racial data enter the UCR numbers only when an arrest is made, so it can be argued that racial comparisons should not be based on UCR data. Different racial groups may report crime to the police at different rates, some groups may be more successful at escaping arrest, and the police may discriminate between racial groups in their arrest efforts. However, although racial bias in arrests is frequently discussed, when investigated the data suggest that arrest rates actually track perpetrator rates (Dilulio, 1996; Wilbanks, 1987). Furthermore, there is an advantage to using UCR data because its racial categories are more detailed. Unlike the NCVS, which reports only "black", "white", and "other", the UCR compiles arrest data on "black", "white", "American Indian/Eskimo", and "Asian/Pacific Islander". These are the only national crime data that make these distinctions. Also, as will be explicated below, UCR arrest data can be compared to other data sources in ways that make it possible to treat Hispanics as a separate ethnic category.

Another good reason to use UCR arrest data (race of persons arrested) is that the racial proportions are actually quite close to those from NCVS survey data (race of perpetrator as reported by victims). For example, according to the UCR, 57 percent of people arrested for robbery in 1997 were black, as were 37 percent of those arrested for aggravated assault (UCR, 1998). According to NCVS data on single-offender crimes, 51 percent of robbers were reported by their victims to be black as were 30 percent of those who committed aggravated assault (USDJ, 1997). Since there is a greater overrepresentation by blacks in NCVS-reported multiple-offender crimes, combining the two sets of figures brings the racial proportions in the NCVS figures extremely close to the racial proportions in UCR arrest numbers. Put differently, police are arresting criminals of different races in very close to the same proportions as Americans say they are victimized by people of those races.

By this measure, who is committing crime in America? . . .

The white rate is always set to one, so if the black rate is three, for example, it means that blacks are arrested at three times the white rate. Once again, it does not mean that three times as many blacks as whites were arrested; it means that if 100 of every 100,000 whites were arrested for a crime, 300 of every 100,000 blacks were arrested for the same crime. The data show a consistent pattern: Blacks are arrested at dramatically higher rates than other racial groups. American Indians and Eskimos (hereinafter "Indians") are arrested at slightly higher rates than whites, and Asians/Pacific Islanders (hereinafter "Asians") are arrested at consistently lower rates. The popular conception of crime in America is correct: rates are much higher among blacks than among whites or other groups.

To return to the view that arrest data reflect police bias rather than genuine group differences in crime rates, police actually have very little discretion in whom they arrest for violent crimes. Except for murder victims, most people can tell the police the race of an assailant. If a victim says she was mugged by a white man, the police cannot very well arrest a black man even if they want to. For this reason, many people accept that police have little discretion in whom they arrest for violent crime, but still believe drug laws are enforced unfairly against minorities. Drug offenses are beyond the scope of this investigation, but here, too, there is independent evidence that arrest rates reflect differences in criminal behavior, not selective law enforcement. The U.S. Department of Health and Human Services keeps records by race of drug-related emergency room admissions. It reports that blacks are admitted at 6.67 times the non-Hispanic white rate for heroin and morphine, and no less than 10.49 times the non-Hispanic white rate for cocaine (Rates for Hispanics are 2.82 and 2.35 times the white rates; information is not reported for American Indians or Asians) (USDJ, 1998b). There is only one plausible explanation for these rates: Blacks are much more likely to be using drugs in the first place. Finally, if racist white police were unfairly arresting non-whites we would expect arrest rates for Asians to be higher than those for whites. Instead, they are lower for almost every kind of crime.

Measuring Hispanic Crime Rates

Any study of crime rates in America is complicated by the inconsistent treatment of Hispanics by different government agencies. For example, the Census Bureau's official estimate for the 1997 population of the United States divides all 268 million Americans into four racial groups: white, black, Indian and Eskimo, and Asian and Pacific Islander. The bureau then explains that among these 268 million people there are 29 million Hispanics who "can be of any race". However, it also counts non-Hispanic whites, non-Hispanic blacks, Indians, etc. Thus we find that although according to the strictly racial classification, there are 221 million whites in the United States, there are only 195 million non-Hispanic whites. When American Hispanics, approximately half of whom are Mexican, are apportioned to the four racial categories, the Census Bureau considers 91 percent to be white, six percent black, one percent American Indian, and two percent Asian.

The treatment of Hispanics can make for odd results. For example, according to the 1990 census, the 3,485,000 people of Los Angeles were 52.9 percent white, 13.9 percent black, 0.4 percent American Indian, and 22.9 percent Asian—which adds up to 100 percent. This makes the city appear to be majority white. However, Los Angeles was also 39.3 percent Hispanic, and if we subtract the 91 percent of them who are classified as whites, the non-Hispanic white population drops to only 16.6 percent.

What does this mean for crime statistics? Because the UCR figures do not treat Hispanics as a separate category, almost all the Hispanics arrested in the United States go into official records as "white". This is contrary to the usual cultural understanding of the term, which is not normally thought to include most Mexicans and Latinos.

If violent crime rates for Hispanics are different from those of non-Hispanic whites, putting Hispanics in the "white" category distorts the results. This is not as serious as in the case of hate crimes, in which the crime itself has to do with the very personal characteristics that are being omitted from the records, but there is no legitimate reason not to make ethnic and racial comparisons as accurate as possible. The UCR tabulates separate data on American Indians and Eskimos—who are less than one percent of the population—but it ignores Hispanics, who are 12 percent of the population.

Some data-gathering agencies do treat Hispanic and non-Hispanic whites separately. The California Department of Justice, which records all arrests within the state, consistently makes this distinction (although it lumps Asians and American Indians into the "other" category) (Calif, 1998). In conjunction with Census Bureau population figures for Hispanics, nonHispanic whites, and non-Hispanic blacks living in California in 1997, we can calculate the arrest rates for the different groups for various crimes. . . . As is the case with national UCR data, blacks are arrested at much higher rates than whites, but Hispanics are also arrested at considerably higher rates.

The different rates at which Hispanics and non-Hispanic whites are held in prisons and jails are another indicator of the differences in crime rates between the two groups. Although the UCR does not treat Hispanics as a separate category for arrest purposes, some government reports on the prison population do consider them separately. For example, the Department of Justice has calculated incarceration rates per 100,000 population for non-Hispanic whites (193), Hispanics (688), and non-Hispanic blacks (1,571) (USDJ, 1998b). Expressed as multiples of the white rate, the Hispanic rate is 3.56 and black rate is 8.14.

These multiples are close to those from the California arrest data, and justify the conclusion that Hispanics are roughly three times more likely than non-Hispanic whites to be arrested for various crimes. By accepting this assumption, we can use the following formula to incorporate this differential into the UCR racial data on white arrests so as to calculate more accurate arrest rates for non-Hispanic whites:

R(Number of non-Hispanic whites) + 3R(Number of white Hispanics) = Actual Number of Arrests.

Here, R is the arrest rate for non-Hispanic whites and 3R is the arrest rate for Hispanics who are categorized as white when they are arrested. Calculations of this sort show that if Hispanics are broken out as a separate ethnic category with an arrest rate three times the non-Hispanic rate, the rate for non-Hispanic whites decreases by 19.5 percent. . . . Due to lack of precise information, the multiple for Hispanics is set to three times the white rate for all crimes even though there is certain to be some variation in the multiples for different types of crimes. . . .

It should be noted here that the NCVS survey data on interracial crime also includes most Hispanics in the "white" category. It is therefore impossible to know how many of the "whites" who committed violent crimes against blacks were actually Hispanic or how many of the "whites" against whom blacks committed violent crimes were Hispanic. If Hispanics commit violent crimes against blacks at a higher rate than whites—and judging from their higher arrest and incarceration rates for violent offenses this seems likely—the NCVS report also inflates the crime rates of non-Hispanic whites.

Men vs. Women, Blacks vs. Whites

Many people resist the idea that different racial groups have substantially different rates of violent crime. However, there are several group differences in crime rates that virtually everyone accepts and, indeed, takes for granted. Men in their late teens and 20s, for example, are much more prone to violence that men beyond their 50s. When young men are arrested more frequently for violent offenses, no one doubts that it is because they commit more violent crime. Likewise, virtually no one disputes the reason for higher arrest rates for men than for women: Men commit more violent crime than women (Wilson & Herrnstein, 1985). This is the case for racial groups as well: Asians are arrested at lower rates than whites because they commit fewer crimes; blacks and Hispanics are arrested at higher rates because they commit more crimes (Levin, 1997; Rushton, 1995; Whitney, 1990).

When it comes to violent crime, blacks are approximately as much more likely to be arrested than whites, as men are more likely to be arrested than women. The multiples of black v. white arrest rates are very close to the multiples of male v. female arrest rates, suggesting that blacks are as much more dangerous than whites as men are more dangerous than women.

What does this mean? Although most people have no idea what the arrest rate multiples may be, they have an intuitive understanding that men are more violent and dangerous than women. If someone in unfamiliar circumstances is approached by a group of strange men she feels more uneasy than if she is approached by an otherwise similar group of strange women. No one would suggest that this differential uneasiness is "prejudice". It is common sense, born out by the objective reality that men are more dangerous than women.

In fact, it is just as reasonable to feel more uneasy when approached by blacks than by otherwise similar whites; the difference in danger as reflected by arrest rates is virtually the same. It is rational to fear blacks more than whites, just as it is rational to fear men more than women. Whatever additional precautions a person would take are justified because a potential assailant was male rather than female are, from a statistical point of view, equally justified if a potential assailant is black rather than white. . . .

Likewise, there is now much controversy about so-called "racial profiling" by the police, that is, the practice of questioning blacks in disproportionate numbers in the expectation that they are more likely than people of other races to be criminals. The philosophical, legal and rational case for racial profiling has been elaborated by the philosopher Michael Levin (Levin, 1997). "Racial" profiling is just as rational and productive as "age" or "sex" profiling. Police would be wasting their time if they stopped and questioned as many little old ladies as they do young black men. It is the job of the police to catch criminals, and they know from experience who is likely to be an offender. Americans who do not question the wisdom of police officers who notice a possible suspect's age and sex should not be surprised to learn those officers also notice race.

Conclusions

Two things can be said about most of the information in this investigation: It is easily discovered but little known. Every year, the FBI issues its report on hate crimes, and distributes thousands of copies to scholars and the media. Why does no one find it odd that hundreds of whites are reportedly committing hate crimes against whites? And why does no one question the wisdom of calling someone white when he is a perpetrator but Hispanic when he is a victim?

For some years there has been an extended national discussion about the prevalence of black-on-black crime—and for good reason. Blacks suffer from considerably more violent crime than do Americans of other races. And yet, amid this national outcry over the extent of black-on-black crime, there appears to be little concern about the fact that there is actually more black-on-white crime. Nor does there seem to be much interest in the fact that blacks are 50 to 200 times more likely than whites to commit interracial crimes of violence. Differences as great as this are seldom found in comparative studies of group behavior, and they cry out for causal investigation and explanation. It is probably safe to say that if the races were reversed, and gangs of whites were attacking blacks at merely four or five times the rate at which blacks were attacking whites the country would consider this a national crisis that required urgent attention.

Everyone knows that young people are more dangerous than old people, and that men are more dangerous than women. We adjust our behavior accordingly and do not apologize for doing so. Why then must we pretend that blacks are no more dangerous than whites or Asians? But of course it is no more than pretense. Everyone knows that blacks are dangerous, and everyone—black and white—takes greater precautions in black neighborhoods or even avoids such neighborhoods entirely.

The answers to these questions lie in the current intellectual climate. Americans are extremely hesitant to "perpetuate stereotypes", and generally take care not to draw or publicize conclusions that may reflect badly on racial minorities. This is understandable, but has reached the point that certain subjects can no longer be investigated without bringing down cries of "racism". Needless to say, research that reflects badly on the majority population is not constrained by the same fears. However, our willingness to ignore sensibilities should not be selective. Violent crime and interracial violence are important, agonizing concerns in this country, and we cannot begin to formulate solutions unless we understand the problems.

References

AP, 1999, Whitman fires State Police superintendent over remarks to newspaper. Trenton NJ: Associated Press, March 1, 1999.

Blumstein, A., and J. Cohen, 1987, Characterizing criminal careers. *Science*, 237: 985–991.

Blumstein, A., and E. Graddy, 1981–82, Prevalence and recidivism in index arrests: A feedback model. *Law and Society Review*, 16: 265–290.

Calif, 1998, Adult and juvenile arrests reported, 1997. Race/ethnic group by specific offense statewide, January through December 1997. California Department of Justice Division of Criminal Justice, Criminal Justice Statistics Center: p. 5939, printed 04/15/98 (unpublished).

Could, R. W., and M.J. Waldren, 1986, London's Armed Police: 1829 to the present. London: Arms and Armour Press.

Dilulio, John J., Jr., 1996, My black crime problem and ours. City Journal, Spring: 14ff.

Drummond, Tammerlin, 1999, It's not just in New Jersey. *Time* 153 (23), June 14, 1999:61.

Ellis, Lee, 1987, The victimful—victimless crime distinction, and seven universal demographic correlates of victimful criminal behavior. Personality and Individual Differences, 91: 525–548.

Francis, Samuel, 1999, Media blackout on black-on-white crime. *Conservative Chronicle*, June 30, 1999: 23.

Hama, Aldric, 1999, Demographic changes and social breakdown: The role of intelligence. (manuscript under review).

Hooton, Earnest Albert, 1939, *Crime and the Man*. Cambridge MA: Harvard University Press.

Levin, Michael, 1997, *Why Race Matters: Race differences and what they mean*. Westport CT: Praeger.

Rushton, J. Philippe, 1985, Differential K theory: The sociobiology of individual and group differences. *Personality and Individual Differences*, 6: 441–452.

Rushton, J. Philippe, 1995, *Race, Evolution, and Behavior. A life history perspective*. New Brunswick, NJ: Transaction.

Taylor, Jared, 1992, *Paved with Good Intentions: The failure of race relations in contemporary America*. New York: Carroll & Graf.

UCR, 1998, Crime in the United States, 1997. Washington DC: U.S. Department of Justice, Federal Bureau of Investigation, USGPO.

USDJ, 1997, Criminal Victimization in the United States, 1994. Washington DC: U.S. Department of Justice, Bureau of Justice Statistics, USGPO.

USDJ, 1998a, Criminal Victimization in the United States, 1997. Washington DC: U.S. Department of Justice, Bureau of Justice Statistics, USGPO.

USDJ, 1998b, Sourcebook of Criminal Justice Statistics, 1997. Washington DC: U.S. Department of Justice, Bureau of Justice Statistics, USGPO.

Whitney, Glayde, 1990, On possible genetic bases of race differences in criminality. In: Ellis, Lee and Harry Hoffman (Eds.), *Crime in Biological, Social, and Moral Contexts*. Westport CT: Praeger. 134–149.

Whitney, Glayde, 1995, Ideology and censorship in behavior genetics. *The Mankind Quarterly*, 35: 327–342.

Wilbanks, William, 1986, *The Myth of a Racist Criminal Justice System*. Monterey CA: Brooks/Cole.

Wilson, James Q. and Richard J. Herrnstein, 1985, *Crime and Human Nature*. New York: Simon & Schuster.

Michael J. Lynch

 **NO**

Misleading "Evidence" and the Misguided Attempt to Generate Racial Profiles of Criminals; Correcting Fallacies and Calculations Concerning Race and Crime in Taylor and Whitney's Analysis of Racial Profiling

In 1999, *The Journal of Social, Political and Economic Studies* published an article written by Taylor and Whitney that endeavored to demonstrate the efficacy of racial profiling of criminals. In that article, Taylor and Whitney made two significant general errors that influenced their conclusions concerning the utility of racial profiling. Their first error threatens the validity of their theoretical position. The second invalidates their statistical results and conclusions. Taken together, these general errors invalidates their position on race and crime.

To be more specific about these errors, Taylor and Whitney ground their argument concerning race and crime on a rather restricted review of extant literature. Excluding their own prior research from considerations, Taylor and Whitney refer approvingly to studies by Hooton, Wilson and Hernnstein, Wilbanks and Rushton, and appear to hold them out as exposing sound criminological explanations of the relationship between race and crime. In truth, the views on race and crime expressed by these authors have been refuted and rejected by the majority of criminologists (for criticism of these researchers and their general views on race see: Cernovsky and Litman, 1993; Gabor and Roberts, 1990; Lynch, 1990, 2000; Neopolitan, 1998; Shipman, 1994; Yee et al., 1993; Zuckerman, 1990).

Taylor and Whitney also make several methodological errors in their analyses of criminological data sources that generate misleading results and conclusions concerning the appropriateness of racial profiling. Specifically, these errors include: the use of prevalence rates rather than incidence rates; the failure to use race-based population-adjusted comparisons for offender and

From *Mankind Quarterly*, vol. 42, issue 3, Spring 2002, pp. 313–329. Copyright © 2002 by Council for Social and Economic Studies.

victimization data; focusing on rare forms of inter-racial crime and generalizing to the entire populations of criminals; and using data useful for addressing racial biases in criminal justice processes (Uniform Crime Report and imprisonment data) to calculate racial differences in offending.

To be sure, Blacks are over-represented in criminal justice data. But, Black over-representation in the criminal justice system (measured against the size of the Black population) cannot be employed as evidence that Blacks are responsible for more crime than Whites because over-representation may be a measure of processing biases (Mann, 1993). In short, observations concerning Black over-representation in criminal justice data do not directly translate into claims related to racial differences in offending. Taylor and Whitney, however, use criminal justice data as evidence of differences in offending by race. They are not the first to make this error and the researchers they site approvingly (Rushton, Wilbanks, Wilson and Hernnstein) have also misinterpreted criminal justice data as indicating race differences in offending.[1] Taylor and Whitney's argument begins with literature based on a misinterpretation of criminal justice data, and justifies this view with what can be described either as purposefully misleading or completely naive analyses of crime and victimization data. In either case, their conclusions are incorrect.

Taylor and Whitney's specific focus centers on the fact that "society" seems to express greater concern over Black-on-Black crime when, in fact, Taylor and Whitney believe that Black-on-White crime is the larger social problem. Had their argument been limited to this minor issue, their point would have some validity (though, as we demonstrate, even this contentions turns out to be incorrect). But, this turns out not to be their point at all. Rather, as they conclude "it is certainly understandable that police should take these statistics into account when searching for suspects, and that they may wish to take more precautions when entering some neighborhoods than others."[2] This conclusion, as we demonstrate below, is the result of the inappropriate use, analysis of and generalizations made from criminal justice data.

Taylor and Whitney make numerous errors in their analysis and use of criminal justice data. It is not our intention to review each of these errors here because these errors are repeated across different sources of data and our comments would become unnecessarily lengthy. Thus, to simplify our analysis, we focus only on one aspect of Taylor and Whitney's analysis: their use of National Crime Victimization Survey (NCVS). To further reduce unnecessary repetition, we have restricted this reanalysis of NCVS data to violent crimes where victims report a single offender.

The NCVS

According to the Bureau of Justice Statistics, The National Crime Victimization Survey is the Nation's primary source of information on criminal victimization. Each year, data are obtained from a nationally representative sample of roughly 50,000 households comprising nearly 100,000 persons on the frequency, characteristics and consequences of criminal victimization in the United States. The survey enables BJS to estimate the likelihood of victimization by rape, sexual assault, robbery, assault, theft, household burglary, and motor vehicle theft for the population as a whole as well as for segments of the population such as women, the elderly, members of various racial groups, city dwellers, or other groups. The NCVS provides the largest national forum for victims to describe the impact of crime and characteristics of violent offenders (http:// www.ojp.usdoj.gov/bjs/cvict.htm#Programs).

Taylor and Whitney report on data from the 1994 NCVS, while this reanalysis reports on 1999 NCVS data. Employing a different year for NCVS should not be problematic or invalidate the our reanalysis. NCVS data do not change dramatically from year to year, and are especially consistent with respect to reports of offender's race. Further, since Taylor and Whitney's goal is to validate racial profiling of criminals, evidence that this profile is stable across time would need to be produced. Consequently, it makes sense to repeat their analysis with several different years of NCVS data.

For the present discussion, we employ 1999 victim reports of offender's race for three violent or personal offenses where victims reported a single or lone offender: rape, robbery and assault. These three crimes are the only ones for which victim reports of offender race are available. These data are available at http://www.ojp.usdoj.gov/bjs/cvict.htm#Programs. The next section provides an overview of these data.

Overview of the 1999 NCVS

In 1999, the NCVS indicated 5,620,080 lone offender victimizations for the crimes of rape, robbery and assault reported by Black and White victims.[3] Approximately eighty-five percent of these victimizations were reported by White victims (N = 4,760,930). The remaining 867,150 victimizations were reported by Blacks.

Taylor and Whitney direct our attention to the inter-racial offenses reported in these data—that is, cases involving Black-offenders and White victims, and cases involving White offenders and Black victims. In 1999, there were 748,058 interracial victimizations (91,050 + 657,008). This figure, which appears to indicate an abundance of Black-on-White crime is misleading on two accounts. First, inter-racial violent crimes are rare events with respect to all crimes, comprising less than 2 percent of all reported criminal victimizations in any given year. Second, inter-racial violence is only one dimension of crime and thus generalizations from these data alone may lead to invalid conclusions.

Of these 748,058 inter-racial acts of violence, 657,008 involved a Black offender-White victim, while 91,050 involved a White offender-Black victim pairing. Taylor and Whitney make much of this finding, claiming that these data illustrate the extensively disproportionate nature of interracial victimizations involving White victims-Black offenders. That fact that nearly 88 percent of violent interracial victimizations involve Black offender-White victim dyads is interesting but, as we demonstrate below, not unexpected given the claims of opportunity theory, which would predict this outcome based upon knowing the racial distribution of the U.S. population.

Employing less than 2 percent of crimes—that is, by focusing on data depicting the extent of interracial crimes of violence—Taylor and Whitney conclude that Black-on-White crimes are serious enough to justify the use of racial profiling. As we have already noted, this conclusion is likely to be misleading because it is generalized from a non-representative sub-sample of all crimes. To get a better understanding of the relationship between race and violent criminal victimizations, it is necessary to analyze a broader portion of NCVS cases for which offender race is reported. The next section begins to address the basis for a reanalysis of NCVS data that presents the "big picture" of crime.

The Bigger Picture of Crime

In 1999, White victims of personal violence reported that 74.5 percent of lone attackers in rape, robbery and assault cases were White (N = 3,546,893), while only 13.3 percent were Black. In other words, the majority of crimes committed against Whites were by White offenders. This is not the conclusion drawn from reading Taylor and Whitney's research.

A similar picture of crime and victimization emerges when we examine Black responses to the NCVS: Blacks report that 80 percent of lone attackers are Black, while 10.5 percent are White. Taken together, these data clearly indicate that for the majority of offenses, crime is an intra-racial phenomenon, involving a victim and offender of the same race. From a crime profiling perspective, these data indicate that racial profiling, if we accept this idea as legitimate, should be performed on the basis of the victim's race because of the high correlation between race of victim and offender. It should be noted, however, that this form of profiling, while legitimate statistically, is hardly practical, since it fails in its mission of reducing the pool of potential suspects sufficiently.

The basic data provided by the NCVS makes it clear that the "crime problem" for each racial group consists of other members of the racial group to which one belongs. This conclusion is not apparent in Taylor and Whitney's research, which consistently points to the threat Black offenders present to Whites. How is it that Taylor and Whitney derive and justify this result? Answering this question requires investigating the proper use of rate standardized crime data that focuses on racial comparisons.

Misleading With Rate Comparisons

Taylor and Whitney mislead readers when they engage in a common criminological practice by using rate standardized data as a basis for comparing crime across racial groups. While it is commonplace for criminologists to standardize crime data and transform them into rates per 100,000 for comparison, racial comparisons based on rate standardization lead to erroneous conclusions. Rate standardization is useful for specific kinds of comparisons. One appropriate use would be to compare the prevalence of crime across locations known to have different sized populations. Doing so, we might address questions of relative safety. Second, we can use a rate comparison when are able to assume that the populations in question may be present in equal proportions.

In the United States, this latter assumption is violated when race is basis of the comparison. Black-White racial compositions vary from place to place. Whites, however, comprise a higher percentage of the US population than Blacks. Locations where the population is represented by an equal number of Blacks and Whites would be rare or unusual (Massey and Denton, 1993). Thus, there would be relatively few place to which racially-specific standardized rates of victimization (or offending) would be applicable.[4]

Taylor and Whitney further compound the prediction error they make by relying on rate standardized race comparisons when they transform these standardized rates into ratios or odds of victimization and offending. For example, Taylor and Whitney calculate the ratio of Black to White rates of inter-racial offending by dividing the rate of White Victim/Black Offenders per 100,000 population by the Black Victim/White Offender rate per 100,000 population. Constructing ratios from standardize rates that depict unequal populations as existing in equal proportions inflates the level of crime attributable to one group, while deflating the level of crime attributed to the other. This procedure, in other words, contains two opposing errors that compound the original error and inflate the ratio substantially. In this case, the ratio is inflated in a way that favors the interpretation that Black-on-White crime is more serious than White-On-Black crime.

Rate standardize data cannot be directly employed to reach conclusions concerning levels of offending by race. Rather, rate data need to be properly adjusted properly before comparisons across races are made, and before we can draw conclusions concerning the contribution of each race to crime. To do so, race specific rates need to be adjusted to reflect race-based population compositions. A corrected example of how race specific rates of offending should be used is provided below.

Turning Race-Specific Rates into Meaningful Data: An Example

The U.S. population is approximately 12 percent Black and 80 percent White. These figures have been rounded to make the calculations which follow simpler. Each calculation is an approximation, and the results reported are valid though not exact.

In 1999, 4,760,930 single offender violent crime victimizations were reported by Whites. Translated into a rate per 100,000, Whites report approximately 2204 victimizations per 100,000 Whites in the populations (Number of victimizations reported by Whites/White Population for the U.S. × 100,000). The comparable victimization rate for Blacks is 2710 victimizations per 100,000 Blacks in the population. These figures tell us that in a population composed of an equal number of Black and Whites (100,000), Blacks are more likely to be the victim of crimes than Whites (2710/2204 = 1.23).

The problem with this comparison is that in most locales the population is not composed of an equal number of Blacks and Whites, and the practice of standardization misrepresents the real victimization ratio. To address this problem of unequivalent populations, we could either rely on raw numbers of victims if available, or adjust the standardized race specific victimization (or offeroing) rate by the population's racial composition. We will illustrate this procedure by applying victimization data to a fictitious city (City X) with a population of 100,000 and a racial composition that reflects the national average for the US: 80 percent White and 12 percent Black. In City X there will be 80,000 Whites and 12,000 Blacks.

Our first step is to calculate the number of White victims from the race-specific standardized victimization rate data and City X population data cited above. We know that the standardized White victimization rate was 2204/100,000. Thus, we can multiple the victimization rate by the White population parameter in City X—80% or .80—to derive the number of White victims ($2204 \times .80$). Doing so, we discover that there are 1763 White victims of interpersonal violence in City X. We then follow the same procedure to calculate the number of Black victims of interpersonal crime in City X. Thus, we take the Black rate of interpersonal victimization (2710/100,000) and multiple this figure by the Black population parameter, 12% or .12, yielding 325. Black victims of interpersonal violence in City X is 325.

Before going any further, let us be clear about the meaning of the figures that were just derived. In City X there are 2088 Black and White victims of violent, interpersonal crimes. Eighty-four percent of these victims are White. The ratio of White to Black victims in City X is 5.4; that is, there are 5.4 White victims for every 1 Black victim of interpersonal violence.

Now that we have derived the total number of victims of each race from population and victimization rate data, we can employ the number of victims we have derived to calculate the number of offenders by race. We do so by multiplying NCVS perceived race of offender data by City X victimization figures. . . .

In total, there are 1850 interpersonal victimizations involving only Black and White victims-offenders (while Black and Whites report a total of 2088 victimizations, 238 of these are committed by members of a racial group other than Black or White). Seventy-one percent of these victimizations were committed against Whites by White offenders (1313/1850). In contrast, 14.5 percent of victimizations (260/1850) are committed by Blacks against Blacks; 13.3 percent are committed by Blacks versus Whites (243/1850); and 1.8 percent are by Whites versus Blacks (34/1850). Overall, Whites commit 73 percent of interpersonal crimes of violence in City X (1313 + 34/1850), which represents an average American city in terms of racial composition and interpersonal victimization and perceived offending by race as described in the NCVS.

What implications do these population adjusted victimization and offending data have for efforts at criminal profiling? They indicate that the offender is White in nearly three out of four crimes of interpersonal violence involving Black or White crime victims. Further, they illustrate that numerically, Black-on-White crimes of interpersonal violence (N = 243) are less likely than Black-on-Black crimes of interpersonal violence (N = 260). This finding from population adjusted rates is important because it directly disproves one of Taylor and Whitney's contentions; namely, that Black-on-White crime is more frequent than Black-on-Black crime. As we argued earlier, Taylor and

Whitney's conclusion was generated by making inappropriate use of criminological data. The use of standardized rates of victimization and offending makes it appear that Whites are more likely to be victimized by violent Black offenders than Black are when, in reality, the situtation is reversed. This occurs because the standardized rate comparison assumes equivalent sized Black and White populations. When we adjust these rates to reflect the real world, the conclusion is reversed.

Taylor and Whitney also employed the use of odds or ratio calculations to reach conclusions concerning Black-on-White and White-on-Black crime. The odds they present are inaccurate and invalid because they are derived from rate standardized data and are not adjusted for real racial population proportions. Below we describe a more valid approach to deriving the ratio of White-on-Black to Black-on-White crimes of violence.

Calculating the Odds of Victimization

Throughout their article, Taylor and Whitney assert that the odds of Black-on-White crime are between 50–200 times greater than the odds of White-on-Black crimes. As Taylor and Whitney admit early on, the figures they represent as odds are not actually odds because of the manner in which they are calculated. Consistent with our earlier argument, we contend that the odds they calculated provide inaccurate estimates because they are based on prevalence rates (rates per 100,000) rather than incidence data.

Taylor and Whitney hinge their argument here on the statement that the odds of a White being victimized by a Black is disproportionate. But, disproportionate to what? Taylor and Whitney fail to define what they mean by the word disproportionate, and we are left to ponder the significance of this idea.

As we have already shown using population adjusted victimization rates, Black-on-White crime is not disproportionate to Black-on-Black crime. This finding fails to support an essential aspect of Taylor and Whitney's argument. Thus, the only remaining means for interpreting this idea of disproportionate racial offending is to compare real victimoffender ratios to expected victimoffender ratios. The justification for doing so is easily derived from the popular criminological position called "opportunity theory" (Cohen and Felson, 1980a, 1980b; Felson and Cohen). Recent evidence supports the utility of opportunity theory for making predictions concerning violent victimizations (Lee, 2000).

Opportunity theory predicts that crime results from an intersection of motivated offenders with suitable targets. The opportunities for crime vary by numerous situational characteristics, but are defined or limited in the absolute sense by the availability of potential targets. The nature of targets varies by the type of crime. For crimes of violence, this opportunity is measured by the availability of potential victims people. The first parameter of opportunity, in this case, is defined by the size of a population.

In the specific case under examination, the opportunity dimension for crime is being defined by racial composition of the population. In other words, if opportunity arguments are correct, and there are no other forces in operation, the opportunity for interracial violent crime ought to be a product of the White/Black population ratio. This is easily calculated. In our hypothetical city—City X—we can divide the White population by the Black population. Doing so, we derive a White/Black population ratio of 6.7 (80,000/12,000). This figure indicates that we would expect Whites to be the victims of more crime more often than Blacks solely on the basis of opportunity for violence. This assumption can be easily assessed as follows.

First, we derive the ratio of victimization by race by creating a ratio of White to Black victimizations. We use the population data derived for our hypothetical city for these calculations which represented an average US city of 100,000 in terms of racial composition, crime and victimization patterns. Total White victimizations in City X was 1556 (1313 + 243); total Black victimization was 294 (260 + 34). The overall race victimization ratio is 1556/294, or 5.3—much lower—20 percent lower—than the expected ratio of 6.7. This figure indicates that in general, White victimizations are below the level predicted simply on the basis of opportunity or availability.

As noted, Taylor and Whitney's arguments specifically and consistently focused only on interracial crimes. The same opportunity ratios can be calculated for interracial crimes of violence. Though these ratios may be misleading because of the relative rare nature of the behavior in question, we estimate these ratios to illustrate the extent to which Taylor and Whitney's odds calculations are inflated by relying on prevalence (rate per 100,000) rather than incidence data.

To calculate the interracial opportunity ratio, we simply take the number of cases involving White-victims and Black offenders (243) and dividing by the number of cases where there are Black-victims and White-offenders (34). The opportunity ratio in this case is 7.2, slightly higher (7%) than the interracial ratio predicted by opportunity theory alone (6.7)[5].

In sum, the disproportionate ratio or odds of Black-on-White violent crime victimization that appear to "shock" Taylor and Whitney are actually a function of their method for calculating odds. Using incidence data and appropriate populations for comparison, we estimated that Black victimizations of Whites are not disproportionate to Black/White population ratios. Indeed, our calculations confirmed the idea that victimization ratios could be explained by opportunity theory as a function of the US population's racial composition.

Conclusion

Taylor and Whitney conclude their article with the following:

> Everyone knows that young people are more dangerous than old people, and that men are more dangerous than women. We adjust our behavior accordingly and do not apologize for doing so. Why then must we pretend that statistics regarding race differences in violent crime are to be ignored?

If Taylor and Whitney's analysis was valid, used appropriate methods for comparing racially-linked criminal justice data, and did not mislead readers by generalizing from a fraction of violent crime to either all violent crimes or all crimes, than we might have to take their question seriously. However, because they either purposefully or unintentionally deceived readers due to their ignorance of the proper use of criminal justice data and specific issues that emerge when making comparisons of standardized race-based crime data, their question can be dismissed as non-sense. Their conclusion, in other words, is as misleading as their analysis and interpretation of victimization, crime, and criminal justice data.

As I have shown, proper use of NCVS data does not support Taylor and Whitney's contentions. Using NCVS data appropriately—focusing on all crimes of violence as the appropriate basis for generalization rather than Taylor and Whitney's focus on a fraction of violent crime—we can clearly see that the majority of victims of violent crime report that their offender was White. This is not a statistical fallacy; there are more White than Black victims of crimes; the majority of Whites—nearly three-quarters—report that their offenders are White, not Black. Further, when we use the NCVS appropriately, one of the lessons we learn is that crime is primarily an intra-racial phenomenon. Whites are more likely to victimize Whites; Blacks are more likely to victimize Blacks. Further, the incidence of inter-racial crime is a function of opportunities for victimization as determined by the racial composition of the US population.

One of Taylor and Whitney's primary concerns is that society concentrates too much attention on Black-on-Black crime while neglecting Black-on-White crime. Their argument seems, then, to express concern for the safety of Whites. Their focus on Black-on-White crimes, however, creates a misleading conclusions concerning the threat Whites face. As we have demonstrated employing NCVS data, the majority of White crime victims are victimized by White offenders. In short, the safety of Whites is more greatly threatened by Whites rather than by Blacks.

Further, if Taylor and Whitney had actually been concerned that society concentrates too strongly on Black-on-Black crime, the correct comparison group for analysis should be White-on-White crime. By using this comparison group we could indeed argue that society's emphasis on Black-on-Black crime is misdirected, and that, instead, society's focus ought to be on White-on-White crimes, which are much more numerous. But, pointing out that the majority of crimes are committed by Whites, and that White victimization frequently comes at the hands of a White offender would not fit the broader research agenda established by these investigators.

Taylor and Whitney's claim that Black-on-White crime is extensive enough to justify racial profiling is based on the misuse of data and inappropriate comparisons and generalizations. As we have argued, the conclusion that racial profiling is acceptable is based on generalizing from less than 2 percent of crime—this 2 percent being the approximate percent of crime that is comprised of inter-racial crimes of violence. No criminologists would find such a procedure legitimate.

Taylor and Whitney also legitimize racial profiling by using prevalence rather than incidence data. Incidence data indicates that most crime are committed by Whites; indeed the ratio of White-to-Black crimes of violence in the NCVS is 2.69 White offenders per every Black offender. Thus, despite the prevalence of crime among Black communities and populations, and despite the fact that Blacks are over-represented in criminal justice data, Whites are the problematic crime population. Consequently, if we favored the use of racial profiling—and we do not—correct calculations of offender incidence indicate that police ought to concentrate their efforts on Whites: as potential offenders Whites far outnumber Blacks. Further, if the police were to use racial profiling, it should be based on the race of the victim. NCVS data makes it clear that the race of the victim and offender are the same more than seventy-five percent of the time. Thus, if a Black victim reports a crime, the police would do well to look for a Black offender based upon odds alone. Likewise, if a White victim reports a crime to police, the police would do well to look for a White offender, based on odds alone.

When people speak of racial profiling, what they mean is the creation of criminal profiles that target Black offenders. As our analysis indicates, the legitimacy of racial profiling—of targeting Black offenders over White offenders—is misleading at best, and at worst, a form of institutionalized racism. Our data indicate that it is high time that the notion of racial profiling be put to rest.

Throughout this article, we have demonstrated that racial profiling is objectionable from a statistical perspective. In closing, it should also be noted that racial profiling is objectionable to criminologists from both a legal and philosophical perspective. Our nation's criminal laws are based on the premise that guilt is determined on a case by case basis as a result of specific evidence. The inquiry that examines this evidence should be carried out without prejudice. Further, crime suspects are to be assumed innocent until proven guilty. Our Constitution, Courts and legal scholars speak to principles including: probable cause, which requires direct evidence rather than a suspicion or hunch based on someone's race or other status; due process of law and the rule of law; and the right to be judged by a juror of peers rather than by police or other actors in the criminal justice system. The idea of racial profiling reverses the important legal and philosophical ideas upon which the American system of democratic justice rests. Taylor and Whitney's support of racial profiling is not only misleading and inaccurate, it strikes at the heart of the American justice system and American democracy.

Notes

1. It bears mention that among Rushton, Wilbanks, Wilson and Hernnstein, only Wilbanks was trained as a criminologist.
2. What police may want to take into account when deciding the dangerousness of a situation is the data on police killings and assaults. Taylor and Whitney's conclusions concerning police safety and race would be considered misleading and inaccurate based on even a cursory reading of these data. For example, between 1988 and 1997, the Sourcebook of Criminal Justice Statistics notes that White offenders (49 percent) are responsible for killing more police officers than Black offenders (42%). While Black killings may be disproportionate to their population composition, this does not eliminate the fact that

police are more likely to be killed by Whites than by Blacks. Further, these data do not take into account the differential treatment Blacks receive that may escalate their reactions to police such as heightened use of force and a greater likelihood of being killed by police than White suspects (Mann 1993).

3. We have excluded other racial groups from consideration to simplify the results and discussion. Including other races would not significantly alter the results reported here.

4. While it may sometimes be useful to employ rate standardized data to compare the prevalence of a behavior among race-groups, a reliance on rate standardized data would still produce misleading results when we employ them to make generalizations concerning the amount of crime each racial group produced. An example of this situation is illustrated in the text of this article.

5. This minor difference in estimation could be due in part to the exclusion of other races from the analysis, and to rounding of population figures used to generate these outcomes. It is also possible that White-on-Black and Black-On-White crime are the product of factors other than opportunity.

References

Cernovsky, Z., and L., Litman. 1993 Reanalysis of Rushton's Crime Data. *Canadian Journal of Criminology*. 35, 1: 31–36.

Cohen, Lawrence and Marcus Felson. 1980a The Property Crime Rate in the United States: A Macro-Dynamic Analysis, 1947–1977, With Ex-Ante Forecasts for the Mid-1980s. *American Journal of Sociology*. 86, 1:90–118.

Gabor, T., and J. Roberts. 1990 Rushton on Race and Crime: The Evidence Remains Unconvincing. *Canadian Journal of Criminology*. 32: 335–343.

Lee, Matthew. 2000 Community cohesion and violent predatory victimization: A theoretical extension and cross-national test of opportunity theory. *Social Forces*. 79.2: 683–706.

Lynch, M. J. 2000 J. Phillippe Rushton on Crime: An Examination and Critique of the Explanation of Crime and Race. *Social Pathology*. 6,3: 228–224.

Lynch, M. J. 1990 "Racial Bias and Criminal Justice: Methodological and Definitional Issues." In B. MacLean and D. Milovanovic's (eds) *Racism, Empiricism and Criminal Justice*. Vancouver: Collective Press.

Mann, Coramae Richey. 1993. *Unequal Justice*. Bloomington, IN: University of Indiana Press.

Massey, Douglas and Nancy Nenton. 1993. *American Apartheid*. Cambridge, MA: Harvard University Press.

Neopolitan, J. 1998. Cross-National Variation in Homicide: Is Race a Factor? *Criminology*. 36, 1: 139–155.

Shipman, Pat. 1994. *The Evolution of Racism: Human Differences and the Use and Abuse of Science*. NY: Simon and Schuster.

Taylor, Jared, and Glayde Whitney. 1999. Crime and Racial Profiling by U.S. Police: Is There any Empirical Evidence? *The Journal of Social, Political and Economic Studies*. 24,4: 485–510.

Yee, A. H. Fairchild, F. Weizmann, and G. Wyatt. 1993. Addressing Psychology's Problems with race. *The American Psychologist*. 48: 1132–1140.

Zuckerman, M. 1990. Some Dubious Premises in Research and Theory on Racial Differences. *The American Psychologist*. 45: 1297–03.

POSTSCRIPT

Is Racial Profiling an Acceptable Law Enforcement Strategy?

Racial issues have a way of generating substantial controversy. One of the more contentious issues in the U.S. justice system in recent years has been whether members of minority groups commit more crime, or if the disparity in official crime statistics among different races reflects a systemic selection bias. In other words, are the members of minority groups selected for arrest and official processing in the U.S. justice system more often than whites?

Taylor and Whitney assert that there is a true difference in the number of crimes committed by different races. In fact, these authors believe that racial profiling is just as rational and productive as age or gender profiling. Because "it is the job of the police to catch criminals, and they know from experience who is likely to be an offender," they are justified in following policies that emphasize race as a predictor of criminal behavior.

Michael J. Lynch believes that racial profiling is not justified by the crime data. Moreover, he contends that racial profiling may be a thinly veiled form of institutional racism and that it is objectionable from a legal and philosophical perspective as well.

The legal problems with racial profiling by law enforcement officials are indeed compelling. In *United States v. Brignoni-Ponce*, 422 U.S. 873 (1975), the U.S. Supreme Court held that stopping subjects because they "appear[ed] to be of Mexican ancestry," violated the Fourth Amendment to the U.S. Constitution. Following this principle, law enforcement practices that target minority group members for investigation due solely to their appearance seem likely to be held unconstitutional by reviewing courts.

Moreover, as Professor Lynch observes, racial profiling by law enforcement officials may be challenged from a philosophical and moral perspective as well. Is it morally permissible to stereotype people based on a group characteristic such as their race or religion? We must remember too that when law enforcement personnel as agents of our government use racial profiling strategies, it lends an official stamp of approval to the practices. Does this not conjure images of governmentally enforced school segregation and institutionalized racism during the Civil Rights era?

The question posed in this section is a challenging one. After reading these articles, which author presents the most compelling arguments? Remember that to justify racial profiling, the government must be able to support these practices on an empirical, legal, and moral basis as well. Based on the available evidence, it would seem that supporters of these practices will face an uphill battle on all levels.

There is a wealth of additional information available on this topic. Please see: David A. Harris, *profiles in Injustice: Why Racial Profiling Cannot Work* (The New Press, 2002); Avram Bornstein, "Antiterrorist Policing in New York City after 9/11: Comparing Perspectives on a Complex Process," *Human Organization* (Spring 2005); P.A.J. Waddington, Kevin Stenson, and David Don, "In Proportion: Race and Police Stop and Search," *The British Journal of Criminology* (November 2004); Bernard E. Harcourt, "Rethinking Racial Profiling: A Critique of the Economics, Civil Liberties, and Constitutional Literature, and of Criminal Profiling More Generally," *The University of Chicago Law Review* (Fall 2004); Thomas Gabor, "Inflammatory Rhetoric on Racial Profiling Can Undermine Police Services," *Canadian Journal of Criminology and Criminal Justice* (July 2004); and Bernard E. Harcourt, "Unconstitutional Police Searches and Collective Responsibility," *Criminology & Public Policy* (July 2004).

ISSUE 7

Should Serious Sex Offenders Be Castrated?

YES: Lawrence Wright, from "The Case for Castration," *Texas Monthly* (May 1992)

NO: Kari A. Vanderzyl, from "Castration as an Alternative to Incarceration: An Impotent Approach to the Punishment of Sex Offenders," *The Northern Illinois University Law Review* (Fall 1994)

ISSUE SUMMARY

YES: Attorney Lawrence Wright argues that while castration may not be an ideal solution, if we treat it as therapy rather than punishment, as help instead of revenge, and if we view offenders as troubled victims, not monsters, then perhaps castration will become an accepted and humane option for sex offender treatment.

NO: Attorney Kari A. Vanderzyl asserts that castration should be rejected as an unacceptable, ineffective, and unconstitutional alternative to imprisonment for sex offenders.

Castration of sex offenders is a frightening issue that for some will conjure images of Joseph Mengele, the Nazi physician who performed horrible experiments on human subjects in concentration camps during World War II. Is it possible to view castration, however, as a voluntary and humane therapeutic solution for serious sex offenders? Moreover, does castration work? If serious offenders are castrated, will they cease committing sex offenses? The articles in this section demonstrate that at least three different issues must be examined before considering castration as a routine form of treatment for sex offenders: the empirical evidence, its constitutionality, and the moral propriety of castrating sex offenders.

The available evidence on castrating sex offenders is interesting indeed. A German study conducted between 1970 and 1980 analyzed 104 individuals who had undergone voluntary castration as a form of treatment. Seventy percent of these individuals were categorized as pedophiles, 25 percent were aggressive sex offenders, 3 percent were exhibitionists, and 2 percent were classified as homosexuals. The control group consisted of individuals who had applied for castration during the same period but did not have the surgery. The researchers

141

found that sexual interest, sex drive, erection, and ejaculation had generally decreased in 75 percent of the cases within six months of the operation. Moreover, the postoperative recidivism rate for sex crimes was 3 percent at most, compared to 46 percent for non-castrated subjects. The authors of the study also concluded that the social adjustment of the castrated subjects appeared to be more favorable than that of the non-castrated individuals. Among the castrated subjects, 70 percent were satisfied with the treatment, 20 percent were ambivalent, and 10 percent were not satisfied.

The U.S. Supreme Court has not expressly considered the issue of the constitutionality of castration as a form of treatment for sex offenders. In *Buck v. Bell*, 274 U.S. 200 (1927), however, a Virginia law was upheld that provided for the involuntary sterilization of persons confined to a state mental institution who were found to be afflicted with a hereditary form of insanity or imbecility. Justice Oliver Wendell Holmes, widely regarded as one of the greatest Supreme Court justices in U.S. history, stated: "It is better for all the world, if instead of waiting to execute degenerate offspring for crime, or to let them starve for their imbecility, society can prevent those who are manifestly unfit from continuing their kind. . . . Three generations of imbeciles is enough."

Fifteen years later, in *Skinner v. Oklahoma*, 316 U.S. 535 (1942), the Court considered a related issue—the constitutionality of an Oklahoma law that provided for the forced sterilization of habitual criminals for committing a third felony involving "moral turpitude." Stated Justice William O. Douglas:

> We are dealing here with legislation which involves one of the basic civil rights of man. Marriage and procreations are fundamental to the very existence and survival of the race. The power to sterilize, if exercised, may have subtle, far-reaching and devastating effects. In evil or reckless hands it can cause races or types which are inimical to the dominant group to wither and disappear. (541).

So, where are we regarding the Supreme Court's likely handling of mandatory sex offender castration laws? Although *Buck v. Bell* has been strongly criticized, more recent state court decisions have upheld compulsory sterilization laws in the context of mentally incompetent individuals. In addition, four states, including Texas, Florida, California, and Montana, have enacted laws to require involuntary chemical or surgical castration of certain convicted sex offenders. It will be very interesting to see whether U.S. courts will uphold *mandatory* castration laws.

What are your views on the issue of castrating serious sex offenders? Should it become a routine form of treatment for all those who cannot control their sexual urges? Or, should it be reserved for particular types of egregious sex offenders, such as pedophiles and serial rapists? Moreover, how should society draw the line between the types of sex offenders who are castrated and those who receive other forms of "treatment"? Is there a moral principle that should limit the use of this form of treatment, regardless of its utility? These are difficult questions. When you read these articles, try to develop a sense of whether this form of treatment is consistent with principles of basic fairness that are the foundation of our justice system.

YES

Lawrence Wright

The Case for Castration

Everybody from Jesse Jackson to feminist leaders told child molester Steve Butler he shouldn't be able to trade his manhood for his freedom. Everybody was wrong.

There is a lesson in every disaster. Now that the hysteria has quieted in Houston, we can survey the ruins left by the Great Castration Fiasco. When a young black man named Steve Allen Butler offered to place his testicles on the scales of justice, he began a debate that spread through Texas and soon across the entire country, illuminating the divisions between classes, races, and genders. Concerns were raised about the Constitution and medical ethics. Charges were hurled and mud was slung. The image of the state of Texas was damaged by the sneering of the national press. And yet the question that no one in this broad argument seemed willing to address was exactly what we should do with our sex offenders.

If one thing is clear in this whole messy episode, it's that what we're doing now is a failure. Again and again, critics have said that castration is not an effective answer to sexual offense. So far no one has asked, "Compared with what?" Today there are nearly eight thousand sex offenders in Texas prisons. Their crimes include indecent exposure, sex with minors, incest, aggravated sexual assault, and rape. Yet only two hundred are receiving counseling—an indication of how little faith we place in therapeutic solutions. Given the turnover in our prisons, most of those offenders will be out on the streets after serving a small portion of their sentences. More than half will be arrested for another sex crime in fewer than three years.

We may despise the people who commit such acts, but we should realize that most of them are victims themselves, not just of childhood sexual abuse but of their own overwhelming sexual impulses. As was evident in the Butler case, some of the offenders are crying out for another form of treatment. They want to be castrated. Until we find a better solution, perhaps voluntary castration of sex offenders is a good idea.

The debate began last fall at a dinner party in Tanglewood. "Like every gathering I've been to in Houston recently, the subject of crime captured the whole conversation," recalls state district judge Michael Mc Spadden. . . .

It was at that dinner party that Dr. Louis J. Girard mentioned his then-unpublished paper on castration. . . . Being a scientist, Girard decided to examine what factors influence criminal behavior. "A lot of crime is based on high levels of testosterone," he concluded. This powerful hormone determines a man's body shape, his hair patterns, the pitch of his voice. "It also produces aggressiveness in the males," Girard told the judge. "It is the reason that stallions are high-strung and impossible to train, the reason male dogs become vicious and start to bite people. It's why boys take chances and chase girls, why they drive too fast and deliberately start fights. In violent criminals, these tendencies are exaggerated and carried to extremes." In Girard's opinion, castration would reduce and possibly eliminate such aggressive impulses. The castrated criminal would be more docile and have a better opportunity to be rehabilitated, educated, and to become a worthwhile citizen," Girard contended.

Girard's idea rang a bell with McSpadden. If there was a painless, inexpensive procedure that would reduce the overflowing prison population, allow criminals to gain control over their violent natures, make them more susceptible to rehabilitation, and also act as a powerful deterrent to other offenders, what could be wrong with that? . . .

The controversy might have died out soon after that except for 27-year-old Steve Butler, who read about it in the paper in October. At the time, Butler was sitting on the fifth floor of the Harris County jail, accused of having had sex with a 13-year-old girl. Butler was already on probation in McSpadden's court for fondling a 7-year-old girl in 1989. The new charge could result in a lengthy prison term. Butler might get life, plus 10 years for violating his probation. He had already rejected the plea bargain offered by the assistant district attorney handling the case, Bill Hawkins, in which Butler would plead guilty to aggravated sexual assault and receive 35 years. Because it was an aggravated charge (meaning that the victim was under 14), Butler would have to serve at least one fourth of his time before he would be eligible for parole. He would spend the next 8 years and 9 months in prison as a convicted child molester, the lowest rung on the criminal hierarchy. . . .

Butler's problem, as he later admitted to psychologists who examined him, was that he had no control aver his sexual impulses. Dr. Michael Cox, a well-respected therapist at Baylor College of Medicine who counsels sex offenders, examined Butler at Judge McSpadden's request. After administering a battery of standard psychological tests, Cox found Butler to be mildly depressed but otherwise sane and competent. Butler "didn't look any different from the garden-variety child molesters I see in the program," says Cox. "He had been abused when he was young. He seemed to be more of a situational offender—in other words, his sexual preference is for adult women. But he does have a drinking problem, and if there is a female child available and he's been drinking, one thing can lead to another." . . .

As for Butler, his motives were varied. "I just think it would help me a whole lot," he admits. "I could be a better person. I could go on with my life and take care of my family." He is also frightened by the idea of going to prison, especially as a child molester. "I've heard stories about it," he says in a near whisper. "Some say it's hard. You have to fight."

⋅⋖◉⋗⋅

"Frankly, I think the judge is titillated by the idea of cutting the balls off a black man," says the Reverend Jew Don Boney, the chairman of the Houston chapter of the Black United Front. "This is McSpadden playing God. It's unprecedented; it's outside of normal legal bounds; and it introduces a whole new level of inhumanity into the criminal justice system." . . .

Castration is a profound symbol of the historic oppression of black men. In 1855 the Territory of Kansas introduced judicial castration of Negroes and mulattoes who raped or attempted to rape white women. In the South, blacks were sometimes castrated before being lynched. "It's a reminder of what I read about in the days of slavery and in the late eighteen-hundreds and early nineteen-hundreds," says Burns. "If this is the best we can come up with in terms of punishing or trying to deal with people guilty of that type of crime, then I'm wondering what changes we have made between 1892 and 1992." "It's just too close to an ugly part of our history," says Robert Newberry. "You would have to have gone through that type of history to really feel the emotional impact of how our forefathers were treated." Newberry recalls seeing a photo of a lynched black man with a bloody gash where his sex organs had been. "This castration issue brings it all back. It stirs up the pain."

For many black people, the contrast between the white judge—maverick Republican who plays tennis at the Houston Racquet Club—and the shine man sitting in the jailhouse seemed to characterize the imbalance of power between the races. One had privilege and the respect of society; the other was a high school dropout with no prospects, the sort of castoff that society notices only when he becomes a statistic in the criminal justice system. What was there left to take away from Steve Butler—except his manliness?

That Butler himself sought castration was rarely commented upon, except to say that he was a victim of judicial coercion. In fact, McSpadden had been elaborately cautious in making sure that Butler's choice was free and informed. He instructed Butler to talk to four psychiatrists and therapists, including Michael Cox, who was outspokenly opposed to the castration option. No one was able to change Butler's mind. He still preferred castration to prison, a choice denounced as "a very dangerous precedent" by Frank Burns. And yet when I asked Burns what he would do if he were in Butler's place, having to choose between a lengthy spell in prison or castration, he said he "may very well" make the same choice: castration and freedom. . . .

"People hear the word 'castration' and it scares them," McSpadden told me one afternoon in his chambers. "They don't realize it is a simple surgical procedure that can be done on an outpatient basis. It's not cutting off the penis. It's far less intrusive than a hysterectomy. What's more, the crime we see in Texas is a direct result of the failure of present punishments to serve their intended purposes of retribution, rehabilitation, and deterrence. If castration does work, then we not only let that person live a normal life because of a simple medical treatment, but we also protect society from that same person for years to come." . . .

⋅≺◉≻⋅

It was clear from the hundreds of calls and letters that the castration issue strikes a deep chord of fear and anger and a longing for revenge. That is exactly what worries Cassandra Thomas, the director of the rape program at the Houston Area Women's Center. "I don't think castration should be used as punishment," she says. "It only buys into the myth that sexual assault is about sex, and so therefore if you get rid of sexual desires you get rid of rape. The reality is that sexual assault is about violence; it's about a need for power and control. It has nothing to do with the genital organs." Castration, she says, is "an empty symbolic gesture." . . .

Many women see rape as a political act, evidence of the male need to control the female. Viewed through that lens, treating the problem by removing the sex organs will only frustrate men and make them, as Thomas argues, "more likely to use violence as a way of dealing with their issues of inadequacy and powerlessness and helplessness that perpetuate sexual assaults in the first place." . . .

⋅≺◉≻⋅

Nearly everyone involved in the Butler case—like nearly everyone in Texas—has had some experience with castrated animals. The district attorney of Harris County, Johnny Holmes, keeps a herd of Longhorns, and he has personally castrated many of them. "My experience is that they get a lot bigger and a lot gentler," says Holmes. Girard castrated bulls when he was young; he also played polo at the Bayou Club. "Believe me, there's a tremendous difference in the amount of control you have between a gelding and a stallion." Recently one of his German shepherds became cantankerous and nipped Girard's daughter and his niece. "So I just castrated him, and he stopped." Michael Cox, the Baylor sex therapist, had his cat castrated. "He doesn't get into fights about female cats, but he still fights over territory." . . .

Voluntary castration became legally permissible in Denmark through the Access to Sterilization law of 1929, which permitted the operation on a "person whose sexual drive is abnormal in power or tendency, thus making him liable to commit crimes." Although the Danish law did permit forced castrations, that provision was never put into practice and was subsequently eliminated. Other European countries implemented similar voluntary programs. In this country, Oklahoma allowed forced castration of repeated felons convicted of crimes involving "moral turpitude"—a larger category than sex offenses—until the U.S. Supreme Court declared its law unconstitutional in 1942. Recently bills were knocked down in Washington, Alabama, and Indiana that would have permitted sex offenders to be castrated in exchange for a reduction in their sentences. The historical associations make it difficult to talk about castration without the specter of government-imposed sterilization becoming a part of the argument. Unfortunately, that is exactly the way Girard and McSpadden have framed their proposal.

Dr. John Bradford of the Royal Ottawa Hospital in Canada says that as a rule, the recidivism rate of sex offenders (that is, their likelihood to offend again) averages 80 percent before castration, dropping to less than 5 percent afterwards. In Europe, many studies on the consequences of therapeutic castration show essentially the same thing—that it is profoundly effective in lowering the rates of repeated sex offenses. A 1973 Swiss study of 121 castrated offenders found that their recidivism rate dropped to 4.3 percent, compared with 76.8 percent for the control group. In Germany, a similar report showed a post-operative recidivism rate of 2.3 percent for sex offenses, compared with 84 percent for non-castrates. Various Danish studies have followed as many as 900 castrated sex offenders for several decades; they show that recidivism rates drop to 2.2 percent. What is also important is that 90 percent of the castrated men reported that they themselves are satisfied with the outcome. "The main conclusion to be derived from all this material on castrated men," wrote Dr. Georg K. Sturup, chief psychiatrist of Denmark's Herstedvester Detention Center, in 1968, "is that a person who has suffered acutely as a result of his sexual drive will, after castration, feel a great sense of relief at being freed from these urges." . . .

꧁◎꧂

Many people who oppose castration believe that the main problem sex offenders have is psychological, not physical. Therefore, they assume, diligent treatment involving therapy and the latest behavior modification techniques should make a difference. In fact, when counseling succeeds, it is only with a very limited group. It's an inside joke among sex counselors that if you want to have a successful program, you fill it with incest perpetrators, whose reoffense rate is about 3 percent, and keep out all the difficult cases, especially the rapists. . . .

No doubt there is progress in the field of sex offender treatment. No doubt some offenders are susceptible to treatment and others are not. But the stark fact is that none of these programs compares in effectiveness with castration.

The cost of our failure to treat sex offenders can't be known or measured, only guessed at. The tendency to sexually offend is usually lifelong. The chances of ever being arrested for a sex crime are very small—2 percent by some measures. "I went twelve years without being arrested, but I never went more than three days without acting out," an exhibitionist told me. The sheer number of offenses buried in the term "recidivate" can be imagined by a ten-year study of 550 sex offenders (many of whom had never been arrested), which asked each perpetrator how many victims he could specifically identify. The tally was 190,000 victims. . . .

꧁◎꧂

The pressure was building on Steve Butler. The Reverend Jesse Jackson came to Houston and was allowed to see Butler, even against Butler's request not to see any visitors. Butler still wouldn't talk about his case. "This is not just a Houston matter, just as Selma was not just for Alabama," Jackson proclaimed outside the jailhouse, thus putting the matter of Butler's voluntary castration on a par with the civil rights movement. "We shall make a broad public appeal here and around the country, because such a precedent would be an ugly and dangerous precedent. Rape is sickness. Castration is sickness. The judge's complicity is sickness. We must break this cycle of sickness." . . .

Meanwhile, in Dallas, a man accused of sexually assaulting two girls seven months after being released from prison, said he would prefer castration to prison. "If you cut off man's desire to have sex whatsoever, that should solve the problem," Andrew Jackson, a 52-year-old white man, told a reporter. The prosecutor refused his offer, but it is clear that the castration issue in Texas isn't going to go away with the Butler case. It is also dear that Butler himself is not going to be castrated, despite his own wishes. The surgeon who had volunteered to perform the operation backed out when the publicity became too intense. Another doctor called the judge's office and left word that he'd be happy to perform the procedure for free, but on investigation the man turned out to be a dentist.

It was, finally, the lack of a surgeon that caused McSpadden to resign from the case. The weekend before he did so, he agreed to meet with Butler's five sisters and their attorney. "I told them step by step what had happened, but they were convinced it was a white conspiracy to railroad their younger brother," says McSpadden. The sisters were demanding that Butler be granted probation, which the prosecution had no interest in offering.

Now Butler's case will go to another court. If the victim's mother agrees to let her testify, Butler may be convicted and sent to prison for a long time. He may decide to reconsider the state's offer of 35 years and expect to be out in about a decade. If the victim doesn't testify, Butler will be a free man—free, but probably unchanged. The likelihood that he will reoffend is high even if he does join the eight thousand sex offenders we are currently incarcerating. Because eventually Butler will be back in society, as will the rest of them. Nothing that we are doing with the offender population has made any real difference in their lives; on the other hand, what sex offenders are doing to us, the rest of society, is seen every day in the courts and hospitals and rape crisis centers and child treatment programs—the circle of tragedy touches us all, somehow, if only in the financial burden of caring for the victims and jailing the perpetrators. We do a sorry job even of that.

Now that the Butler case is out of the news, perhaps it's time to think about whether voluntary castration has a place in the treatment of sex offenders. It is a mistake to make castration a punishment, as Girard and McSpadden have proposed; the Supreme Court would probably rule it unconstitutional, and in any case it is simply too offensive to too many people. Moreover, it should be limited to sex offenders. Castration does lower testosterone, which influences aggressive and violent behavior, but taking away the sex drive won't make a bad man good. It should be reserved for those men with uncontrollable sexual urges. In the case of pedophiles, when they exercise their sexuality they violate the law, not to mention the damage: they do to the children. What good is their sexuality to them? If they want to be relieved of it, why can't they be?

Most sex offenders are white; this is a crime where blacks are not overly represented in the prison system. There is no reason for this to be a race issue or even a class issue, since sex offenses cut across economic lines as well. "If I saw some semblance of evidence that this would work, I'd be for it," Robert Newberry admitted after the Butler case cooled off, "but let it start with a white man." Given the history of castration in this country, that may be a fair request.

Finally, it is a foolish consistency to castrate women for sexual or other crimes. There can be a change in behavior after such an operation, but so far it has never been correlated with sex crimes. That said, the fact is that women can have their Fallopian tubes tied as a contraceptive measure or their entire uterus removed as treatment for premenstrual syndrome, while men who rape or molest children or expose themselves up to thirty times a day can't be castrated because that would be barbarous.

"Why can't it be like abortion, available on demand?" one offender asks. That seems a reasonable question. As it stands now, the only way Butler could be castrated is if he gets a sex-change operation. Society poses no object ion to that.

We should acknowledge that men who seek castration are making a sacrifice. The way we can do so is by reducing their prison time and giving them adequate adjustment counseling. The critics may be right that some men may reoffend, but everything we know about the subjects suggests that castration works better than any other approach. Why can't we honor the plea of Steve Butler and many other men and give them the help they are begging for? Castration may not be an ideal solution, but if we treat it as therapy rather than punishment, as help instead of revenge, and if we view offenders as troubled victims, not monsters, then perhaps the castration option will be seen as evidence of our wisdom and humanity, not of our backwardness and cruelty.

 **NO**

Castration as an Alternative to Incarceration: An Impotent Approach to the Punishment of Sex Offenders

The use of castration as a punitive measure, practiced for centuries by other cultures, has enjoyed newfound prominence in this country's criminal justice system as a potential remedy for the proliferation of sex offenses. Not surprisingly, the implementation of castration as an alternative to incarceration has generated considerable debate, including questions regarding its constitutionality and desirability from a public policy standpoint. Fueling the controversy, several recently convicted sex offenders have requested that they be castrated rather than receive lengthy prison sentences.

In March of 1992, Steven Allen Butler, a convicted rapist, stood before Texas District Court Judge Michael McSpadden and requested that the judge order surgical castration rather than sentencing him to prison. Judge McSpadden initially assented to the request, but ultimately withdrew approval in the wake of national publicity and protests by civil libertarians. Physicians in the area refused to perform the operation, and even Butler found himself reconsidering his unusual request.

In Great Britain, a man with a forty-year history of child sex abuse privately arranged for his own surgical castration after prison authorities ignored his repeated pleas for the operation. The subject, a sixty year old former coal miner, has served numerous prison terms for sex offenses against children and has threatened suicide, gone on hunger strikes and even attempted to castrate himself. Although officials at a psychiatric hospital offered to administer chemical castration, the offender refused such treatment, considering chemical castration a temporary, and therefore inadequate, solution to his deviant behavior.

Sharing this desire for sterilization, a thirty-eight year old convicted rapist sentenced in McLean County, Illinois, expressed a preference for castration rather than a prison sentence. Despite the offender's request for sterilization,

From *Northern Illinois University Law Review*, 15 N. III University Law Review 107 (Fall 1994). Copyright © 1994 by Kari A. Vanderzyl. Reprinted by permission. All notes and citations in the original have been omitted. Ellipses in the article reflect material that has been omitted from the original text.

the sentencing judge concluded that castration was not a viable alternative to incarceration and sentenced the repeat offender to a thirty-seven year term of imprisonment.

This [article] addresses the legal implications of castration as a punitive measure, tracing the development of compulsory sterilization from its origins in the eugenics movement in the early twentieth century to its present status as an alternative to imprisonment. In particular, the first section explores the rise of eugenics legislation in the United States, the Supreme Court's legitimization of compulsory sterilization and the current practice among the courts of upholding sterilization legislation for the mentally retarded. Within the second section, the use of castration as a punitive measure both in the United States and abroad is discussed. In addition, the second section describes methods of male sterilization, including surgical castration, vasectomy and the non-surgical alternative, chemical castration. The third section analyzes common constitutional challenges to compulsory castration and asserts that the use of castration as an alternative to incarceration violates the rights of privacy and procreation, and may also violate the Eighth Amendment protection against cruel and unusual punishment. In the fourth section, the reasonable relationship test is applied to castration as a term of probation, yielding mixed results. The informed consent objection presented in the fifth section suggests that castration as an alternative to a prison sentence violates the voluntariness requirement of the informed consent doctrine. Finally, section six explores the economic and social policy considerations implicated by sterilization in the punitive context, focusing on the financial burdens to society and the failure of castration to address the uncontrollable hostility manifesting itself in acts of sexual violence. The article concludes by asserting that castration in any form constitutes an ineffective, unconstitutional alternative to incarceration.

Background

Historical Framework: Eugenics and the Socially Unfit

Compulsory sterilization is not a novel concept. The controversy over a court's or state agency's authority to destroy an individual's ability to procreate has persisted for over a century, since the notion of involuntary sterilization originated with the eugenics movement. Defined by its creator, Sir Francis Galton, as "the science which deals with all influences that improve the unborn qualities of the race . . . [and] develop them to the utmost advantage," eugenics seeks to achieve the elimination of social ills through biological reformation. American eugenicists relied upon Darwin's theory of evolution and Mendel's genetics experimentation to provide scientific support for their movement. Borrowing from the research of Darwin and Mendel, eugenicists theorized that feeble-mindedness and other negative qualities resulted from inferior genes. Operating on this premise, proponents of eugenics linked every existing social problem to heredity and concluded that the solution to the country's social ills required control over human reproduction. Through lecture tours and written propaganda, positive eugenics encouraged individuals with superior genes to select mates from within their own ranks and to maximize family size. Negative eugenics utilized a different approach, calling for the implementation of a program of sterilization to eliminate procreation of the unfit. Before 1900, compulsory sterilization of the unfit enjoyed limited popular support. Surgical castration, that era's prevailing method of sterilization, produced hormonal imbalance and psychological and physiological effects. With the emergence of two less severe methods, vasectomy and salpingectomy, compulsory eugenics sterilization grew in popularity.

Compulsory Sterilization Legislation

Inspired by the eugenics rationale that played on the pervasive fear of a growing mentally retarded citizenry, in the early 1900's, a number of states enacted compulsory sterilization legislation. State laws mandated sterilization for punitive and therapeutic purposes, with surgical procedures such as castration, vasectomies and salpingectomies performed to punish convicted felons and rehabilitate mentally retarded individuals in state institutions. State officials invoked the doctrine of *parens patriae* to justify the involuntary sterilization of the mentally retarded, claiming to act in the best interests of the institutionalized individuals. Under the doctrine of *parens patriae*, the state bears the responsibility of caring for citizens incapable of protecting their own interests. Despite legislators' efforts to legitimize the practice of involuntary sterilization through reliance on the *parens patriae* justification, the courts nevertheless established a pattern of invalidating compulsory sterilization laws as violations of equal protection or due process.

"Three Generations of Imbeciles. . .": *Buck V. Bell* and the Aftermath

At the height of the United States eugenics movement, proponents found an unlikely ally in the nation's highest court. In the now famous case of an institutionalized sixteen year old girl facing compulsory sterilization pursuant to a Virginia statute, the Court upheld the legislation as a valid exercise of the state's police power. Writing for the majority, Justice Holmes reasoned that it would be "better for all the world, if instead of waiting to execute degenerate offspring for crime, or to let them starve for their imbecility, society can prevent those who are manifestly unfit from continuing their kind. . . . Three generations of imbeciles are enough." . . .

Castration as a Punitive Measure

While the involuntary sterilization of mentally retarded persons remains a prominent issue, the greatest and most recent controversy regarding procreative rights has arisen in the punitive context. As an alternative to imprisonment, male sex offenders may elect to undergo castration as punishment for their crimes, raising a number of legal, social and moral issues. . . .

Constitutional Challenges to Sterilization in the Punitive Context

The sterilization of individuals for punitive purposes raises a number of constitutional issues. Government interference with an individual's ability to reproduce implicates constitutional rights to privacy and procreation and the guarantee against cruel and unusual punishment. To achieve recognition as a legitimate, viable alternative to incarceration, male sterilization must pass constitutional muster in each of the areas implicated. . . .

Castration and the Right to Privacy

Although the Constitution contains no explicit mention of a privacy right, the Supreme Court has acknowledged an implied right to privacy under the Fourteenth Amendment protecting an individual's autonomy in making decisions concerning childbearing and contraception. In *Griswold v. Connecticut,* the Court held that a state statute barring married persons' use of contraceptives violated the Fourteenth Amendment's Due Process Clause, reasoning that the penumbras of the Bill of Rights' enumerated protections created a "zone of privacy." The Court in *Griswold* characterized an individual's privacy interest as a fundamental right upon which the state cannot intrude in the absence of a compelling governmental interest. The Supreme Court further articulated the protected realm of privacy in *Eisenstadt v. Baird,* concluding that to have any meaning at all, the right of privacy must include the "right of any individual, married or single, to be free from unwarranted governmental intrusion" into his or her decision of whether or not to have children. . . .

An interference with an individual's ability to reproduce, whether permanent or temporary, clearly implicates the constitutional right of privacy. By offering castration to convicted sex offenders as an alternative to imprisonment, legislatures and courts intrude upon an offender's decision whether or not to have children, a decision the (U.S. Supreme) Court . . . deemed protected from unwarranted governmental invasion under the Fourteenth Amendment. Just as a state may not prohibit married and single persons from using contraception, so it should not be allowed to compel individuals to practice contraception. Proponents of the use of castration as a form of punishment for sex offenders may argue that because the offender has the opportunity to reject sterilization and choose incarceration instead, no intrusion of protected privacy rights occurs. However, the inherently coercive nature of the choice between freedom through castration and an extended prison sentence renders voluntary consent to sterilization an impossibility. The privacy right primarily implicated by castration in the punitive context is the fundamental right of procreation, a privacy interest meriting a separate discussion that includes analysis under the strict scrutiny standard.

The Fundamental Right of Procreation

Castration as an alternative to incarceration, whether surgical or chemical, violates the right of procreative freedom. To render a convicted sex offender sterile is to deprive him of his right to procreate, a right characterized by Justice Douglas in *Skinner [v. Oklahoma]* as "one of the basic civil rights of man." Castration, like a vasectomy, eliminates the offender's capacity for procreation. However, castration by surgery or injections represents a more intrusive procedure than the vasectomy at issue in *Skinner* because it results in the cessation of the sexual drive. . . .

Castration as Cruel and Unusual Punishment

Another objection to male sterilization as an alternative to incarceration may be premised on the prohibition against cruel and unusual punishment provided by the Eighth Amendment. An Eighth Amendment analysis of castration as punishment for convicted sex offenders requires an examination of . . . whether the procedure constitutes cruel and unusual punishment. . . .

While the Eighth Amendment may have been originally intended to protect against punishment deemed inhuman and barbarous, the Supreme Court has construed the provision more broadly. In *Weems v. United States,* for example, the Court focused on the disproportionality between the penalty and offense to determine whether the defendant's sentence constituted cruel and unusual punishment. Not merely a static concept, the Eighth Amendment "must draw its meaning from the evolving standards of decency that mark the progress of a maturing society." Despite its seeming reluctance to explicitly define the limits of the provision prohibiting cruel and unusual punishment, the Court has established some guidelines for determining Eighth Amendment violations. The Court has incorporated three interrelated tests to identify cruel and unusual punishment: (1) whether the punishment is inherently cruel; (2) whether the punishment is disproportionate to the offense; and (3) whether the punishment exceeds the extent necessary to achieve the legitimate governmental objectives. . . .

[T]he Supreme Court of South Carolina voided the suspended sentence of a sex offender where the suspension and probation were conditioned on the offender's submission to surgical castration. According to the court in *State v. Brown,* because castration constitutes physical mutilation, it satisfies the cruelty requirement of the prohibition against cruel and unusual punishment. While the *Brown* decision seems to focus on the physical suffering associated with castration, "mutilation" as used by the court also suggests an element of degradation, consistent with earlier courts' analysis of cruelty. . . .

The preceding analysis of constitutional objections to castration demonstrates that sex offenders possess the fundamental right to be free from unwarranted governmental intrusion into their decision-making concerning procreation. Because castration is not the least restrictive means available to effectuate the governmental interest of protecting society, sterilization as a punitive measure violates offenders' Fourteenth Amendment privacy rights.

Additionally, offenders enjoy a constitutionally protected liberty interest to refuse unwanted medical treatment in the form of surgical or pharmacological castration, or vasectomy. Finally, castration implicates the Eighth Amendment prohibition against cruel and unusual punishment. Failing to qualify as treatment, when subjected to scrutiny under any of the established tests, castration would most likely be found to constitute cruel and unusual punishment violative of the Eighth Amendment. . . .

Policy Considerations

In addition to its constitutional and common law implications, castration raises several significant policy considerations. Most important to a determination of its viability as an alternative to incarceration is its effectiveness as a punitive measure. According to recent studies, approximately forty percent of rapists and pedophiles will repeat their crimes. A primary criticism of castration as a form of punishment for sex offenders is that it fails to address the anger and hatred motivating sex offenses against women and children. To take away an offender's ability to procreate is merely to eliminate one channel of aggression. While advocates of chemical castration hail its five percent recidivism rate as evidence of the program's success, that statistic may be misleading. A high percentage of sex crimes go unreported, and further, most treatment programs track participants' progress for only a short time after the termination of treatment, when the risk of relapse is the lowest.

Critics also attack castration as a sanctioning alternative for its seeming lenience. Instead of serving thirty years in prison, a convicted sex offender may elect to undergo surgical castration, vasectomy, or chemical castration and retain his freedom. Victims of serious sex offenses would most likely not be reassured knowing that the violent offender who injured them will escape incarceration upon completion of a sterilization procedure. Moreover, castration merely validates the offender's distorted self-portrait, that he is a victim who cannot help himself. The source of the violence, the uncontrollable anger and hostility, will remain long after the scalpel or injection removes the offender's capability to procreate.

Finally, the cost to society of practicing compulsory castration may also undermine its viability. Admittedly, the state would incur minimal expense in surgically castrating sex offenders in relation to the money spent keeping those same offenders in prison. However, castrated offenders may very well vent their aggression in other criminal ways and therefore ultimately require incarceration. Similarly, those offenders undergoing chemical castration and counseling present a financial burden. Not only must the state cover the cost of the drug for those offenders unable to pay for their own treatment, but financial resources must also be used to provide counseling services. A counseling staff must be funded in order to treat and monitor the progress of chemically castrated offenders. Such a program requires a great deal of both time and money to operate effectively. Viewed in terms of the above social and economic considerations, sterilization does not appear to be a viable alternative to incarceration.

Conclusion

Castration should be rejected as an unacceptable, ineffective and unconstitutional alternative to imprisonment. A lingering spectre from the American eugenics movement at the turn of the century, the sterilization of criminals has enjoyed limited legislative and judicial support in contemporary society. However, relatively recent technological developments resulting in the marketing of hormone suppressers has added a new dimension to the issue of sterilization of sex offenders and has received support for its non-surgical method of temporarily reducing the sexual drives of paraphiliac offenders. Despite the procedural differences, however, chemical castration and its surgical equivalents share constitutional flaws which render them inappropriate substitutes for incarceration.

The prevailing forms of male sterilization interfere with an offender's ability to produce offspring, and, as a consequence, violate the offender's constitutionally protected privacy rights, including the fundamental right of procreation. Moreover, the offender maintains a liberty interest in exercising his right to refuse unwanted medical treatment. A state is therefore precluded from forcing an offender to undergo sterilization unless it demonstrates a legitimate interest overriding the offender's right of self-determination. Subjected to Eighth Amendment analysis, castration in any form fails to qualify as treatment and instead constitutes cruel and unusual punishment. . . .

Finally, policy considerations mandate the elimination of punitive sterilization practices for sex offenders. The seemingly low recidivism rate hailed by proponents as evidence of chemical castration's success fails to reflect the high number of sex crimes that go unreported each year. Proponents additionally ignore the substantial administrative costs associated with implementing a treatment program of chemical castration for criminals who cannot pay for it themselves and who may likely have to continue treatment for long periods of time. Not only does this procedure drain valuable public resources, but at the same time, it subjects the offenders to potentially dangerous side effects, the full extent of which remains unknown. In a society besieged by crime and the fear it begets, where prison overcrowding has grown to massive proportions and society is desperate for a cure, castration may seem to be the definitive remedy. Nevertheless, a remedy which necessitates the deprivation of fundamental rights and personal liberties and which fails to address the source of the problem must be rejected as an unacceptable solution.

POSTSCRIPT

Should Serious Sex Offenders Be Castrated?

$\mathbf{A}$t first glance, castrating serious sex offenders seems to be a radical and somewhat Orwellian solution to a difficult social problem. But, what if it works? If we can significantly reduce serious sex offender recidivism by castrating them and eliminating their sexual urges, is it a good social policy?

Kari A. Vanderzyl asserts that a primary criticism of castration is that it fails to address the anger and hatred motivating sex offenses against women and children. Thus, castration merely eliminates one channel of an offender's aggression. Vanderzyl asserts that the source of the violence, anger, and hostility will remain. She believes as well that the low recidivism rates reported in castration studies may be misleading. A high number of sex offenses go unreported, and most treatment programs track offender progress for only a short time. Moreover, Vanderzyl believes that castration as a form of treatment conjures an image of eugenics movements and is a deprivation of fundamental rights and personal liberties.

Lawrence Wright argues, however, that even though castrating sex offenders is not an ideal solution, it works better than any other approach. In addition, it may be a more humane form of sex offender treatment because it will help offenders control their behavior and reduce prison time.

Castration as a form of sex offender treatment does appear to be gaining some momentum in the United States. It will be interesting to see whether the public and the courts are receptive to this form of treatment, or if it will be rejected as an approach that is barbaric and unacceptable in society.

There are a number of additional resources that may shed light on the issues discussed in this section. See, for example, J. Michael Bailey and Aaron S. Greenberg, "The Science and Ethics of Castration: Lessons from the *Morse* Case," *Northwestern University Law Review* (Summer 1998); William Winslade, "Castrating Pedophiles Convicted of Sex Offenses Against Children: New Treatment or Old Punishment?" *Southern Methodist University Law Review* (1998, vol. 51, p. 349); Douglas J. Besharov and Andrew Fachhs, "Sex Offenders: Is Castration an Acceptable Punishment?" *American Bar Association Journal* (July 1992); Nickolaus Heim and Carolyn J. Hursch, "Castration for Sex Offenders: Treatment or Punishment? A Review of Recent European Literature," *Archives of Sexual Behavior* (1979, vol. 8); and Christopher Meisenkothen, "Chemical Castration—Breaking the Cycle of Paraphiliac Recidivism," *Social Justice* (Spring 1999).

Additional resources include: Reinhard Wille and Klaus M. Beier, "Castration in Germany," *Annals of Sex Research* (1989, vol. 2, pp. 103–133), which examined the results of a treatment program for a sample of 104 men who underwent voluntary castration over a 10-year period. This study found a post-operative recidivism rate of approximately 3 percent. Other resources are Marjorie A. Fonza, "A Review of Sex Offender Treatment Programs," *ABNF Journal* (Mar/Apr 2001); Catherine A. Gallagher, David B. Wilson, Paul Hirshfield, Mark B. Coggeshall, and Doris L. MacKenzie, "A Quantitative Review of the Effects of Sex Offender Treatment on Sexual Reoffending," *Corrections Management Quarterly* (Fall 1999); Craig Turk, "Kinder Cut," *The New Republic* (Aug. 25, 1997); and J. Paul Federoff and Beverly Moran, "Myths and Misconceptions About Sex Offenders," *The Canadian Journal of Human Sexuality* (1997, vol. 6, issue 4).

ISSUE 8

Should Juvenile Courts Be Abolished?

YES: Barry C. Feld, from *Bad Kids: Race and the Transformation of the Juvenile Court* (Oxford University Press, 1999)

NO: Vincent Schiraldi and Jason Ziedenberg, from *The Florida Experiment: An Analysis of the Impact of Granting Prosecutors Discretion to Try Juveniles As Adults* (July 1999)

ISSUE SUMMARY

YES: Law professor Barry C. Feld contends that the entire concept of a separate juvenile court system was wrong from the start. The results have been unanticipated negative consequences for America's children and for justice, including denial of due process, confusing of court functions, and terrible punishments purporting to be treatment.

NO: Vincent Schiraldi, director of the Justice Policy Institute, and researcher Jason Ziedenberg bemoan the increasing trend to transfer juveniles to adult courts. They feel that states in which prosecutors decide if children are to be tried as adults are especially pernicious in harming youngsters. Moving thousands of kids into adult courts, they argue, is unnecessary, harmful, and racist.

In the 1890s Judge Ben Lindsey, with the help of socially prominent and active citizens and their wives, helped to establish the juvenile court movement. His work was hailed as innovative and compassionate. Horror tales and news exposés of the dreadful treatment of America's youngsters in adult prisons, as well as in the adult courts that often processed them as if they were common criminals, were well-known. Something had to be done, progressive elements among the rich and the intellectuals maintained. They felt that child criminals and criminal children needed help, guidance, love, an opportunity for a second chance, and education, not punishment, humiliation, degradation, additional undeserved pain, and torment.

Soon states around the country had separate facilities for treating juvenile offenders as well as separate facilities for incarcerating them. In some areas judges were called "Masters" and were encouraged to be kindly and sympathetic, not gruff, procedural, and legalistic. *Parens patriae* (state as parents) became the role of the juvenile court procedures. Guilt or innocence was not the issue, nor was "punishment." The goal was to determine through case studies what the needs of referred youngsters were, then, if necessary, to provide for these needs through a juvenile facility. Such needs could include food, shelter, education, separation from terrible families or neighborhoods, separation from peers who smoked, and so on.

Since the function of the proceedings was to ascertain and provide needs, legalities such as determining guilt or innocence or even a specific sentence were ignored. Often youngsters who were not initially charged with criminal offenses but were status offenders were sentenced to juvenile facilities. Status offenses included truancy, running away from home, hanging out on the street, and sassing teachers or social workers. Some more progressive states had a classification system distinguishing such offenders. These terms included *CINS* (children in need of supervision) and *PINS* (persons in need of supervision). However, often they were housed under the same administrative roof as youngsters who were charged with more serious offenses.

The age range for juveniles varied from state to state; some classified juveniles as anyone who is 19 or younger, and most demarcated children from adults at age 18 or 16. Many juvenile facilities, though, would keep offenders until they were 21 "for their own good." Since the purpose of the juvenile system was to "help" youngsters, a 12-year-old who had been truant could be held in custody until he was 18 or even 21. Until Supreme Court decisions in the 1960s provided some basic constitutional rights, children were not entitled to an attorney, could not appeal their sentences, and could he held incommunicado indefinitely.

Yet the juvenile courts were almost universally considered progressive. Eventually, some had second thoughts. It was theorized that the real function of the courts and juvenile system was to "Americanize" the children of immigrants and to more smoothly pipe marginal American children (poor white ethnics and blacks) into mainstream industrial society. According to this perspective, the juvenile court system, along with required public school education, functioned as socializing agencies more than as helping ones. Meanwhile, word slowly leaked out that many juvenile reformatories were quite different from what many people thought. Treatment was often nonexistent, and a variety of cruelties were typical.

As we enter the twenty-first century still carrying the weight of a very conservative, get-tough-with-all-delinquent-kids mode, to some the question becomes, which is the lesser of two evils, juvenile courts or adult courts for criminal children? The issue is in many ways a very sad one for the protagonists. Barry C. Feld, who has worked to help troubled youth for many years, reluctantly advocates abolishing juvenile courts. He is convinced that trying to salvage the existing system will only enable the get-tough side to do even worse things to delinquents. Vincent Schiraldi, who is arguably America's top advocate for the compassionate treatment of children, is convinced that additional transfers of juveniles into adult courts will be a disaster. He and coauthor Jason Ziedenberg draw from empirical research to document their concerns.

YES

Barry C. Feld

Abolish the Juvenile Court

In the three decades since *Gault*,[1] judicial decisions, legislative amendments, and administrative changes have transformed the juvenile court from a nominally rehabilitative welfare agency into a scaled-down, second-class criminal court for young people. These revisions have converted the historical ideal of the juvenile court as a social welfare institution into a penal system that provides young offenders with neither therapy nor justice. Even as legal reforms foster increased punitiveness and convergence with criminal court, juvenile courts deflect, co-opt, ignore, or accommodate constitutional procedural mandates with minimal institutional change. They use courtroom procedures under which no adult would consent to be tried if she faced the prospect of confinement and then incarcerate youths in prisonlike settings for substantial terms.

Popular concerns about youth crime, especially drugs, guns and violence, bolster policies to repress rather than to rehabilitate young offenders. . . . Indeed, public unwillingness to provide for the welfare of all children, much less for those who commit crimes, forces us to question whether the juvenile court can or should be rehabilitated.

. . . [Y]ouths whom judges remove from home or incarcerate in institutions for terms of months or years receive substantially fewer procedural safeguards than do adults convicted of comparable crimes. As a result, juvenile courts punish delinquents in the name of treatment but deny to them protections available to criminals. In view of this convergence with criminal courts, do we need a separate, procedurally deficient justice system simply to punish middle-level younger offenders?

Most juvenile justice scholars and practitioners recognize juvenile courts' functional convergence with criminal courts but recoil at the prospect of abolishing them and trying and sentencing all offenders in criminal court. They argue that significant developmental differences exist between young people and adults or that rehabilitation still differs from punishment and urge policymakers to maintain the distinctions between delinquents and criminals. . . . [P]roponents of a separate juvenile justice system invoke the Progressives' fallback position—despite juvenile courts' procedural deficiencies and substantive bankruptcy, criminal courts constitute even worse places to try and sentence younger offenders.

From Barry C. Feld, *Bad Kids: Race and the Transformation of the Juvenile Court* (Oxford University Press, 1999). Copyright © 1999 by Oxford University Press. Reprinted by permission of Oxford University Press. References omitted.

. . . Because we do not regard young people as the moral equals of adults, then why and how do we blame, punish, protect, or treat young offenders differently?

This [selection] explores three possible resolutions to the dilemma posed when the child is a criminal and the criminal is a child: a "rehabilitative" juvenile court, a juvenile version of a criminal court, and an integrated criminal court. Proponents of a welfare-oriented juvenile court urge that we "reinvent juvenile justice" and restructure juvenile courts to pursue their original rehabilitative purposes. Advocates of a juvenile version of a criminal court propose that we honestly acknowledge juvenile courts' criminal social control functions, incorporate punishment as a legitimate component of delinquency sanctions, and provide all criminal procedural safeguards but in judicially separate delinquency proceedings. Advocates of an integrated criminal court recommend that we abolish juvenile court jurisdiction over criminal conduct, try all offenders in criminal courts, and introduce certain procedural and substantive modifications to accommodate the youthfulness of younger offenders.

In this [selection], I endorse an integrated criminal court as a better solution to the conundrum posed when a child is a criminal. I will first explain why neither a rehabilitative juvenile court nor a juvenile version of criminal court can "work" as their proponents envision. I argue that traditional juvenile courts' deficiencies reflect a fundamental flaw in their conception rather than *simply* a century-long failure of implementation. Juvenile courts attempt to combine social welfare and criminal social control in one agency and inevitably do both badly because of the inherent contradiction in those two missions. On the other hand, a juvenile version of a criminal court is an institution without a rationale. Because we already have criminal courts, without some other social welfare rationale, a juvenile version of a criminal court simply would be redundant and a temporary way station on the road to fill integration.

If we uncouple social welfare from criminal social control, then we can abolish juvenile courts and formally recognize youthfulness as a mitigating factor in criminal sentencing to accommodate the reduced culpability of younger offenders. Young people differ from adults in their breadth of experience, temporal perspective, willingness to take risks, maturity of judgment, and susceptibility to peer influences. These generic and developmental characteristics of adolescents affect their opportunity to learn to be responsible, to develop fully a capacity for self-control, and provide compelling policy rationale to mitigate their criminal sentences. I propose an age-based "youth discount" of sentences—a sliding scale of developmental and criminal responsibility—to implement the lesser culpability of young offenders in the legal system. Only an integrated justice system can avoid the legal dichotomies and contradictory policies inherent in all current binary formulations—either adult or child, either punishment or treatment. . . . [A]dvantages include enhanced protection for the many young offenders whom criminal courts already sentence as adults; affirmation of individual responsibility; . . . elimination of the sentencing disparities associated with waiver decision making; rejection of the ideology of individualized justice that fosters racial, gender, and geographic disparities; and, ultimately, simple honesty about the reality of criminal social control in the juvenile court.

Rehabilitate the "Rehabilitative" Juvenile Court?

The *parens patriae* juvenile court rests on the dual ideas of "treatment" and "children." It provided a mechanism to protect, reform, and treat "innocent" children and rejected the criminal law's jurisprudence of guilt, blameworthiness, and punishment. It affirmed deterministic models of behavior and adopted paternalistic policies to treat the child as an object for adults to shape and manipulate in her "best interests," rather than as an autonomous and responsible person. . . . [H]owever, ideological and jurisprudential changes have blurred both the "treatment-punishment" and "child-adult" dichotomies. Increasingly the juvenile court functions as a system of criminal social control to protect society from young offenders, rather than as a welfare agency to nurture and protect vulnerable children from a wrathful community. In this revised formulation of adolescence, the justice systems more often emphasize young people's "almost adult" status rather than their "childlike" qualities. When these agencies encounter "other people's children," especially poor and minority youths, the ambivalence and conflict experienced when the child is a criminal "[are] easily converted to hostility and take institutional form in social policies to control and incarcerate youth rather than to enhance their development."

Inadequate Social Welfare

. . . State agencies, rather than juvenile courts, control the institutions and programs to which judges send delinquents. From their inception, these correctional facilities have had more in common with prisons than with hospitals or clinics. By the time of *Gault*, the juvenile courts' failures of implementation were readily apparent.

Juvenile courts lack necessary resources because providing for child welfare is a societal responsibility, not simply a judicial one. Historically and currently, public officials deny juvenile courts adequate resources because of pervasive public antipathy to their clients, those who are poor, disadvantaged, and minority offenders. Thus, any proposal to reinvigorate the juvenile court as a social welfare agency first must address why political leaders who have failed to provide minimally adequate resources and personnel for the past century now will do so. The ideological shift from treatment to punishment and the accompanying "criminalizing" of the juvenile court may portend a more fundamental shift from public responsibility for citizens' welfare to private individual responsibility.

Proponents of a rehabilitative juvenile court also must account for and avoid the failures of earlier generations of juvenile court reforms. Many reforms reflect organizational responses to crises of legitimacy and serve primarily to deflect or neutralize critics. For example, . . . the escalation in youth homicide fostered extensive policy debate about only the relative merits of different ways to "crack down" and transfer more youths to criminal court and thereby to preserve the juvenile court for the "less bad" remaining delinquents. Juvenile justice specialists frame policy options within a "scientific paradigm" of expertise and professional competence to assert a veneer of legitimacy. The ensuing technical tinkering narrows the range of debate, produces symbolic rather than substantive reforms, and fails to address issues of discretion and penal social control or the relationships between social structure and crime, gun, or social welfare policies. . . .

Others attribute the failures of child welfare policies to contradictions embedded in *parens patriae* ideology and divisions between public and private obligations toward young people. Because parents bear primary responsibility to raise their own children, public programs to assist other people's children stipulate that parents demonstrably must fail at the task as a prerequisite of receiving public assistance. But, stigmatizing and clients and social programs by making failure a requirement of eligibility undermines public support for those programs and ensures their inadequacy. . . .

If we formulated a child social welfare policy ab initio, would we select a juvenile court as the most appropriate agency through which to deliver social services and make criminality a condition precedent to the receipt of services? If we would not create a court to deliver social services, then does the fact of a youth's criminality confer on it any special competency as a welfare agency? Many young people who do not commit crimes desperately need social services, and many youths who commit crimes do not require or will not respond to the meager services available. Because our society chooses to deny adequate social welfare services to meet the "real needs" of all young people, juvenile courts' treatment ideology serves primarily to legitimate the exercise of judicial coercion of some *because of their criminality*. In short, little commends the *idea* of a juvenile court as a social welfare delivery system except bureaucratic inertia.

Individualized Justice and the Rule of Law

Quite apart from its unsuitability as a social welfare agency, the individualized justice of a rehabilitative juvenile court fosters lawlessness and thus detracts from its role as a court of law. Despite statutes and procedural rules, juvenile court judges purport to decide each case to achieve a child's best interests. But a treatment ideology without a scientific foundation breeds lawlessness. . . . Unlike punishment, which implies limits, treatment may continue "for the duration of minority." Thus, juvenile courts in theory and in practice sentence or treat minor offenders severely and sanction serious offenders mildly. . . .

If judges possess neither practical scientific bases by which to classify youths for treatment nor demonstrably effective programs to prescribe for them, then the exercise of "sound discretion" simply constitutes a euphemism for idiosyncratic subjectivity. Racial, gender, geographic, and socioeconomic disparities constitute almost inevitable corollaries of an individualized treatment ideology. At the least, judges will sentence youths differently based on extraneous personal characteristics for which they bear no responsibility. If juvenile courts provided exclusively benign and effective services, then perhaps differential processing of male and female, urban and rural, or black and white juveniles might be tolerable. At the worst, however, judges impose haphazard, unequal, and discriminatory punishment on similarly situated offenders without any effective procedural or appellate checks.

Is the discretion that judges exercise to classify for treatment warranted? Do the successes of rehabilitation justify its concomitant lawlessness? Do the incremental benefits of juvenile court intervention for some youths outweigh the inevitable inequalities and racial disparities that result from the exercise of individualized discretion for others? . . . Although some treatment does "work" for some youths, states do not routinely provide . . . model demonstration services universally for ordinary, run-of-the-mill delinquents. . . . [I]n the face of unproven efficacy and uncertain resources, the possibility that rehabilitation may occur does not justify incarcerating young offenders with fewer procedural safeguards than we provide to adults charged, convicted, and confined for crimes.

Procedural informality constitutes an essential adjunct of a "welfare" court's substantive discretion; juvenile courts predicate their informal process on the promise of benign and effective treatment. . . . The informal and confidential nature of delinquency proceedings reduces the visibility and accountability of the process and precludes external checks on coercive interventions. As long as the mythology prevails that juvenile court intervention constitutes only benign coercion and that, in any event, children should not expect more, youths will continue to receive the "worst of both worlds."

Failure of Implementation Versus Conception

The fundamental shortcoming of the juvenile court's welfare *idea* reflects a failure of conception rather than *simply* a failure of implementation. The juvenile court's creators envisioned a social service agency in a judicial setting and attempted to fuse its social welfare mission with the power of state coercion. The juvenile court *idea* that judicial clinicians successfully can combine social welfare and penal social control in one agency represents an inherent conceptual flaw and an innate contradiction. Combining social welfare and penal social control functions only ensures that the court performs both functions badly. Providing for child welfare is a societal responsibility, not a judicial one, and the polity declines to provide those necessary resources because juvenile courts' clients are poor, disproportionately minorities, *and* criminal offenders. As a result, juvenile courts subordinate social welfare concerns to crime control considerations.

The conflicted impulses engendered between concern for child welfare and punitive responses to criminal violations form the root of the ambivalence embedded in the juvenile court. The hostile reactions that people experience toward other people's children whom they regard as a threat to themselves and their own children undermine benevolent aspirations and elevate concerns for their control. Juvenile justice personnel simultaneously profess child-saving aspirations but more often function as agents of criminal social control. Because they possess few resources besides the power to incarcerate for crimes, juvenile courts function as agencies of social control. . . .

Because juvenile courts operate in a societal context that does not provide adequate social services for children in general, juvenile justice intervenes in the lives of those who commit crimes for purposes of social control rather than of social welfare. This in-built contradiction places the juvenile court in an untenable position. . . .

Neither juvenile court judges nor any other criminal justice agencies realistically can ameliorate the social ills that afflict young people or significantly reduce youth crime.

A Juvenile Version of a Criminal Court: Due Process and Reduced Punishment

. . .[I]f we acknowledge that juvenile courts punish young offenders, then we assume an obligation to provide them with all criminal procedural safeguards. . . . [T]o punish juveniles in the name of treatment, and to deny them basic safeguards foster a sense of injustice that thwarts any reform efforts.

The current juvenile court provides neither therapy nor justice *and* cannot be rehabilitated. The alternative policy options are either to make juvenile courts more like criminal courts or to make criminal courts more like juvenile courts. Whether we try young offenders in a separate juvenile court or in a unified criminal court, we must reconsider basic premises and address issues of substance and procedure. Issues of substantive justice include developing and implementing a doctrinal rationale—diminished responsibility, reduced capacity, immaturity of judgment, or truncated self-control—to sentence young offenders differently, and more leniently, than older defendants. Issues of procedural justice include providing youths with *all* the procedural safeguards adults receive *and* additional protections that recognize their immaturity and vulnerability in the justice process.

Many analysts acknowledge that "the assumptions underlying the juvenile court show it to be a bankrupt legal institution" that functions as an extension of criminal courts and requires a new rationale to justify its continued existence. Rather than abolishing the juvenile court, however, they propose to transform it into an explicitly penal juvenile justice system that provides enhanced procedural protections and imposes less-severe punishment than do criminal courts because of youths' reduced culpability. . . .

Proponents of a juvenile version of a criminal court point to the manifold deficiencies of criminal courts. . . . However, . . . charges of excessive caseloads, ineffective defense counsel, inadequate sentencing options, inattention to children's real needs, and assembly-line justice apply equally to juvenile courts. An unsentimental comparison of the relative quality of juvenile and criminal "justice" leaves little basis on which to decide whether either system treats young people or adult defendants justly and fairly. If the state charged you with a crime, under which system of procedures would you rather be tried? . . .

Young Offenders in Criminal Courts: Youthfulness As a Mitigating Factor

. . . If the child is a criminal and the "real" reason he appears in court is for formal social control, then states could abolish juvenile courts' delinquency jurisdiction and try youths in criminal courts alongside their adult counterparts. But if the criminal is a child, then states must modify their sentencing provisions to accommodate the youthfulness of some defendants. Politically popular sound bites—"old enough to do the crime, old enough to do the time" or "adult crime, adult time"—do not analyze adequately the complexities of a youth sentencing policy. My proposal to abolish the juvenile court constitutes neither a mindless endorsement of punishment nor a primitive throwback to earlier centuries' views of young people as miniature adults. Rather, it honestly acknowledges that juvenile courts currently exercise criminal social control, asserts that young offenders in a criminal justice system *deserve* less-severe consequences for their misdeeds than do more mature offenders simply because they are young and addresses the many problems created by trying to maintain binary, dichotomous, and contradictory criminal justice systems based on an arbitrary age classification of a youth as a child or an adult.

Formulating a youth sentencing policy entails two tasks. First, . . . a rationale to sentence young offenders differently, and *more leniently,* than older defendants. Explicitly punishing young offenders rests on the premise that adolescents possess sufficient cognitive capacity and volitional controls to be responsible for their behavior, albeit not to the same extent as adults. . . . Second, I . . . propose a "youth discount" as a practical administrative mechanism to institutionalize the principle of youthfulness in sentencing. A sentencing policy that recognizes youthfulness as a mitigating factor and provides a youth discount fosters greater honesty about the role of the justice system and greater realism about young people's developmental capacity and criminal responsibility. . . .

Juveniles' Criminal Responsibility

. . . Quite apart from decisions about guilt or innocence, individual capacity and criminal responsibility also affect appropriate sentences. . . .

A formal mitigation of punishment based on youthfulness constitutes a necessary component of a criminal justice system in order to avoid the equally undersirable alternatives of either excessively harsh penalties disproportionate to culpability on the one hand or of nullification and excessive leniency on the other. Youthfulness provides a rationale to mitigate sentences to some degree without excusing criminal conduct.

Shorter sentences for young people do not require a separate justice system in which to try them. Both juvenile and criminal courts separate determinations of guilt or innocence from sentencing and restrict consideration of individual circumstances largely to the latter phase. Criminal courts may impose lenient sentences on young offenders when appropriate. . . .

Sentencing policies can and should protect young people from the adverse consequences of their developmentally less competent decisions. . . .

Reduced Culpability

. . . [I]n *Thompson v. Oklahoma* (487 U.S. 815 [1988]), the Supreme Court analyzed the criminal responsibility of young offenders and provided some additional support for shorter sentences for reduced culpability for youths older than the common-law infancy threshold of age fourteen. The *Thompson* plurality vacated Thompson's capital sentence because the Court concluded that a fifteen-year-old offender could not act "with the degree of culpability that can justify the ultimate penalty" (486 U.S. at 834). Although the Court provided several rationales for its decision, it explicitly decided that juveniles are less culpable for the same crimes that are their adult counterparts. Also, *Thompson* reaffirmed several earlier decisions that also emphasized that youthfulness constitutes an important mitigating factor when judges sentence young defendants. . . .

Administering Youthfulness As a Mitigating Factor at Sentencing: The "Youth Discount"

. . . A statutory sentencing policy that integrates youthfulness and limited opportunities to learn self-control with principles of proportionality and reduced culpability would provide younger offenders with categorical fractional reductions of adult sentences. . . .

This categorical approach would take the form of an explicit "youth discount" at sentencing. A fourteen-year-old offender might receive, for example, 25 to 33 percent of the adult penalty; a 16-year-old defendant, 50 to 66 percent; and an eighteen-year-old adult, the full penalty, as is presently the case. The "deeper discounts" for younger offenders correspond to the developmental continuum and their more limited opportunities to learn self-control and to exercise responsibility.

. . . [Y]oung offenders commit their crimes in groups to a much greater extent than do adults. Although the law treats all participants in a crime as equally responsible and may sentence them alike, young people's susceptibility to peer group influences requires a more nuanced assessment of their degree of participation, personal responsibility, and culpability. . . . The group nature of youth crime affects sentencing policy in several ways. Because of susceptibility to peer influences, the presence of a social audience may induce youths to participate in criminal behavior in which they would not engage if alone. Even though the criminal law treats all accomplices as equally guilty, they may not all bear equal responsibility for the actual harm inflicted and may *deserve* different sentences. . . . Thus, the group nature of adolescent criminality requires some formal mechanism to distinguish between active participants and passive accomplices with even greater "discounts" for the latter.

Virtue of Affirming Partial Responsibility for Youth

. . . The juvenile court's rehabilitative ideal elevated determinism over free will, characterized delinquent offenders as victims rather than perpetrators, and envisioned a therapeutic institution that resembled more closely a preventive, forward-looking civil commitment process rather than a criminal court. By denying youth's personal responsibility, juvenile court's treatment ideology reduces offenders' duty to exercise self-control, erodes their obligation to change, and sustains a self-fulfilling prophecy that delinquency occurs inevitably for youths from certain backgrounds.

Affirming responsibility encourages people to learn the virtues of moderation, self-discipline, and personal accountability. Acknowledging that we *punish* young offenders for their misconduct "becomes part of a complex of cultural forces that keep alive the moral lessons, and the myths, which are essential to the continued order of society. . . . A culture that values autonomous individuals must emphasize both freedom and responsibility.

While the paternalistic stance of the traditional juvenile courts rests on the humane desire to protect young people from the adverse consequences of their bad decisions, protectionism disables young people from the opportunity to learn to make choices and to be responsible for their natural consequences. . . .

Age-Segregated Dispositional Facilities and "Room to Reform"

Questions about young offenders' criminal liability or their degree of accountability differ from issues about the appropriate place of confinement or the services or resources the state should provide to them. Even explicitly punitive sentences do not require judges or correctional authorities to confine young people with adults in jails and prisons, as is the current practice for waived youths, or to consign them to custodial warehouses or "punk prisons." States should maintain separate, age-segregated youth correctional facilities to protect both younger offenders and older inmates. . . . Insisting on humane conditions of confinement can do as much to improve the lives of incarcerated youths as the "right to treatment" or the rehabilitative ideal. Some research indicates that youths sentenced to juvenile correctional facilities may reoffend somewhat less often, seriously, or rapidly than comparable youths sentenced to adult facilities. If consistently replicated, these findings provide modest support for a separate youth correctional system, rather than for an entire separate juvenile justice system. . . .

Eliminate Civil Disabilities

. . . [Y]oung first-or second-time offenders need not suffer all the disabilities and losses of rights associated with a conviction. A legislature can provide young offenders with relief from collateral consequence, restore civil rights, or nullify the effects of felony convictions upon the conclusion of a sentence and supervision.

Conclusion

. . . Even far-reaching justice system changes can have only a modest effect on social problems as complex as crime and violence. . . .

A proposal to abolish the juvenile court and to try all young offenders in an integrated justice system makes no utilitarian claims but represents a commitment to honesty about state coercion. States bring young offenders who break the law to juvenile court for social control and to punish them. Juvenile courts' rehabilitative claims fly in the face of their penal reality, undermine their legitimacy, and impair their ability to function as judicial agencies. . . .

[C]haracterizing penal coercion as "social welfare" seems both dangerous and dishonest. The *idea* of rehabilitation inherently and seductively expands, widens nets of social control, and promotes abuse through self-delusion. . . . [U]ltimately, youths incarcerated in the name of treatment recognize that the justice system had deceived them.

The shortcomings of the rehabilitative juvenile court run far deeper than inadequate resources or unproven treatment techniques. Rather, the flaw lies in the very *idea* that the juvenile court can combine successfully criminal social control and social welfare in one system. . . .

I propose to abolish the juvenile court with considerable trepidation. On the one hand, combining enhanced procedural safeguards with a youth discount in an integrated criminal court provides young offenders with greater protections and justice than they currently receive in the rehabilitative juvenile system and more proportional and humane consequences than judges presently inflict on them as adults in the criminal justice system. Integration may foster a more consistent crime control response than the current dual system permits to violent and chronic young offenders at various stages of the developmental and criminal career continuum. On the other hand, politicians may ignore the significance of youthfulness as a mitigating factor and instead use these proposals to escalate the punishment of young people. Although abolition of the juvenile court, enhanced procedural protections, and a youth discount constitute essential components of a youth sentencing policy package, nothing can prevent get-tough legislators from selectively choosing only those elements that serve their punitive agenda, even though doing so unravels the threads that make coherent a proposal for an integrated court.

In either event, the ensuing debate about a youth sentencing policy would require public officials to consider whether to focus primarily on the fact that young offenders are *young* or *offenders*. A public policy debate when the child is a criminal and the criminal is a child forces a long overdue and critical reassessment of the entire social construction of "childhood." . . . .

Most people tolerate an intolerable juvenile justice because they believe that it will affect only other people's children—children of other colors, classes, and cultures—and not their own. Juvenile courts tap a resonant legitimating theme because they invoke *parens patriae* and child welfare ideals even as they impose penal controls on young offenders.

Editor's Note

1. In *In re Gault,* Gerald Gault, a juvenile, challenged the constitutionality of the Arizona Juvenile Code, which led to his being sentenced to six years in an industrial school after he was found guilty of making obscene phone calls. As an adult, he would have been entitled to representation by a lawyer and would have had the opportunity to be confronted by the person who charged him. However, since he was a juvenile, he was not entitled to these rights. In a 7–2 decision, the Supreme Court granted children some but not all of these rights.—Ed.

**Vincent Schiraldi and
Jason Ziedenberg**

The Florida Experiment

"Anthony Laster is the kind of kid who has never been a danger to anyone. A 15-year-old, eighth grader with an IQ of 58, Anthony is described by relatives as having the mind of a five-year-old. Late last year, a few days after his mother died, Anthony asked another boy in his class at a Florida middle school to give him lunch money, claiming he was hungry. When the boy refused, Anthony reached into his pocket and took $2. That's when Anthony ran smack into Palm Beach County prosecutor Barry Kirscher's brand of compassionless conservatism. Rather than handling the case in the principal's office, where it belonged, Mr. Kirscher decided to prosecute Anthony as an adult for this, his first arrest. Anthony spent the next seven weeks—including his first Christmas since his mother died—in custody, much of it in an adult jail."[1]

Introduction

Anthony Laster was one of 4,660 youth who Florida prosecutors sent to adult court last year under the wide ranging powers they enjoy with the state's direct file provisions. Florida is one of 15 states that allow prosecutors—not a judge—to decide whether children arrested for crimes ranging from shoplifting to robbery should be dealt with in the juvenile justice or criminal justice system.[2] While 43 states have changed their laws to make it easier for judges to send children into the adult criminal system since 1993, Florida is leading the nation in using prosecutors to make the decision to try children as adults. In 1995 alone (Figure 1), Florida prosecutors sent 7,000 case to adult court nearly matching the number of cases judges sent to the criminal justice system nationwide that year.[3]

A juvenile crime bill currently being considered by the U.S. Congress (House-Senate Conference Committee) would give U.S. Attorneys even greater powers than those enjoyed by prosecutors in Florida.

The change in federal law would remove judges from the process of deciding which justice system would serve young people, and transfer that power to the sole discretion of prosecutors. The Justice Department also appears to support giving prosecutors expanded powers to try youth as

Figure 1

In 1995, Florida Prosecutors Rival Judges in the Rest of
U.S. in Sending Youth to Adult Court

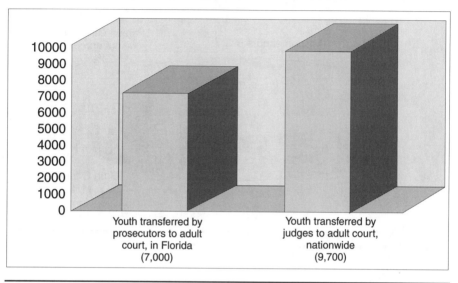

Source: The Urban Institute, 1998

adults in federal court.[4] Given the current legislative drive, it is worthwhile
to examine the Florida experience to see what the future will hold for
the nation.

Profile: Who Are Prosecutors Sending to Adult Court in Florida?

I. Offense Category

When prosecutorial waiver was introduced in 1981, the percentage of delinquency cases transferred to adult court in Florida soared from 1.2% to
nearly 9% by 1987.[5] In fiscal year 1997–98, 6,425 of the 94,693 cases dis-
posed of by judicial processing in Florida resulted in transfer to adult court.
While these waiver provisions were originally designed to ensure that violent juvenile offenders were being detained, a 1991 study of two representative Florida counties showed that only 28% of the youths prosecutors
waived to adult court were for violent crimes.[6] More than half (55%) of the
youths prosecutors sent to adult court were charged with property offenses
that involved no violence, and fully 5% were tried as adults for misdemeanors (Figure 2). Almost a quarter of the cases waived were first time, low
level offenders.[7]

Figure 2

Most Youth Transferred by Prosecutors in Florida Were
Charged With Non-Violent Offenses

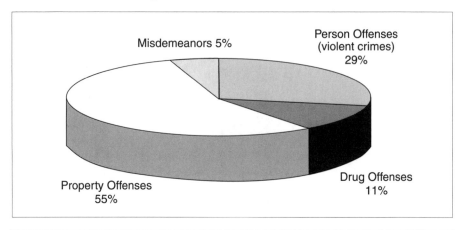

Source: Notre Dame Journal of Law, Ethics, and Public Policy (1996)

II. Disproportionate Minority Confinement

The most striking feature of Florida's transferred youth population profile is the extent to which minority youth are overrepresented in the ranks of the youth being referred to adult court. One study conducted by the Florida Department of Juvenile Justice found that black youths were 2.3 times more likely than white youth to be transferred in Florida.[8] Even though non-whites account for 24% of the 10–17 age bracket in Florida, they currently represent 74% of those 10–17 held in the Florida prison system.[9] "I think the way the system sets up programs shows some institutional bias," is the way one candid Florida prosecutor describes it.[10]

Policy Impact in Florida

I. Sentencing: Longer Terms for Youths in Adult Court?

While some have suggested that huge numbers of children are being held in adult facilities across the state, it is not clear that youth going to adult court via prosecutorial waiver are serving long sentences. A study published in the *Notre Dame Journal of Law, Ethics and Public Policy* found that, of the youth who were incarcerated after disposition, half received short sentences, some shorter than they would have received in the juvenile justice system. The majority (54%) of those sentenced to prison were released within three years.[11] A 1998 survey of the Florida transferred population shows that a majority of youth prosecutors sent to adult court for property, drug and weapons offenses received jail sentences or probation terms well within the range of what could have been prescribed to them in the juvenile court.[12] The same study showed that in 1995, 61% of the youth found guilty in adult court were incarcerated, but only 31% were served prison terms.[13]

II. More Youths to Adult Jail and to Juvenile Detention

While it might be expected that prosecutorial waiver would reduce the number of youths being funneled into Florida's juvenile justice system, the opposite has been true. Between 1993 and 1998, the number of annual commitments to Florida's juvenile justice system increased by 85% despite its liberal use of waiver to adult court. Florida has the sixth highest incarceration rate for youth per 100,000 in the nation, and detains young people at a rate 25% greater than the national average.[14] This happened during a time when the number of waiver cases was increasing, and the number of felony referrals to the juvenile justice system was decreasing. This is happening, despite the fact that youths waived to adult court are held before trial in adult jails, further skackening the numbers that would need to be held in juvenile detention. Rather than the happy prospect of devoting more resources in the juvenile justice system to fewer youths, the system has widened its "net of control" by committing youth for lower level offenses.[15]

Crime Control Impact

I. Recidivism: Adult Court Prosecution Increases Propensity for Crime

Quantitative: Studies and Data
A number of studies have shown that youth sent to adult court generally recidivate at a higher rate than they do if they are sent to the juvenile justice system. A series of studies in Florida have analyzed what happens to youth referred to adult court—90% of whom are referred there directly by a prosecutor. A study published in the journal *Crime and Delinquency* showed that youth transferred to adult court in Florida were a third more likely to reoffend than those sent to the juvenile justice system.[16] The transferred youths reoffended almost twice as fast as those who were sent to juvenile detention.[17] Of those who committed new crimes, the youth who had previously been tried as adults committed serious crimes at double the rate of those sent to juvenile court.[18] While a 1997 study by the same authors showed that property offenders were slightly less likely to recidivate when transferred to adult court, the authors note: "Once the effect of offense type was controlled, the logistic regression analysis indicated that transfer led to more recidivism. Moreover, the transferred youths who subsequently reoffended were rearrested more times and more quickly than were the non-transferee youth who reoffended regardless of the offense for which they

were prosecuted . . . although property felons who were transferred may have been less likely to reoffend, when they did reoffend they reoffended more often and more quickly."[19]

JUVENILE OFFENDERS GENERALLY FOLLOW ONE OF THREE PATHS TO ADULT COURT

Judicial Waiver: A juvenile court judge waives jurisdiction over the case after considering the merits of transfer for the individual youth.

Legislative Exclusion: A state legislature determines that an entire class of juvenile crimes should be sent to adult court automatically, usually serious and violent offenses.

Prosecutorial Discretion: A state or local prosecutor has the authority to file charges against some juveniles directly in adult court.

Source: The Urban Institute, 1998

Qualitative: Interviews With Youths in Deep End Juvenile Programs
The same authors recently conducted in-depth interviews with fifty youths sent to prison by Florida prosecutors, versus fifty who were sent to a state "maximum risk" juvenile detention facility.[20] This study found that the youth themselves recognized the rehabilitative strengths of the juvenile justice system in contrast to the adult prison system.

Sixty percent of the sample sent to juvenile detention said they expect would not reoffend, 30% said they were uncertain whether they would reoffend, while 3% said they would likely reoffend. Of those expected not to reoffend, 90% said good juvenile justice programming and services were the reason for their rehabilitation. Only one of the youths in juvenile detention said they were learning new ways to commit crimes. Most reported at least one favorable contact with a staff person that helped them. As such, the juvenile justice system responses were overwhelmingly positive:

A: "This place is all about rehabilitation and counseling. . . . This place here, we have people to listen to when you have something on your mind . . . and need to talk. They understand you and help you."

B: "They helped me know how to act. I never knew any of this stuff. That really helped me, cause I ain't had too good a life."[21]

By contrast, 40% of the transferred youth said they were learning new ways to commit crimes in prison. Most reported that the guards and staff in prisons were indifferent, hostile, and showed little care for them. Only 1/3 of the youths in prison said they expected not to reoffend. Not surprisingly, the youths sent to prison by prosecutors responded in an overwhelmingly despondent and negative way:

C: "When I was in juvenile programs, they were telling me that I am somebody and that I can change my ways, and get back on the right tracks. In here, they tell me I am nobody and I never will be anybody."

D: "In the juvenile systems, the staff and I were real close. They wanted to help me. They were hopeful for me here. They think I am nothing but a convict now."

II. Crime Control Impact: Crime Rate

Despite having prosecutorial waiver on the books since 1981, Florida has the second highest overall violent crime rate of any state in the country, and that status has remained virtually unchanged throughout the 1990s.[22] Florida's violent juvenile crime rate is fully 48% higher than the national average (Figure 3).[23]

Though Florida leads the nation in using prosecutorial waiver, the other 14 states which allow states attorneys discretion to send youth to criminal court do not fare much better. Of the 15 states that currently employ prosecutorial waiver provisions, five (Florida, Arizona, Massachusetts, the District of Columbia and Louisiana) are among the ten states with the highest violent crime arrest rate (age 10–17). While the rest of the nation enjoyed a decline in juvenile crime between 1992 and 1996, five states that employ prosecutorial waiver—Arkansas, Nebraska, Arizona, Virginia and New Hampshire—actually experienced an increase in their violent juvenile crime rates.[24]

Figure 3

Florida Has the Second Highest Violent Crime Rate in the Country, 48% Higher Than the National Average

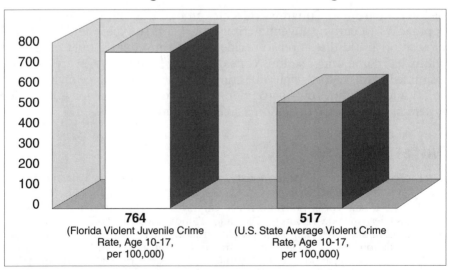

	764	517
	(Florida Violent Juvenile Crime Rate, Age 10-17, per 100,000)	(U.S. State Average Violent Crime Rate, Age 10-17, per 100,000)

Source: Office of Juvenile Justice and Delinquency Prevention, 1997

The Risks Youth Face in Adult Jails

The children who prosecutors are sending to adult court in Florida face greater threats to their life, limb and future when they enter Florida's adult jail and prison systems. These well-documented risks affect both the youth who are convicted in adult court, and those (like Anthony Laster) who are merely being held in pre-trial detention in jail, on crimes of which they may be exonerated.

One study has shown that youths are five times more likely to report being a victim of rape when they are held in an adult facility versus juvenile detention.[25] Youth in adult jails are also twice as likely to report being beaten by staff and 50% more likely to be attacked with a weapon. A Justice Department study done in 1981 showed that the suicide rate of juveniles in adult jails is 7.7 times higher than that of youth in juvenile detention centers.[26]

The Will of the People?: Public Opinion and Prosecutorial Waiver

A survey published in the journal *Crime and Delinquency* found that a majority of Americans oppose changing federal law to allow for prosecutorial waiver of youth to adult court.[27] When asked, "Would you agree strongly, agree somewhat, disagree somewhat, or disagree strongly that federal prosecutors should have total discretion to try juveniles as adults for all felonies?," 56% of a nationally representative sample of Americans disagreed or disagreed strongly with the idea (41% agreed, and 3% said they had no opinion). Nearly twice as many respondents were strongly opposed to the idea compared to those who strongly supported it (29% vs. 16%).[28]

Conclusion

As the United States Congress and states around the country weigh various approaches to curbing juvenile crime, the "Florida Experiment" of giving prosecutors broad discretion to decide whether juveniles should be tried as adults has come under serious consideration.[29] On almost every measure examined in this report—statewide crime control, individual recidivism, racial equity and the youth's own perception of future offense behavior—the Florida system of prosecutorial discretion waiver was found wanting.

Notes

1. Schiraldi, Vincent. "Prosecutorial Zeal vs. America's Kids." The Christian Science Monitor, March 22, 1999.
2. The 15 states or jurisdictions which employ Direct File (prosecutorial discretion waiver) include Arkansas, Colorado, Florida, Georgia, Louisiana, Michigan, Nebraska, New Hampshire, Vermont, Arizona, Massachusetts, Montana, Oklahoma, Virginia, and the District of Columbia. Griffin, P., Torbet, P., and Szymanski, L. 1998. "Trying Juveniles as Adults in Criminal Court: Analysis of State Transfer Provisions." Washington, D.C.: U.S. Department of Justice, Office of Justice Programs, Office of Juvenile Justice and Delinquency Prevention.

3. Butts, Jeffrey A. and Adele V. Harrell. "Delinquents or Criminals: Policy Options for Young Offenders." Washington, D.C.: The Urban Institute, 1998, p. 6.

4. "In our view, the system should be fundamentally altered so that, in appropriate circumstances, the prosecutor alone determines whether to prosecute the juvenile as an adult." Gregory, Kevin V. Deputy Assistant Attorney General, in Testimony before the Subcommittee on Crime, Committee on the Judiciary, U.S. House of Representatives, March 10, 1999.

5. 1999 Annual Report and Juvenile Justice Fact Book, Florida Juvenile Justice Accountability Board, February, 1999.

6. Bishop, Donna M. and Charles E. Frazier. "Transfer of Juveniles to Criminal Court: A Case Study and Analysis of Prosecutorial Discretion." The Notre Dame Journal of Law, Ethics and Public Policy, Vol. 5: p. 281–302, 1991.

7. Ibid.

8. Department of Juvenile Justice-Management Report, No. 42. March 24, 1996.

9. Inmate Population: Current Inmate Age. Agency Annual Report, Department of Corrections, 1998.

10. Bishop, Donna M. and Charles E. Frazier, "Race Effects in Juvenile Justice Decision Making: Findings of a Statewide Analysis." The Journal of Criminal Law and Criminology, Vol. 86, 1996.

11. Bishop, et al., 1991.

12. Bishop, Donna M. and Charles E. Frazier, "The Consequences of Transfer" in The Changing Borders of Juvenile Justice: Transfer of Adolescents to the Criminal Court. Chicago: University of Chicago Press [in press].

13. Bishop, Donna M., Charles E. Frazier, Lonn Lanza-Kaduce and Henry George White. "Juvenile Transfers to Criminal Court Study: Phase I Final Report." Washington, D.C.: Office of Juvenile Justice and Delinquency Prevention, 1998.

14. Snyder, Howard N. and Melissa Sickmund. "Juvenile Offenders and Victims: Update on Violence." Washington, DC: Office of Juvenile Justice and Delinquency Prevention, 1998.

15. Bishop and Frazier [in press].

16. Bishop, Donna M. et al. "The Transfer of Juveniles to Criminal Court: Does It Make a Difference?" Crime & Delinquency, Vol. 42, No. 2, April 1996.

17. Ibid.

18. Ibid.

19. Bishop, Donna M., Charles E. Frazier, Lonn Lanza-Kaduce and Lawrence Winner. "The Transfer of Juveniles to Criminal Court: Reexamining Recidivism Over the Long Term." Crime and Delinquency, Vol. 43, No. 4, October 1997.

20. Bishop and Frazier, Office of Juvenile Justice and Delinquency Prevention, 1998.

21. Ibid, and keynote address, National Association of Sentencing Advocates Conference, Miami, Florida, April 15, 1999.

22. Snyder, p. 22.

23. Ibid.

24. Kathleen Maguire and Ann L. Pastore, eds., Sourcebook of Criminal Justice Statistics 1997. U.S. Department of Justice, Bureau of Justice Statistics, 1997; (1996); (1995). U.S. Department of Justice, Bureau of Justice Statistics. Washington, D.C., USGPO, 1998 (1997); (1996).

25. Fagan, Jeffrey, Martin Forst and T. Scott Vivona. "Youth in Prisons and Training Schools: Perceptions and the Consequences of the Treatment Custody Dichotomy." Juvenile and Family Court, No. 2, 1989, p. 10.

26. Flaherty, Michael G. "An Assessment of the National Incidences of Juvenile Suicides in Adult Jails, Lockups and Juvenile Detention Centers." The University of Illinois, Urbana, Champaign, 1980.

27. Schiraldi, Vincent and Mark Soler. "The Will of the People: The Public's Opinion of the Violent and Repeat Juvenile Offender Act of 1997." Crime and Delinquency, Vol. 44., No. 4, October, 1998.

28. Ibid.

29. For example, in March, 2000, Californians will be voting on the "Gang Violence and Juvenile Crime Prevention Act of 1998" initiative, which will give prosecutors discretion to try certain juveniles as adults at the age of 14.

POSTSCRIPT

Should Juvenile Courts Be Abolished?

As the public and politicians increasingly reflect intolerance toward criminals, especially violent ones, might Feld's proposal be viewed as an extreme one rising from desperation? That is, if we lived in different times, needed monies and staffing for juvenile courts, facilities, and services in the community would be provided. Is Feld's "sliding scale" fair for youngsters in adult courts? Can it be argued that because it is impossible to tell precisely how emotionally "developed" a youth is, it is ethically and legally unacceptable to sentence one youngster to a longer term than another youngster who did the same crime? Is Feld correct when he asserts that the juvenile court concept itself is untenable because it is impossible to have both the goal of crime control and treatment simultaneously? For instance, Schiraldi and Ziedenberg could argue that if courts were sympathetic toward and knowledgeable of youth, programs could be developed to treat children and consequently to reduce their involvement in crime.

For the most part, Schiraldi, and Ziedenberg base their arguments on a Florida study. Is that a good basis for suggesting national policy, especially since Florida is an extreme case? Are the authors confusing the issues of waivering kids to adult courts and incarcerating kids in adult jails and prisons? Does their drawing from tear-jerking testimonies of selected child cases really serve to clarify the issue? For instance, might one just as easily juxtapose their reports with sad statements from victims of juvenile violence?

Can the two positions by synthesized? If federal monies were provided for randomly selected states to experiment with abolishing juvenile courts for, say, 20 years, would that be a better basis for deciding what is best for society and for child criminals? Meanwhile, should juvenile courts be abolished, as Feld says, or should the traditional system be maintained, as Schiraldi and Ziedenberg suggest?

Among the many works by Feld pertaining to the issue is his *Readings in Juvenile Justice Administration* (Oxford University Press, 1999). Among the many publications of the Justice Policy Institute, which is directed by Schiraldi, is *Second Chances: One Hundred Years of the Children's Court* (1999).

A positive though balanced overview is "Juvenile Justice: A Century of Experience," by S. Drizin, *Current* (November 1999). Several highly favorable articles on juvenile courts can be found in the special issue of *Juvenile Justice* entitled "100th Anniversary of the Juvenile Court, 1899–1999" (December 1999), published by the Office of Juvenile Justice and Delinquency Prevention (OJJDP). Several other relevant reports are available from the OJJDP, including *From the Courthouse to the Schoolhouse: Making Successful Transitions* (March 2000).

Focus on Accountability: Best Practices for Juvenile Court and Probation (1999), and *Offenders in Juvenile Court, 1996* (1999). Two helpful overviews of female offenders and the system are *Women Offenders* by L. greenfeld and T. Snell (December 1999), published by the Bureau of Justice Statistics, and *Juvenile Justice Journal Volume VI, Number 1 (Investing in Girls: A Twenty-First Century Strategy)* (October 1999), published by the OJJDP. An alternative system that neither of the protoganists address is teen courts, which are explored in J. Butts, D. Hoffman, and J. Buck, *Teen Courts in the United States: A Profile of Current Programs* (1999), also available from the OJJDP.

An excellent source from the federal level is S. G. Mezey's *Children in Court: Public Policymaking and Federal Court Decisions* (State University of New York Press, 1996). A brief discussion of a judge's analysis is "Judge Recommends Overhaul of Juvenile Supervision System," *Criminal Justice Weekly* (August 3, 1999). Two news articles that outline problems and prospects of the juvenile court system are "Regrettable Regression in the Way We Treat Young Criminals," by L. Dodge, *The Washington Post* (August 29, 1999) and "Juvenile Court Comes of Age," by C. Wetzstein, *The Washington Times* (August 29, 1999). An analysis of gender differences can be found in "Explaining the Gender Difference in Adolescent Delinquent Behavior: A Longitudinal Test of Mediating Mechanisms," by X. Liu and H. B. Kaplan, *Criminology* (February 1999).

ISSUE 9

Are the Dangers of Internet Child Pornography Exaggerated?

YES: Julia Wilkins, from "Protecting Our Children from Internet Smut: Moral Duty or Moral Panic?" *The Humanist* (September/ October 1997)

NO: Bob Trebilcock, from "Child Molesters on the Internet: Are They in Your Home?" *Redbook* (April 1997)

ISSUE SUMMARY

YES: Julia Wilkins, a writer of books and articles on educating children, argues that claims of Internet dangers are simply an example of "moral panic" causing otherwise sensible people to overreact.

NO: Magazine writer Bob Trebilcock contends that the Internet is a real danger to children because it provides easy access to pornography, encourages the creation and dissemination of child pornography, and provides pedophiles with a new crop of children to prey upon.

I have sworn upon the altar of God, eternal hostility against every form of tyranny over the mind of man.

—Thomas Jefferson

Congress shall make no law respecting an establishment of religion, or prohibiting the free exercise thereof; or abridging the freedom of speech, or of the press.

—First Amendment of the U.S. Constitution

In spite of these valiant declarations, there have always been restraints on speech and writing with both practical and legal supports. Not that the issue of freedom of expression (including speaking, writing, publishing, painting, photography, and, more recently, Internet communications) has ever been close to a settled one. To the literate and the cultural elite, the very idea of outside constraints on expression is unacceptable. To the religious right and a variety of special interest groups, society simply could not function if there were no regulations on communication that might threaten decency.

Chief Justice Oliver Wendell Holmes ruled over 70 years ago that the First Amendment does not allow someone the right to shout "Fire!" in a crowded theater because of the harm that such an act could cause. This ruling, though frequently ignored in current debates, supports advocates of Internet control. It also reflects the thinking of a growing number of scholars and activists who insist that words and images can be psychologically or even physically harmful and hence should be illegal.

What are the dangers of the Internet with regard to child pornography? Do we need special safeguards? In 1997 the U.S. Supreme Court ruled that the Communications Decency Act (CDA) passed by Congress violated the First Amendment. The Court did *not* say that existing laws prohibiting obscenity, child pornography, libel, copyright infringements, and the like do not apply to the Internet. The Court simply decided that the CDA was far more restrictive of free speech than was constitutional.

Hundreds of concerned citizens, especially parents, are forming coalitions. They are demanding legal actions to close down Web sites that are perceived as dangerous and to control computer use and programs in all public arenas, especially public libraries and schools. Since 1995 "Innocent Images," and FBI operation with 10 offices devoted to catching cyberstalkers, has arrested 487 pornographers and men attempting to "date" children contacted through the Internet. Convictions are around 95 percent. Some people argue that the operation engages in entrapment. Others contend that the 487 arrested individuals represent only the tip of the iceberg—that there are perhaps thousands of individuals who successfully exploit children via the Internet. Still others insist that such exploitation (as well as pornography itself) could be successfully controlled through better training of children and utilization of computer technology, such as content filtering software.

In 1922 the sociologist William Ogburn (1886–1959) identified a "culture lag" between social norms, values, and institutions and material aspects of human societies. In the 1950s the British writer C. P. Snow warned about the divide between science and technology and the humanities. Technological innovations generate strains. Computers and the Internet, despite already going through several technological generations, are still remarkably new. Their influence, however, could be as pervasive as any other invention of the past 200 years.

As you read the following selections by Julia Wilkins and Bob Trebilcock, reflect on your own experiences with computers and the Internet. Is access to pornography as difficult to block as Trebilcock implies? Will Wilkins's ideas for parental control work? How does the issue relate to broader conceptual arguments over technology? In what ways are the problems identified in this issue related to problems in other media, such as pornographic books and magazines? In what ways do they differ? Is the revolution resulting from Internet communication creating more serious crime problems?

YES

Julia Wilkins

Protecting Our Children
from Internet Smut

The term *moral panic* is one of the more useful concepts to have emerged from sociology in recent years. A moral panic is characterized by a wave of public concern, anxiety, and fervor about something, usually perceived as a threat to society. The distinguishing factors are a level of interest totally out of proportion to the real importance of the subject, some individuals building personal careers from the pursuit and magnification of the issue, and the replacement of reasoned debate with witchhunts and hysteria.

Moral panics of recent memory include the Joseph McCarthy anti-communist witchhunts of the 1950s and the satanic ritual abuse allegations of the 1980s. And, more recently, we have witnessed a full-blown moral panic about pornography on the Internet. Sparked by the July 3, 1995, *Time* cover article "On a Screen Near You: Cyberporn," this moral panic has been perpetuated and intensified by a raft of subsequent media reports. As a result, there is now a widely held belief that pornography is easily accessible to all children using the Internet. This was also the judgment of Congress, which, proclaiming to be "protecting the children," voted overwhelmingly in 1996 for legislation to make it a criminal offense to the send "indecent" material over the Internet into people's computers.

The original *Time* article was based on its exclusive access to Marty Rimm's *Georgetown University Law Journal* paper, "Marketing Pornography on the Information Superhighway." Although published, the article had not received peer review and was based on an undergraduate research project concerning descriptions of images on adult bulletin board systems in the United States. Using the information in this paper, *Time* discussed the type of pornography available online, such as "pedophilia (nude pictures of children), hebephelia (youths) and . . . images of bondage, sadomasochism, urination, defecation, and sex acts with a barnyard full of animals." The article proposed that pornography of this nature is readily available to anyone who is even remotely computer literate and raised the stakes by offering quotes from worried parents who feared for their children's safety. It also presented the possibility that pornographic material could be mailed to children without their parents' knowledge. *Time*'s example was of a ten-year-old boy who supposedly received pornographic images in his e-mail

From Julia Wilkins, "Protecting Our Children from Internet Smut: Moral Duty or Moral Panic?" *The Humanist* (September/October 1997). Copyright © 1997 by Julia Wilkins. Reprinted by permission.

showing "10 thumbnail size pictures showing couples engaged in various acts of sodomy, heterosexual intercourse and lesbian sex." Naturally, the boy's mother was shocked and concerned, saying, "Children should not be subject to these images." *Time* also quoted another mother who said that she wanted her children to benefit from the vast amount of knowledge available on the Internet but was inclined not to allow access, fearing that her children could be "bombarded with X-rated pornography and [she] would know nothing about it."

From the outset, Rimm's report generated a lot of excitement—not only because it was reportedly the first published study of online pornography but also because of the secrecy involved in the research and publication of the article. In fact, the *New York Times* reported on July 24, 1995, that Marty Rimm was being investigated by his university, Carnegie Mellon, for unethical research and, as a result, would not be giving testimony to a Senate hearing on Internet pornography. Two experts from *Time* reportedly discovered serious flaws in Rimm's study involving gross misrepresentation and erroneous methodology. His work was soon deemed flawed and inaccurate, and *Time* recanted in public. With Rimm's claims now apologetically retracted, his original suggestion that 83.5 percent of Internet graphics are pornographic was quietly withdrawn in favor of a figure less than 1 percent.

Time admitted that grievous errors had slipped past their editorial staff, as their normally thorough research succumbed to a combination of deadline pressure and exclusivity agreements that barred them from showing the unpublished study to possible critics. But, by then, the damage had been done: the study had found its way to the Senate.

Government Intervention

Senator Charles Grassely (Republican–Iowa) jumped on the pornography bandwagon by proposing a bill that would make it a criminal offense to supply or permit the supply of "indecent" material to minors over the Internet. Grassley introduced the entire *Time* article into the congressional record, despite the fact that the conceptual, logical, and methodological flaws in the report had already been acknowledged by the magazine.

On the Senate floor, Grassley referred to Marty Rimm's undergraduate research as "a remarkable study conducted by researchers at Carnegie Mellon University" and went on to say:

> The university surveyed 900,000 computer images. Of these 900,000 images, 83.5 percent of all computerized photographs available on the Internet are pornographic. . . . With so many graphic images available on computer networks, I believe Congress must act and do so in a constitutional manner to help parents who are under assault in this day and age.

Under the Grassley bill, later known as the Protection of Children from Pornography Act of 1995, it would have been illegal for anyone knowingly or recklessly transmit indecent material to minors. This bill marked the beginning of a stream of Internet censorship legislation at various levels of government in the United States and abroad.

The most extreme and fiercely opposed of these was the Communications Decency Act, sponsored by former Senator James Exon (Democrat–Nebraska) and Senator Dan Coats (Republican–Indiana). The CDA labeled the transmission of "obscene, lewd, lascivious, filthy, indecent, or patently offensive" pornography over the Internet a crime. It was attached to the Telecommunications Reform Act of 1996, which was then passed by Congress on February 1, 1996. One week later, it was signed into law by President Clinton. On the same day, the American Civil Liberties Union filed suit in Philadelphia against the U.S. Department of Justice and Attorney General Janet Reno, arguing that the statute would ban free speech protected by the First Amendment and subject Internet users to far greater restrictions than exist in any other medium. Later that month, the Citizens Internet Empowerment Coalition initiated a second legal challenge to the CDA, which formally consolidated with *ACLU v. Reno*. Government lawyers agreed not to prosecute "indecent" or "patently offensive" material until the three-judge court in Philadelphia ruled on the case.

Although the purpose of the CDA was to protect young children from accessing and viewing material of sexually explicit content on the Internet, the wording of the act was so broad and poorly defined that it could have deprived many adults of information they needed in the areas of health, art, news, and literature—information that is legal in print form. Specifically, certain medical information available on the Internet includes descriptions of sexual organs and activities which might have been considered "indecent" or "patently offensive" under the act—for example, information on breastfeeding, birth control, AIDS, and gynecological and urinological information. Also, many museums and art galleries now have websites. Under the act, displaying art like the Sistine Chapel nudes could be cause for criminal prosecution. Online newspapers would not be permitted to report the same information as is available in print media. Reports on combatants in war, at the scenes of crime, in the political arena, and outside abortion clinics often provoke images or language that could be constituted "offensive" and therefore illegal on the net. Furthermore, the CDA provided a legal basis for banning books which had been ruled unconstitutional to ban from school libraries. These include many of the classics as well as modern literature containing words that may be considered "indecent."

The act also expanded potential liability for employers, service providers, and carriers that transmit or otherwise make available restricted communications. According to the CDA, "knowingly" allowing obscene material to pass through one's computer system was a criminal offense. Given the nature of the Internet, however, making service providers responsible for the content of the traffic they pass on to other Internet nodes is equivalent to holding a telephone carrier responsible for the content of the conversations going over that carrier's lines. So, under the terms of the act, if someone sent an indecent electronic comment from a workstation, the employer, the e-mail service provider, and the carrier all could be potentially held liable and subject to up to $100,000 in fines or two years in prison.

On June 12, 1996, after experiencing live tours of the Internet and hearing arguments about the technical and economical infeasibility of complying with the censorship law, the three federal judges in Philadelphia granted the request for a preliminary injunction against the CDA. The court determined that "there is no evidence that sexually oriented material is the primary type of content on this new medium" and proposed that "communications over the Internet do not 'invade' an individual's home or appear on one's computer screen unbidden. Users seldom encounter content 'by accident.'" In a unanimous decision, the judges ruled that the Communications Decency Act would unconstitutionally restrict free speech on the Internet.

The government appealed the judges' decision and, on March 19, 1997, the U.S. Supreme Court heard oral arguments in the legal challenge to the CDA, now known as *Reno v. ACLU*. Finally, on June 26, the decision came down. The Court voted unanimously that the act violated the First Amendment guarantee of freedom of speech and would have threatened "to torch a large segment of the Internet community."

Is the panic therefore over? Far from it. The July 7, 1997, *Newsweek*, picking up the frenzy where *Time* left off, reported the Supreme Court decision in a provocatively illustrated article featuring a color photo of a woman licking her lips and a warning message taken from the website of the House of Sin. Entitled "On the Net, Anything Goes," the opening words by Steven Levy read, "Born of a hysteria triggered by a genuine problem—the ease with which wired-up teenagers can get hold of nasty pictures on the Internet—the Communications Decency Act (CDA) was never really destined to be a companion piece to the Bill of Rights." At the announcement of the Court's decision, anti-porn protesters were on the street outside brandishing signs which read, "Child Molesters Are Looking for Victims on the Internet."

Meanwhile, government talk has shifted to the development of a universal Internet rating system and widespread hardware and software filtering. Referring to the latter, White House Senior Adviser Rahm Emanuel declared, "We're going to get the V-chip for the Internet. Same goal, different means."

But it is important to bear in mind that children are still a minority of Internet users. A contract with an Internet service provider typically needs to be paid for by credit card or direct debit, therefore requiring the intervention of an adult. Children are also unlikely to be able to view any kind of porn online without a credit card.

In addition to this, there have been a variety of measures developed to protect children on the Internet. The National Center for Missing and Exploited Children has outlined protective guidelines for parents and children in its pamphlet, *Child Safety on the Information Superhighway*. A number of companies now sell Internet newsfeeds and web proxy accesses that are vetted in accordance with a list of forbidden topics. And, of course, there remain those blunt software instruments that block access to sexually oriented sites by looking for keywords such as *sex, erotic,* and *X-rated*. But one of the easiest solutions is to keep the family computer in a well-traveled space, like a living room, so that parents can monitor what their children download.

Fact or Media Fiction?

In her 1995 *CMC* magazine article, "Journey to the Centre of Cybersmut," Lisa Schmeiser discusses her research into online pornography. After an exhaustive search, she was unable to find any pornography, apart from the occasional commercial site (requiring a credit card for access), and concluded that one would have to undertake extensive searching to find quantities of explicit pornography. She suggested that, if children were accessing pornography online, they would not have been doing it by accident. Schmeiser writes: "There will be children who circumvent passwords, Surfwatch software, and seemingly innocuous links to find the 'adult' material. But these are the same kids who would visit every convenience store in a five-mile radius to find the one stocking *Playboy*." Her argument is simply that, while there is a certain amount of pornography online, it is not freely and readily available. Contrary to what the media often report, pornography is not that easy to find.

There *is* pornography in cyberspace (including images, pictures, movies, sounds, and sex discussions) and several ways of receiving pornographic material on the Internet (such as through private bulletin board systems, the World Wide Web, newsgroups, and e-mail). However, many sites just contain reproduced images from hardcore magazines and videos available from other outlets, and registration fee restrictions make them inaccessible to children. And for the more contentious issue of pedophilia, a recent investigation by the *Guardian* newspaper in Britain revealed that the majority of pedophilic images distributed on the Internet are simply electronic reproductions of the small output of legitimate pedophile magazines, such as *Lolita*, published in the 1970s.

Clearly the issue of pornography on the Internet is a moral panic—an issue perpetuated by a sensationalistic style of reporting and misleading content in newspaper and magazine articles. And probably the text from which to base any examination of the possible link between media reporting and moral panics is Stanley Cohen's 1972 book, *Folk Devils and Moral Panic*, in which he proposes that the mass media are ultimately responsible for the creation of such panics. Cohen describes a moral panic as occurring when "a condition, episode, person or group of persons emerges to become a threat to societal values and interest; . . . the moral barricades are manned by editors . . . politicians and other 'right thinking' people." He feels that, while problematical elements of society can pose a threat to others, this threat is realistically far less than the perceived image generated by mass media reporting.

Cohen describes how the news we read is not necessarily the truth; editors have papers to sell, targets to meet, and competition from other publishers. It is in their interest to make the story "a good read"—the sensationalist approach sells newspapers. The average person is likely to be drawn in with the promise of scandal and intrigue. This can be seen in the reporting of the *National Enquirer* and *People*, with their splashy pictures and sensationalistic headlines, helping them become two of the largest circulation magazines in the United States.

Cohen discusses the "inventory" as the set of criteria inherent in any reporting that may be deemed as fueling a moral panic. This inventory consists of the following:

Exaggeration in reporting   Facts are often overblown to give the story a greater edge. Figures that are not necessarily incorrect but have been quoted out of context, or have been used incorrectly to shock, are two forms of this exaggeration.

Looking back at the original *Time* cover article, "On a Screen Near You: Cyberporn," this type of exaggeration is apparent. Headlines such as "The Carnegie Mellon researchers found 917,410 sexually explicit pictures, short stories and film clips online" make the reader think that there really is a problem with the quantity of pornography in cyberspace. It takes the reader a great deal of further exploration to find out how this figure was calculated. Also, standing alone and out of context, the oft-quoted figure that 83.5 percent of images found on Usenet Newsgroups are pornographic could be seen as cause for concern. However, if one looks at the math associated with this figure, one would find that this is a sampled percentage with a research leaning toward known areas of pornography.

The repetition of fallacies   This occurs when a writer reports information that seems perfectly believable to the general public, even though those who know the subject are aware it is wildly incorrect. In the case of pornography, the common fallacy is that the Internet is awash with nothing but pornography and that all you need to obtain it is a computer and a modem. Such misinformation is integral to the fueling of moral panics.

Take, for example, the October 18, 1995, *Scotland on Sunday*, which reports that, to obtain pornographic material, "all you need is a personal computer, a phone line with a modem attached and a connection via a specialist provider to the Internet." What the article fails to mention is that the majority of pornography is found on specific Usenet sites not readily available from the major Internet providers, such as America Online and Compuserve. It also fails to mention that this pornography needs to be downloaded and converted into a viewable form, which requires certain skills and can take considerable time.

Misleading pictures and snappy titles   Media representation often exaggerates a story through provocative titles and flashy pictorials—all in the name of drawing in the reader. The titles set the tone for the rest of the article; the headline is the most noticeable and important part of any news item, attracting the reader's initial attention. The recent *Newsweek* article is a perfect example. Even if the headline has little relevance to the article, it sways the reader's perception of the topic. The symbolization of images further increases the impact of the story. *Time*'s own images in its original coverage—showing a shocked little boy on the cover and, inside, a naked man hunched over a computer monitor—added to the article's ability to shock and to draw the reader into the story.

Through sensationalized reporting, certain forms of behavior become classified as *deviant.* Specifically, those who put pornography online or those who download it are seen as being deviant in nature. This style of reporting benefits the publication or broadcast by giving it the aura of "moral guardian" to the rest of society. It also increases revenue.

In exposing deviant behavior, newspapers and magazines have the ability to push for reform. So, by classifying a subject and its relevant activities as deviant, they can stand as crusaders for moral decency, championing the cause of "normal" people. They can report the subject and call for something to be done about it, but this power is easily abused. The *Time* cyberporn article called for reform on the basis of Rimm's findings, proclaiming, "A new study shows us how pervasive and wild [pornography on the Internet] really is. Can we protect our kids—and free speech?" These cries to protect our children affected the likes of Senators James Exon and Robert Dole, who took the *Time* article with its "shocking" revelations (as well as a sample of pornographic images) to the Senate floor, appealing for changes to the law. From this response it is clear how powerful a magazine article can be, regardless of the integrity and accuracy of its reporting.

The *Time* article had all of Cohen's elements relating to the fueling of a moral panic: exaggeration, fallacies, and misleading pictures and titles. Because certain publications are highly regarded and enjoy an important role in society, anything printed in their pages is consumed and believed by a large audience. People accept what they read because, to the best of their knowledge, it is the truth. So, even though the *Time* article was based on a report by an undergraduate student passing as "a research team from Carnegie Mellon," the status of the magazine was great enough to launch a panic that continues unabated— from the halls of Congress to the pulpits of churches, from public schools to the offices of software developers, from local communities to the global village.

Child Molesters on the Internet

Like many parents of young children, I'd read the headlines about pedophiles trying to seduce kids and swapping pornography on the Internet. This sort of deviant behavior, I assumed, must lurk in deep, all-but-impenetrable recesses of cyberspace. But when I got this assignment to report on the 'Net's red-light district, I decided to see what an on-line novice like myself could find.

Armed with a hint or two from a computer consultant, I turned on the standard-issue computer in my family room and clicked on Usenet, a section of the World Wide Web, where anyone can post or access messages and photographs related to a specific topic, and typed in the words "alt.sex.incest." In less than a minute, I was scrolling through hundreds of brief tent messages from guys who offered to swap photographs or described their sexual fantasies with children. One message was repeated four times: "subject: Re: z9 × 7 I lookin' 4 cindys series. . . ." I clicked my mouse.

The text came up quickly, a request for a series of photos. "I only have cindy 1, 2, 8, 15, 17 . . . if someone can repost 'em all . . . thanx."

Underneath was a reply from another user: "Here's 3, 4, and 5. Enjoy! Rick." Below the text, a color image appeared on my screen, slowly unrolling from top to bottom like a window blind. As the first image formed, I took a sharp, deep breath. At the top of the photo, a pair of chubby, dimpled knees was spread apart. Naked from the waist down, Cindy was lying on her back, legs apart. It was a typical centerfold pose, but Cindy was no typical centerfold model. She was not much older than 6.

Eleven more shots formed on my screen, the same little girl performing oral sex on an adult male. As I exited the file, my hands were shaking and my stomach was churning.

I looked at my watch. In less than 15 minutes, without any special software or expert knowledge, I'd found a deviant world without sexual boundaries, one that could be located by curious teenagers and potential child molesters alike. Though I called the police to report what I'd seen, I still didn't sleep well that night. Who was Cindy? Who was forcing her to do those things? And, given the rash of recent headlines about computer-related sex crimes, is any child safe from sexual exploitation in the age of the mouse and the modem?

Make no mistake about it: The Internet is a powerful tool that levels the information playing field. On-line in your home, you can view the Louvre's art collection, chat with David Bowie on his fiftieth birthday, and access research from top academic institutions across the country. No wonder the 'Net is growing so explosively. In just three years, America Online, the largest commercial service provider, has expanded from 1 million to 8 million households, and, globally, 30 million people are estimated to be logging on-line.

Granted, the vast majority of what's on the Internet is entertaining, informative, if not educational. But the 'Net does have a dark side. "I call the Internet the playground of the nineties for pedophiles," says Donna Rice Hughes, director of marketing and communications for Enough Is Enough, a Fairfax, Virginia, nonprofit group that campaigns to make the Internet safe for children.

Hughes may have a point. In addition to housing pictures of dozens of children, like the ones of Cindy, the Internet has spawned sites featuring snapshots of children—unwittingly photographed while at play in parks and at the beach—who serve as pedophiles' love objects; kids-only chat rooms where child molesters prowl; and electronic support groups in which "boy-lovers" validate each other's most disturbed impulses.

Could these pedophiles be reaching right into your home via the family PC? What are authorities doing to regulate this booming and, at times, unsettling new forum? And what can you, as a parent, do to protect your children?

Can We Talk? The Danger of Chat Rooms

"How old are u?"

The words appeared simultaneously on screens in New Hampshire and California.

"I am 14," the user in California replied.

"love to do u then," the man in New Hampshire typed.

"I would like that," the boy replied.

The man's name was Alan Hicks. A 46-year-old mechanical engineer and one-time Big Brother, Hicks was also a convicted pedophile who had served time for molesting young boys. After his release on parole, Hicks joined a treatment group and agreed to make a training film about his life for the benefit of law enforcement officials.

He also discovered the Internet. During one year on-line, he befriended numerous boys in chat rooms. When the boys were willing, Hicks took the conversations private, where he talked graphically about sex and E-mailed pornographic photos. In return, he asked for favors—a pair of underwear, even samples of boys' urine and semen.

"WHY PEDOPHILES GO ON-LINE": ONE CONVICT'S STORY

"Child pornography is the pedophile's rock cocaine. It's a quick fix. It's cheap, and thanks to the Internet, it's everywhere."

The speaker's name is "Bob," and he's a computer expert in his forties. He's also a recovering pedophile who has spent 20 years on the wrong side of the law. Talking to me by phone from a southern state he will not identify, Bob says he's watched the explosive growth of pedophiles on the Internet from both sides of the fence.

Why is the Internet so enticing for pedophiles? "It's created easily accessible stimulation for child molesters," says Bob. "You can download pictures in complete anonymity. You do not have to make any kind of human contact."

Anonymity is so crucial, says Bob, because your average pedophile "is not the dirty old man in a trench coat, but a teacher at your local elementary school. The Internet becomes his outlet."

Bob acknowledges that chat rooms pose the greatest physical danger to your child on-line. However, he notes, "On the computer, the search for a victim is an arduous task that's fraught with danger due to the intensity of law enforcement."

"Besides," he adds, "victims are too easy to find in other places." Successful pedophiles, he explains, "are better with your children than you are. They give them more attention. They are your swim coach, your Sunday school teacher—people you trust to come into contact with your child every single day."

Which children, I ask, were safe from these predators? Kids who got a lot of love, attention, and time from their parents, Bob said, were least likely to be curious about what another adult might offer.

Hicks would probably still be on-line today if he hadn't sent a nude photo of himself to a police informant who turned it over to James McLaughlin, a Keene, New Hampshire, police detective currently working with federal authorities on a nationwide probe of child exploitation on the Internet. By coincidence, Detective McLaughlin recognized Hicks from that training film he made, and helped return him to jail last November.

The Hicks case illustrates the most palpable danger to children on-line: child molesters lurking in chat rooms devoted to innocent subjects like sports and music. "Ultimately," McLaughlin says, "pedophiles will try to get the kids to agree to phone or mail contact, and then arrange for a meeting."

The scary truth is, some succeed. Last November, Cary Bodenheimer, a 30-year-old engineer for a major aircraft manufacturer in the Philadelphia area, pled guilty to having had sex in an Illinois motel room with a 13-year-old girl he had met over the Internet. A year earlier, James Heigh, 29, of Keizer, Oregon, was convicted of third-degree rape after he met a 14-year-old girl on-line, engaged her in lengthy phone calls, and then had sex with her.

Granted, the number of cases is relatively small, and only 23 incidents involving chat rooms were reported between 1994 and 1996, according to the National Center for Missing and Exploited Children. But warns J. Robert Flores, senior trial attorney with the Department of Justice Child Exploitation and Obscenity Section, "This is a new crime that's just three or four years old. Not all law enforcement agencies are reporting their numbers."

Insidiously, these overtures by pedophiles are often made while mom and dad are in the next room, pleased that their child is learning to use the computer rather than watching mindless TV. Teens, for their part, are often bolder on-line than they would be in the real world. "Sex is on the minds of a lot of 12- and 13-year-olds," says Gary Hewitt, a psychotherapist in Rochester, New York, who has worked with children who were abducted and exploited by strangers. "They'll go on-line and open up. A pedophile will then tell that child whatever he or she wants to hear to bond with them."

To safeguard children from these anonymous predators, America Online has added guards to monitor the kids-only chat rooms for suspicious dialogue. A good first step, but private messages—invisible to the rest of the chat room—cannot be screened, and that's where a pedophile is likely to begin forging a relationship with a child.

Experts agree that the best way to keep your child safe in cyberspace is the same as keeping your child safe in the real world: parental involvement. Says Sergeant Nick Battaglia, former supervisor of the child exploitation unit of the San Jose Police Department, and an expert on computer-related sex crimes, "Just like you wouldn't let your child play alone in an urban park for three hours, you shouldn't let them play alone on the Internet."

Battaglia urges parents to keep the computer in a central location, limit how much time your child spends on-line, and educate yourself about the technology so you can monitor what your child is doing. Most critically, go on-line with your child as often as possible to help her identify inappropriate requests, and emphasize that people encountered in chat rooms are strangers, just like the ones you've warned them about in the real world. Finally, insist that your child never give out personal information—home address, phone number, school name—on-line without first asking your permission, and never agree to meet someone in person without a parent being present.

Kiddie Porn's New Life On-Line

While on-line chat rooms pose a new threat to our children, authorities also credit the Internet with reviving an old foe: child pornography. The problem is pressing enough that the FBI formed the "Innocent Images" task force, a three-year undercover investigation focusing on the use of on-line computer services to distribute kiddie porn which has led to about 70 felony convictions. But to be candid, FBI spokesperson Larry Foust admits, they have only scratched the surface.

Indeed, it's never been a better time to be a pedophile: The Internet has opened up a new, anonymous way for pedophiles to exchange and expand their collections of porn, says Don Huycke, program manager of the Child Pornography Enforcement Program for the U.S. Customs Service, the long-standing experts in kiddie porn, since so much of it has been produced overseas. "They'll say: I want two little girls age 6 to 9 having sex. We find guys making 40 to 50 downloads per night of child pornography."

The resurgence of kiddie porn marks an end to one of law enforcement's success stories. In 1982, a Supreme Court decision approved the ban on the distribution of material depicting children engaged in sexual conduct, virtually shutting down the U.S. kiddie porn industry by the end of the decade. By

1993, all that had changed with the mushrooming popularity of the internet: In the last fiscal year, the number of search warrants issued by Customs involving child pornography increased by 220 percent, with the majority of those cases involving the use of computers. Though most child pornography on-line has been culled from magazines produced in the seventies and early eighties, some experts hint that the Internet encourages new images to be created. Thanks to new technology, like digital cameras, porn can be produced directly on-line, without leaving the literal paper trail that photos do when developed and published.

Child porn is dangerous, the experts say, not just because kids are molested during the production but because pedophiles use the images to convince children that sex with adults is enjoyable and natural. What's more, mental health professionals worry about the long-term impact of child pornography on the Internet. Says David N. Greenfield, Ph.D., a Hartford, Connecticut, psychologist who has studied the phenomenon of Internet addiction, "I'm concerned about kids being exposed to this material when they are too young to realize it's an unrealistic portrayal of sexual behavior. Seeing child pornography on the 'Net legitimizes it, which is dangerous."

Can anything be done to wipe this sort of material off the Internet? Authorities hope so. Last year, Congress passed the Communications Decency Act, which prohibits the knowing distribution of indecent material to minors by computer. A bill introduced by Senator Orrin G. Hatch, which passed in September 1996, makes it illegal to produce "morphed" child pornography, in which perfectly innocent pictures of children are altered by computer to show them engaged in sex acts, say, by grafting the head of a child onto the body of a nude, slender adult.

Enforcing the law, however, is the real challenge. Given the millions of web sites—and the ability of pedophiles to encrypt photos, or put them in a code that can only be translated with special software—most police departments are ill-equipped to find such pornography. Until the police catch up with the child pornographers, parents can rely on "net nanny" software programs (similar to the V-chip for your television set) to control the sites a child can browse on the web. Some service providers, such as America Online, perform the same function.

Could My Child's Photo Be on the 'Net?

More alarmingly, authorities are finding that even children with absolutely no connection to child pornography are turning up on-line as love objects for pedophiles. Consider the case of George Chamberlain, a 56-year-old pedophile serving a 35-year sentence in Minnesota for child sexual assault. In 1995, authorities seized a prison computer used by Chamberlain as part of a computer programming and telemarketing business run by prison inmates. Connected to the information superhighway, he also swapped child pornography and E-mail messages with other pedophiles on the Internet.

Worse still, investigators discovered a list stored on computer with the names, ages, and addresses of 3,000 children, culled from seemingly harmless listings in local newspapers. Though Chamberlain denied compiling the names, to investigators, they looked like a virtual catalog of potential abuse victims. The list's mere existence raises the question: Could my child be on the Internet without my knowledge?

Though unlikely, the answer is yes. Circulating in Usenet groups are photos of fully clothed cheerleaders, gymnasts, and little girls at play, snapped by pedophiles' cameras and posted in files labeled "erotica"—clearly, someone's fantasy material. On the World Wide Web, some sites created by self-described "boy-lovers"—men infatuated with young or teenage boys—receive almost a quarter-million visitors in a given four-month period. Visit the "Boys in the Real World" site to see photos of prepubescent boys at play taken at Disneyland , Sea World, and the San Diego Zoo. At ComQuest Boys, a message by the web page's producer describes how he took his photos of boys frolicking on a Santa Monica beach: "I had to get within about 12 feet of my unsuspecting subjects in order to fill the frame, which is a challenge to say the least. If I . . . visit a beach . . . again, I hope to get beautiful boys to volunteer to be photographed and show their smiling faces and newly forming muscles."

Authorities stress that these photos serve solely as fantasy material for pedophiles who are unlikely to try to find or make contact with the children depicted. Yet, as a cop and a parent, Nick Battaglia admits, "Those sites are very upsetting, because someone's taking your privacy and exploiting your child." Unfortunately, he adds, "there's nothing illegal about it." And there's very little you can do to protect your family, beyond confronting anyone who seems to be taking inappropriate photos of your—or anyone else's—child.

How Child Molesters Network in Cyberspace

Beyond trading fantasy material, pedophiles have even formed on-line support groups, in which they bolster one another's egos and share tips. "Boy-lovers with integrity and courage can use the resources of the Internet . . . to break through the boundaries that others would impose in this culture," asserts the NAMBLA Bulletin, the voice of the North American Man/Boy Love Association. In the past, pedophiles were fundamentally an isolated group. Thanks to the Internet, that's changing—and fast—as pedophile support groups spring up on-line. One site, alt.support.boy-lovers, provides answers to frequently asked questions like "What do boy-lovers feel?" and recommends literary works with a boy-lover theme, such as Thomas Mann's *Death in Venice*. The site's mission: to provide acceptance "for boy-lovers who do not consider themselves in need of conversion to an orientation other than their natural one."

The quest for acceptance is precisely what concerns law enforcement officers and mental health professionals. Chris Hatcher, Ph.D., a clinical professor of psychology at the University of California in San Francisco who studies pedophiles and child abductors, has coined the phrase "virtual validation" to describe the burgeoning network of pedophiles on-line. "They're able to be in contact with sometimes hundreds of other people with similar beliefs," explains Dr. Hatcher. "That is a level of validation they were never able to obtain before."

Coupled with the availability of child pornography on the 'Net, Dr. Hatcher argues that the virtual validation pedophiles find on-line may encourage someone who has not yet molested a child to do so. "Pedophiles who make contact with children have a developmental pattern," says Dr. Hatcher. It begins with fantasy, moves to gratification through pornography, then voyeurism, and finally to contact. "The 'Net accelerates that pattern. It gives them a level of virtual validation that would have otherwise taken years to obtain." Adds Gary Hewitt, "The support group sites give pedophiles a real sense of power, and the impetus to go out and molest someone." Protected by First Amendment rights, these cyberspace support-group sites are difficult to restrict.

What's Next?

Last April, a 10-year-old girl was invited to a slumber party at the home of another little girl in Greenfield, California. What her parents didn't know: The friend's father, Ronald Riva, was a member of the Orchid Club, an on-line group of men who met in pedophile chat rooms and used the Internet to swap pornography and true-life stories of child molestation.

That night, Riva and another club member, who was visiting, awoke the girl, then fondled her in front of a digital camera attached to a computer. The images of her molestation were broadcast to other members of the group, who watched the live event on their computers and responded interactively, typing in what they'd like to see happen next.

This shocking crime led to an investigation by U.S. Customs and other agencies, ending in the indictments of 16 members of the Orchid Club. The first known example of pedophiles using the Internet for real-life abuse of a child, the Orchid club might be a barometer of where we are headed on the Internet.

Most experts agree that the Internet phenomenon is still too new to predict the future danger to children. As more people become familiar with the 'Net, and the potential dangers of this otherwise positive medium, kids may be safer than ever. Or the threat could snowball. Technology like digital cameras and video conferencing that download images directly into the computer may create more homegrown child pornography, as in the Orchid Club case.

Despite the high-tech wizardry employed by the Orchid Club members, the case serves as a cautionary reminder about how pedophiles always have— and probably always will—operate. The 10-year-old victim met her molesters in the neighborhood. Observes Burt G. Hollenbeck Jr., Ph.D., a New Hampshire psychologist who has treated around 400 pedophiles, "The focus on computers as a threat to our children obscures the fact that the real danger is in our backyards. As a society, we'd rather think the molester is some faceless guy at a computer terminal. But, every guy at a PC has another identity. He's also grandpa, the teacher, or our next-door neighbor."

POSTSCRIPT

Are the Dangers of Internet Child Pornography Exaggerated?

Wilkins identifies notable exaggerations of Internet smut dangers, including the 1995 *Time* story alleging that "83.5 percent of Internet graphics are pornographic." Some suggest that an unfortunate result of living in a highly moralized and politicized age is that people who should know better will resort to lies to make their points. Yet Trebilcock is correct that serious cases of child cyberporn and other sex problems are surfacing on the Internet. These include virtually all of the traditional kiddie porn practices as well as Internet innovations such as "morphed" pornography and chat-room conversations that become private and obscene.

Are parent-level practices such as keeping the home computer in plain view, utilizing "nanny nets" to block objectionable material on the Internet, and explaining to youngsters potential dangers and trusting them not to take risks (e.g., giving out their names or phone numbers) enough? Many insist that they are, especially with vigorous enforcement. Some, such as *Wired* magazine editor Jon Katz, say that we do our children a disservice by not trusting them, after proper training, to use the Internet wisely. Some people note that when shopping over the Internet began—especially shopping for big-ticket items that required immediate payment by credit card—corporations were quick to develop controls to prevent card numbers from becoming public. Otherwise, potential customers would be fearful of shopping over the Internet, and on-line sales would cease. Can the same type of thing be done for pornography? For example, a current federal bill proposes to cut off funds for public libraries that do not put effective content filters in their computers. Would such a law effectively screen children from Internet pornography?

Among the rapidly growing literature on children, pornography, and the Internet is the Office of Juvenile Justice and Delinquency Prevention report *Use of Computers in the Sexual Exploitation of Children* by D. Armagh, N. Battaglia, and K. Lanning (June 1, 1999). Summaries of recent legal clarifications include "Ninth Circuit Strikes Federal 'Virtual' Child Pornography Law on First Amendment Grounds," *Criminal Justice Weekly* (December 21, 1999). Among the many debates over library censorship are M. Herring, "X-Rated Libraries," *Weekly Standard* (July 12, 1999) and "The Case for Censorship," by D. Lowenthal, as well as several rebuttals to Lowenthal, *Weekly Standard* (August 23, 1999). Also see Wendy Kaminer's attack on censorship in "The Politics of Sanctimony," *The American Prospect* (November 23, 1999).

Correctional Service of Canada

The Correctional Service of Canada (CSC), as part of the criminal justice system and respecting the rule of law, contributes to the protection of society by actively encouraging and assisting offenders to become law-abiding citizens, while exercising reasonable, safe, secure, and humane control. Learn how the CSC operates, obtain facts and statistics about corrections in Canada, and find out about Canada's federal penetentiaries.

`http://www.csc-scc.gc.ca/text/home_e.shtml`

Criminal Offenders Statistics

At this site, the U.S. Department of Justice's Bureau of Justice Statistics (BJS) provides a variety of statistics on criminal offenders, including characteristics of state prison inmates, recidivism rates, and statistics on women offenders. This site also links to BJS reports.

`http://www.ojp.usdoj.gov/bjs/crimoff.htm`

Koch Crime Institute

The Koch Crime Institute (KCI), based in Topeka, Kansas, is a nonpartisan organization that is committed to research and policy analysis that identifies and promotes meaningful strategies in crime reduction and prevention. The KCI consults and partners with communities, other states, organizations, and well-known institutions that are interested in fighting crime in the most effective and economical ways possible.

`http://www.kci.org`

HIV InSite: Prisons

This HIV InSite page provides numerous categorized links to statistics, news reports, legal cases, and organizations related to HIV and prisons. Categories include epidemiology, sexual assault, policy and legal materials, compassionate release, women in prisons, global dimensions, and more.

`http://hivinsite.ucsf.edu/topics/prisons/`

PART 3

Prison Programs and Alternatives

*S*ince *the 1950s scholars have supported the idea that imprisonment, especially for the young, should be avoided. If incarceration is required, according to this viewpoint, then it should be for the purpose of rehabilitation, not punishment, deterrence, or incapacitation. Yet today America's fear of crime is extremely high, and U.S. incarceration rates are greater than they have ever been. As a result, the penal issues have shifted dramatically. The presence of AIDS, the notorious recidivism rates, and other factors have changed the rules, if not the incarceration game itself. What should be done to imprisoned offenders, particularly those who will probably assault again or worse upon release?*

- Is the Segregation of HIV-Positive Inmates Ethical?

- Are Conjugal and Familial Visitations Effective Rehabilitative Concepts?

- Should Serial Killers and Violent Sexual Predators Be Quarantined for Life?

ISSUE 10

Is the Segregation of HIV-Positive Inmates Ethical?

YES: Penny A. Robinette, from "Is the Segregation of HIV-Positive Inmates Ethical? Yes," *The Prison Journal* (March 1999)

NO: Billy Long, from "Is the Segregation of HIV-Positive Inmates Ethical? No," *The Prison Journal* (March 1999)

ISSUE SUMMARY

YES: Penny A. Robinette, an administrator at Presbyterian Child Welfare Services in Richmond, Kentucky, contends that riskier behavior, significantly higher increases in AIDS cases, and the difficulties of controlling and treating AIDS within America's prisons all justify mandatory testing and segregation of HIV-positive inmates.

NO: Assistant professor of criminal justice Billy Long argues that the risks and incidence of AIDS in prisons have been greatly exaggerated. Moreover, she contends, mandatory testing and segregation of inmates will have more negative than positive consequences.

Historically, there have been many philosophical justifications for incarcerating society's criminals. The major ones include deterrence, incapacitation, and retribution. The guilty have wronged society, so they should be punished, according to this prevalent view. A fourth reason that, until recently, was pre-dominant among progressive scholars and administrators is incarceration for rehabilitation and treatment; that is, prisons would function to help offenders through drug programs, education, occupational training, teaching of interactional skills, and so on. Although it looked good theoretically, the latter fell far short in most training schools and prisons. Treatment programs, even when they existed, often could do little to overcome the many negative influences of an inmate's life prior to imprisonment nor could they neutralize the many negative aspects of the prison itself, including punitive guards and the inmate subcultures. In many states, with the drastic cut-back of funding for rehabilitation, there was sometimes not even a pretense of rehabilitation.

Yet it has never been the avowed goal of most prison systems to intentionally cause physical or psychological harms, although prisons frequently do exactly that. The criminal justice equivalent of the medical problem of iatrogenic outcomes (physician-induced illness) has usually been less visible. In addition, while society has not followed exactly the utilitarian norm of "the greatest good for the greatest number," all social systems will do things to protect themselves and to ensure survival against perceived threats.

Medically, quarantining patients with deadly, contagious diseases, requiring youngsters and others to be innoculated against dangerous illnesses, and regulating foods, drugs, and plants that might carry disease have been common practices for years. Indeed, some worry that citizens are now being overly medicalized to the point that individual freedoms are unnecessarily being taken away.

The issue of testing and segregating prison inmates on the basis of being seropositive for human immunodeficiency virus (HIV) combines both philosophies of incarceration concerns and medical control problems. On the one hand is the medical problem of how to help sick people more effectively. To do this, the sick people must first be identified. If their illnesses are contagious and potentially deadly, then others should be protected. On the other hand, especially in terms of HIV-positive prison inmates, are the questions of whether or not knowing who they are is really necessary and whether or not these prisoners, even those with full-blown acquired immunodeficiency syndrome (AIDS), are necessarily medically better off in isolation.

Does forcing sick inmates into segregation unduly add to their punishment? Or, asking the other side of the question, does allowing AIDS victims to share cells with healthy inmates unfairly add to the punishment of the noninfected prisoners? Moreover, are guards being unfairly penalized by not being told which inmates have AIDS or by being forced to work with AIDS-infected inmates? Also, what is the most effective management strategy for dealing with prisoners with AIDS? If doing or not doing anything about inmates with AIDS might violate Eighth Amendment Rights (to not be subjected to cruel and unusual punishment), what liability factors need to be addressed? Who is likely to end up suing whom? Currently, the majority of prisons in the United States are under litigation, so this is a serious problem.

In the following selections, Penny A. Robinette argues that segregation of HIV-positive inmates is justified. Billy Long maintains that such segregation will have more negative effects than positive ones.

Penny A. Robinette

 **YES**

Is the Segregation of HIV-Positive Inmates Ethical?

Acquired Immunodeficiency Syndrome (AIDS) is a lethal communicable disease that reduces and inhibits the functioning of the immune system. Once contracted, this disease attacks the body's natural immune system making it susceptible to recurrent pneumonia, pulmonary tuberculosis, invasive cancers, and other debilitating and deadly illnesses. AIDS is caused by the Human Immunodeficiency Virus (HIV). HIV seropositivity can be detected through an individual blood test. HIV can be present long before any symptoms appear and, once detected, can continue for many years before leading to AIDS. There has not been research that can conclude that HIV positivity does not always develop into AIDS. HIV is transmitted through exchange of bodily fluid, but only specific and highly intrusive forms of exchange have been proven to transmit this virus. Those forms include blood transfusions, sexual intercourse, and use of previously infected hypodermic needles.

Prisoner Behavior and HIV

Prison inmates engage in more of the behaviors conducive to the transfer of this virus and engage in them more frequently than does the general population. A study by the Bureau of Justice Statistics found that between 1991 and 1995, one in three prisoner deaths was attributable to AIDS, whereas 1 in 10 died from AIDS in the general population (Maruschak, 1997). Risk factors within prison include needle sharing, anal intercourse, tattooing, history of multiple sexual partners, history of multiple sexually transmitted diseases, poor physical and mental health, and risk-taking personalities (Pagliaro & Pagliaro, 1992).

The greatest of these risk factors for the prison population is the use of contaminated needles. Due to an increase in mandatory sentencing guidelines for drug use, the prisons have seen an increase in numbers of intravenous (IV) drug users. A leading national study revealed that more than 50% of state prison inmates had used a major drug within the month previous to incarceration (Durham, 1994). These inmates will find ways to continue their drug use in prison. With the lack of availability of needles, it is more likely

From Penny A. Robinette, "Is the Segregation of HIV-Positive Inmates Ethical? Yes," *The Prison Journal*, vol. 79, no. 1 (March 1999). Copyright © 1999 by Sage Publications, Inc. Reprinted by permission.

that prisoners will share contaminated needles (Severson, 1993). This also supports the research that has indicated that female inmates are at a higher risk of contracting HIV in prison than males, with the use of shared needles being the greatest risk-taking behavior as opposed to homosexual activity. In 1995, 2.3% of all male state prisoners were confirmed HIV positive, whereas 4.0% of all female state prisoners were confirmed (Maruschak, 1997).

Homosexual activity in prison is a known risk behavior for its frequent association with violence and contraction of sexually transmitted diseases. Research has indicated that prevalence of homosexual activity for male inmates ranges from 30% to 60% (Durham, 1994). This sexual involvement does not hinge on sexual orientation as it does in the general population but most frequently is due to the gender-specific nature of prison facilities (Severson, 1993). Homosexual activity is especially dangerous to prison inmates because it is the most widely known risk behavior in both prison and general populations regarding the spread of HIV. Homosexual activity has been a growing basis for both discrimination and domination regarding inmates' HIV statuses.

The problems that are facing correctional services with regard to HIV/ AIDS in prison are not diminishing. The most common solutions discussed are testing of inmates, segregation of HIV-positive or AIDS inmates, and education for all inmates. Questions of care, treatment, and prevention are growing. Who should be tested for HIV seropositivity and who should be informed of the results? Should everyone testing positive be quarantined within the prison? Should inmates with full-blown AIDS be paroled? Is HIV a great enough risk that it warrants limiting the rights of an individual? What are the care and safety issues with regard to correctional staff? What are the prisons' responsibilities to the families and sexual partners of HIV-infected inmates?

The HIV-Positive Population in Prison

From 1991 to 1995, there was a 36% increase in the prison population. During that same time period, there was a 38% increase in the number of known HIV-positive prisoners (Maruschak, 1997). Only 16 state facilities mandate testing of all inmates at some time during their incarceration. The rate of increase of seropositivity could be even higher than 38%. According to the Bureau of Justice Statistics, in 1995 for every 100,000 inmates, 100 died of AIDS-related causes (Maruschak, 1997). There also has been some evidence to suggest that AIDS inmates are dying an average of 8 months before AIDS patients in the general population (Severson, 1993).

In 1994, 2.4% of the overall custody population of both state and federal prisons was reported to be HIV positive. In 1995, this percentage actually dropped to 2.3%. This difference is due to a decrease in the number of reported HIV-positive inmates in federal prisons. There are no federal facilities that mandate a blanket testing policy for inmates. The decrease reported by federal prisons is based on figures generated from testing based on voluntary requests, on clinical indicator referrals, and upon release of inmates. The percentage of state inmates with AIDS/HIV increased by 14% between 1993 and 1995 (Maruschak, 1997).

It has been shown that a significantly greater percentage of female inmates (4.0%) are contracting HIV than are males (2.3%). This rate was higher for women in every region and far greater than the majority of states. In the northeast region, five states reported rates of greater than 10% of female inmates known to be HIV positive. The statistics for women show an even more disproportionate trend when compared from 1991 to 1995 when male HIV positivity increased 28% and female HIV positivity increased 88% (Maruschak, 1997). The impact is complicated for facilities serving female inmates with HIV due to the increase of HIV-infected newborns (Prendergrast, 1997).

Those states with the highest reported percentage of HIV-positive male inmates included New York (13.9%), Connecticut (5.1%), and Rhode Island (4.4%). Actual numbers of AIDS cases within correctional facilities were also highest in New York (1,182), then Florida (692) and Texas (495).

Screening and Segregation

Due to the number of inmates who have been notably involved in high-risk behavior associated with the transference of HIV, increasing numbers of facilities are implementing some form of mass or blanket screening policy. Many of those facilities are overlapping those testing policies so that a particular inmate may, for example, be tested upon entrance, again upon evidence of high-risk behavior, and then again upon being released. Use of a blanket testing policy was recommended by the American Medical Association, and as much as 88% of the general population is in agreement (Blumberg & Langston, 1995). Blanket testing is seen as the most accurate means of identifying HIV-positive inmates. Even with the risk of false negatives and false positives, mass screening is the best indicator of who should be eligible for treatment.

Segregation has been proposed as an alternative for HIV-positive inmates for several reasons. T. M. Hammett disclosed the position in favor of segregation in a study from 1987 and 1988. Segregation allows identification of HIV-positive inmates and the ability to more closely monitor those inmates' health for treatment purposes (Vlahov, 1990). Observation of high-risk behaviors and an ability to target specific areas of education and counseling for inmates also are increased with segregation. The greatest purpose for segregation is to separate those known HIV-positive inmates from potentially spreading the virus to noninfected prisoners, but it also serves to protect the HIV-positive inmates from discrimination, which is commonly expressed with violence.

Testing and segregation are both sensible solutions for retarding the progression of AIDS within correctional facilities. It is the negative implementation of these programs, not the concept of segregation itself, that has prevented the success of segregation. Criticism has been introduced when segregation has been used as an opportunity to label, deny rights, and/or restrict services. It has been well documented that numerous HIV-positive and AIDS prisoners have been segregated in a discriminatory manner from all religious services, recreations, work opportunities, and early release time. Segregation for any prisoner testing positive for any communicable disease should only limit contact, not prisoners' rights. The concept of rights, however, must include not only the prisoners but also everyone who comes into contact with those prisoners, from other prisoners to prison employees to family members to the community upon those prisoners' release. Segregation used appropriately should reduce the risk of HIV/AIDS to all populations. It should not be used as a method of punishment or as a means of reduction of care for inmates. It should be coupled with education, medical treatment, and continuation of the level of care and services provided to other inmates as well as the provision of an educational component for the general prison population regarding communicable diseases.

Many opponents to testing and segregation have stated that voluntary testing and educational programs can work together to eliminate the spread of HIV more effectively. Studies using inmates who remain in the general prison population have found that only 85% of those who believe to have possibly contracted the disease consented to being tested. Only 66% elected to attend counseling and education programs (Carroll, 1992). Left to their own voluntary decisions to adhere to testing, the inmates who will not consent to testing are most fearful of the outcome. Although 85% are in agreement to undergo testing voluntarily, it is the 15% who refuse who understand the disease least, have the most uneducated bias against the disease itself, and are frequently at the greatest risk to contract the disease. For some, this stigma is so high that they even refuse treatment of AIDS once symptoms become prevalent (Severson, 1993). Mass testing prior to counseling and education would allow both the individual inmates and the facilities to design these programs according to the needs of both the HIV-positive and non-HIV-positive populations. Segregation further would allow the design of education and counseling programs to be tailored to those needs.

Some of the persons against a blanket policy on testing and segregation have indicated that segregation only should be used for those persons who upon having been counseled, continue to show high-risk behavior and disregard for others (Carroll, 1992). The majority of persons confined to prison were arrested for high-risk behavior. The best measures for inmates would be to test each prisoner upon entrance, segregate those who are HIV positive, and then implement intensive counseling and educational programs focusing on instructing those who know they are HIV positive.

Why have testing and segregation become the alternative to educational programs? Why can they not be beneficial to each other? It has been proven that separating those individuals who are active members of a group for educational purposes allows them a certain freedom to participate at a more intimate, level. Most support groups and therapy groups are based on this theory. This would apply to HIV-positive inmates as well. They would be able to be educated and counseled on dealing with their disease without an attached stigma as opposed to the education in prevention that nonpositive inmates would receive.

As stated earlier, most decisions in correctional facilities are based on cost-effectiveness. In the past, programs have been implemented in part on meeting necessary goals but are as much based on bottom-line dollar figures. The most recent research has shown that per state, it would be more cost-beneficial to detect HIV as early as possible and administer medical preventive treatments within the prisons. This method would be much less costly to society than the eventual treatment of AIDS in emergency status. Even the treatment of HIV prior to the onset of AIDS costs $2,000 to $3,000 less for prison inmates than for members of the general public (Severson, 1993).

Part of the problem in dealing with AIDS has been the stigma that has accompanied this disease. From its outbreak in the United States, when it was specifically attached to homosexual practices, AIDS has created fear, not simply as a lethal disease but also by the contact through which the disease was contracted. Although that stigma has changed in the medical field, it is slow to change in the general population and continues to persist strongly in the prison community. In the beginning, most programs such as segregation were implemented out of fear of the disease as much as to provide assistance to inmates.

AIDS is a disease that attacks and kills using other diseases. Tuberculosis (TB) has made such a resurgence in correctional facilities that it is the number two cause of death for AIDS inmates and the most recurring disease contracted in conjunction with HIV. Prisons have become the perfect incubator for TB and other airborne communicable diseases due to the overcrowded conditions and a general lack of ventilation. Coupled with pneumonia, TB is the greatest reason for segregating HIV-positive inmates and screening for both HIV and TB upon entering the prison system. Tuberculosis is generally high where HIV is high. This is evidenced by New York's 27% TB positivity and 13.9% HIV positivity (Blumberg & Langston, 1995; Maruschak, 1997).

Legal and Constitutional Perspectives

In 1985, 42% of prison facilities had segregation programs for HIV-positive and/or AIDS inmates (Blumberg & Langston, 1995). Currently, 6 states have segregation policies strictly for HIV-positive prisoners, 16 have policies for inmates with AIDS, and 1 has even constructed a separate prison unit to hold segregated AIDS inmates (Haas, 1993). Segregation policies have been eliminated and reestablished over time, with legal challenges made from HIV-positive inmates, non-HIV-positive inmates, correctional staff, and family members of inmates. The majority of these cases have been decided in favor of the correctional administration (for an in-depth discussion, see Haas, 1993).

Newly generated issues from the 8th Amendment have brought about a broadening scope with regard to Constitutional protection. If the Constitution pertains to prisoners and the public, to inmates and staff, to family and non-HIV-positive people, who is to be protected by the federal and state correctional facilities? The court cases are beginning to shift away from HIV-positive inmates filing charges and toward other types of individuals charging grievances. Those grievances have included, for example, non-HIV-positive inmates suing prisons for failing to test and segregate HIV-positive inmates, correctional staff filing against facilities for failure to warn, and families of HIV-positive inmates making motions against facilities for failure to warn.

Correctional officers have argued that segregation of HIV-positive and AIDS inmates would allow them to act with more caution in performing their duties. Although there has been no reported case of a correctional officer contracting HIV through job-related tasks, there are risks taken daily within this type of employment. The risk behaviors feared by officers specific to HIV include spitting, biting, and needle punctures. It has been estimated that the risk to officers is less than 1%, but it would be ignorance to assume that this case would never happen (Durham, 1994).

Another group with emerging issues has been the family and friends visiting inmates. General visitation should not provide any threat for families or friends. Conjugal visits for HIV-positive inmates now are being questioned. Correctional facilities are limited in their ability to inform visitors of inmates' HIV statuses. For correctional facilities to make every effort to limit the potential for spreading HIV, segregation must extend to protection of the general public. This includes either informing persons before conjugal visits or not allowing the visitation at all. Duty currently lies with the HIV-positive individuals to provide information to friends or family members. However, the correctional facilities have an obligation to protect the general public from harm from potentially dangerous prisoners.

Conclusion

Testing and segregation are the safest and most beneficial options for resolving the issues of HIV and AIDS in state and federal prisons. Mandatory testing and segregation are not viable options for the general public because it is assumed that the general public is aware of the risks of HIV and the behaviors associated with contracting the disease. Most important, however, it is assumed that the general public would not intentionally and repeatedly act out these high-risk behaviors. The prison community is different from the general population in this manner. It is much more likely that inmates will participate in these behaviors. It is therefore in the best interest of the general population to test each prisoner, segregate all HIV-positive inmates, and use the average of 2.5 to 3 years of time served to educate and counsel the inmates about their disease—how it affects them and the community.

It is becoming increasingly important to detect HIV and begin treatment as soon as possible. The cost-benefit of this early intervention spreads to the community as well. Also, the earlier education and counseling begin in the course of the disease, the better individuals are able to cope with the accompanying changes in life.

Currently, the federal courts have remained supportive of prison officials' expertise in resolving issues related to communicable diseases. The expertise used by each facility not only has been different according to region but also has repeatedly changed. The future series of cases brought before the courts will likely change the perspective for testing and segregation again as more members of the general public become victims to prison policy or the lack thereof.

References

Blumberg, M., & Langston, D. (1995). The impact of HIV/AIDS and tuberculosis on corrections. In K. C. Hass & G. P. Alpert (Eds.), *The dilemmas of corrections: Contemporary readings* (3rd ed., pp. 572–584). Prospect Heights, IL: Waveland.

Carroll, L. (1992). AIDS and human rights in the prison: A comment on the ethics of screening and segregation. In C. A. Hartjen & E. E. Rhine (Eds.), *Correctional theory and practice* (pp. 162–77). Chicago: Nelson-Hall.

Durham, A. M., III. (1994). *Crisis and reform: Current issues in American punishment* (pp. 67–104). Boston: Little, Brown.

Haas, K. C. (1993). Constitutional challenges to the compulsory HIV testing of prisoners and the mandatory segregation of HIV-positive prisoners. *Prison Journal, 73,* 391–422.

Hammett, T. M. (1990). *Update 1989: AIDS in correctional facilities.* Washington, DC: National Institute of Justice.

Maruschak, L. (1997). *AIDS in correctional institutions.* Washington, DC: U.S. Department of Justice.

Pagliaro, L. A., & Pagliaro, A. M. (1992, April). Sentenced to death? HIV infection and AIDS in prisons: Current and future concerns. *Canadian Journal of Criminology,* 201–214.

Prendergast, M. L., Wellisch, J. & Falkin, G. P. (1997). Assessment of and services for substance-abusing women offenders in community and correctional settings. In J. W. Marquart & J. R. Sorensen (Eds.), *Correctional contexts: Contemporary and classical readings* (pp. 318–326). Los Angeles: Roxbury.

Severson, M. (1993). Protection or prevention: Testing the prisoner population for communicable diseases. *Criminal Justice Review, 18,* 203–220.

Vlahov, D. (1990). HIV-1 infection in the correctional setting. *Criminal Justice Policy Review, 4,* 306–318.

NO

Billy Long

Is the Segregation of HIV-Positive Inmates Ethical?

Acquired immune deficiency syndrome (AIDS) is perhaps the single most devastating medical and social problem of this era. It has precipitated fear, resulted in hundreds of thousands of deaths in America, and led to discrimination against those who have been affected by the disease.

AIDS, more recently referred to as HIV (Human Immunodeficiency Virus) disease, also has presented the correctional community with numerous problems. This is because correctional facilities house many people who exhibit high-risk characteristics. While attempting to address problems generated by HIV disease, prison administrators have grappled with issues such as mandatory testing, segregation of seropositive inmates, confidentiality of and access to serum test results, and the construction of AIDS education programs. Prison officials also have had to decide potential responses to the threat of HIV and AIDS, such as whether to make condoms available for safer sex, to provide bleach for the sterilization of needles, or to offer clean needles (Braithwaite, Hammett, & Mayberry, 1996).

Fortunately, the prevalence of HIV disease in prison has not reached levels once predicted. In fact, the frequency of intraprison seroconversion is rare (Horsburgh, Jarvis, McArthur, Ignacia, & Stock, 1990), making it highly unlikely that inmates will become infected while incarcerated. Nevertheless, HIV infection is far more common in America's prisons than in the general public, as 11,565 cases have been reported (Hammett, Harrold, Gross, & Epstein, 1994).

The segregation of HIV-positive inmates, once a relatively standard practice, fortunately has declined dramatically since 1985 (Braithwaite et al., 1996). This is due in part to the fact that much of the hysteria and irrational fears about seropositive persons generally, and inmates specifically, have subsided. Segregation is no longer viewed as a sensible strategy to reduce the spread of HIV (Braithwaite et al., 1996). However, there are at least four other factors as to why segregating HIV-positive inmates has fallen out of favor: (a) the need to avoid stigmatizing those with HIV, (b) the hazards of mass screening for HIV, (c) the logistical problems with segregated housing, and (d) the extremely remote possibility of transmitting the virus via casual contact.

From Billy Long, "Is the Segregation of HIV-Positive Inmates Ethical? No," *The Prison Journal*, vol. 79, no. 1 (March 1999). Copyright © 1999 by Sage Publications, Inc. Reprinted by permission.

Stigmatizing Seropositive Inmates

When seropositive inmates are ostracized intentionally from the rest of the prison population, inferior health care is inevitable. There are, in effect, two correctional systems, one for seronegative inmates and one for those who are seropositive. Prison-based medical care providers typically grimace at the prospect of dealing with inmates who manifest symptoms of HIV disease. Jeffery (1989) refers to this problem as the *typification* of patients. Health care providers who do not have private practices (e.g., those who work in community clinics and/or prisons) classify patients into one of two groups: good patients and rubbish. Good patients are those who have illnesses that allow medical providers the opportunity to practice their chosen specialty and to test the competence and maturity of the staff (as defined by the staff). This generally means that good patients exhibit acute, severe, or rare disorders that require surgery, present the appearance of imminent death, or otherwise challenge the staff to perform noteworthy medical procedures to bring the patients back to health.

On the surface, it may appear that HIV disease/AIDS would be desirable because it satisfies the necessary requirement to be good patients (i.e., imminent death). However, this is not the case. Remember, to be good patients, the patients must afford the staff members an opportunity to bring the patients back to health. In the case of HIV disease/AIDS, this is not possible (at least in a long-term sense). All AIDS patients ultimately die. Thus, the symptoms exhibited by AIDS patients are deemed *rubbish* by the medical professionals. Furthermore, in the prison setting, many female-specific illnesses (e.g., reproductive tract symptoms) are viewed as mundane or routine. Patients "guilty" of exhibiting these ailments are referred to as *rubbish* (Jeffery, 1989). Although caring for prisoners with AIDS is inevitable with or without segregation, the problem of stigmatizing inmates invariably will be worse if they are forced to live in special HIV units. This attitude inescapably leads to inferior medical care for inmates.

Segregation Requires Mass Screening

If correctional institutions have as a policy the segregation of seropositive inmates, it follows that all inmates would have to be screened for HIV antibodies. This is necessary to identify those who will be isolated. This is unwise for several reasons. First, the accuracy of test results is in question. One potential problem is that the results of HIV tests are simply in error. This could result in the isolation of inmates who are not seropositive. Furthermore, there is a time lag between exposure to HIV and the presence of antibodies. An inmate, for example, could have HIV when tested but be deemed seronegative because the virus has not had sufficient time to be detected.

This inevitably would result in having seropositive inmates in the general prison population. This could have very serious consequences. A policy of mass screening, accompanied with a policy of isolating known seropositives, creates a false sense of security in the general prison population. Prisoners will feel as though they know who has and does not have HIV disease. This being the case, risky behavior may be more likely. Because inmates "know" that all seropositives are kept in isolation, there must be no danger in engaging in intravenous (IV) drug use or unprotected, passive anal intercourse. Because mass screening invariably will miss some seropositives, this means that some HIV-infected inmates may engage in risky behavior while in the general prison population that could lead to the spread of the virus. Other problems associated with mass screening include (a) cost and (b) the undermining of educational programs; that is, attempting to identify all seropositives inevitably will lead to "targeted" educational efforts aimed at the "dangerous classes" of inmates (e.g., known homosexuals, IV drug users). This is not consistent with the view that prison-based AIDS education efforts should be aimed at all inmates. Targeted programs inescapably suggest that HIV disease is salient only for certain groups.

Duplication of Services

A policy of segregating inmates results in a duplication of correctional services. That is, if seropositive inmates are isolated from the general prison population, special efforts will have to be made to provide various services. At one prison, seropositives who have been quarantined have experienced severe restrictions on such basic functions as psychosocial and medical services. Also, there have been reports of segregated seropositives being restricted in terms of their visitation privileges, recreational activities, vocational training, and educational programs. It also has been discovered that isolated seropositive inmates have suffered in the area of earned "good time credit." For example, seropositives may be designated as *unprogrammed and unclassified*, be housed in special units, and receive only one third of good time, whereas general population inmates earn one half of good time credit (Greenspan, 1996; Randy Weathers, personal communication, November 1997).

Even if these types of services are provided, there must be a duplication of efforts to make them available. In effect, departments of correction (DOCs) have to provide the services in the seronegative (again recognizing the hazards of this type of classification) and the seropositive populations. Once again, the costs associated with segregating inmates become prohibitive.

Transmitting HIV

Proponents of isolating HIV-positive inmates often suggest that it is necessary to ensure that the virus is not spread to other inmates or staff. Thus, once inmates exhibit antibodies for HIV, they are to be kept in special units so as to avoid contact with noninfected persons. This argument is faulty for several reasons. First, a substantial amount of evidence suggests that HIV cannot be transmitted casually. Peterman (1988) reported that the risk of transmission through direct casual contact (e.g., hugging, kissing, shaking hands, sharing drinking glasses) and indirect casual contact (e.g., food preparation) is extremely low. For example, he studied families of transfusion-infection cases and found that with the exception of sexual partners, family members never became infected. Even when examining the sexual mode of transmission, he found that many spouses of transfusion-infection cases remained HIV negative even after 3 years of unprotected sex. This strengthens the argument that HIV requires more than casual contact for transmission (Peterman, 1988). In sum, segregating inmates for the purpose of preventing HIV infection is not justified. There are other avenues that should be pursued to achieve this objective.

For example, people in service oriented occupations (e.g., the police and correctional officers, health care workers) have been urged to use universal precautions. Initially designed to prevent hepatitis, these precautions should be followed while engaging in job-related activities in which there is a risk of infection. Universal precautions require that all blood products be treated as if they contain an infectious agent. Employees are encouraged to wear gloves when there is any potential for contact with bodily fluids, and masks are to be used to perform acts such as mouth to mouth resuscitation. Spills involving bodily fluids should be cleaned up immediately using disinfectants (Hammett, 1991). Distinctions are made with reference to bodily fluids as they relate to the use of universal precautions. Dangerous fluids include blood, any fluid containing blood, semen, vaginal secretions, as well as cerebrospinal, synovial, pericardial, and amniotic fluids. Bodily fluids that need not be treated with universal precautions include feces (although fluids found in feces may be dangerous), urine, sweat, tears, vomitus, nasal secretions, saliva, and sputum (Centers for Disease Control and Prevention [CDC], 1988).

What Should Be Done?

It is widely believed that it is necessary to provide inmates with the appropriate barriers for protection (see, e.g., Braithwaite et al., 1996). It is scurrilous for any authority figure to understand the modes of HIV transmission and to withhold resources that can prevent infection. It is a foregone conclusion that sex takes place in prison. It is therefore recommended that DOCs make condoms readily available to inmate populations. This should not be done on a piecemeal basis, however. Inmates should not be given condoms on a one per visit basis to the infirmary or during an AIDS counseling session. Indeed, condoms should be made available in open containers whereby inmates can obtain them without being observed. This practice currently is being used in French prisons, where there are no reports of negative fallout, and in Canada, 82% of prison officers surveyed said that condom availability caused no problems at their institutions (Expert Committee on AIDS and Prisons, 1994). Correctional officials must begin to moderate their views that characterize the prison system strictly in terms of security maintenance and stifling adherence to regulations. They must recognize that current policies "that prohibit sexual activity between inmates [are] unrealistic and inhumane" (Gaiter, 1996, p. 2). A more functional approach would be to view the prison more from a public health model. Rather than viewing condom distribution as encouraging sex in prisons or condoms as vehicles for smuggling contraband, condoms should be viewed as barriers for protection against a deadly virus. As Braithwaite et al. (1996) concluded:

> In the systems with condom availability, there have been few if any problems with condoms being used as weapons or for smuggling contraband, despite suggestions by opponents that this would occur. (p. 85)

IV Drugs

IV drug use is another area of risk reduction in which explicit instruction is imperative. It is not appropriate to simply tell inmates that cleaning needles reduces their risk. Inmates need to have detailed information on how to clean needles. For example, they need to be told exactly how to clean needles (e.g., how long to leave the bleach solution in the syringe, the proper uses of rinse water, etc.). The following quote illustrates the type of information that must be provided to inmates with regard to IV drug use and HIV.

> The CDC's revised procedure calls for rinsing with clean water, then with full-strength bleach, then with clean water again at least three times, shaking the syringe for thirty seconds during each rinsing. Although proper cleaning with bleach does significantly reduce the risk of HIV transmission, the only way to be certain that there is no infected blood in a needle or syringe is to use new sterile equipment every time. Bleach is only recommended when no other safer options are available. (CDC, 1993, p. 1)

To educate inmates this way is consistent with the theory of harm reduction. Here, it is assumed that inmates must be convinced that they are capable of implementing strategies that will reduce their risk of infection for any behavioral change to take place. Correctional officials must acknowledge the fact that many inmates are from extremely deprived backgrounds and use IV drugs as a means of coping. Therefore, it is inappropriate for prisons to force inmates into accepting a dichotomy: IV drug use on the outside and complete abstinence on the inside. Harm reduction theory takes the inmates at whatever point they are in their lives and stresses how the individual can become safer but only in an incremental fashion (Harm Reduction Coalition, 1995). This approach can be implemented easily without segregating those with HIV.

The obvious recommendation from this is for correctional officials to increase the safety of IV drug use by making bleach available to clean needles. Although a needle exchange program would provide the optimum amount of safety, there is the real possibility of needles being used as weapons. Nevertheless, bleach tablets as part of an HIV prevention kit can be made available to reduce the hazards associated with needle sharing. Any prison-based AIDS education effort must inform the inmates about how to clean needles, where to obtain the necessary protection barriers, and how to obtain drug treatment. Bleach is already available in prisons as a general cleaning agent; thus, making it more readily available for needle cleaning would not require a drastic change of policy. The greatest positive effect of this change would be that it would increase the self-efficacy of the inmates.

If given the necessary tools for infection prevention, they will begin to feel as though they have control of their lives (Braithwaite et al., 1996). Along the same lines, drug treatment opportunities must be made more available to male and female inmates. IV drug use is the leading cause of HIV infection among inmates. There are more IV drug users in American correctional institutions than in drug treatment centers, so prisons are convenient places to reach these individuals (Dixon, 1993).

In sum, segregation of HIV-positive inmates is not necessary to achieve the desired result (i.e., low seroconversion in prison). Resources should be used to educate inmates concerning HIV disease and its modes of transmission as well as to provide inmates with the appropriate barrier protection. This is a far more effective way of dealing with the spread of HIV than to resort to cruel and demoralizing policies that isolate inmates simply because they carry a virus.

References

Braithwaite, R., Hammett, T., & Mayberry, R. (1996). *Prisons and AIDS: A public health challenge.* San Francisco: Jossey-Bass.

Centers for Disease Control and Prevention. (1988). Update: Universal precautions for prevention of transmission of Hepatitis B virus and other blood borne pathogens in health-care settings. *Morbidity and Mortality Weekly Report, 37,* 377–388.

Centers for Disease Control and Prevention. (1993). HIV/AIDS surveillance report, 1992. *Morbidity and Mortality Weekly Report, 5*(3), 1–19.

Dixon, P. (1993). Infection with HIV in prisoners: Meeting the health care challenge (Review). *American Journal of Medicine, 95,* 629–635.

Expert Committee on AIDS in Prisons. (1994, February). *HIV/AIDS in prisons: Final report of the expert committee on AIDS and prisons.* Montreal: McGill Centre for Ethics, Medicine and the Law.

Gaiter, J. (1996). Improving HIV/AIDS prevention in prisons is good public health policy. *American Journal of Public Health, 85*(9), 1–3.

Greenspan, J. (1996). *AIDS in prison: The new death row for prisoners?* Oakland, CA: HIV/AIDS in Prison Project.

Hammett, T. (1991). *1990 update: AIDS in correctional facilities.* Washington, DC: National Institute of Justice.

Hammett, T., Harrold, L., Gross, M., & Epstein, J. (1994). *1992 update: HIV/AIDS in correctional facilities: Issues and options.* Washington, DC: U.S. Department of Justice.

Harm Reduction Communication. (1995). New York: Harm Reduction Coalition (HRC).

Horsburgh, C., Jarvis, J., McArthur, T., Ignacia, T., & Stock, P. (1990). Seroconversion to immunodeficiency virus in prison inmates. *American Journal of Public Health, 80,* 209–210.

Jeffery, R. (1989). Normal rubbish: Deviant patients in casualty departments. In D. Kelly (Ed.), *Deviant behavior* (pp. 291–307). New York: St. Martin's.

Peterman, T. (1988). Risk of HIV transmission from heterosexual adults with transfusion-associated infections. *Journal of the American Medical Foundation, 259,* 55–58.

POSTSCRIPT

Is the Segregation of HIV-Positive Inmates Ethical?

Some countries, such as Cuba, resolve the AIDS problem in the general population by placing AIDS patients in humane but separate areas. Medically and rationally it seems that segregating prisoners with AIDS, especially those in maximum security lock-ups, is both ethical and sensible. Yet the issue is not that clear-cut. Long argues that the increase in AIDS within America's prisons has not been significant. Apparently, inmates know the risks and take precautions to prevent dangerous contacts.

Long raises a parallel problem for AIDS treatment in the free world: mandatory testing—or, in the case of prisons, segregation—is liable to cause people to take the problem "underground." That is, HIV-infected people will not seek help or will try to cover up the fact that they are infected. With any medical problem, the cooperation of the sick is imperative. Long also contends that AIDS inmates formerly unknown as such will become objects of abuse. Robinette turns that argument around to justify segregation as a form of protection for both the sick and the healthy.

Could some compromise be reached? For example, many prisons segregate older inmates, usually at their requests, from younger, more dangerous ones. Could segregation be voluntary? Or could there be degrees (e.g., full-blown AIDS inmates would be separated, while those who only test positive for HIV would be given a choice)? Some worry about the added costs of duplicating services. Should this be a consideration in a potential life-and-death situation as this? Is the segregation of HIV-positive inmates ethical?

A cutting-edge overview of AIDS research and its spread is *Social Networks, Drug Injectors' Lives and HIV-AIDS* by S. R. Friedman, R. Curtis, and A. Neaigus (Plenum, 1999). A useful overview of this and other related prison issues is *From AIDS to the Internet: Correctional Realities* (American Correctional Association, 1999). An excellent source of relevant statistics is *HIV in Prisons 1997*, published by the Bureau of Justice Statistics (November 1999).

Discussions of the broader issue of crime control from female inmates' perspectives can be found in "The Implications of Crime Control Policy on HIV/AIDS Related Risk Among Women Prisoners," *Crime and Delinquency* (October 1998) and *Breaking the Walls of Silence: AIDS and Women in a New York State Maximum Security Prison* by the AIDS Counseling and Education Program of the Bedford Hills Correctional Facility (Overlook Press, 1998). A good overview of health issues of incarcerated females is "Adjudicated Health: Incarcerated Women and the Social Construction of Health," by M. Maeve, *Crime, Law and Social Change* (vol. 1, 1999).

ISSUE 11

Are Conjugal and Familial Visitations Effective Rehabilitative Concepts?

YES: Jill Gordon, from "Are Conjugal and Familial Visitations Effective Rehabilitative Concepts? Yes," *The Prison Journal* (March 1999)

NO: Elizabeth H. McConnell, from "Are Conjugal and Familial Visitations Effective Rehabilitative Concepts? No," *The Prison Journal* (March 1999)

ISSUE SUMMARY

YES: Assistant professor of criminal justice Jill Gordon identifies and defends several humanitarian and practical reasons for allowing family visitations in adult prisons. She argues that they are rehabilitative for inmates and good for their families.

NO: Associate professor of criminal justice Elizabeth H. McConnell maintains that although more wardens now favor conjugal visits than in the past, there is little empirical support that they are useful for either inmates or their families or that they necessarily reduce prison tensions. Also, she says, they are costly and probably unfair to other inmates.

$\mathbf{A}$t a broad cultural or value level of analysis, this issue is tricky, although statistically it is relatively insignificant because only eight states even allow conjugal visits. This issue is difficult also because family visits often lead to sexual interaction (although probably far less frequently than most people assume). When incarcerated felons are allowed to have sex with their wives, a significant number of citizens will be angered. First, for some the idea of such intimacies, however fleeting and rare, within the prison setting is highly offensive. Second, those who reflect the retribution model of incarceration feel that prisons exist to punish, not to serve as "hotels."

Hence, at the cultural level of analysis the issue goes beyond inmates' having weightrooms, college courses, the right to smoke, and such. Logistically, there are many problems with any program that allows outsiders to interact freely and behind closed doors with inmates, even after they are searched thoroughly. Contraband, whispered plans for escape, negotiations regarding criminal deals on the street, to mention a few contingencies, always exist. In addition, pregnancies, sexually transmitted diseases, and even AIDS could result from conjugal visits. The costs of maintaining private visitation areas is a factor as well.

Others argue that, especially when children's participation in visits is considered, such opportunities are good. According to this line of reasoning, familial visitations will strengthen the family and provide the inmate with strong ties to facilitate his returning to the community when released. Most inmates spend less than three years in prison for any one adjudication. In spite of a rapidly aging prison population, most prisoners are well under 30 and, defenders say, would benefit from visits not only with their wives and children over a one- to three-day period but with their parents and siblings as well.

At the international level, many countries, such as Mexico, openly endorse conjugal visits. Some of their major problems, however, have to do with the fact that to have this chance, guards have to be bribed. Often prostitutes can be imported for the right bribe, along with alcohol and drugs. America's inhibitions against such "normal" and "natural" visits is viewed with disbelief and astonishment in other countries.

Many criminologists over the years have pointed out the seeming irony that Mississippi was possibly the first state to sanction conjugal visits, which it did around 1918. Yet the initial right was only for black male inmates. This reflected the stereotypes of the day that such inmates were overly sexual and therefore "needed" private interactions strictly to release tension and make controlling them easier. Obviously, the rationale for supporters of conjugal and family visitations has changed to encompass family maintenance, humanitarian purposes, and to weaken the influence of the inmate subculture.

As you study this debate, consider the reasons offered by Jill Gordon and Elizabeth H. McConnell for and against familial visitations. What evidence informs the various reasons for allowing or not allowing conjugal visits? Who would such visits be most helpful for, and how could they be arranged? Could the argument be made that female inmates (who are almost never allowed conjugal visits) would also benefit? How about teenagers in juvenile facilities with girlfriends or gay adult partners of inmates? Is it fair to have such visits for married inmates only? How might such visits positively affect rehabilitation? How might they impede it?

Jill Gordon  **YES**

Are Conjugal and Familial Visitations Effective Rehabilitative Concepts?

During the past few decades, the idea of conjugal visitations has been expanded and now centers on family visitation programs (commonly referred to as *family reunion programs*). In general, these allow inmates and their families to have extended visits on the prison grounds in a private facility that is separate from the institution. The primary objective of family reunion programs is to maintain and strengthen family ties during the inmates' periods of incarceration.

Ten states have implemented or currently are implementing a type of extended visitation program. There are some common themes found among the various extended visitation programs (Goetting, 1982a, 1982b). Each state has a number of inmate eligibility criteria that center on the inmates' behavioral patterns and the amount of time served at the facilities, and inmates must be excluded from participation in the home furlough program. The visits can last from less than 1 day to a maximum of 3 days and occur at designated places on the institution property. The visitors allowed to participate in the program vary by state, but visitors typically include spouses, children, and parents of convicted offenders.

Many inmates and some of their spouses have raised legal issues (based on prohibiting cruel and unusual punishment, the right to privacy, religious practice, and equal protection) with regard to conjugal and extended family visits. Although the courts have not granted extended visitation on constitutional issues, the programs are beneficial. Family reunion programs can offer a rehabilitative benefit to inmates and their families.

Benefits of Conjugal and/or Familial Visitation

The Inmate

Incarceration can produce emotional, physical, and psychological responses for inmates. The inmates' reactions to incarceration often encompass feelings of loneliness, isolation, guilt, anger, and despair. These emotional responses can lead to loss of sleep, restlessness, and loss of hunger. These reactions (both

From Jill Gordon, "Are Conjugal and Familial Visitations Effective Rehabilitative Concepts? Yes," *The Prison Journal,* vol. 79, no. 1 (March 1999). Copyright © 1999 by Sage Publications, Inc. Reprinted by permission.

physical and emotional) can cause more serious psychological difficulties, such as depression, paranoia, anxiety, and suicidal tendencies. The majority of these reactions are a result of the loss of or separation from family and friends. This isolation often forces inmates to adapt to the inmate subculture, which means the indoctrination and acceptance of the values, norms, and culture of inmate life. The subculture formulates rules for the inmates to follow that usually are counter to the general institutional rules and norms. Therefore, the inmate subculture may reduce the influence of the institutional social control measures. In addition, the transition process back into the community becomes more difficult because the inmates' value system is different from that of the outside community, and the ties inmate once had with the community may be severed.

Incarceration also causes practical problems for some offenders, such as maintaining parent-child and marital relationships. Prison life decreases the role incarcerated offenders have in their children's lives. Specifically, barriers occur with regard to decision making, financial contribution, supervision, and general knowledge of the children's activities and well-being. More important, these issues can lead to incarcerated parents losing custody of children. This has an impact not only on families but also on society because child welfare agencies often must find suitable foster care situations for these children.

Similarly, incarceration creates a strain on marriages. The spouses of incarcerated offenders must assume additional roles and responsibilities. A reduction in the amount and types of communication and contact combined with the additional burdens often lead to divorce of the couples.

Family reunion programs can reduce these strains on the inmates' relations with their families and improve the inmates' postrelease success. Carlson and Cervera (1992) examined the types of activities that occur during extended family visits. The researchers found that families engaged in conversations, played games, cooked, watched television, and had some sexual relations (reported as the least-occurring activity). The inmates in this study reported that they enjoyed the visits, felt part of the family, and felt closer to their wives. The wives reported improved relations between the children and the incarcerated spouses. These elevated feelings may improve the inmates' self-esteem while incarcerated and may decrease the potential for the inmates to become fully indoctrinated into the inmate subculture. Therefore, this sense of well-being felt by the inmates can carry over to the general operations of the institution.

The institutional benefit of a decreased feeling of isolation or loss among the inmates can be a higher degree of social control. For example, research shows that among the inmates who participate in family reunion programs, their disciplinary records improved compared to nonparticipants (Howser, Grossman, & MacDonald, 1983; Howser & MacDonald, 1982). In addition, participation in the extended visitation program serves as an incentive for inmates to comply with institutional rules and regulations (due to eligibility requirements). Therefore, the program can be an effective management tool for correctional officers and administrators (Goetting, 1982a, 1982b).

Research suggests that extended family visitation and/or conjugal visitation programs do maintain family ties that can influence the postrelease success of inmates; specifically, studies have shown that inmates who participate in conjugal and/or family visits have a higher likelihood of being employed upon release (Fox, 1981), a positive parole outcome (see Goetting, 1982b), and a lower likelihood of recidivism upon release from the institution (Howser et al., 1983; LeClair, 1978). These results reveal that the offenders are affected by the extended visitation program both during and after the periods of incarceration.

The Family

Extended visitation programs can help reduce the effects of having incarcerated family members. The incarceration of family members negatively affects the entire family system and tends to create a large strain on family systems that in turn "punishes" families. Families must reassign roles, rework daily schedules and activities, and reevaluate their financial statuses. These issues combined with the stigmatization often felt by families and the neglect of support from social service agencies create several emotional, practical, and economic dilemmas. Research has examined the impact of incarceration on wives and children of inmates.

Most of the roles once accomplished by incarcerated offenders are absorbed by their wives. In addition, the wives of the inmates experience high amounts of stress in coping with financial pressures, child care issues, and housing issues (Fishman, 1990). These women may cope better when they receive support from local agencies and their family, friends, and others in the same situation. The level of adjustment may increase with the use of family reunion programs because families may still function, in some regard, as family units.

Carlson and Cervera (1992) examined the consequences of a family reunion program on inmates and their wives. The wives who participated in the program reported that their relationships with their husbands changed in a positive direction, the wives wanted longer and more frequent contacts, the visits helped the relationships, and the visits improved family-child relationships. Although these visits seem to have had a positive response for the families, the researchers point out that the levels of cohesiveness, adaptability, and satisfaction with the marriages were not statistically significant between those who participated versus those who did not participate in the extended visit program. However, it appears that the family ties were strengthened in various ways for most of the families who participated.

Parental incarceration can have a serious impact on children. Some of the negative responses by the children of incarcerated offenders include feelings of anger, rejection, confusion, and a loss of identity. If these feelings are not addressed, the children become highly susceptible to emotional and cognitive problems that may lead to juvenile delinquency (Johnston, 1995). Although visiting incarcerated parents may reduce these reactions, many social service professionals and caregivers shield children from visiting incarcerated parents because of the possible negative effects found in the institutional environment (Bloom & Steinhart, 1993; Hairston, 1989; Johnston, 1995). The traditional visitation scenario—a noisy, well-guarded environment that does not allow or limits the extent of contact between the inmates and their visitors—can increase the negative feelings of the children; thus, it is essential to create an environment that enables the families to interact among themselves. The family reunion program creates an environment that permits families to act and function as systems and is more conducive to eliminating the children's negative reactions. Extended family visits reassure children that their parents are doing fine and also can reduce or abolish the negative feelings (guilt, rejections) the children posses's (Johnston, 1995).

Another strain on the families is finding the time and finances to visit incarcerated family members for the brief time allowed for typical visits. Many institutions are not located in close proximity to the inmates' areas of residence, so the families often spend more time traveling to the institutions than visiting with the inmates. Thus, for many, the cost outweighs the benefit. The extended family visits are more advantageous because the program allows for the families to spend more time together and interact as families; thus, the benefit can outweigh the cost.

Recommendations for Current and Future Extended Visitation Programs

Several benefits of extended visitation programs have been outlined above; however, there are some recommendations for the program. The rehabilitative impact may be heightened by providing inmates and their families with counseling. The family systems often have previous problems that become enhanced because of the incarceration of family members. Offering counseling in conjunction with the extended family visits can allow each family member to understand how they affect the family system and the overall problem of criminal behavior. Strategies that identify problems and offer solutions can enhance the overall functioning of the family systems and possibly improve the postrelease success of the offenders.

Extended visitation programs can renew and enrich families by offering counseling services. The programs cannot be expected to affect the poor behavioral functioning of families by simply increasing the length of the visits. However, the family systems can improve through the use of well-grounded and supported methods of identifying family patterns as well as by finding solutions to overcome the maladaptive systems.

Another recommendation is to study the impact of extended family visitations more fully. Researchers need to examine the effectiveness of extended family visitation programs in terms of daily institutional occurrences (i.e., disciplinary infractions among the inmates); the impact on spouses, parents, and/or children (i.e., the adjustment process and occurrence of negative reactions); the impact on the family systems (i.e., the quality of the interactions); and the postrelease behavior of the inmates (i.e., employment, recidivism, and so forth) for one family reunion program. It is essential to examine simultaneously all of these components to accurately assess the effectiveness of such a program. In addition, the research on extended family programs must consider the impact on both the male and female institutional populations.

Conclusions

Incarceration creates an enormous amount of stress for inmates and their families. This stress combined with the limited help provided to the families often leads to a breakdown in family relations. This is not what the criminal justice system, politicians, or society should hope for, because the strength of families' relations frequently serves as a principal way of eliminating offenders' future criminal activity.

Extended family visitation programs allow family members to visit inmates for more than a couple of hours and enable the families to engage in "family" activities (i.e., cooking together, reading to their children, discussing family issues). At minimum, these programs will sustain inmates' ties to their families. At maximum, the programs can strengthen and enhance the families' relationships and improve the offenders' postrelease behavior, thus reducing any future burdens on the criminal justice system.

References

Bloom, B., & Steinhart D. (1993). *Why punish the children? A reappraisal of the children of incarcerated mothers in America.* San Francisco: National Council on Crime and Delinquency.

Carlson, B. E., & Cervera, N. (1992). *Inmates and their wives incarceration and family life.* Westport, CT: Greenwood.

Fishman, L. T. (1990). *Women at the wall: A study of prisoners' waivers doing time on the outside.* Albany: State University of New York Press.

Fox, G. (1981). The family and the ex-offender: Potential for rehabilitation. In S. Martin, L. Sechrest, & R. Redner (Eds.), *New directions in the rehabilitation of criminal offenders.* Washington, DC: National Academy Press.

Goetting, A. (1982a). Conjugal association in prison: Issues and perspectives. *Crime and Delinquency, 28,* 52–71.

Goetting, A. (1982b). Conjugal association in prison: The debate and its resolution. *New England Journal on Prison Law, 8,* 141–154.

Hairston, C. (1989). Men in prison: Family characteristics and family views. *Journal of Offender Counseling, Services and Rehabilitation, 14,* 23–30.

Howser, J., Grossman, J., & MacDonald, D. (1983). Impact of family reunion program on institutional discipline. *Journal of Offender Counseling, Services and Rehabilitation, 8,* 27–36.

Howser, J., & MacDonald, D. (1982). Maintaining family ties. *Corrections Today, 44,* 96–98.

Johnston, D. (1995). Parent-child visitation in the jail or prison. In K. Gabel & D. Johnston (Eds.), *Children of incarcerated parents* (pp. 135–143). New York: Lexington Books.

LeClair, D. (1978). Home furlough program effects on rates of recidivism. *Criminal Justice and Behavior, 5,* 249–259.

NO

Elizabeth H. McConnell

Are Conjugal and Familial Visitations Effective Rehabilitative Concepts?

The merits of conjugal visits for prisoners have been debated for many years in the United States, often with little consideration of their rehabilitative properties. Historically, a number of reoccurring arguments challenging conjugal visitation have been presented, including, for example, concerns about morality, its fairness with regard to unmarried inmates, and whether it diminishes same-sex assaults in prison. Since the 1980s, several new challenges to its use have surfaced, such as health and liability concerns that relate to HIV/ AIDS. The following is a brief overview of the more noted challenges to conjugal and familial visitation as an effective rehabilitative concept.

Does the Lack of Consensus About the Morality of Conjugal Visits Diminish Its Rehabilitative Effectiveness?

One of the chief objections to conjugal visit programs is the belief that they are incompatible with existing mores. This objection is based on the belief that the primary focus of the programs is the physical dimension of the sexual relationship between married couples (Hopper, 1969; Johns, 1971; Task Force on Corrections, 1973). In fact, prison administrators have been among those who object to conjugal visits on a moral basis, with some suggesting that conjugal visits would make penal institutions nothing more than legal houses of prostitution.

Inmates and their spouses also have concerns about conjugal visits, as evidenced by their unwillingness to participate in the conjugal visit program at Parchman, Mississippi (Hopper, 1969). They often reported that the process was too embarrassing for them and their wives. According to Ballough (1964), only 13% of American prison wardens who responded to a national survey supported conjugal visits. Many of the respondents believed that conjugal visits were immoral and without rehabilitative merit. However, Bennett's (1989) findings indicate that correctional administrators' attitudes about conjugal visits have changed. Bennett surveyed two groups of prison wardens, those in most of the penal institutions in eight states with conjugal visit programs (California, Connecticut, Minnesota, Mississippi, New Mexico, New York, Washington, and Wyoming) and a random sample of wardens from states without conjugal visit programs. He found that almost one half of the wardens endorsed private family visiting programs. This included the wardens (34%) from states that did not allow conjugal visiting. Bennett further reported that the wardens not only supported programs characterized by "suitable security safeguards" but also predicted that "private family visiting programs would increase in the next ten years," (Silverman & Vega, 1996, p. 456).

Does the Exclusive Nature of Conjugal Visitation Programs Diminish Their Rehabilitative Effectiveness?

Another objection regarding the rehabilitative effectiveness of conjugal visits stems from the fact that all unmarried inmates and most married female inmates are excluded from participation in conjugal visitation programs. Although no official documentation exists that indicates when conjugal visitation was implemented by the Mississippi State Penal System at Parchman, correctional staff reported that "conjugal visits were allowed as long ago as 1918" for African American males (Hopper, 1969, p. 52). By the early 1960s, those who were eligible to participate in conjugal visitations at Parchman included married male inmates of all races, with single males and all females being excluded, still a common practice in those states that currently have conjugal visitation programs. Although many inmates are excluded, the courts have held that providing conjugal visits for some inmates and not others does not violate the equal protection clause (Palmer, 1991).

Some critics argue that exclusion from conjugal visitation programs contributes to institutional problems, as inmates who are not eligible to participate in conjugal visitation programs harbor negative attitudes about their exclusion (Silverman & Vega, 1996). However, research findings based on data collected from inmates in Mississippi in 1963 and again in 1984 indicate that less than 15% of the unmarried inmates had concerns about married inmates having conjugal visits (Hopper, 1989).

A more paramount concern about exclusion from conjugal visitation programs and its impact on their rehabilitative effect is centered around the fact that an overwhelming majority of the inmate population is excluded from participation in the programs. Statistical data on offender characteristics indicate that less than one fifth (18%) of the prison population is married and that this figure has decreased from 22% in 1979 (Beck, Bonczar, & Gilliard, 1993; Innes, 1988). Rehabilitative effectiveness is considerably challenged when one acknowledges the small numbers of inmates who are eligible to participate in conjugal visitation programs. This leaves one to doubt the rehabilitative effectiveness of these programs when assessment is based on economic costs.

Do Conjugal Visitation Programs Reduce Consensual Same-Sex Relationships, Sexual Assault, or Other Violence in Prisons?

Several researchers have examined the relationship between conjugal visitation and the behaviors of incarcerated inmates. Bennett (1989) found that prison administrators did not believe that consensual same-sex relationships, violence, or sexual assaults in prisons were reduced by conjugal visitation programs. On the other hand, Hopper (1989) and Burstein (1977) found that inmates, especially those participating in conjugal visitation programs, believed that same-sex behaviors were reduced. It is noted that although some inmates engage in consensual same-sex relationships due to loneliness or as a sexual outlet, it is reasonable to assume that conjugal visitation opportunities meet these needs for participating inmates, thus reducing consensual same-sex relationships.

However, sexual assaults and other violent behaviors among inmates are not likely to decrease due to conjugal visits, as sexual assaults and other acts of violence generally are motivated by inmates' needs to dominate one another or for the expression of anger and aggression. Hopper (1969) says that

> married inmates who could satisfactorily engage in conjugal visits are those who can adjust best to prison life even without sex relations; likewise, those inmates who present the greatest sexual problems, i.e., homosexuals and other sex deviates, are the ones least likely to benefit from conjugal visits. (pp. 13–14)

Thus, neither solutions to sexual tensions nor sexual assaults and other acts of violence of excluded prisoners are addressed by conjugal visit programs.

Is a Negative Effect of Conjugal Visitation an Increase in Prison Contraband and Escapes?

Another argument against conjugal visitation as an effective rehabilitative practice stems from the belief that it contributes to the introduction of drugs and other contraband into the institution as well as enhances inmates' attempts to escape. Some critics argue that it has a corrupting nature in that it provides added opportunities for inmates to be corrupted and to corrupt the correctional staff who supervise visitation. The visits allow private meetings between wives and husbands during which contraband items can be exchanged or escapes can be planned. The degree of privacy and length of meeting contribute to the greater likelihood that items can be exchanged. Programs such as this seem ideal for smuggling drugs into the prison and the money made from drugs out of the prison. Inmates and the families of inmates who participate in family visitation programs could be subjected to pressure from those who engage in contraband enterprises.

Bennett (1989) acknowledged that prison administrators reported concerns about drug smuggling with regard to conjugal visits; however, the administrators believed that the use of standard precautionary measures is all that is necessary to alleviate these concerns. This attitude by prison administrators seems overly optimistic when one considers the magnitude of contraband in prisons today.

Does HIV/AIDS Negate the Rehabilitative Effect of Conjugal Visitation?

Many correctional personnel are concerned about the viability of conjugal visits as an effective rehabilitative approach while taking into consideration concerns about HIV/AIDS. Based on official statistics, it has been determined that inmates have AIDS at 10 times the rate of the general population. By the end of 1993, 11,565 inmate AIDS cases were reported by state and federal correctional authorities (Hammett, Harrold, Gross, & Epstein, 1994). It was reported further that the incidence rate for AIDS among institutionalized inmates was 195 cases per 100,000. The increasing number of inmates who test positive for HIV or who have AIDS has presented diverse problems and challenges to correctional personnel.

One pressing concern for correctional administrators is the spread of this deadly disease. Because it is commonly spread through sexual contact, correctional administrators must be concerned about institutional programs that are characterized by behaviors that could facilitate the spread of this life-threatening disease, either from inmates to their spouses and families or vice versa. Prior to implementing conjugal visitation programs, correctional administrators have a duty to address these problems. For example, is the state financially liable when an infected inmate infects a noninfected spouse or other family member through agency-approved contact? Who is liable if the infected spouse or family member transmits the disease to someone else in society? Is the state liable when an inmate who is infected by his or her spouse transmits the disease to another inmate or to institutional personnel? Who will pay for the medical care of infected inmates and inmates' spouses and families? When AIDS babies are born as a result of a conjugal visit contact, who will pay for their medical care? Is it legal to require HIV/AIDS testing of men and women who participate in conjugal visitation programs? How can the institution be sure that participants in conjugal visit programs are taking precautionary measures to protect themselves from infection? These are but a few concerns about HIV/AIDS and how it affects conjugal visitation.

According to Hammett (1988), correctional agencies must have policies and procedures for their employees and clients to follow that will protect them from infectious contamination. The Centers for Disease Control (CDC) has identified universal precautions to reduce the spread of infectious diseases, several of which appear to be problematic in terms of conjugal visits. For example, one must wear gloves when contact with blood or body fluids is likely; avoid smoking, eating, drinking, nail-biting, and all hand-to-mouth, hand-to-nose, and hand-to-eye actions while working in areas contaminated with blood or body fluids; and clean up any spills of blood or body fluids thoroughly and promptly, using a 1:10 household bleach dilution (Silverman & Vega, 1996). The CDC also recommends that all personnel treat all prisoners as though they are HIV infected to protect staff and inmates from the possibility of becoming exposed to the HIV virus. The recommendations by the CDC appear to negate the viability of conjugal visit programs.

Is the Rehabilitative Effect of Conjugal Visits Diminished by Pregnancy Concerns?

Pregnancy is another medical and/or health concern associated with conjugal visitation programs. Does the state have legal authority to exert control over the reproductive rights of inmates and their spouses? If not, who will provide financial support for children conceived through conjugal visits? Is it reasonable to ask tax payers to assume this added financial burden? Is it ethical to knowingly provide opportunities for children to be born into single-parent families? When female inmates participate in conjugal visitation programs, what is the state's response when the female inmate becomes pregnant? Is abortion an option or a requirement? Who will pay for the pregnant inmates' health care and that of their infants? Is it ethical to require that infants be born in prison? Who protects the rights of the children?

Does the Justice Model Encompass Rehabilitative Programs Such As Conjugal and Familial Visitation?

Many people believe that the overriding purpose of imprisonment is to punish and that offenders are punished by being deprived of the benefits associated with living in society, for example, by limiting their social relationships. Supporters of the "just desert" or the punishment model believe that prisons should be painful places and that conjugal visit programs and the like are suspect to the extent that they diminish the punitive effects of incarceration.

At present, the majority of society seems to support the justice model, a model that is characterized by the tenet that lawbreakers deserve to be punished and that punishment is not intended to provide social benefits (Fogel, 1979). If one subscribes to the punishment model then inmates should suffer for their antisocial behaviors and should not be provided rehabilitation programs.

Are Cohesive, Adaptive, and Close Families a Rehabilitative Effect of Conjugal and Familial Visitations?

Researchers who have analyzed the impact of conjugal and familial visitation on incarcerated offenders' relationships with their families are almost nonexistent. Some researchers have determined that one rehabilitative effect of conjugal visitation programs is that they act as incentives for inmates to maintain good behavior while incarcerated and that inmates who participated in familial visitation programs were significantly less likely to be reincarcerated than were nonparticipants (Howser, Grossman, & MacDonald, 1984). In an evaluation of New York State's family reunion program, Carlson and Cervera (1991) compared two groups, inmates and their families who participated in familial visitation and inmates and their families who did not participate in familial visitation, to determine if the two groups differed in terms of cohesiveness, adaptiveness, and closeness. No statistical group differences in terms of cohesiveness, adaptiveness, and closeness were evident when the data were analyzed. This resulted in the researchers concluding that for the two groups examined, familial visitation did not result in measurable differences in cohesiveness, adaptiveness, and closeness. In other words, inmates and inmates' families who did not participate in the family reunion program were just as cohesive, adaptive, and close as the inmates and inmates' families who did.

Based solely on the previous information, it is argued that conjugal visits result in a number of serious problems for corrections personnel and offenders. In fact, it appears that more harm is done when compared to the positive results of family visitation programs. Because the negative impacts of the programs appear to be greater than their positive contributions, we must conclude that correctional systems should research other methods of achieving offender rehabilitation.

References

Balough, J. K. (1964). Conjugal visitations in prison: A sociological perspective. *Federal Probation, 27,* 52–58.

Beck, A. J., Bonczar, T. P., & Gilliard, D. K. (1993). *Jail inmates 1992.* Washington, DC: Bureau of Justice Statistics.

Bennett, L. A. (1989). Correctional administrators' attitudes toward private family visiting. *Prison Journal, 66,* 110–114.

Burstein, J. Q. (1977). *Conjugal visits in prison.* Lexington, MA: Heath Publishing.

Carlson, B. E., & Cervera, N. (1991). Inmates and their families: Conjugal visits, family contact, and family functioning. *Criminal Justice and Behavior, 18,* 318–333.

Fogel, D. (1979). *We are the living proof. The justice model for corrections.* Cincinnati: Anderson.

Hammett, T. M. (1988). *AIDS in correctional facilities: Issues and opinions* (3rd ed.). Washington, DC: National Institute of Justice.

Hammett, T. M. Harrold, L., Gross, M., & Epstein, J. (1994). *1991 Update: AIDS in correctional institutions—Issues and opinions.* Cambridge, MA: Abt Associates.

Hopper, C. B. (1969). *Sex in prison: The Mississippi experiment with conjugal visiting.* Baton Rouge: Louisiana State University Press.

Hopper, C. B. (1989). The evolution of conjugal visiting in Mississippi. *Prison Journal, 66,* 103–109.

Howser, J., Grossman, J., & MacDonald, D. (1984). Impact of family reunion programs on institutional discipline. *Journal of Offender Counseling, Services, and Rehabilitation, 8,* 27–36.

Innes, C. A. (1988, January). *BJS special report: Profile of state prison inmates, 1986.* Washington, DC: Department of Justice.

Johns, D. R. (1971). Alternatives to conjugal visiting. *Federal Probation, 36,* 48–52.

Palmer, J. W. (1991). *Constitutional rights of prisoners.* Cincinnati: Anderson.

Silverman, I. J., & Vega, M. (1996). *Corrections: A comprehensive view.* St. Paul, MN: West.

Task Force on Corrections. (1973). *Corrections.* Washington, DC: National Advisory Commission on Criminal Justice Standards and Goals.

POSTSCRIPT

Are Conjugal and Familial Visitations Effective Rehabilitative Concepts?

Who do you agree with? On what grounds? Moral? Humanitarian? Practical? Rehabilitative? Since less than 20 percent of all inmates are married, and since many of these have wives and families who live many miles away from the prison and who may have problems taking time off from work, the inmate pool for conjugal visitations is considerably narrow. Would this very small figure justify the costs of separate facilities, monitoring, and so on? Are familial visitation rights fair to the general inmate population, including singles, gay inmates, and lifers who might like to have outside visitors overnight?

McConnell argues that homosexuals and others are left out of the eligibility pool but that they are often the most difficult prisoners to control. However, many prisons have "girls' wards," or cells for openly homosexual inmates. Often wardens separate these inmates from others over their objections because they "flirt" and can contribute to heterosexual prisoners' fighting over their women. Would a partial solution to this problem be to arrange and supervise visits between inmates who are interested in being alone together?

Gordon contends that inmates who are allowed family visits are more malleable, while McConnell asserts that there is little hard empirical support of this belief. Would making conjugal visits a "reward" requiring good conduct rather than a "right" add to visitations' strengthening control over participating inmates? Would appropriate tools or props be useful for strengthening visits and make them more likely to be rehabilitative? For example, films, bikes, or fishing opportunities for prisoners and their children might be helpful. How could some of the problems identified by both authors be minimized? Are conjugal and familial visitations helpful? It so, for whom? Among earlier studies of this issue are J. Q. Burstein, *Conjugal Visits in Prison: Psychological and Social Consequences* (Lexington Books, 1977); C. B. Hopper, *Sex in Prison: The Mississippi Experiment With Conjugal Visiting* (Louisiana State University Press, 1969); and a follow-up cited by McConnell, "The Evolution of Conjugal Visiting in Mississippi," by C. B. Hopper, *The Prison Journal* (vol. 6, 1989), pp. 103–109.

More recent works that emphasize the broader issue of family relations include C. L. Blinn's *Material Ties: A Selection of Programs for Female Offenders* (American Correctional Association, 1997); *Parents in Prison: Addressing the Needs of Families* by J. Boudouris (American Correctional Association, 1996); and K. Gabel and D. Johnston, eds., *Children of Incarcerated Parents* (Free Press, 1995).

ISSUE 12

Should Serial Killers and Violent Sexual Predators Be Quarantined for Life?

YES: Frank M. Ochberg, from "Quarantine Them Beyond Their Jail Terms," *The Washington Post* (December 5, 1999)

NO: Howard Zonana, from "We're Doctors—Not Judges, Juries or Jailers," *The Washington Post* (December 5, 1999)

ISSUE SUMMARY

YES: Professor of psychiatry Frank M. Ochberg argues that a class of violent offenders are incurable and ought to be confined for life to mental hospitals rather than released from prison upon completion of their sentences.

NO: Professor of psychiatry and law Howard Zonana contends that doctors have no business becoming jailers for those who are perceived as dangerous by legal authorities.

Commentators on modern societies often point to the rule of law, however imperfect, as one of the greatest achievements of civilizations. Democracies in particular are praised for seeking justice and social control while striving to maintain due process, fairness, and legal consistency and protections for the accused. In America's tripartite system of government, the presidency, Congress, and the courts exist to maintain checks and balances so that no single group usurps the rights of others. The courts are especially important safeguards of individual rights and liberties.

Animated by the U.S. Constitution, including the Bill of Rights, the different levels of the courts traditionally have functioned as an insulator between external threats, such as elected officials and other powerful interests, and the "common man or woman," including those accused of doing terrible things. The courts also function to protect individuals from other components of the criminal justice system, including the police and prisons. At the very least, legal scholars say, the courts protect the accused from the public, which, following horrible criminal acts against individual citizens, can become vigilantes and even form lynch mobs. During such extreme situations politicians, prosecutors, prison administrators, and even medical professionals can give in to the cries for vengeance. This becomes strikingly pernicious, Howard Zonana argues in the second of the following selections, when the criminal justice system itself participates in the public's clamors by coopting medical professionals to inflict additional confinement on criminals with no intention of treating them.

Yet there are very dangerous individuals who have done great harm to others, including children, and who seem to be quite capable and ready to do it again. These "lethal predators," Frank M. Ochberg argues in the following selection, are often not legally insane; they are "evil." If this contention is true, shouldn't medical experts such as psychiatrists draw from their stock of knowledge to identify dangerous people and assist the criminal justice system in quarantining them beyond their legal sentences to protect the public?

As you read this debate, consider whether or not the trade-off between constitutional protections for all (including those who are accused of terrible crimes) and the likelihood of additional harm being done if legal protections are maintained is worth it. How many people might be affected by Ochberg's proposal? Think about Zonana's concern that once rights are suspended a potential floodgate of abuses could follow. At a more formal level of analysis, what is the role of psychiatrists and other professionals in criminal justice? Should they be healers or jailers?

Frank M. Ochberg

Quarantine Them Beyond Their Jail Terms

There is a certain small group of serial killers who are cruel, ritualistic and devoid of conscience, whose crimes have a strong sexual component and often involve rape or torture. They are outwardly normal and often very intelligent. They are difficult to apprehend and convict because they cover their tracks and improve their methods with each calculated crime. Because of that difficulty, they sometimes are able to plead guilty to lesser offenses and thus avoid maximum sentences. When they are released, it is almost certain they will kill again. Those of us who study them call them "lethal predators."

These people are not legally insane; they understand their misbehavior and can choose when to act upon their urges. Rather, they are mentally abnormal—"a rare blend of psychopathy combined with predatory sexual violence," in the words of Canadian psychologist Robert Hare.

FBI profilers Alan C. Brantley and Mary Ellen O'Toole estimate that there are approximately 100 such criminals in American prisons who are eligible to be paroled or released in less than a decade. And that should not be allowed to happen. Lethal predators serving less than a life sentence should be confined *beyond* the terms imposed in criminal court. This is not double jeopardy (two punishments for the same offense). It is a constitutional way to save innocent lives.

State by state, legislators can pass laws to accomplish this goal. This has been feasible since 1997, when the U.S. Supreme Court declared that Kansas's Sexually Violent Predator Act was constitutional. Kansas was one of several states that passed laws allowing the involuntary hospitalization of certain sexual predators after they complete their criminal sentences. Various state courts found those laws unconstitutional. Double jeopardy was one reason. Another was the fact that most of these criminals could not be effectively treated, and, in the words of an earlier Supreme Court ruling, "Absent treatment, confinement is imprisonment." This is ironic: If they can't be treated, why should these criminals be sent back into society?

But in the case of *Kansas v. Hendricks,* the Supreme Court said states could "quarantine" criminals who have a "mental abnormality" that results in predation, even though they had already served their sentences. Such hospitalization must be humane and nonpunitive, the court said; treatment may be offered, but a cure need not be expected. The court drew a parallel between such a predator and a person whose contagious disease poses a grave risk to others; either should be isolated, curable or not.

Although such civil commitment after confinement is now constitutional, only a handful of states have enacted legislation that would make that possible. More states need to do so.

I never thought I'd be a partisan in this debate. After many years in state and federal mental health administration, since 1981 I have been studying and treating the victims of violence, and avoiding the perpetrators. But then the case of Donald Gene Miller landed on my doorstep.

Miller was a 23-year-old criminal justice student and youth minister in East Lansing, Mich., when his fiancee disappeared on New Year's Day 1977. Two years later, Miller was convicted of raping and nearly strangling a 14-year-old girl, then stabbing her 13-year-old brother. Local prosecutors were sure Miller was responsible for the disappearances of his fiancee and at least three other women, but they lacked admissible evidence.

So the prosecutors offered a deal: Miller would lead authorities to the bodies of his victims and he would plead guilty to four counts of manslaughter. In exchange, his sentence for those killings would run concurrently with that for rape and attempted murder of the teenage girl—30 to 50 years.

Miller accepted the bargain, the bodies were identified, and he went to prison. Due to statutory sentencing guidelines, including mandatory time off for good behavior, Miller was to be freed in February 1999.

In 1997, my colleagues in the Michigan Victim Alliance asked me to help: Can't we do something, they said, to keep this serial killer from coming back to East Lansing?

As former mental health director for the state of Michigan, I was able to assemble a group of detectives, judges, legislators, prosecutors, prison psychologists and victim advocates. For two years, we debated Miller's diagnosis, prognosis and dangerousness. We interviewed experts who had interviewed him, including Earl James, a state police homicide detective and author of the book "Catching Serial Killers." "Clearly," James said, "he fit the profile of the intelligent, organized predator who escalates from fantasy to torture, murder and necrophilia." Nothing concentrates the mind like knowing a man like this is coming home—and his home is in your neighborhood.

Could Miller be confined in a mental hospital? Not under Michigan law—he wasn't insane; he was evil. Could Miller be tried in federal court for civil rights violations (crimes against women)? Not with existing evidence and binding non-disclosure agreements.

Ultimately, we discovered that Miller could be charged with a prison felony. Authorities sometime earlier had found a garrote in his cell and had given him a slap on the wrist—docking two years of his earned "good time." Our committee got prosecutors to bring this offense to criminal court. Miller was convicted. At sentencing, we were able to introduce evidence of his sadistic psychopathy because Michigan has a habitual offender statute and this was his third felony conviction. The court tacked on 20 to 40 more years.

Obviously, we were lucky. Other communities across America, facing the releases of their Donald Millers, are very much at risk.

The National Center for the Analysis of Violent Crime, a unit of the FBI, is now working with members of our Michigan team to reduce that risk. We are summarizing the scientific findings on the dangerousness and recidivism of predators, developing protocols for use in identifying incarcerated lethal predators, and helping state legislators frame appropriate laws.

Although the Supreme Court found the Kansas statute constitutional, it is not an ideal model, since it is broad enough to allow indefinite hospitalization of thousands of sexual deviants, including relatively harmless habitual exhibitionists. Laws that are too broad could be too costly, overwhelm the mental health system, and remove incentives for treatment where treatment *is* possible.

These are some of the valid reasons cited by the American Psychiatric Association and the American Civil Liberties Union for their objection to the *Kansas v. Hendricks* precedent.

·◄◎►·

But it is possible for states to write effective statutes that affect only a small group of genuinely dangerous killers. They can define lethal predators and require that such prisoners be evaluated for post-release civil commitment.

The inmate obviously would have to be lethal—he must have killed—and he must be a predator—that is, he must have left evidence of repetitious predatory acts, whether or not they resulted in criminal convictions. One essential feature of predation is its motivation: The perpetrator gets a sexual pleasure—usually involving arousal—while causing pain to the victim. Another feature is the crime's ritualistic quality.

A lethal predator also must demonstrate mental abnormality, usually a combination of sexual sadism and psychopathy. A psychologist or psychiatrist can evaluate sexual sadism to a high degree of reliability using standard tests, clinical interviews and evaluation of corroborated evidence. Psychopathy can also be determined. (This is not to be confused with psychosis, in which a person is out of touch with reality; psychotic criminals were judged mentally ill and confined long before *Kansas v. Hendricks.*) A psychopath understands right from wrong but has no conscience. Canadian psychologist Hare developed a commonly used method for establishing this condition, which consists of 20 items that trained assessors can rate according to a carefully constructed formulation.

At the civil commitment trial, a judge or jury would hear the testimony of police investigators and psychologists or psychiatrists, and then decide whether the inmate fit the statute. The standard of proof should be "clear and convincing" rather than "beyond reasonable doubt," since this is a civil, not a criminal determination. Predators should be confined in a secure setting, but separate from nonpredatory mentally ill patients. Each individual's case could be reviewed at set intervals.

By limiting the scope of new laws to the most dangerous class of predators, objections based upon cost and mental health policy will be avoided. Lives will be saved. And our state legislators will be spared the embarrassment of releasing lethal predators back home—to where we live.

Howard Zonana  **NO**

We're Doctors—Not Judges, Juries or Jailers

Physicians who promote the extension of sexual predator statutes, or even endorse them, must have lost their moral compass. It is not hard to understand the public's wish to see repeat offenders locked up and prevented from inflicting further harm upon society. The public probably couldn't care less whether the confinement is in a prison or a mental hospital, though people might have a few qualms if they understood that the hospital costs are two to five times higher.

It is harder to understand, however, why physicians would be willing to use their medical authority for preventive detention and punishment. Involuntary hospitalization was designed to ensure that those who are seriously mentally ill receive humane care and treatment when they are unable to care for themselves. It was not designed to be an arm of the criminal justice system.

Recently, some states have created a new kind of civil commitment that permits a class of criminals—repeat sexual offenders—to be transferred at the end of their sentences from prisons to hospitals and detained there until they can prove they are no longer dangerous. The decision to commit can be made on the basis of the behavior that resulted in their original arrest. No evidence of recent dangerous behavior is required. The laws are so broad as to include exhibitionists as well as sexual sadists and other criminals, as long as there was a sexual component to the crime. Now, some justice and mental health officials want to extend this to certain murderers so that they, too, would be indefinitely confined under the label of "mentally abnormal."

Because the element of mental abnormality is so vague, it allows the state to select the criminal behavior it would like to target and then find some disorder that will be present in certain felons. It is not that it is impossible to diagnose potentially dangerous mental abnormalities; it is that the process is an abuse of psychiatry.

About 15 states have adopted these "sexually violent predator" commitment statutes, upheld in 1997 as constitutional by a 5-to-4 U.S. Supreme Court decision in *Kansas v. Hendricks*. Leroy Hendricks is a pedophile who was arrested and imprisoned several times for molesting children. After he had finished serving his time—and although he had consistently been found

From Howard Zonana, "We're Doctors—Not Judges, Juries or Jailers," *The Washington Post* (December 5, 1999). Copyright © 1999 by Howard Zonana. Reprinted by permission of the author.

legally sane and competent—he was sent to a state hospital for the criminally mentally ill based on his mental disorder of pedophilia and presumed continuing inability to control his behavior. This amounts to using physicians and the mental health system to extend a criminal's prison sentence indefinitely.

Repeat sex offenders have always outraged the public. In an earlier era of therapeutic optimism—roughly the 1940s and '50s—more than half the states had laws confining such criminals to hospitals instead of prisons so that they could obtain treatment. When treatment did not work well enough, most states repealed or suspended these statutes and used "indeterminate" sentences such as "one day to life" to keep such offenders in prison.

But in the '70s, sentencing reforms repudiated a system that could be so prone to abuse. It was replaced with "determinate sentencing," wherein convicted felons receive fixed sentences and are required to serve the entire time in prison.

But the inflexibility of determinate sentencing, in turn, set the stage for the release of offenders who may repeat patterns of antisocial behavior. Following a particularly vicious crime by a sadistic pedophile who had already served his full "determinate sentence" in Washington, that state and others began to pass sexual predator laws.

What is problematic about these statutes is that the confinement in a mental hospital would begin only *after* the offender's entire prison sentence was served.

An additional problem, from a medical viewpoint, is the statutes' broad definition of mental disorder. It could be met by a diagnosis, such as antisocial personality disorder (APD), that generally has not been used as a basis for civil commitment. APD can be diagnosed when there is a history of childhood behavioral problems coupled with later adult criminal activity. It is not very precise or reliable; in fact, most criminals could be given this diagnosis. Since many are also recidivists, it could be argued that they are candidates for commitment at the end of their sentences.

In its Task Force Report on Sexually Dangerous Offenders this year, the American Psychiatric Association said that the new statutes are a misuse of psychiatry because they have the effect of defining criminal behavior as a mental illness. Moreover, they do not base criteria for hospitalization on psychiatric research or therapeutic findings.

꧁◉꧂

While the Kansas case specifically involved a pedophile, statutes in other states, such as Wisconsin, have included rapists with antisocial personality disorder. Now we are seeing proposed extensions to other criminal behavior, such as murder. Why stop there? In some countries, political dissidents have been labeled as mentally ill.

There are a host of problems surrounding the implementation of these civil commitment programs. Aside from the additional expenses of screening, legally adjudicating and civilly committing these inmates, there are enormous logistical problems. These "patients" require maximum-security settings. They cannot be mixed with actual mentally ill patients, since they often abuse them.

There are many unmet health needs in our prisons as it is. We need to identify serious psychiatric disorders that warrant treatment regardless of the crime committed. The proposed programs for murderers, however, are not seen as a mechanism to provide necessary treatment but rather to extend punishment and protect society. These statutes cloak their quasi-punitive intent in the language of medical treatment. These are appropriate societal goals but not at the expense of undermining the legitimacy of the medical model of commitment.

Criminal recidivists pose an enormous social problem to society. But it is a problem that needs to be addressed by the criminal justice system—not the medical profession. The system needs to be given resources to craft broader criminal penalty statutes, enabling longer sentences, as well as to provide better probation and parole monitoring of such individuals.

Mental health treatment may be a helpful adjunct in some cases where the individual is interested or the diagnosis warrants it, but is should not be distorted into being used as a tool of the state. Just as physicians should not participate in legally authorized executions, we should not condone the misuse of our professional values and erode patient trust by transforming our roles from healers to jailers.

POSTSCRIPT

Should Serial Killers and Violent Sexual Predators Be Quarantined for Life?

This issue parallels similar ones pervading criminal justice systems in modern societies. For example, many become outraged when convicted murderers are freed because of legal technicalities, when child molesters receive lenient sentences, and when known criminals are allowed to move into nice neighborhoods. In philosophy, the following ethical question is sometimes raised: If a terrorist knows where a bomb is planted on an airplane with dozens of people aboard, should the police have the right to torture him to get the information to save innocent lives? What rights do killers and violent offenders have? Should "evil" people be allowed to roam our streets?

Some people argue that framing the discourse in this way is absurd. They ask, What is "evil"? Aren't corporate heads who knowingly pollute streams, dictators who murder their own citizens, and Pentagon generals who participate in napalming villages equally "evil"? In an imperfect world where vengeance is far more "natural" than justice, should responsible citizens even consider responding to the serious problem of violent crime with further labeling and name calling? Others worry that medical experts do not have the ability to identify predators, let alone predict who will commit crimes in the future.

Ochberg argues that some serious violent sex offenders are incurable. Historically, sex offenders are likely to be recidivists. However, the new view holds that with relapse treatment (i.e., programs similar to those used to treat alcoholism) significant modifications in sexually deviant behavior are possible. However, offenders are never cured completely and must watch for relapses; and offenders must be highly motivated to cease such conduct, show empathy for victims, and be remorseful.

For a pointed attack on Kansas's 1994 Sexually Violent Predator Act, see S. Lally's "Steel Beds v. Iron Bars: New Laws Muddle How to Handle Sex Offenders," *The Washington Post* (July 27, 1997). Among the many excellent U.S. Department of Justice publications are *Sex Offenses and Offenders* (January 1997) and *Childhood Victimization: Early Adversity, Later Psychopathology* by C. S. Widom (January 2000). Male violence is linked with culture in *Masculinities, Violence and Culture* by S. E. Hatty (Sage Publications, 1999). Works that look at imprisonment processes are M. Welch's *Punishment in America: Social Control and the Ironies of Imprisonment* (Sage Publications, 1999); *Crime and Punishment: Inside Views* edited by R. Johnson and H. Toch (Roxbury, 2000); and George E. Rush's *Inside American Jails and Prisons* (Copperhouse, 1997), an outstanding survey of state and federal prisons and jails.

On the Internet . . .

Federal Bureau of Investigation

The home page of the FBI leads to the 10 most wanted criminals, uniform crime reports, FBI case reports, major investigations, and more.

http://www.fbi.gov

Sourcebook of Criminal Justice Statistics Online

Data about all aspects of criminal justice in the United States is available at this site, which includes over 655 tables and figures from more than 100 sources.

http://www.albany.edu/sourcebook/

Gun Owners of America

Gun Owners of America is a gun lobby organization based in Springfield, Virginia. Their site links to current national alerts and state-wide alerts about gun owners' rights, proposed gun-control legislation, and other gun-related information.

http://www.gunowners.org

Handgun Control, Inc.

Handgun Control, Inc., is a nonpartisan, not-for-profit organization that lobbies in favor of commonsense gun regulations at both state and national levels. This site offers action alerts, information on gun laws and legislation, and advice on how to avoid becoming a victim of handgun violence.

http://www.handguncontrol.org

NYPD Crime Strategies

This site from the chief of the New York Police Department details several crime strategies adopted by the department, including "Reclaiming the Public Spaces of New York City," which is based on the broken windows theory.

http://www.ci.nyc.ny.us/html/nypd/html/
chfdept/strategies.html

Community Policing: A List of Programs

This site contains a "mega-list" of Community Policing and Problem Solving (COPPS) programs and a description of each. Some program titles link to sites that further detail the programs or provide examples of the programs in action.

http://faculty.ncwc.edu/toconnor/comlist.htm

PART 4

Criminal Justice Research, Evaluation, and Policy Analysis

*A*lthough research—in particular, its interpretations and applications—can be highly problematic, it remains a core task for criminologists and criminal justice scholars. Among the most important criminological research findings of the past 25 years is that a relatively small core of criminals commit a disproportionate amount of crime. Also important to criminal justice is the development and utilization of technology, such as DNA technology, computer units in police cars, and innovations in investigation techniques. Yet just how helpful is this research?

Questions addressed in this selection ask, Why haven't increased executions reduced violent crime? Is it possible that more guns in the hands of Americans could actually lead to less crime? And, lastly, Will zero tolerance policing solve much of America's cities' crime problems? Perhaps researching crime and then deciding how to use the results is one of criminology's biggest problems.

- Is Capital Punishment Bad Public Policy?

- Do More Guns Lead to Less Crime?

- Should the Police Enforce Zero-Tolerance Laws?

ISSUE 13

Is Capital Punishment Bad Public Policy?

YES: David Von Drehle, from "Miscarriage of Justice: Why the Death Penalty Doesn't Work," *The Washington Post Magazine* (February 5, 1995)

NO: Ernest van den Haag, from "The Ultimate Punishment: A Defense," *Harvard Law Review* (May 1986)

ISSUE SUMMARY

YES: David Von Drehle, a writer and the arts editor for the *Washington Post,* examines specific capital punishment cases, statistics, and statements made by U.S. Supreme Court justices and prosecutors reversing their support of the death penalty and concludes that capital punishment is bad policy.

NO: Ernest van den Haag, a professor of jurisprudence and public policy (now retired), analyzes a number of objections to capital punishment, ranging from its unfair distribution to its excessive costs and its brutal nature. He rejects claims that capital punishment is unfair and barbaric, and he maintains that the death penalty does deter criminals and is just retribution for terrible crimes.

In 1968 only 38 percent of all Americans supported the death penalty for certain crimes. In 1972, when the U.S. Supreme Court handed down its decision in *Furman v. Georgia* stating that capital punishment violated the Eighth Amendment, which prohibits cruel and unusual punishment, many Americans were convinced that capital punishment was permanently abolished. After all, even though there were 500 inmates on death row at the time, there had been a steady decline in the number of executions in the United States: In the 1930s there were on average 152 executions per year; in 1962 there were 47 executions; and in 1966 there was 1. Polls in the late 1960s showed that most Americans opposed the death penalty, and virtually every other Western industrial nation had long since eliminated the death sentence or severely modified its use.

Polls taken in the 1990s showed that 75–80 percent of all Americans support capital punishment. In 1990, 23 people were executed; in 1999, 98 were.

Since 1976, when capital punishment was restored, over 600 people have been executed. Currently, there are approximately 3,500 people on death row. Eighteen states allow executions of defendants who are as young as 16, and there are currently over 60 juveniles on death row. Texas leads the nation in executions: 36 percent of all executions in 1999 were held in that state. Of the 1999 executions, 94 were by lethal injection, and 3 were by electrocution.

What has happened since the 1960s? We will probably never know the full answer to this question, but there are some clues. To begin with, in *Furman v. Georgia,* the Supreme Court did not really ban capital punishment because it was cruel and unusual in itself. It simply argued that it was unconstitutional for juries to be given the right to decide arbitrarily and discriminatorily on capital punishment. Thus, if states can show that capital punishment is not arbitrary or discriminatory and that the sentencing process is performed in two separate stages—first guilt or innocence is established, and *then* the determination of the sentence occurs—then some offenses are legally punishable by death. This was the Supreme Court's ruling in 1976 in *Gregg v. Georgia,* which effectively restored the death penalty.

Since the late 1960s Americans have become more conservative. Fear of crime has greatly increased, although the number of crimes may not have changed. Moreover, many of the measures taken under the Omnibus Safe Streets Act to reduce crime, speed up judicial processes, and rehabilitate criminals are now viewed by professionals and laypeople alike as failures. The national mood is now solidly behind "getting tough" on criminals, especially drug dealers and murderers. Support and utilization of capital punishment make sense within the logic of the present cultural and political situation.

There is a movement among criminologists to reassess studies done before the 1960s that indicated that states in which capital punishment prevailed had homicide rates that were just as high as those in which it was not a penalty and that executions did not deter others from committing crimes. Isaac Ehrlich, for instance, in an extensive statistical analysis of executions between 1933 and 1967, reached very different conclusions. He contends not only that the executions reduced the murder rate but also that one additional execution per year between 1933 and 1967 would have resulted in seven or eight fewer murders per year!

Many scholars have bitterly attacked Ehrlich's empirical findings. Most attempt to fault his methods, but others assert that even if he is empirically correct, the trade-off is not worth it. The state should not have the right to extract such a primitive "justice" as the murder of a human being, even a convicted killer. Other scholars emphasize the fact that there have been a disproportionate number of blacks executed (between 1930 and 1967, 2,066 blacks were executed as opposed to 1,751 whites, even though blacks constituted only 10 percent of the total population then). Some counter that this simply indicates that more whites need to be executed as well!

Is capital punishment bad policy? If not, what crimes should it be reserved for? Murder? Rape? Espionage? Drug dealing? Kidnapping? How should it be carried out?

David Von Drehle  **YES**

Miscarriage of Justice: Why the Death Penalty Doesn't Work

$\mathbf{A}$s a boy of 8, the son of good, poor parents, James Curtis "Doug" McCray had limitless dreams; he told everyone he met that someday he would be president of the United States. Soon enough, he realized that poor black children did not grow up to be president, but still he was a striver. At Dunbar High School in Fort Myers, Fla., he was an all-state receiver on the football team, an all-conference guard in basketball and the state champion in the 440-yard dash. He made the honor roll, and became the first and only of the eight McCray kids to attend college.

His was a success story, but for one flaw. McCray had a drinking problem. He washed out of college and joined the Army. A year and a half later, the Army gave him a medical discharge because he had been found to suffer from epilepsy. McCray married, fathered a son, tried college again; nothing took. He wound up back home, a tarnished golden boy.

On an October evening in 1973, an elderly woman named Margaret Mears was at home in her apartment, picking no trouble, harming no one, when someone burst in, stripped and raped her, then beat her to death. A bloody handprint was matched to Doug McCray's. He insisted that he had no memory of the night in question, and his jury unanimously recommended a life sentence. But McCray had the bad fortune to be tried by Judge William Lamar Rose.

... To him, the murder of Margaret Mears was precisely the type of savagery the law was intended to punish: committed in the course of another felony, and surely heinous, surely atrocious, surely cruel. Rose overruled the jury and banged the gavel on death.

When McCray arrived at Florida State Prison in 1974, nine men awaited execution and he made 10. His case entered the appeals process, and as the years went by, McCray wept for his best friend on death row, John Spenkelink, who became the first man in America executed against his will under modern death penalty laws. He watched as a young man named Bob Graham became governor of Florida and led the nation in executing criminals. Eight years

From David Von Drehle, "Miscarriage of Justice: Why the Death Penalty Doesn't Work," *The Washington Post Magazine* (February 5, 1995). Copyright © 1995 by *The Washington Post.* Reprinted by permission.

later, he watched Gov. Bob Martinez take Graham's place and sign 139 death warrants in four years. McCray saw the infamous serial killer Ted Bundy come to the row, and almost 10 years later saw him go quietly to Old Sparky.

Living on death row, McCray saw men cut, saw men burned, even saw a man killed. He saw inmates carried from their cells after committing suicide, and others taken away after going insane. He saw wardens and presidents come and go. Death row got bigger and bigger. By the time Spenkelink was executed in May 1979, Jacksonville police officers printed T-shirts proclaiming "One down, 133 to go!" . . .

Doug McCray watched as death row doubled in size, and grew still more until it was not a row but a small town, Death Town, home to more than 300 killers. Nationwide, the condemned population climbed toward 3,000. The seasons passed through a silver of dirty glass beyond two sets of bars outside McCray's tiny cell on the row, which was very cold in the winter and very hot in the summer, noisy at all times and stinking with the odor of smoking, sweating, dirty, defecating men. Four seasons made a year, and the years piled up: 5, 10, 15, 16, 17 . . .

All this time, Doug McCray was sentenced to death but he did not die. Which makes him the perfect symbol of the modern death penalty.

People talk a great deal these days about getting rid of government programs that cost too much and produce scant results. So it's curious that one of the least efficient government programs in America is also among the most popular. Capital punishment is favored by more than three-quarters of American voters. And yet, in 1994, the death row population nationwide exceeded 3,000 for the first time ever; out of all those condemned prisoners, only 31 were executed. There are hundreds of prisoners in America who have been on death row more than a decade, and at least one—Thomas Knight of Florida—has been awaiting execution for 20 years. Every cost study undertaken has found that it is far more expensive, because of added legal safeguards, to carry out a death sentence than it is to jail a killer for life. Capital punishment is the principal burden on the state and federal appellate courts in every jurisdiction where it is routinely practiced. The most efficient death penalty state, Texas, has a backlog of more than 300 people on its death row. It manages to execute only about one killer for every four newly sentenced to die—and the number of executions may drop now that the U.S. Supreme Court has ordered Texas to provide lawyers for death row inmate appeals. Overall, America has executed approximately one in every 20 inmates sentenced to die under modern death penalty laws.

This poor record of delivering the punishments authorized by legislatures and imposed by courts has persisted despite a broad shift to the right in the federal courts. It has resisted legislative and judicial efforts to streamline the process. It has outlasted William J. Brennan Jr. and Thurgood Marshall, the Supreme Court's strongest anti-death penalty justices. It has endured countless campaigns by state legislators and governors and U.S. representatives and senators and even presidents who have promised to get things moving. If New York reinstates the death penalty this year, as Gov. George Pataki has promised, there is no reason to believe things will change; New York is unlikely to see another execution in this century. Congress extended the death penalty to cover more than 50 new crimes last year, but that bill will be long forgotten before Uncle Sam executes more than a handful of prisoners.

Most people like the death penalty in theory; virtually no one familiar with it likes the slow, costly and inefficient reality. But after 20 years of trying to make the death penalty work, it is becoming clear that we are stuck with the reality, and not the ideal.

⋅◆⋅

To understand why this is, you have to understand the basic mechanics of the modern death penalty. The story begins in 1972.

For most of American history, capital punishment was a state or even a local issue. Criminals were tried, convicted and sentenced according to local rules and customs, and their executions were generally carried out by town sheriffs in courthouse squares. Federal judges took almost no interest in the death penalty, and even state appeals courts tended to give the matter little consideration.

Not surprisingly, a disproportionate number of the people executed under these customs were black, and the execution rate was most dramatically skewed for the crime of rape. As sensibilities became more refined, however, decent folks began to object to the spectacle of local executions. In Florida in the 1920s, for example, a coalition of women's clubs lobbied the legislature to ban the practice, arguing that the sight of bodies swinging in town squares had a brutalizing effect on their communities. Similar efforts around the country led to the centralizing of executions at state prisons, where they took place outside the public view, often at midnight or dawn.

Still, the death penalty remained a state matter, with the federal government extremely reluctant to exert its authority. Washington kept its nose out of the death chambers, just as it steered clear of the schools, courtrooms, prisons and voting booths. All that changed, and changed dramatically, in the 1950s and '60s, when the Supreme Court, in the era of Chief Justice Earl Warren, asserted more vigorously than ever that the protections of the U.S. Constitution applied to actions in the states. For the first time, federal standards of equality were used to strike down such state and local practices as school segregation, segregation of buses and trains, poll taxes and voter tests. The lengthened arm of the federal government reached into police stations: For example, in *Miranda v. Arizona*, the Supreme Court required that suspects be advised to their constitutional rights when arrested. The long arm reached into the courtrooms: In *Gideon v. Wainwright*, the high court declared that the federal guarantee of due process required that felony defendants in state trials be provided with lawyers.

Opponents of capital punishment urged the courts to reach into death rows as well. Anthony Amsterdam, at the time a Stanford University law professor, crafted arguments to convince the federal courts that the death penalty violated the Eighth Amendment (which bars "cruel and unusual punishments") and the 14th Amendment (which guarantees "equal protection of the laws"). Amsterdam's arguments won serious consideration in the newly aggressive federal courts, and on January 17, 1972, the greatest of Amsterdam's lawsuits, *Furman v. Georgia,* was heard in the Supreme Court.

Amsterdam delivered a brilliant four-pronged attack on capital punishment. He began by presenting statistical proof that the death penalty in America was overwhelmingly used against the poor and minorities. Next, Amsterdam argued that the death penalty was imposed arbitrarily, almost randomly. Judges and juries meted out their sentences without clear standards to guide them, and as a result men were on death row for armed robbery, while nearby, murderers served life, or less. Discretion in death sentencing was virtually unfettered. Amsterdam's third point was his most audacious, but it turned out to be crucial: The death penalty was so rarely carried out in contemporary America that it could no longer be justified as a deterrent to crime. In the years leading up to Amsterdam's argument, use of the death penalty had steeply declined. What made this argument so daring was that the sharp drop in executions was partly a result of Amsterdam's own legal campaign to abolish the death penalty. He was, in effect, challenging a state of affairs he had helped to create.

In closing, Amsterdam argued that the death penalty had become "unacceptable in contemporary society," that the "evolving standards" of decent behavior had moved beyond the point of legal killing. This was the weakest of his arguments, because nearly 40 states still had death penalty laws on the books, but previous Supreme Court decisions suggested that the shortest route to abolishing the death penalty would be to convince a majority of the justices that "standards of decency" had changed. Amsterdam had to try.

Behind closed doors, the nine justices of the court revealed a wide range of reactions to Amsterdam's case—from Brennan and Marshall, the court's liberal stalwarts, who voted to abolish capital punishment outright, to Justice William H. Rehnquist, the new conservative beacon, who rejected all of the arguments. Justice William O. Douglas was unpersuaded by the notion that standards of decency had evolved to the point that capital punishment was cruel and unusual punishment, but he agreed the death penalty was unconstitutionally arbitrary. Chief Justice Warren E. Burger and Justice Harry A. Blackmun both expressed personal opposition to capital punishment—if they were legislators, they would vote against it—but they believed that the language of the Constitution clearly left the matter to the states. That made three votes to strike down the death penalty, and three to sustain it.

Justice Lewis F. Powell Jr. also strongly objected to the court taking the question of the death penalty out of the hands of elected legislatures. This would be an egregious example of the sort of judicial activism he had always opposed. Though moved by Amsterdam's showing or racial discrimination, Powell believed this was a vestige of the past, and could be rectified without a sweeping decision in Furman. Powell's vote made four to sustain the death penalty. Justice Potter Stewart, painfully aware of the more than 600 prisoners whose lives were dangling on his vote, moved toward Douglas's view that the death penalty had become unconstitutionally arbitrary. Stewart's vote made four to strike down the death penalty as it existed.

That left Justice Byron R. White, known to observers of the court as a strict law-and-order man. In his brusque opinions, White backed prosecutors and police at almost every turn. But he was deeply impressed by Amsterdam's presentation; he told his law clerks that it was "possibly the best" oral argument he had ever heard. The point that had won White was Amsterdam's boldest: that the death penalty was applied too infrequently to serve any purpose. White cast the deciding vote to strike down the death penalty not because he wanted to see an end to capital punishment, but because he wanted to see more of it.

The product of these deliberations was one of the most difficult decisions in the history of the U.S. Supreme Court. The broad impact of *Furman v. Georgia,* striking down hundreds of separate laws in nearly 40 separate jurisdictions, was unprecedented. Rambling and inchoate—nine separate opinions totaling some 50,000 words—it remains easily the longest decision ever published by the court. But for all its wordy impact, Furman was almost useless as a precedent for future cases. It set out no clear legal standards. As Powell noted in his stinging dissent:

"Mr. Justice Douglas concludes that capital punishment is incompatible with notions of 'equal protection' that he finds 'implicit' in the Eighth Amendment . . . Mr. Justice Brennan bases his judgment primarily on the thesis that the penalty 'does not comport with human dignity' . . . Mr. Justice Stewart concludes that the penalty is applied in a 'wanton' and 'freakish' manner . . . For Mr. Justice White it is the 'infrequency' with which the penalty is imposed that renders its use unconstitutional . . . Mr. Justice Marshall finds that capital punishment is an impermissible form of punishment because it is 'morally unacceptable' and 'excessive' . . .

"I [will not] attempt to predict what forms of capital statutes, if any, may avoid condemnation in the future under the variety of views expressed by the collective majority today."

In other words, totally missing from the longest Supreme Court decision in history was any clear notion of how the death penalty might be fixed.

⋅⁂⋅

That painfully splintered 5-to-4 vote turned out to be a high-water mark of the Supreme Court's willingness to intervene in the business of the states. In Furman, the justices were willing to abolish the death penalty as it existed. But the justices were not willing to forbid executions forever. They kicked the question of whether the death penalty was "cruel and unusual" back to the state legislatures. For nearly 20 years, the states—especially the Southern states—had felt pounded by the Supreme Court. Rarely did they get the chance to answer. The court did not ask what they thought about school desegregation, or voting rights, or the right to counsel. But *Furman v. Georgia* invited the states to respond to a hostile Supreme Court decision.

Florida was the first state to craft an answer, after calling its legislature into special session. Blue-ribbon panels appointed by the governor and legislature struggled to make sense of Furman—but how? On the governor's commission, legal advisers unanimously predicted that no capital punishment law would ever satisfy the high court, but the membership turned instead to a nugget from Justice Douglas's opinion. Douglas wrote that the problem with the pre-Furman laws was that "under these laws no standards govern the selection of the penalty." Douglas seemed to be saying that judges and juries needed rules to guide their sentencing.

The legislative commission reached a different conclusion, simply by seizing on a different snippet from the Furman ruling. Figuring that Byron White was the most likely justice to change his position, commission members combed his opinion for clues. White had complained that "the legislature authorizes [but] does not mandate the penalty in any particular class or kind of case . . ." That phrase seemed crucial: "Authorizes but does not mandate." Apparently, White would prefer to see death made mandatory for certain crimes.

Furman was as cryptic as the Gnostic gospels. Robert Shevin, Florida's attorney general at the time, was just as confused. He summoned George Georgieff and Ray Marky, his two top death penalty aides, to explain the ruling. "I've been reading it since it came out," Marky told his boss, "and I still have no idea what it means."

Gov. Reubin Askew refused to go along with mandatory sentences—he considered them barbaric. And so it was that while rank-and-file lawmakers made interminable tough-on-crime speeches, in the last month of 1972 Florida's power brokers hashed out a deal behind closed doors. Their new law spelled out "aggravating" circumstances—such as a defendant's criminal record and the degree of violence involved in the crime—which, if proven, would make a guilty man eligible for the death penalty. The law also spelled out "mitigating" circumstances, such as a defendant's age or mental state, that might suggest a life sentence instead. After a defendant was found guilty of a capital offense, the jury would hear evidence of aggravating and mitigating factors. By majority vote, the jurors would recommend either life in prison or the death penalty. Then the judge would be required to reweigh the aggravating and mitigating factors and impose the sentence, justifying it in writing. As a final safeguard, the sentence would be reviewed by the state's highest court. In this way, perhaps, they could thread the Furman needle: setting standards, limiting discretion, erasing caprice—all while avoiding mandatory sentences.

They were a few men in a back room, trading power and guessing over an incoherent Supreme Court document. It was not a particularly promising effort. Nevertheless, their compromise passed overwhelmingly, giving America its first legislative answer to Furman. Immediately, officials from states across the country began calling Florida for advice and guidance. And very soon, lawyers and judges began to discover that the law drafted in confusion and passed in haste was going to be hell to administer.

⋅❦⋅

The problem was that underneath the tidy, legalistic, polysyllabic, etched-in-marble tone of the new law was a lot of slippery mishmash. The aggravating and mitigating factors sounded specific and empirical, but many of them were matters of judgment rather than fact. A murderer was more deserving of the death penalty, for example, if his actions involved "a great risk of death to many persons"—but where one judge might feel that phrase applied to a drive-by killer who sprays a whole street with gunfire, another might apply it to a burglar who stabs a man to death while the victim's wife slumbers nearby. How much risk makes a "great" risk, and what number of persons constitutes "many"?

Another aggravating circumstance was even harder to interpret—"especially heinous, atrocious or cruel." The idea was to identify only the worst of the hundreds of murders each year in Florida. But wasn't the act of murder itself "heinous, atrocious or cruel"? Again, this aggravating circumstance was very much in the eye of the beholder: To one judge, stabbing might seem more cruel than shooting, because it involved such close contact between killer and victim. Another judge, however, might think it crueler to place a cold gun barrel to a victim's head before squeezing the trigger. One jury might find it especially heinous for a victim to be killed by a stranger, while the next set of jurors might find it more atrocious for a victim to die at the hands of a trusted friend. And so forth. It was an attempt to define the undefinable.

The imprecision was even more obvious on the side of mitigation, where it weighed in a defendant's favor if he had no "significant history" of past criminal behavior. How much history was that? "The age of the defendant" was supposed to be considered under the new law—but where one jury might think 15 was old enough to face the death penalty, another might have qualms about executing a man who was "only" 20. What about elderly criminals? Was there an age beyond which a man should qualify for mercy—and if so, what was it?

Clearly, a lot of discretion was left to the judge and jury. Even more discretion was allowed in tallying the aggravating versus the mitigating circumstances, and still more in deciding what weight to give each factor. The jury was supposed to render an "advisory" opinion on the proper sentence, death or life in prison, but how much deference did the judge have to pay to that advice? The law said nothing. After the judge imposed a death sentence, the state supreme court was required to review it. But what standards was the court supposed to apply? The law said nothing.

These questions might have seemed tendentious and picayune, except for the fact that Doug McCray and dozens of others were quickly sent to death row, and these seemingly trivial questions became the cruxes of life-and-death litigation. The law, shot through with question marks, became a lawyer's playground. After all, laws were supposed to be clear and fixed; they were supposed to mean the same thing from day to day, courtroom to courtroom, town to town. And given that their clients were going to be killed for breaking the law, it seemed only fair for defense lawyers to demand that simple degree of reliability.

In 1976, when the U.S. Supreme Court returned to the question of capital punishment, the justices agreed that the laws must be reliable. By then some 35 states had passed new death penalty laws, many of them modeled on Florida's. In a string of rulings the high court outlawed mandatory death sentences and affirmed the complex systems for weighing specified factors in favor of and against a death sentence.

But in striking down mandatory sentences, the court made consistency a constitutional requirement for the death penalty; the law must treat "same" cases the same and "different" cases differently. The thousands of capital crimes committed each year in America raised a mountain of peculiarities—each criminal and crime was subtly unique. Somehow the law must penetrate this mountain to discern some conceptual key that would consistently identify cases that were the "same" and cull ones that were "different." Furthermore, the court decided, the Constitution requires extraordinary consistency from capital punishment laws. "The penalty of death is qualitatively different from a sentence of imprisonment, however long," Justice Potter Stewart wrote. "Because of that qualitative difference, there is a corresponding difference in the need for reliability . . ."

Each year, some 20,000 homicides are committed in America, and the swing justices expected the death penalty laws to steer precisely and consistently through this carnage to find the relatively few criminals deserving execution. Somehow, using the black-and-white of the criminal code, the system must determine the very nature of evil. King Solomon himself might demur.

"The main legal battle is over," declared the New York Times in an editorial following the 1976 decisions. In fact, the battles were only beginning.

After Doug McCray was sentenced to die in 1974, his case went to the Florida Supreme Court for the required review. . . . In October 1980, the Florida Supreme Court agreed that Doug McCray should die. The following year the U.S. Supreme Court declined to review the state court's decision.

Through all this, McCray continued to insist that he had no memory of murdering Margaret Mears. He passed a lie detector test, and though such tests are not admissible in court, there was another reason to believe what he said. It was possible that McCray's epilepsy, which had first emerged in several powerful seizures during his Army basic training, was the type known as "temporal lobe seizure disorder." This disease often emerges in late adolescence; it is known to cause violent blackouts; and it can be triggered by alcohol. The possibility had not come out at McCray's trial, nor was it properly researched in preparation for his hearing on executive clemency. The hearing, held on December 16, 1981, went badly for McCray. An attorney, Jesse James Wolbert, had been appointed to represent him, but Wolbert did not bother to read the trial record, let alone prepare a compelling case for mercy. Perhaps he had other things on his mind: By the time McCray's death warrant was signed three months later, Wolbert had drained another client's trust fund and become a federal fugitive.

Wolbert's disappearance turned out to be a blessing for McCray, because an anti-death penalty activist named Scharlette Holdman persuaded Bob Dillinger of St. Petersburg to take the case, and Dillinger was a damn good lawyer. He filed a hasty appeal in the Florida Supreme Court asking for a stay of execution. The result was amazing: Having affirmed McCray's death sentence

18 months earlier, the justices now ordered a new trial. The sentence, they ruled, had been based on the theory that the murder had been committed in conjunction with a rape. "Felony murder," this is called—murder coupled with another felony. In 1982, the Florida Supreme Court, by a vote of 4 to 3, declared that the underlying felony, rape, had not been proven beyond a reasonable doubt. Eight years after the original sentence, Doug McCray was going back to trial.

Except that something even more amazing happened a few weeks later. The state supreme court granted the prosecution's request for a rehearing, and Justice Ray Ehrlich abruptly changed his mind. His vote made it 4 to 3 in favor of upholding McCray's death sentence. In the course of six months, Ehrlich had gone from believing McCray's sentence was so flawed that he should have a new trial to believing that his sentence was sound enough to warrant his death. The court contacted the company that publishes all its decisions and asked that the first half of this flip-flop—the order for a new trial—be erased from history.

Gov. Bob Graham signed a second death warrant on May 27, 1983. By this time, Bob Dillinger had located his client's ex-wife in California, where she lived with her son by Doug McCray. The son was what his father had once been: bright as a whip, interested in current events, a devourer of books, good at games. The ex-wife, Myra Starks, was mystified by the course her husband's life had taken. They had been high school sweethearts, and she had married him certain that he was upward bound. When McCray had left school to join the Army, Starks had clung to that vision, picturing a steady string of promotions leading to a comfortable pension. Then came the seizures and the medical discharge, and her husband's behavior changed horribly. He drank heavily, and sometimes when he was drunk he struck out at her violently—though after each of these outbursts, he insisted he remembered nothing. Myra Starks did not make a connection between the medical discharge and the change in her man; instead, she packed up their baby boy and moved out. Within a year, McCray was on trial for murder.

In addition to locating Starks, Bob Dillinger also arranged for a full-scale medical evaluation of his client, and the doctor concluded that McCray indeed suffered from temporal lobe seizure disorder. It all came together: the violent blackouts, triggered by drink. In prison, after a number of seizures, McCray was put on a drug regimen to control his disease: Dilantin, a standard epilepsy treatment, in the mornings, and phenobarbital, a sedative, at night. When Dillinger arranged for Myra Starks to see her ex-husband, after a decade apart, she exclaimed, "He's just like the old Doug!"

But he was scheduled to die. Following established procedure, Dillinger returned to the Florida Supreme Court. It was the fifth time the court had considered McCray's case. This time, the justices concluded that the new medical evidence might be important in weighing whether death was the appropriate sentence. They ordered the trial court to hold a hearing and stayed the execution while this was done.

Doug McCray had lived on death row nine years. . . .

In all that time, though, his case had not moved past the first level of appeals. The Florida Supreme Court had weighed and reweighed his case, and with each weighing the justices had reached a different conclusion.

❧

McCray's case was far from unusual. Every death penalty case winds up on spongy ground, even the most outrageous. It took nearly a decade for Florida to execute serial killer Ted Bundy, and even longer for John Wayne Gacy to reach the end in Illinois. The courts routinely reverse themselves, then double back again. The same case can look different with each fresh examination or new group of judges. Defenders have learned to exploit every possible advantage from the tiniest detail to the loftiest constitutional principle. A conscientious defense attorney has no choice—especially if any question remains as to whether the condemned man actually committed the crime for which he was sentenced. The effort involves huge expenditures of time and resources, and results are notoriously uncertain. . . .

❧

By the time Doug McCray's case returned to the trial court for a new sentence in 1986, the hanging judge, William Lamar Rose, was gone. So many years had passed. But in his place was another stern man who was no less outraged at the enormity of McCray's crime. . . .

McCray had, over the years, become a favorite of death penalty opponents, because he seemed so gentle and redeemable. Frequently, they argued that not all death row prisoners are "like Ted Bundy," and McCray was the sort of prisoner they were talking about. The harshest word in his vocabulary was "shucks." He read every book he could get his hands on. There was a poignant vulnerability to him.

But the new judge focused, as the old one had done, on the crime: A defenseless, innocent, helpless woman alone, terrorized, apparently raped, then killed. He sentenced McCray to death once more. And the case returned to the Florida Supreme Court for a sixth time. In June 1987, after a U.S. Supreme Court decision in favor of another Florida inmate, the justices sent McCray's case back because the judge had overruled the jury's advisory sentence. What was his justification? The judge's justification was an elderly woman savagely murdered. Once again, he imposed the death sentence.

So the case of Doug McCray returned for the seventh time to the Florida Supreme Court. Did he deserve to die? Four times, a trial judge insisted that he did. Twice, the state's high court agreed. And four times, the same court expressed doubts. A single case, considered and reconsidered, strained and restrained, weighed and reweighed. A prism, a kaleidoscope, a rune of unknown meaning. The life of a man, viewed through the lens of a complex, uncertain, demanding law. Should he live or die?

In May 1991, after weighing his case for the seventh time in 17 years, the Florida Supreme Court reversed McCray's death sentence and imposed a sentence of life in prison. For 17 years, two courts had debated—the trial court and the state supreme court. No liberal outsiders stalled the process, no bleeding hearts intervened. Even the lawyers added little to the essential conundrum, which was in the beginning as it was in the end: Doug McCray, bad guy, versus Doug McCray, not-quite-so-bad guy. The case was far from aberrant. It was one of hundreds of such cases.

•◄❍►•

Some politicians and pundits still talk as if the confusion over the death penalty can be eliminated by a healthy dose of conservative toughness, but among the people who know the system best that explanation is losing steam. More than 20 years have passed since *Furman v. Georgia;* courts and legislatures have gotten tougher and tougher on the issue—but the results have remained negligible. The execution rate hovers at around 25 or 30 per year, while America's death row population has swelled past 3,000. It makes no real difference who controls the courts, as California voters learned after they dumped their liberal chief justice in 1986. The court turned rightward, but 7½ years later, California had executed just two of the more than 300 prisoners on its death row. (One of the two had voluntarily surrendered his appeals.) No matter how strongly judges and politicians favor capital punishment, the law has remained a mishmash.

It is hard to see a way out. The idea that the death penalty should not be imposed arbitrarily—that each case should be analyzed by a rational set of standards—has been so deeply woven into so many federal and state court rulings that there is little chance of it being reversed. Courts have softened that requirement, but softening has not solved the problem. Proposals to limit access to appeals for death row inmates have become staples of America's political campaigns, and many limits have been set. But it can take up to a decade for a prisoner to complete just one trip through the courts, and no one has proposed denying condemned inmates one trip.

. . . [E]ven the most vicious killers . . . cannot be executed quickly. Gerald Stano, who in the early 1980s confessed to killing more than two dozen women, is alive. Thomas Knight, who in 1980 murdered a prison guard while awaiting execution for two other murders, is alive. Jesus Scull, who in 1983 robbed and murdered two victims and burned their house around them, is alive. Howard Douglas, who in 1973 forced his wife to have sex with her boyfriend as he watched, then smashed the man's head in, is alive. Robert Buford, who in 1977 raped and beat a 7-year-old girl to death, is alive. Eddie Lee Freeman, who in 1976 strangled a former nun and dumped her in a river to drown, is alive. Jesse Hall, who in 1975 raped and murdered a teenage girl and killed her boyfriend, is alive. James Rose, who in 1976 raped and murdered an 8-year-old girl in Fort Lauderdale, is alive. Larry Mann, who in 1980 cut a little girl's throat and clubbed her to death as she crawled away, is alive.

And that's just in Florida. The story is the same across the country.

In 1972, Justice Harry Blackmun cast one of the four votes in favor of preserving the death penalty in *Furman v. Georgia,* and he voted with the majority to approve the new laws four years later. For two decades, he stuck to the belief that the death penalty could meet the constitutional test of reliability. But last year Blackmun threw up his hands. "Twenty years have passed since this Court declared that the death penalty must be imposed fairly and with reasonable consistency or not all," he wrote. ". . . In the years following Furman, serious efforts were made to comply with its mandate. State legislatures and appellate courts struggled to provide judges and juries with sensible and objective guidelines for determining who should live and who should die . . . Unfortunately, all this experimentation and ingenuity yielded little of what Furman demanded . . . It seems that the decision whether a human being should live or die is so inherently subjective, rife with all of life's understandings, experiences, prejudices and passions, that it inevitably defies the rationality and consistency required by the Constitution . . . I feel morally and intellectually obligated simply to concede that the death penalty experiment has failed."

Also last year, an admiring biography of retired Justice Lewis Powell was published. Powell was one of the architects of the modern death penalty. As a swing vote in 1976, he had helped to define the intricate weighing system that restored capital punishment in America. Later, as the deciding vote in a 1987 case, *McCleskey v. Kemp,* Powell had saved the death penalty from the assertion that racial disparities proved the system was still arbitrary. Now Powell was quoted as telling his biographer, "I have come to think that capital punishment should be abolished." The death penalty "brings discredit on the whole legal system," Powell said, because the vast majority of death sentences are never carried out. Biographer John C. Jeffries Jr. had asked Powell if he would like to undo any decisions from his long career. "Yes," the justice answered. "McCleskey v. Kemp."

No one has done more than Ray Marky to make a success of the death penalty. As a top aide in the Florida attorney general's office, he worked himself into an early heart attack prosecuting capital appeals. Eventually, he took a less stressful job at the local prosecutor's office, where he watched, dispirited, as the modern death penalty—the law he had helped write and had struggled to enforce—reached its convoluted maturity. One day a potential death penalty case came across his new desk, and instead of pushing as he had in the old days, he advised the victim's mother to accept a life sentence for her son's killer. "Ma'am, bury your son and get on with your life, or over the next dozen years, this defendant will destroy you, as well as your son," Marky told her. Why put the woman through all the waiting, the hearings and the stays, when the odds were heavy that the death sentence would never be carried out? "I never would have said that 15 years ago," Marky reflected. "But now I will, because I'm not going to put someone through the nightmare. If we had deliberately set out to create a chaotic system, we couldn't have come up with anything worse. It's a merry-go-round, it's ridiculous; it's so clogged up only an arbitrary few ever get it.

"I don't get any damn pleasure out of the death penalty and I never have," the prosecutor said. "And frankly, if they abolished it tomorrow, I'd go get drunk in celebration."

Ernest van den Haag  **NO**

The Ultimate Punishment: A Defense

In an average year about 20,000 homicides occur in the United States. Fewer than 300 convicted murders are sentenced to death. But because no more than thirty murderers have been executed in any recent year, most convicts sentenced to death are likely to die of old age.[1] Nonetheless, the death penalty looms large in discussions: it raises important moral questions independent of the number of executions.

The death penalty is our harshest punishment. It is irrevocable: it ends the existence of those punished, instead of temporarily imprisoning them. Further, although not intended to cause physical pain, execution is the only corporal punishment still applied to adults. These singular characteristics contribute to the perennial, impassioned controversy about capital punishment.

I. Distribution

Consideration of the justice, morality, or usefulness, of capital punishment is often conflated with objections to its alleged discriminatory or capricious distribution among the guilty. Wrongly so. If capital punishment is immoral *in se*, no distribution among the guilty could make it moral. If capital punishment is moral, no distribution would make it immoral. Improper distribution cannot affect the quality of what is distributed, be it punishments or rewards. Discriminatory or capricious distribution thus could not justify abolition of the death penalty. Further, maldistribution inheres no more in capital punishment than in any other punishment.

Maldistribution between the guilty and the innocent is, by definition, unjust. But the injustice does not lie in the nature of the punishment. Because of the finality of the death penalty, the most grievous maldistribution occurs when it is imposed upon the innocent. However, the frequent allegations of discrimination and capriciousness refer to maldistribution among the guilty and not to the punishment of the innocent.

Maldistribution of any punishment among those who deserve it is irrelevant to its justice or morality. Even if poor or black convicts guilty of capital offenses suffer capital punishment, and other convicts equally guilty of the same crimes do not, a more equal distribution, however desirable,

From Ernest van den Haag, "The Ultimate Punishment: A Defense," *Harvard Law Review*, vol. 99 (May 1986). Copyright © 1986 by The Harvard Law Review Association. Reprinted by permission.

would merely be more equal. It would not be more just to the convicts under sentence of death.

Punishments are imposed on persons, not on racial or economic groups. Guilt is personal. The only relevant question is: does the person to be executed deserve the punishment? Whether or not others who deserved the same punishment, whatever their economic or racial group, have avoided execution is irrelevant. If they have, the guilt of the executed convicts would not be diminished, nor would their punishment be less deserved. To put the issue starkly, if the death penalty were imposed on guilty blacks, but not on guilty whites, or, if it were imposed by a lottery among the guilty, this irrationally discriminatory or capricious distribution would neither make the penalty unjust, nor cause anyone to be unjustly punished, despite the undue impunity bestowed on others.

Equality, in short, seems morally less important than justice. And justice is independent of distributional inequalities. The ideal of equal justice demands that justice be equally distributed, not that it be replaced by equality. Justice requires that as many of the guilty as possible be punished, regardless of whether others have avoided punishment. To let these others escape the deserved punishment does not do justice to them, or to society. But it is not unjust to those who could not escape.

These moral considerations are not meant to deny that irrational discrimination, or capriciousness, would be inconsistent with constitutional requirements. But I am satisfied that the Supreme Court has in fact provided for adherence to the constitutional requirement of equality as much as possible. Some inequality is indeed unavoidable as a practical matter in any system.[2] But, *ultra posse neo obligatur.* (Nobody is bound beyond ability.)

Recent data reveal little direct racial discrimination in the sentencing of those arrested and convicted of murder. The abrogation of the death penalty for rape has eliminated a major source of racial discrimination. Concededly, some discrimination based on the race of murder victims may exist; yet, this discrimination affects criminal victimizers in an unexpected way. Murderers of whites are thought more likely to be executed than murderers of blacks. Black victims, then, are less fully vindicated than white ones. However, because most black murderers kill blacks, black murderers are spared the death penalty more often than are white murderers. They fare better than most white murderers. The motivation behind unequal distribution of the death penalty may well have been to discriminate against blacks, but the result has favored them. Maldistribution is thus a straw man for empirical as well as analytical reasons.

II. Miscarriages of Justice

In a recent survey Professors Hugo Adam Bedau and Michael Radelet found that 7000 persons were executed in the United States between 1900 and 1985 and that 25 were innocent of capital crimes. Among the innocents they list Sacco and Vanzetti as well as Ethel and Julius Rosenberg. Although their data may be questionable, I do not doubt that, over a long enough period, miscarriages of justice will occur even in capital cases.

Despite precautions, nearly all human activities, such as trucking, lighting, or construction, cost the lives of some innocent bystanders. We do not give up these activities, because the advantages, moral or material, outweigh the unintended losses. Analogously, for those who think the death penalty just, miscarriages of justice are offset by the moral benefits and the usefulness of doing justice. For those who think the death penalty unjust even when it does not miscarry, miscarriages can hardly be decisive.

III. Deterrence

Despite much recent work, there has been no conclusive statistical demonstration that the death penalty is a better deterrent than are alternative punishments. However, deterrence is less than decisive for either side. Most abolitionists acknowledge that they would continue to favor abolition even if the death penalty were shown to deter more murders than alternatives could deter. Abolitionists appear to value the life of a convicted murderer or, at least, his nonexecution, more highly than they value the lives of the innocent victims who might be spared by deterring prospective murderers.

Deterrence is not altogether decisive for me either. I would favor retention of the death penalty as retribution even if it were shown that the threat of execution could not deter prospective murderers not already deterred by the threat of imprisonment.[3] Still, I believe the death penalty, because of its finality, is more feared than imprisonment, and deters some prospective murderers not deterred by the threat of imprisonment. Sparing the lives of even a few prospective victims by deterring their murderers is more important than preserving the lives of convicted murderers because of the possibility, or even the probability, that executing them would not deter others. Whereas the lives of the victims who might be saved are valuable, that of the murderer has only negative value, because of his crime. Surely the criminal law is meant to protect the lives of potential victims in preference to those of actual murderers.

Murder rates are determined by many factors; neither the severity nor the probability of the threatened sanction is always decisive. However, for the long run, I share the view of Sir James Fitzjames Stephen: "Some men, probably, abstain from murder because they fear that if they committed murder they would be hanged. Hundreds of thousands abstain from it because they regard it with horror. One great reason why they regard it with horror is that murderers are hanged." Penal sanctions are useful in the long run for the formation of the internal restraints so necessary to control crime. The severity and finality of the death penalty is appropriate to the seriousness and the finality of murder.

IV. Incidental Issues: Cost, Relative Suffering, Brutalization

Many nondecisive issues are associated with capital punishment. Some believe that the monetary cost of appealing a capital sentence is excessive. Yet most comparisons of the cost of life imprisonment with the cost of execution, apart from their dubious relevance, are flawed at least by the implied assumption that life prisoners will generate no judicial costs during their imprisonment. At any rate, the actual monetary costs are trumped by the importance of doing justice.

Others insist that a person sentenced to death suffers more than his victim suffered, and that this (excess) suffering is undue according to the *lex talionis* (rule of retaliation). We cannot know whether the murderer on death row suffers more than his victim suffered; however, unlike the murderer, the victim deserved none of the suffering inflicted. Further, the limitations of the *lex talionis* were meant to restrain private vengeance, not the social retribution that has taken its place. Punishment—regardless of the motivation—is not intended to revenge, offset, or compensate for the victim's suffering, or to be measured by it. Punishment is to vindicate the law and the social order undermined by the crime. This is why a kidnapper's penal confinement is not limited to the period for which he imprisoned his victim; nor is a burglar's confinement meant merely to offset the suffering or the harm he caused his victim; nor is it meant only to offset the advantage he gained.[4]

Another argument heard at least since Beccaria is that, by killing a murderer, we encourage, endorse, or legitimize unlawful killing. Yet, although all punishments are meant to be unpleasant, it is seldom argued that they legitimize the unlawful imposition of identical unpleasantness. Imprisonment is not thought to legitimize kidnapping; neither are fines thought to legitimize robbery. The difference between murder and execution, or between kidnapping and imprisonment, is that the first is unlawful and undeserved, the second a lawful and deserved punishment for an unlawful act. The physical similarities of the punishment to the crime are irrelevant. The relevant difference is not physical, but social.[5]

V. Justice, Excess, Degradation

We threaten punishments in order to deter crime. We impose them not only to make the threats credible but also as retribution (justice) for the crimes that were not deterred. Threats and punishments are necessary to deter and deterrence is a sufficient practical justification for them. Retribution is an independent moral justification. Although penalties can be unwise, repulsive, or inappropriate, and those punished can be pitiable, in a sense the infliction of legal punishment on a guilty person cannot be unjust. By committing the crime, the criminal volunteered to assume the risk of receiving a legal punishment that he could have avoided by not committing the crime. The punishment he suffers is the punishment he voluntarily risked suffering and, therefore, it is no more unjust to him than any other event for which one knowingly volunteers to assume the risk. Thus, the death penalty cannot be unjust to the guilty criminal.

There remain, however, two moral objections. The penalty may be regarded as always excessive as retribution and always morally degrading. To regard the death penalty as always excessive, one must believe that no crime—no matter how heinous—could possibly justify capital punishment. Such a belief can be neither corroborated nor refuted; it is an article of faith.

Alternatively, or concurrently, one may believe that everybody, the murderer no less than the victim, has an imprescriptible (natural?) right to life. The law therefore should not deprive anyone of life. I share Jeremy Bentham's view that any such "natural and imprescriptible rights" are "nonsense upon stilts."

Justice Brennan has insisted that the death penalty is "uncivilized," "inhuman," inconsistent with "human dignity" and with "the sanctity of life," that it "treats members of the human race as nonhumans, as objects to be toyed with and discarded," that it is "uniquely degrading to human dignity" and "by its very nature, [involves] a denial of the executed person's humanity." Justice Brennan does not say why he thinks execution "uncivilized." Hitherto most civilizations have had the death penalty, although it has been discarded in Western Europe, where it is currently unfashionable probably because of its abuse by totalitarian regimes.

By "degrading," Justice Brennan seems to mean that execution degrades the executed convicts. Yet philosophers, such as Immanuel Kant and G. F. W. Hegel, have insisted that, when deserved, execution, far from degrading the executed convict, affirms his humanity by affirming his rationality and his responsibility for his actions. They thought that execution, when deserved, is required for the sake of the convict's dignity. (Does not life imprisonment violate human dignity more than execution, by keeping alive a prisoner deprived of all autonomy?)

Common sense indicates that it cannot be death—or common fate—that is inhuman. Therefore, Justice Brennan must mean that death degrades when it comes not as a natural or accidental event, but as a deliberate social imposition. The murderer learns through his punishment that his fellow men have found him unworthy of living; that because he has murdered, he is being expelled from the community of the living. This degradation is self-inflicted. By murdering, the murderer has so dehumanized himself that he cannot remain among the living. The social recognition of his self-degradation is the punitive essence of execution. To believe, as Justice Brennan appears to, that the degradation is inflicted by the execution reverses the direction of causality.

Execution of those who have committed heinous murders may deter only one murder per year. If it does, it seems quite warranted. It is also the only fitting retribution for murder I can think of.

Notes

1. Death row as a semipermanent residence is cruel, because convicts are denied the normal amenities of prison life. Thus, unless death row residents are integrated into the prison population, the continuing accumulation of convicts on death row should lead us to accelerate either the rate of executions or the rate of commutations. I find little objection to integration.

2. The ideal of equality, unlike the ideal of retributive justice (which can be approximated separately in each instance), is clearly unattainable unless all

guilty persons are apprehended, and thereafter tried, convicted and sentenced by the same court, at the same time. Unequal justice is the best we can do; it is still better than the injustice, equal or unequal, which occurs if, for the sake of equality, we deliberately allow some who could be punished to escape.

3. If executions were shown to increase the murder rate in the long run, I would favor abolition. Sparing the innocent victims who would be spared, *ex hypothesi,* by the nonexecution of murderers would be more important to me than the execution, however just, of murderers. But although there is a lively discussion of the subject, no serious evidence exists to support the hypothesis that executions produce a higher murder rate. *Cf.* Phillips, *The Deterrent Effect of Capital Punishment: New Evidence on an Old Controversy,* 86 AM. J. Soc. 139 (1980) (arguing that murder rates drop immediately after executions of criminals).

4. Thus restitution (a civil liability) cannot satisfy the punitive purpose of penal sanctions, whether the purpose be retributive or deterrent.

5. Some abolitionists challenge: if the death penalty is just and serves as a deterrent, why not televise executions? The answer is simple. The death even of a murderer, however well-deserved, should not serve as public entertainment. It so served in earlier centuries. But in this respect our sensibility has changed for the better, I believe. Further, television unavoidably would trivialize executions, wedged in, as they would be, between game shows, situation comedies and the like. Finally, because televised executions would focus on the physical aspects of the punishment, rather than the nature of the crime and the suffering of the victim, a televised execution would present the murderer as the victim of the state. Far from communicating the moral significance of the execution, television would shift the focus to the pitiable fear of the murderer. We no longer place in cages those sentenced to imprisonment to expose them to public view. Why should we so expose those sentenced to execution?

POSTSCRIPT

Is Capital Punishment Bad Public Policy?

One of the most striking elements about the issue of capital punishment is that most of the public, the politicians, and even many criminological scholars do not seem to be fazed by empirical evidence. Each side marshalls empirical evidence to support its respective position. Opponents of capital punishment often draw from Thorsten Sellin's classic study *The Penalty of Death* (Sage Publications) to "prove" that the number of capital offenses is no lower in states that have the death penalty as compared to states that have abolished executions.

Almost all of the major presidential candidates in early 2000 support the death penalty. In fact, most political candidates seem to support capital punishment nowadays. Supporters of capital punishment draw from numerous studies, including I. Ehrlich's "The Deterrent Effect of Capital Punishment," *American Economic Review* (vol. 65, 1975), pp. 397–417, and his "Capital Punishment and Deterrence: Some Further Thoughts and Additional Evidence," *Journal of Political Economy* (vol. 85, 1977), pp. 741–788. They also draw from W. Berns's *For Capital Punishment: Crime and the Morality of the Death Penalty* (Basic Books, 1979).

Generally, the empirical research indicates that the death penalty cannot conclusively be proven to deter others from committing homicides and other serious crimes. Entire scientific commissions have been charged with the responsibility of determining the deterrent effects of the death penalty (for example, the National Academy of Sciences in 1975). The gist of their conclusions was that the value of the death penalty as a deterrent "is not a settled matter."

As is typical with most aspects of human behavior, including crime and crime control, the issue is filled with much irony, paradox, and contradiction. First, clashing views over capital punishment rely largely on emotion. The public's attitudes, politicians' attitudes, and even scholarly attitudes are frequently shaped more by sentiment and preconceived notions than by rational discourse. As F. Zimring and G. Hawkins indicate in *Capital Punishment and the American Agenda* (Cambridge University Press, 1986), very few scholars have ever changed their opinions about capital punishment.

However, a remarkable transformation occurred in February 2000: Governor George Ryan (R-Illinois) stopped executions in his state after 13 condemned criminals were exonerated while on death row. Twelve inmates had been executed in Illinois since 1976. Ryan and others now wonder if perhaps some of them had been innocent as well.

As we enter the twenty-first century, capital punishment remains a divisive issue. And despite dramatic opposition, such as Governor Ryan's, it probably has growing support. One useful, recent work in strong opposition to the practice is A. Sarat, ed., *The Killing State: Capital Punishment in Law, Politics, and Culture* (Oxford University Press, 1998). Also see "The Cruel and Ever More Unusual Punishment," *The Economist* (May 15, 1999).

An interesting book that looks at both sides of the issue is *The Death Penalty: For and Against* (Rowman & Littlefield, 1997), with J. Reiman attacking and coauthor L. Pojman defending executions as retribution. An empirical study of a neglected aspect of the issue is "An Empirical Examination of Commutations and Executions in Post-*Furman* Capital Cases," by W. Pridemore, *Justice Quarterly* (March 2000). Another series of research articles can be found in the issue of *Criminal Justice Policy Review* entitled "Special Issue on the Death Penalty" (vol. 10, no. 1, 1999). A recent work by a longtime critic of capital punishment is R. M. Bohn's *Deathquest: An Introduction to the Theory and Practice of Capital Punishment in the United States* (Anderson, 1999).

For a take on Hollywood's many films on executions, see "Death Row, Aisle Seat," by A. Sarat, *The American Prospect* (February 14, 2000). A good overview dealing with women and the death penalty is K. A. O'Shea's *Women and the Death Penalty in the United States, 1900–1998* (Greenwood, 1999). In addition to the many studies by Victor Streib on executing children, see *A Review of Juvenile Executions in America* by R. L. Hale (Edwin Mellen Press, 1997). A concise overview of relevant statistics through December 1999 is *Capital Punishment 1998*, a Bureau of Justice Statistics Bulletin (December 1999).

Two studies of the deterrence issue are "Capital Punishment and the Deterrence of Violent Crime in Comparable Countries," by D. Cheatwood, *Criminal Justice Review* (August 1993) and "Deterrence or Brutalization?" by J. Cochran et al., *Criminology* (February 1994). For a survey of the attitudes toward capital punishment among politicians, see M. Sandys and E. McGarrell, "Attitudes Toward Capital Punishment Among Indiana Legislators," *Justice Quarterly* (December 1994). A popular media account of a death penalty sentence given to a mentally impaired individual is "Untrue Confessions," by J. Smolowe, *Time* (May 22, 1995). An interesting comparison of the effects of publicized executions on whites and blacks is "The Impact of Publicized Executions on Homicide," by S. Stack, *Criminal Justice and Behavior* (June 1995). The *Bureau of Justice Statistics Bulletin* routinely updates death penalty statistics. For an outstanding description of death row, see Von Drehle's *Among the Lowest of the Dead: The Culture of Death Row* (Times Books, 1995).

L. K. Gillespie's *Dancehall Ladies: The Crimes and Executions of America's Condemned Women* (University Press of America, 1997) is a solid historical discussion. D. A. Cabana's *Death at Midnight: The Confessions of an Executioner* (Northeast University Press, 1996) is an insightful insider's account. A helpful legal overview is *Death Penalty Cases: Leading U.S. Supreme Court Cases on Capital Punishment* by B. Latzer (Butterworth-Heinemann, 1998). Finally, two outstanding articles that provide both historical and theoretical background for understanding violence and capital punishment as an extension of inequalities maintenance are Roberta Senechal de la Roche, "Collective Violence As Social Control," *Sociological Forum* (March 1996) and "The Sociogenesis of Lynching," in W. F. Brundae, ed., *Under Penalty of Death: Essays on Lynching in the South* (University of North Carolina Press, 1997).

ISSUE 14

Do More Guns Lead to Less Crime?

YES: John R. Lott, Jr., from *More Guns, Less Crime: Understanding Crime and Gun-Control Laws* (University of Chicago Press, 1998)

NO: Franklin E. Zimring and Gordon Hawkins, from *Crime Is Not the Problem: Lethal Violence in America* (Oxford University Press, 1997)

ISSUE SUMMARY

YES: John R. Lott, Jr., the John M. Olin Visiting Law and Economics Fellow at the University of Chicago Law School, contends that gun ownership reduces crime, not increases it, for several documentable reasons. He asserts that the handgun-armed-citizen-scaring-off-criminals thesis is generating enormous controversy on both empirical and ideological grounds.

NO: Franklin E. Zimring and Gordon Hawkins, director and senior fellow, respectively, of the Earl Warren Legal Institute, drawing from European and U.S. data comparing lethal violence rates, conclude that possession and use of handguns drives the vastly disproportionate number of homicides in the United States.

According to some estimates, one in every three households in the United States contains one or more guns. Because of the growing fear of crime, many citizens express increased unwillingness to give up their guns. Guns are seen as necessary to protect home and family. An excellent example of this is the complicated situation that the nationally syndicated columnist Carl Rowan confronted. A well-known supporter of strict firearm controls, he was allegedly threatened by an intruder in his own backyard. Rowan quickly produced a pistol and shot the intruder. While conservatives (who consistently support the right to bear arms and oppose most kinds of gun control) jeered Rowan for his hypocrisy, other Americans were sympathetic. Rowan was later acquitted of criminal charges in the incident. He, like approximately 50 million other Americans, continues to possess a handgun.

This reflects another paradox in U.S. society. On the one hand, many, if not most, Americans support handgun control. On the other hand, most also feel that law-abiding citizens should have the right to possess a gun, at least inside their own homes, and to use it to protect themselves and their families. The argument is that weapons are needed for simple protection.

Simple assault is the most common crime of violence, followed by aggravated assault, which is the use of or threat of a weapon to inflict bodily harm. Other than robbery, most violent crimes are not committed with a gun. Knives, fists, and blunt instruments are more likely to be the weapons of choice. Homicide is the least frequent form of assault in the United States.

Traditionally, the debate over gun control has centered largely around the control of, if not the elimination of, "Saturday Night Specials" (inexpensive, .22-caliber pistols). However, the issue has become more complicated in the 1990s. Not only is the fear and frustration over assaults and homicides being fueled by the significant numbers of young people being arrested for possession of arms, use of arms, and threats with arms, but the power of the weapons on the streets and the types of weapons available have changed dramatically. Uzis, AK-47 assault rifles, MAC-11 assault pistols, .357 Magnums, .45-caliber semiautomatics, and other semiautomatic weapons are frequently being used in deadly assaults. The consequences are an increase of public fear and an increase in fatalities because these weapons, newer to the criminal street scene, are far deadlier than "mere" Saturday Night Specials.

Gun control is now very much part of the cultural war landscape. Reminiscent (only in reverse) of the charges in the 1920s that Prohibition (of alcohol) was the triumph of the conservative, mean-spirited, rural religious right over the fun-loving, ethnically diverse, liberal city dwellers, some charge today that gun control laws represent the efforts of urban politicians and scholars to suppress rural hunters and other Americans. Many gun owners nowadays interpret gun control as a deliberate attempt to export to America's heartland the violence and chaos of the cities. Certainly such sentiments pervade far right militants who openly call for war on various government agencies. It seems that this issue is spreading and growing uglier.

With some U.S. states passing legislation requiring gun makers to produce only weapons with locks on them, the president calling for strict gun control, and the clamor for zero tolerance of guns in the wake of school killings, it seems logical to conclude that there is now very little research-informed support of gun ownership, especially handguns and concealed weapons. However, in the following selection, John R. Lott, Jr., insists that his research proves beyond a reasonable scholarly doubt that the right to bear concealed arms is an important deterrent to assaults and robberies. In the second selection, Franklin E. Zimring and Gordon Hawkins, reflecting the traditional view that guns breed violence and other crimes, argue that without guns the homicide rate in America, one of the highest in the world, would drop significantly.

As you read this debate, consider if anecdotal evidence of "vigilante grannies" who scares off thugs with their handguns illuminate the issue. While Zimring and Hawkins acknowledge that guns-as-protection theory exists, they largely discount it. They also admit that their research shows correlations, not necessarily causes. As you read both arguments, consider the differences between correlations and causes and how you might ascertain actual causes so that more rational policies could be made.

John R. Lott, Jr.  **YES**

More Guns, Less Crime

Introduction

American culture is a gun culture—not merely in the sense that 75 to 86 million people own a total of about 200 to 240 million guns, but in the broader sense that guns pervade our debates on crime and are constantly present in movies and the news. How many times have we read about shootings, or how many times have we heard about tragic accidental gun deaths—bad guys shooting innocent victims, bad guys shooting each other in drug wars, shots fired in self-defense, police shootings of criminals, let alone shooting in wars? We are inundated by images through the television and the press. Our kids are fascinated by computer war games and toy guns.

So We're obsessed with guns. But the big question is: What do we really know? How many times have most of us actually used a gun or seen a gun being used? How many of us have ever seen somebody in real life threatening somebody else with a gun, witnessed a shooting, or seen people defend themselves by displaying or firing guns?

The truth is that most of us have very little firsthand experience with using guns as weapons. Even the vast majority of police officers have never exchanged shots with a suspect. Most of us receive our images of guns and their use through television, film, and newspapers.

Unfortunately, the images from the screen and the newspapers are often unrepresentative or biased because of the sensationalism and exaggeration typically employed to sell news and entertainment. A couple of instances of news reporting are especially instructive in illustrating this bias. In a highly publicized incident, a Dallas man recently became the first Texas resident charged with using a permitted concealed weapon in a fatal shooting. Only long after the initial wave of publicity did the press report that the person had been savagely beaten and in fear for his life before firing the gun. In another case a Japanese student was shot on his way to Halloween party in Louisiana in 1992. It made international headlines and showed how defensive gun use can go tragically wrong. However, this incident was a rare event: in the entire United States during a year, only about 30 people are accidentally killed by private citizens who mistakenly believe the victim to be an intruder. By comparison, police accidentally kill as many as 330 innocent individuals annually.

In neither the Louisiana case nor the Texas case did the courts find the shootings to be criminal.

While news stories sometimes chronicle the defensive uses of guns, such discussions are rare compared to those depicting violent crime committed with guns. Since in many defensive cases a handgun is simply brandished, and no one is harmed, many defensive uses are never even reported to the police. I believe that this underreporting of defensive gun use is large, and this belief has been confirmed by the many stories I received from people across the country after the publicity broke on my original study. On the roughly one hundred radio talk shows on which I discussed that study, many people called in to say that they believed having a gun to defend themselves with had saved their lives. For instance, on a Philadelphia radio station, a New Jersey woman told how two men simultaneously had tried to open both front doors of the car she was in. When she brandished her gun and yelled, the men backed away and fled. Given the stringent gun-control laws in New Jersey, the woman said she never thought seriously of reporting the attempted attack to the police. . . .

Philip Van Cleave, a former reserve deputy sheriff in Texas, wrote me, "Are criminals afraid of a law-abiding citizen with a gun? You bet. Most cases of a criminal being scared off by an armed citizen are probably not reported. But I have seen a criminal who was so frightened of an armed, seventy-year-old woman that in his panic to get away, he turned and ran right into a wall! (He was busy trying to kick down her door, when she opened a curtain and pointed a gun at him.)" . . .

If national surveys are correct, 98 percent of the time that people use guns defensively, they merely have to brandish a weapon to break off an attack. Such stories are not hard to find: pizza deliverymen defend themselves against robbers, carjackings are thwarted, robberies at automatic teller machines are prevented, and numerous armed robberies on the streets and in stores are foiled, though these do not receive the national coverage of other gun crimes. Yet the cases covered by the news media are hardly typical; most of the encounters reported involve a shooting that ends in a fatality.

A typical dramatic news story involved an Atlanta woman who prevented a carjacking and the kidnapping of her child; she was forced to shoot her assailant:

> A College Park woman shot and killed an armed man she says was trying to carjack her van with her and her 1-year-old daughter inside, police said Monday . . .
> She fired after the man pointed a revolver at her and ordered her to "move over," she told police. She offered to take her daughter and give up the van, but the man refused, police said.
> "She was pleading with the guy to let her take the baby and leave the van, but he blocked the door," said College Park Detective Reed Pollard. "She was protecting herself and the baby." . . .

Although the mother saved herself and her baby by her quick actions, it was a risky situation that might have ended differently. Even though there was no police officer to help protect her or her child, defending herself was not necessarily the only alternative. She could have behaved passively, and the criminal might have changed his mind and simply taken the van, letting the mother and child go. Even if he had taken the child, he might later have let the baby go unharmed. Indeed, some conventional wisdom claims that the best approach is not to resist an attack. According to a recent *Los Angeles Times* article, "'active compliance' is the surest way to survive a robbery. Victims who engage in active resistance . . . have the best odds of hanging on to their property. Unfortunately, they also have much better odds of winding up dead."

Yet the evidence suggests that the College Park woman probably engaged in the correct action. While resistance is generally associated with higher probabilities of serious injury to the victim, not all types of resistance are equally risky. By examining the data provided from 1979 to 1987 by the Department of Justice's National Crime Victimization Survey, Lawrence Southwick, confirming earlier estimates by Gary Kleck, found that the probability of serious injury from an attack is 2.5 times greater for women offering no resistance than for women resisting with a gun. In contrast, the probability of women being seriously injured was almost 4 times greater when resisting without a gun than when resisting with a gun. In other words, the best advice is to resist with a gun, but if no gun is available, it is better to offer no resistance than to fight. . . .

Although usually skewed toward the dramatic, news stories do shed light on how criminals think. Anecdotes about criminals who choose victims whom they perceive as weak are the most typical. While "weak" victims are frequently women and the elderly, this is not always the case. For example, in a taped conversation with police investigators reported in the *Cincinnati Enquirer* (October 9, 1996, p. B2), Darnell "Bubba" Lowery described how he and Walter "Fatman" Raglin robbed and murdered musician Michael Bany on December 29, 1995:

> Mr. Lowery said on the tape that he and Walter "Fatman" Raglin, who is also charged with aggravated robbery and aggravated murder and is on trial in another courtroom, had planned to rob a cab driver or a "dope boy."
>
> He said he gave his gun and bullets to Mr. Raglin. They decided against robbing a cab driver or drug dealer because both sometimes carried guns, he said.
>
> Instead, they saw a man walking across the parking lot with some kind of musical instrument. He said as he looked out for police, Mr. Raglin approached the man and asked for money.
>
> After getting the money, Mr. Raglin asked if the man's car was a stick or an automatic shift. Then Mr. Raglin shot the man.

Criminals are motivated by self-preservation, and handguns can therefore be a deterrent. The potential defensive nature of guns is further evidenced by the different rates of so-called "hot burglaries," where a resident is at home when a criminal strikes. In Canada and Britain, both with tough gun-control laws, almost half of all burglaries are "hot burglaries." In contrast, the United States, with fewer restrictions, has a "hot burglary" rate of only 13 percent. Criminals are not just behaving differently by accident. Convicted American felons reveal in surveys that they are much more worried about armed victims than about running into the police. The fear of potentially armed victims causes American burglars to spend more time than their foreign counterparts "casing" a house to ensure that nobody is home. Felons frequently comment in these interviews that they avoid late-night burglaries because "that's the way to get shot."

To an economist such as myself, the notion of deterrence—which causes criminals to avoid cab drivers, "dope boys," or homes where the residents are in—is not too surprising. We see the same basic relationships in all other areas of life: When the price of apples rises relative to that of oranges, people buy fewer apples and more oranges. To the noneconomist, it may appear cold to make this comparison, but just as grocery shoppers switch to cheaper types of produce, criminals switch to attacking more vulnerable prey. Economists call this, appropriately enough, "the substitution effect."

Deterrence matters not only to those who actively take defensive actions. People who defend themselves may indirectly benefit other citizens. In the Cincinnati murder case just described, cab drivers and drug dealers who carry guns produce a benefit for cab drivers and drug dealers without guns. In the example involving "hot burglaries," homeowners who defend themselves make burglars generally wary of breaking into homes. These spillover effects are frequently referred to as "third-party effects" or "external benefits." In both cases criminals cannot know in advance who is armed.

The case for allowing concealed handguns—as opposed to openly carried handguns—relies on this argument. When guns are concealed, criminals are unable to tell whether the victim is armed before striking, which raises the risk to criminals of committing many types of crimes. On the other hand, with "open-carry" handgun laws, a potential victim's defensive ability is readily identified, which makes it easier for criminals to choose the more vulnerable prey. In interviews with felony prisoners in ten state correctional systems, 56 percent claimed that they would not attack a potential victim who was known to be armed. Indeed, the criminals in states with high civilian gun ownership were the most worried about encountering armed victims.

Other examples suggest that more than just common crimes may be prevented by law-abiding citizens carrying concealed handguns. Referring to the July, 1984, massacre at a San Ysidro, California, McDonald's restaurant, Israeli criminologist Abraham Tennenbaum described

> what occurred at a [crowded venue in] Jerusalem some weeks before the California McDonald's massacre: three terrorists who attempted to machine-gun the throng managed to kill only one victim before being shot down by handgun-carrying Israelis. Presented to the press the next day, the surviving terrorist complained that his group had not realized that Israeli civilians were armed. The terrorists had planned to machine-gun a succession of crowd spots, thinking that they would be able to escape before the police or army could arrive to deal with them.

. . . Obviously, arming citizens has not stopped terrorism in Israel; however, terrorists have responded to the relatively greater cost of shooting in public places by resorting to more bombings. This is exactly what the substitution effect discussed above would predict. Is Israel better off with bombings instead of mass public shootings? . . .

Substitutability means that the most obvious explanations may not always be correct. For example, when the February 23, 1997, shootings at the Empire State Building left one person dead and six injured, it was not New York's gun laws but Florida's—where the gun was sold—that came under attack. New York City Mayor Rudolph W. Giuliani immediately called for national gun-licensing laws. While it is possible that even stricter gun-sale regulations in Florida might have prevented this and other shootings, we might ask, Why did the gunman travel to New York and not simply remain in Florida to do the shooting? It is important to study whether states that adopt concealed-handgun laws similar to those in Israel experience the same virtual elimination of mass public shootings. Such states may also run the risk that would-be attackers will substitute bombings for shootings, though there is the same potential downside to successfully banning guns. The question still boils down to an empirical one: Which policy will save the largest number of lives?

The Numbers Debate and Crime

Unfortunately, the debate over crime involves many commonly accepted "facts" that simply are not true. For example, take the claim that individuals are frequently killed by people they know. . . . [A]ccording to the FBI's *Uniform Crime Reports,* 58 percent of the country's murders were committed either by family members (18 percent) or by those who "knew" the victims (40 percent). Although the victims' relationship to their attackers could not be determined in 30 percent of the cases, 13 percent of all murders were committed by complete strangers.

Surely the impression created by these numbers has been that most victims are murdered by close acquaintances. Yet this is far from the truth. In interpreting the numbers, one must understand how these classifications are made. In this case, "murderers who know their victims" is a very broad category. A huge but not clearly determined portion of this category includes rival gang members who know each other. In larger urban areas, where most murders occur, the majority of murders are due to gang-related turf wars over drugs.

The Chicago Police Department, which keeps unusually detailed numbers of these crimes, finds that just 5 percent of all murders in the city from 1990 to 1995 were committed by nonfamily friends, neighbors, or roommates. This is clearly important in understanding crime. The list of nonfriend acquaintance murderers is filled with cases in which the relationships would not be regarded by most people as particularly close: for example, relationships between drug pushes and buyers, gang members, prostitutes and their clients, bar customers, gamblers, and cabdrivers killed by their customers.

While I do not wish to downplay domestic violence, most people do not envision gang members or drug buyers and pushers killing each other when they hear that 58 percent of murder victims were either relatives or acquaintances of their murderers. If family members are included, 17 percent of all murders in Chicago for 1990–95 involved family members, friends, neighbors, or roommates. While the total number of murders in Chicago grew from 395 in 1965 to 814 in 1995, the number involving family members, friends, neighbors, or roommates remained virtually unchanged. What has grown is the number of murders by nonfriend acquaintances, strangers, identified gangs, and persons unknown.

Few murders could be classified as previously law-abiding citizens. In the largest seventy-five countries in the United States in 1988, over 89 percent of adult murderers had criminal records as adults. Evidence for Boston, the one city where reliable data have been collected, shows that, from 1990 to 1994, 76 percent of juvenile murder victims and 77 percent of juveniles who murdered other juveniles had prior criminal arraignments.

Claims of the large number of murders committed against acquaintances also create a misleading fear of those we know. To put it bluntly, criminals are not typical citizens. As is well known, young males from their mid-teens to mid-thirties commit a disproportionate share of crime, but even this categorization can be substantially narrowed. We know that criminals tend to have low IQs as well as atypical personalities. For example, delinquents generally tend to be more "assertive, unafraid, aggressive, unconventional, extroverted, and poorly socialized," while nondeliquents are "self-controlled, concerned about their relations with others, willing to be guided by social standards, and rich in internal feelings like insecurity, helplessness, love (or its lack), and anxiety." Other evidence indicates that criminals tend to be more impulsive and put relatively little weight on future events. Finally, we cannot ignore the unfortunate fact that crime (particularly violent crime, and especially murder) is disproportionately committed against blacks by blacks.

The news media also play an important role in shaping what we perceive as the greatest threats to our safety. Because we live in such a national news market, we learn very quickly about tragedies in other parts of the country. As a result, some events appear to be much more common than they actually are. For instance, children are much less likely to be accidentally killed by guns (particularly handguns) than most people think. Consider the following numbers: in 1995 there were a total of 1,400 accidental firearm deaths in the entire country. A relatively small portion of these involved children: 30 deaths involved children up to four years of age and 170 more deaths involved five- to fourteen-year-olds. In comparison, 2,900 children died in motor-vehicle crashes, 950 children lost their lives from drowning, and over 1,000 children were killed by fire and burns. More children die in bicycle accidents each year than die from all types of firearm accidents.

. . . [T]rade-offs exist for gun-control issues, such as gun locks. As President Clinton has argued many times, "We protect aspirin bottles in this country better than we protect guns from accidents by children." Yet gun locks require that guns be unloaded, and a locked, unloaded gun does not offer ready protection from intruders. The debate is not simply over whether one wants to save lives or not; it involves the question of how many of these two hundred accidental gun deaths would have been avoided under different rules versus the extent to which such rules would reduce people's ability to defend themselves. Without looking at data, one can only guess the net effects. Unfortunately, despite the best intentions, evidence indicates that child-resistant bottle caps actually have resulted in "3,500 additional poisoning of children under age 5 annually from [aspirin-related drugs] . . . [as] consumers have been lulled into a less-safety-conscious mode of behavior by the existence of safety caps." If President Clinton were aware of such research, he surely wouldn't refer to aspirin bottles when telling us how to deal with guns.

Another common argument made in favor of banning guns involves the number of people who die from guns each year: there were 17,790 homicides and 18,169 suicides in 1992 alone. Yet just because a law is passed to ban guns, it does not automatically follow that the total number of deaths will decline. Given the large stock of guns in the country, and given the difficulties the government faces in preventing other illegal items, such as drugs, from entering the country, it is not clear how successful the government would be in eliminating most guns. This raises the important question of whether the law would primarily reduce the number of guns held by law-abiding citizens. How would such a law alter the relative balance of power between criminals and law-abiding citizens?

Suppose it were possible to remove all guns. Other questions would still arise. Would successfully removing guns discourage murders and other crimes because criminals would find knives and clubs poor alternatives? Would it be easier for criminals to prey on the weakest citizens, who would find it more difficult to defend themselves? Suicide raises other questions. It is simply not sufficient to point to the number of people who kill themselves with guns. The debate must be over what substitute methods are available and whether they appear sufficiently less attractive. Even evidence about the "success rate" of different methods of suicide is not enough, because questions arise over why people choose the method that they do. If people who were more intent than others on successfully killing themselves previously chose guns, forcing them to use other methods might raise the reported "success rate" for these other methods. Broader concerns for the general public also arise. For example, even if we banned many of the obvious ways of committing suicide, many methods exist that we could never really control. These substitute methods might endanger others in ways that shootings do not—for example, deliberately crashing one's car, throwing oneself in front of a train, or jumping off a building.

[We] attempt . . . to measure the same type of trade-off for guns. Our primary questions are the following: Will allowing citizens to carry concealed handguns mean that otherwise law-abiding people will harm each other? Will the threat of self-defense by citizens armed with guns primarily deter criminals? Without a doubt, both "bad" and "good" uses of guns occur. The question isn't really whether both occur; it is, rather, Which is more important? In general, do concealed handguns save or cost lives? Even a devoted believer in deterrence cannot answer this question without examining the data, because these two different effects clearly exist, and they work in opposite directions.

To some, however, the logic is fairly straightforward. Philip Cook argues that "if you introduce a gun into a violent encounter, it increases the chance that someone will die." A large number of murders may arise from unintentional fits of rage that are quickly regretted, and simply keeping guns out of people's reach would prevent deaths. Others point to the horrible public shootings that occur not just in the United States but around the world, from Tasmania, Australia, to Dunblane, Scotland.

The survey evidence of defensive gun use weighs importantly in this debate. At the lowest end of these estimates, again according to Philip Cook, the U.S. Department of Justice's National Crime Victimization Survey reports that each year there are "only" 80,000 to 82,000 defensive uses of guns during assaults, robberies, and household burglaries. Other national polls weight regions by population and thus have the advantage, unlike the National Crime Victimization Survey, of not relying too heavily on data from urban areas. These national polls should also produce more honest answers, since a law-enforcement agency is not asking the questions. They imply much higher defensive use rates. Fifteen national polls, including those by organizations such as the *Los Angeles Times*, Gallup, and Peter Hart Research Associates, imply that there are 760,000 to 3.6 million defensive uses of guns per year. Yet even if these estimates are wrong by a very large factor, they still suggest that defensive gun use is extremely common.

Some evidence on whether concealed-handgun laws will lead to increased crimes is readily available. Between October 1, 1987, when Florida's "concealed-carry" law took effect, and the end of 1996, over 380,000 licenses had been issued, and only 72 had been revoked because of crimes committed by license holders (most of which did not involve the permitted gun). A state-wide breakdown on the nature of those crimes is not available, but Dade County records indicate that four crimes involving a permitted handgun took place there between September 1987 and August 1992, and none of those cases resulted in injury. Similarly, Multnomah County, Oregon, issued 11,140 permits over the period from January 1990 to October 1994; only five permit holders were involved in shootings, three of which were considered justified by grand juries. Of the other two cases, one involved a shooting in a domestic dispute, and the other involved an accident that occurred while a gun was being unloaded; neither resulted in a fatality.

In Virginia, "Not a single Virginia permit-holder has been involved in violent crime." In the first year following the enactment of concealed-carry legislation in Texas, more than 114,000 licenses were issued, and only 17 have so far been revoked by the Department of Public Safety (reasons not specified). After Nevada's first year, "Law enforcement officials throughout the state could not document one case of a fatality that resulted from irresponsible gun use by someone who obtained a permit under the new law." Speaking for the Kentucky Chiefs of Police Association, Lt. Col. Bill Dorsey, Covington assistant police chief, concluded that after the law had been in effect for nine months, "We haven't seen any cases where a [concealed-carry] permit holder has committed an offense with a firearm," In North Carolina, "Permit-holding gun owners have not had a single permit revoked as a result of use of a gun in a crime." Similarly, for South Carolina, "Only one person who has received a pistol permit since 1989 has been indicated on a felony charge, a comparison of permit and circuit court records shows. That charge, . . . for allegedly transferring stolen property last year, was dropped by prosecutors after evidence failed to support the charge."

During state legislative hearings on concealed-handgun laws, the most commonly raised concerns involved fears that armed citizens would attack each other in the heat of the moment following car accidents or accidentally shoot a police officer. The evidence shows that such fears are unfounded: although thirty-one states have so-called nondiscretionary concealed-handgun laws, some of them decades old, there exists only one recorded incident of a permitted, concealed handgun being used in a shooting following a traffic accident, and that involved self-defense. No permit holder has ever shot a police officer, and there have been cases where permit holders have used their guns to save officers' lives.

Let us return to the fundamental issue of self-protection. For many people, the ultimate concern boils down to protection from violence. Unfortunately, our legal system cannot provide people with all the protection that they desire, and yet individuals are often prevented from defending themselves. . . .

Others find themselves in a position in which either they no longer report attacks to the police when they have used a gun to defend themselves, or they no longer carry guns for self-defense. Josie Cash learned this lesson the hard way, though charges against her were ultimately dropped. "The Rockford [Illinois] woman used her gun to scare off muggers who tried to take her pizza delivery money. But when she reported the incident to police, they filed felony charges against her for carrying a concealed weapon." . . .

As a Chicago cabdriver recently told me, "What good is a police officer going to do me if you pulled a knife or a gun on me right now?" Nor are rural, low-crime areas immune from these concerns. Illinois State Representative Terry Deering (Democrat) noted that "we live in areas where if we have a state trooper on duty at any given time in a whole county, we feel very fortunate. Some countries in downstate rural Illinois don't even have 24-hour police protection." The police cannot feasibly protect everybody all the time, and perhaps because of this, police officers are typically sympathetic to law-abiding citizens who own guns.

Mail-in surveys are seldom accurate, because only those who feel intensely about an issue are likely to respond, but they provide the best information that we have on police officers' views. A 1996 mail survey of fifteen thousand chiefs of police and sheriffs conducted by the National Association of Chiefs of Police found that 93 percent believed that law-abiding citizens should continue to be able to purchase guns for self-defense. The Southern States Police Benevolent Association surveyed its eleven thousand members during June of 1993 (36 percent responded) and reported similar findings: 96 percent of those who responded agreed with the statement, "People should have the right to own a gun for self-protection," and 71 percent did not believe that stricter handgun laws would reduce the number of violent crimes. A national reader survey conducted in 1991 by *Law Enforcement Technology* magazine found that 76 percent of street officers and 59 percent of managerial officers agreed that all trained, responsible adults should be able to obtain handgun-carry permits. By similarly overwhelming percentages, these officers and police chiefs rejected claims that the Brady law would lower the crime rate.

The passage of concealed-handgun laws has also caused former opponents in law enforcement to change their positions. Recently in Texas, "vocal opponent" Harris County District Attorney John Holmes admitted, "I'm eating a lot of crow on this issue. It's not something I necessarily like to do, but I'm doing it on this." Soon after the implementation of the Florida law, the president and the executive director of the Florida Chiefs of Police and the head of the Florida Sheriff's Association all admitted that they had changed their views on the subject. They also admitted that despite their best efforts to document problems arising from the law, they have been unable to do so. The experience in Kentucky has been similar; as Campbell County Sheriff John Dunn says, "I have changed my opinion of this [program]. Frankly, I anticipated a certain type of people applying to carry firearms, people I would be uncomfortable with being able to carry a concealed weapon. That has not been the case. These are all just everyday citizens who feel they need some protection."

If anything, the support among rank-and-file police officers for the right of individuals to carry guns for self-protection is even higher than it is among the general population. A recent national poll by the Lawrence Research group (September 21–28, 1996) found that by a margin of 69 to 28 percent, registered voters favor "a law allowing law-abiding citizens to be issued a permit to carry a firearm for personal protection outside their home." Other recent national polling by the National Opinion Research Center (March 1997) appears even more supportive of at least allowing some law-abiding citizens to carry concealed handguns. They found that 53.5 percent supported "concealed carry only for those with special needs," while 45 percent agreed that permits should be issued to "any adult who has passed a criminal background check and a gun safety course." Perhaps just as telling, only 16 percent favored a ban on handguns.

The National Opinion Research Center poll also provides some insights into who supports tighter restrictions on gun ownership; it claims that "the less educated and those who haven't been threatened with a gun are most supportive of gun control." If this is true, it appears that those most supportive of restrictions also tend to be those least directly threatened by crime.

State legislators also acknowledge the inability of the police to be always available, even in the most public places, by voting to allow themselves unusually broad rights to carry concealed handguns. During the 1996 legislative session, for example, Georgia "state legislators quietly gave themselves and a few top officials the right to carry concealed guns to places most resident can't: schools, churches, political rallies, and even the Capitol." Even local prosecutors in California strenuously objected to restrictions on their rights to carry concealed handguns.

Although people with concealed handgun permits must generally view the police as offering insufficient protection, it is difficult to discern any pattern of political orientation among celebrities who have concealed-handgun permits: Bill Cosby, Cybill Shepherd, U.S. Senator Dianne Feinstein (D–California),

Howard Stern, Donald Trump, William F. Buckley, Arthur O. Sulzberger (chairman of the *New York Times*), union bosses, Laurence Rockefeller, Tom Selleck, Robert De Niro, and Erika Schwarz (the first runner-up in the 1997 Miss America Pageant). The reasons these people gave on their applications for permits were quite similar. Laurence Rockefeller's reason was that he carries "large sums of money"; Arthur Sulzberger wrote that he carries "large sums of money, securities, etc."; and William Buckley listed "protection of personal property when traveling in and about the city" as his reason. Some made their decision to carry a gun after being victims of crime. Erika Schwarz said that after a carjacking she had been afraid to drive at night.

And when the *Denver Post* asked Sen. Ben Nighthorse Campbell (R–Colo.) "how it looks for a senator to be packing heat," he responded, "You'd be surprised how may senators have guns." . . .

Emotion, Rationality, and Deterrence

. . . The notion of "irrational" crime is enshrined by forty-seven states that recognize insanity defenses. Criminal law recognizes that emotions can overwhelm our normal judgments in other ways. For example, under the Model Penal Code, intentional homicide results in the penalty for manslaughter when it "is committed under the influence of extreme mental or emotional disturbance for which there is reasonable explanation or excuse." These mitigating factors are often discussed in terms of the "heat of passion" or "cooling time," the latter phrase referring to "the interval in which 'blood' can be expected 'to cool' " or the time required for "reason to reassert itself." . . .

Some academics go beyond these cases or laws to make more general claims about the motives behind crime. Thomas Carroll, an associate professor of sociology at the University of Missouri at Kansas City, states that "murder is an irrational act, [and] we don't have explanations for irrational behavior." From this he draws the conclusion that "there's really no statistical explanation" for what causes murder rates to fluctuate. Do criminals respond to disincentives? Or are emotions and attitudes the determining factors in crime? If violent acts occur merely because of random emotions, stronger penalties would only reduce crime to the extent that the people least able to control such violent feelings can be imprisoned.

There are obvious difficulties with taking this argument against deterrence to its extreme. For example, as long as "even a handful" of criminals respond to deterrence, increasing penalties will reduce crime. Higher probabilities of arrest or conviction as well as longer prison terms might then possibly "pay" for themselves. . . . [C]riminal decisions—from when to break into a residence, whom to attack, or whether to attack people by using guns or bombs—appear difficult to explain without reference to deterrence. Some researchers try to draw a distinction between crimes that they view as "more rational," like robbery and burglary, and others, such as murder. If such a distinction is valid, one might argue that deterrence would then at least be effective for the more "rational" crimes.

Yet even if we assume that most criminals are largely irrational, deterrence issues raise some tough questions about human nature, questions that are at the heart of very different views of crime and how to combat it. Still it is important to draw a distinction between "irrational" behavior and the notion that deterrence doesn't matter. One doesn't necessarily imply the other. For instance, some people may hold strange, unfathomable objectives, but this does not mean that they cannot be discouraged from doing things that bring increasingly undesirable consequences. . . .

Evidence of responding to disincentives is not limited to "rational" humans. Economists have produced a large number of studies that investigate whether animals take the costs of doing things into account. Animal subjects have included both rats and pigeons, and the typical experiment measures the amount of some desired treat or standard laboratory food or fluid that is consumed in relation to the number of times the animal must push a lever to get the item. Other experiments alter the amount of the item received for a given number of lever pushes. . . . The results from these experiments consistently show that as the "cost" of obtaining the food increases, the animal obtains less food. In economic terms, "Demand curves are downward sloping."

As for human beings, a large economics literature exists that overwhelmingly demonstrates that people commit fewer crimes if criminal penalties are more severe or more certain. . . . [T]he National Research Council of the U.S. National Academy of Sciences established the Panel of Research on Deterrent and Incapacitative Effects in 1978 to evaluate the many academic studies of deterrence. The panel concluded as follows: "Taken as a whole, the evidence consistently finds a negative association between crime rates and the risks of apprehension, conviction or imprisonment. . . . the evidence certainly favors a proposition supporting deterrence more than it favors one asserting that deterrence is absent."

This debate on incentives and how people respond to them arises repeatedly in many different contexts. Take gun-buyback programs. Surely the intention of such programs is good, but whey should we believe that they will greatly influence the number of guns on the street? True, the guns purchased are removed from circulation, and these programs may help to stigmatize gun ownership. Yet if they continue, one effect of such programs will be to increase the return to buying a gun. The price that a person is willing to pay for a gun today increases as the price for which it can be sold rises. In the extreme case, if the price offered in these gun-buyback programs ever became sufficiently high, people would simply buy guns in order to sell them through these programs. I am sure this would hardly distress gun manufacturers, but other than creating some socially useless work, the programs would have a dubious effect on crime. Empirical work on this question reveals no impact on crime from these programs.

An Overview

. . . Does gun ownership save or cost lives, and how do the various gun laws affect this outcome?

To answer these questions I use a wide array of data. For instance, I have employed polls that allow us to track how gun ownership has changed over time in different states, as well as the massive FBI yearly crime rate data for all 3,054 U.S. counties from 1977 to 1992. I use additional, more recently available data for 1993 and 1994 later to check my results. Over the last decade, gun ownership has been growing for virtually all demographic groups, though the fastest growing group of gun owners is Republican women, thirty to forty-four years of age, who live in rural areas. National crime rates have been falling at the same time as gun ownership has been rising. Likewise, states experiencing the greatest reductions in crime are also the ones with the fastest growing percentages of gun ownership.

Overall, my conclusion is that criminals as a group tend to behave rationally—when crime becomes more difficult, less crime is committed. Higher arrest and conviction rates dramatically reduce crime. Criminals also move out of jurisdictions in which criminal deterrence increases. Yet criminals respond to more than just the actions taken by the police and the courts. Citizens can take private actions that also deter crime. Allowing citizens to carry concealed handguns reduces violent crimes, and the reductions coincide very closely with the number of concealed-handgun permits issued. Mass shootings in public places are reduced when law-abiding citizens are allowed to carry concealed handguns.

Not all crime categories showed reductions, however. Allowing concealed handguns might cause small increases in larceny and auto theft. When potential victims are able to arm themselves, some criminals turn away from crimes like robbery that require direct attacks and turn instead to such crimes as auto theft, where the probability of direct contact with victims is small.

There were other surprises as well. While the support for the strictest gun-control laws is usually strongest in large cities, the largest drops in violent crime from legalized concealed handguns occurred in the most urban counties with the greatest populations and the highest crime rates. Given the limited resources available to law enforcement and our desire to spend those resources wisely to reduce crime, the results of my studies have implications for where police should concentrate their efforts. For example, I found that increasing arrest rates in the most crime-prone areas led to the greatest reductions in crime. Comparisons can also be made across different methods of fighting crime. Of all the methods studied so far by economists, the carrying of concealed handguns appears to be the most cost-effective method for reducing crime. Accident and suicide rates were unaltered by the presence of concealed handguns.

Guns also appear to be the great equalizer among the sexes. Murder rates decline when either more women or more men carry concealed handguns, but the effect is especially pronounced for women. One additional woman carrying a concealed handgun reduces the murder rate for women by about 3–4 times more than one additional man carrying a concealed handgun reduces the murder rate for men. This occurs because allowing a woman to defend herself with a concealed handgun produces a much larger change in her ability to defend herself than the change created by providing a man with a handgun.

While some evidence indicates that increased penalties for using a gun in the commission of a crime reduce crime, the effect is small. Furthermore, I find no crime-reduction benefits from state-mandated waiting periods and background checks before people are allowed to purchase guns. At the federal level, the Brady law has proven to be no more effective. Surprisingly, there is also little benefit from training requirements or age restrictions for concealed-handgun permits.

Franklin E. Zimring and
Gordon Hawkins

NO

Firearms and Lethal Violence

When discussing American lethal violence with any foreign criminologist, guns are always the first factor to be mentioned as an explanation of
the distinctively high rates of death in the United States. What sets the foreign criminologists' comments apart from our American colleagues is not
the unanimity with which they focus on guns, however, because this topic
in inevitably mentioned by American criminologists as well. But our
foreign colleagues are frequently unwilling to discuss any other feature of
American society or government *except* gun ownership and use. In Europe
or Japan, any mention of social, demographic, or economic factors as a
cause of homicide is commonly regarded as an evasion of the most obvious
reason why American violence is specially dangerous. This singular preoccupation with guns and gun use overstates the degree to which U.S. lethal
violence can be explained by a single cause, but not by much. Firearms use
is so prominently associated with the high death rate from violence that
starting with any other topic would rightly be characterized as an intentional evasion.

This [selection] discusses the role of firearms use in explaining the high
rate of lethal interpersonal violence in the United States. This is but one element of a complex set of issues that concerns that relationship between guns
and violence in the United States. Self-inflicted and accidental gun-shot cases
are excluded from this analysis. We will not discuss general patterns of gun
ownership and use . . . or survey the many different types of control strategy
that might reduce gun violence. The central concern here is whether and to
what extent our distinctive patterns of gun use explain the high death rates
from American violence.

The first section of the analysis discusses the way in which the topic and
method of this study push firearms to a position of central importance. The
second part . . . examines what we call global approaches to firearms as a
contributing cause to lethal violence. The third section . . . sets out a variety of
different explanations for why firearms use increases the death rate from violence and surveys what is known about each of those mechanisms. A concluding section talks about issues of causation, in discussions of the relationship
between gun use and lethal violence.

Why Guns?

There are two features of the approach [here] that put special emphasis on gun use: the emphasis on lethal violence and the frequent use of cross-national comparisons. . . . [T]he special connection between gun use and deadly violence in the United States [can be demonstrated] by comparing the proportion of police-reported gun use in total index felonies, violent felonies in the crime index, and killings resulting from intentional injury.

. . . [E]stimates . . . probably understate gun use in index and violent felonies recorded because gun use is not reported for forcible rape and cannot be assessed for noncontact property crime. But the conclusions to be drawn are far too robust to be seriously affected by this problem. The 4 percent estimate for the proportion of total index offenses involving guns confirms what the National Rifle Association has been insisting upon for some time: only a very small proportion of all criminal offenses in the United States are known to involve guns. If all crimes are of equally serious concern to citizens and policy makers, the low prevalence of firearms in serious crime would be a significant reason to look for other instrumentalities and approaches when attempting to reduce crime.

. . . [W]hen the crimes analyzed are restricted to those that threaten or inflict bodily injury—homicide, rape, robbery, and aggravated assault—the proportion of gun involvement increases fivefold, from 4 to 20 percent. When the subject of the inquiry shifts again to criminal injuries that take life, the prevalence of guns jumps again, this time rising to 70 percent. A shorthand way of communicating the importance of the shift to lethal violence as the focus of inquiry is this: If crime is nominated as the problem, guns are involved in one of every twenty-five cases, if lethal violence is nominated as the problem, then guns are implicated in seven of every ten cases.

The contrast between the one-in-five share of violent felonies committed with guns and the 70 percent gun share for American homicide makes guns appear very much more important when the focus shifts from all violence to lethal violence; this contrast also provides a preliminary basis for concluding that attacks with guns are more dangerous than attacks with other weapons. The 20 percent share of violent crime committed with guns in the United States is significant, but very far from cornering the market. The majority of robberies, rapes, and criminal assaults are committed with personal force, knives, or blunt objects. Even the elimination of all firearms incidents would leave a very high volume of violent offenses. But the 70 percent of all lethal attacks committed with firearms represents a statistical dominance that is difficult to ignore or to minimize. Guns alone account for more than twice as much homicide in the United States as all other means combined.

And the contrasting percentage of gun use for lethal and nonlethal violence also provides circumstantial evidence that guns are far more dangerous than any other instruments when used in violent assaults. If 25 percent of all aggravated assaults produce 70 percent of the lethal outcomes, then that 25 percent of gun attacks are seven times more likely to produce death on the average than the 80 percent of all serious assault that does not involve guns and that cumulatively accounts for only 30 percent of all killings. These are only preliminary indications, because gun attacks may be the product of different motives and situations from attacks employing other means. But the dominance of gun cases in the whole of the lethal violence category makes firearms use a necessary first step in the explanation of American lethal violence.

While solely domestic statistics implicate firearms as a dominant cause of American lethal violence, . . . international statistical comparison . . . also calls attention to firearms. No large industrial democracy other than the United States reports firearms as the cause of a majority of its homicides. Thus, scholars engaging in international comparison are confronted with two extraordinary distinctions between homicide in the United States and in the rest of the developed Western world: very much higher rates of homicide in the United States, and a uniquely high percentage of gun use in U.S. violence. Concluding that the elevated gun use is a cause of the distinctively high homicide experience seems natural.

One example of this reasoning from a statistical comparison may be found in an essay by Ronald V. Clarke and Pat Mayhew, "The British Gas Suicide Story and Its Criminological Implications." Clarke and Mayhew compare homicide rates per one million population for England and Wales and the United States for firearms, handguns (also counted in the firearms category), and all means other than firearms. Their results are set out in a table, which is reproduced here as Table 1.

All forms of homicide are more frequent in the United States than in England and Wales. Killings by all means other than guns occur in the United States at a rate per million population that is 3.7 times the nongun homicide rate reported in England and Wales. But homicides by handguns occur in the United States at a rate per million population that is 175 times as great. This comparison leads the authors to conclude that "there is little doubt that

Table 1

Gun and Nongun Homicides, England and Wales and the United States, 1980–1984

Type of murder	Homicides		Average annual rate per one million population[a]		England and Wales to United States ratio
	England and Wales	United States	England and Wales	United States	
All gun[b]	213	63,218	0.86	54.52	1 to 63.4
Handgun[b]	57	46,553	0.23	40.15	1 to 174.6
Nongun[b]	2,416	41,354	9.75	35.67	1 to 3.7
Total[c]	2,629	104,572	10.61	90.19	1 to 8.5

[a] Annual average population for 1980–1984: United States, 231.9 million; England and Wales, 49.55 million.
[b] Figures for the United States involved some extrapolation from homicides for which weapon was known.
[c] Figures for England and Wales relate to offenses currently recorded as homicide.

Source: Clarke and Mayhew 1988, Table 2, p. 107.

limiting the availability of firearms in the United States would have a substantial effect on homicide and probably also on other violent crime." Even though this conclusion cannot be established solely from population statistics of the sort presented in Table 1, the tendency to reach it is inevitable when both the magnitude of gun use and the aggregate death toll differences are that high. The fact that homicide rates with handguns in the United States are 175 times as high as in Great Britain may be only coincidental to the large difference in total homicide rates between the two countries. But few who have studied these international differences are willing to accept the coincidence hypothesis. Instead, those who analyze American violence by first making international comparisons tend to be adamant in their belief that gun use is a major explanation of the elevated death toll from violence. As we have said, it is hard to get them to consider anything else.

And the obvious conclusion about the relationship between firearms and lethal violence in the United States is also the correct one. High levels of gun use in assault and robbery are a very important contributory cause to elevated U.S. death rates from violence. While the magnitude of the difference that can be attributed solely to gun use cannot be determined with precision, as much as half of the difference between American and European homicide rates may be explained by differential resort in the United States to the most lethal of the commonly used instruments of violence.

On Global Comparisons

The type of data featured in . . . Table 1 are global statistical comparisons that show the extent of the overlap between firearms and violence in the United States. We use the phrase "global comparison" to denote efforts to estimate the impact of gun use on the death rate from violence by obtaining a correlation between variations in gun use and variations in homicide rates. Such comparisons do not directly address issues of causation. A further limitation of most global comparative analyses is that they do not directly distinguish what features of firearms use might contribute to elevating death rates from those associated with other types of violent attack. So the global comparative approach should never be the endpoint of any analysis of firearms and violence. Nevertheless, the cautious use of basic comparison can tell us a great deal about the extent to which gun use increases death rates from violence.

One early test of global relationship was reported by Stephen Seitz in 1972. Seitz observed a 0.98 correlation between the firearms homicide rate in a U.S. state in 1967 and the total rate of homicide experienced in that state, so that a higher-than-average death rate from firearms injury would almost predict a higher-than-average death rate from injury by all means. The interpretation of this relationship was: "[I]t is almost impossible to conclude that the relation between firearms and criminal homicide is merely coincidental."

The problem with inferring a causal connection between gun homicide and total homicide from this sort of correlation is that this type of relationship studied by Seitz has been categorized as a "part–whole correlation." Gun homicides constitute the majority of all homicides in the United States. Thus, if a state has a higher-than-average gun homicide rate, the total homicide rate would automatically tend to vary in the same direction as the gun homicide statistics.

The problem can be illustrated by imagining a study of the effect of weight loss strategies that found that those men and women who lost the largest amount of weight from their thighs, legs, and feet during a diet period also tended to lose the largest total amount of body weight. Does this tell us that a priority strategy of a diet regime should be weight reduction in the thighs, legs, and feet? The alternative to concluding that thighs are of special significant in weight reduction is understanding that the bottom half of the body is an important part of the body's weight and for that reason alone persons who lost considerable weight from their legs would have lost more total weight on a diet than those who lost a smaller percentage of their southern extremity poundage. Losing a substantial amount of weight in the legs, far from being an independent variable causing success in a dietary regime, is one of the major effects of having been on a diet.

Is there a way of eliminating the impact that death rates from firearms would have on total homicide rates only because they are such a substantial part of the homicide total? One promising approach would be to measure the influence, not of the number of people killed by guns in any give state, but of the proportionate use of guns rather than other methods of inflicting death. Suppose we compare, for each state, the proportion of fatal attacks using firearms with the total homicide rate for the particular state instead of comparing the rate of gun deaths with the total rate of all deaths, the notorious part–whole correlation. We are now predicting that a high proportionate use of guns will yield a higher-than-average homicide rate while states with lower relative gun use in deadly attacks will also have smaller-than-average total homicide rates. The correlation when we use a percentage homicide variable rather than the gun homicide rate for the fifty states in 1967 is 0.55, suggesting that gun use explains about 30 percent of cross-state variations in homicide in the year that the Seitz analysis was run.

There are a variety of different global comparisons of gun use and death rates that point to gun use as a positive influence on homicide rates. One strategy is to study the relationship between gun use and homicide rates over time in the United States. The correlation between total gun share of homicide and total homicide rates in the United States for the years 1964–1990 is 0.77, indicating that years in which the proportion of all killings committed by guns is high are associated with high total homicide rates by all means, and vice versa.

To the same effect, a recent research note by one of us finds the correlation over time between percentage gun use and total homicide rate for offenders under eighteen was 0.9 over the years 1977–1992, and that changes in gun use were also efficient predictors of which age groups would exhibit the largest increase in homicide.

Even this variety of correlational study results cannot establish a definitive causal sequence. Perhaps both the rate of gun use and the death rate from attacks increase because more people who intend to kill their victims select guns to achieve that goal. Because the proportion of all assaults committed with guns may signal changes in the nature of violent attackers as well as in violent attacks, it is not possible to isolate firearms as a cause of increases in death rate through the use of this kind of comparison.

In the second place, even if we believe that global comparisons make it probable that gun use causes an increased death rate, this kind of global statistical analysis cannot reveal what characteristics of guns or their use in attacks is the operative cause of increased lethality. What is there about guns that produces more homicides than other weapons when they are used in assaults? Simply knowing that those periods of maximum gun use in the recent history of the United States are associated with much higher death rates from intentional injury cannot produce any insight into why gun assaults acquire their extra measure of dangerousness. In this sense, then, global statistical comparison is important as an estimate of the strength of the general relationship between gun use and death from homicide and as a precursor to more specific investigation of the mechanism of guns and the effect of these on violent assault.

The basic problem that limits the policy significance of the global comparison is that changes in gun use may signal changed intentions by attackers as well as increasing the chances that an attack will result in death because the gun is a more lethal instrument. When Clarke and Mayhew assert that reducing gun availability will reduce deaths, they either assume that more deadly intentions are not the cause of a high rate of death from gun assault or believe that the absence of available guns will modify or frustrate an attacker's lethal intentions.

The prudent conclusion from global comparison is that when gun use increases, both the larger capacity of firearms to cause death and the greater manifest desire of the attacker to risk a victim's death will increase the death rate. The global comparison can estimate the joint impact of altered instruments and intentions, but cannot apportion any effects on death rate between these two elements.

As to the magnitude of the relationship between gun use and homicide rates, studies over time in the United States are associated with substantial estimates of gun use effects. More than half of the variations of homicide rates in the United States are linked systematically to variations in the proportion of shooting fatalities in the 0.77 correlated reported previously. And parallel statistics for selected cities and subgroups produce even larger correlations.

No matter how large the noted association between guns and homicide, however, the global comparison is a self-limiting methodology. The more likely it is that such comparisons implicate gun use as a cause of homicide, the more important it becomes to supplement such statistics with different empirical strategies that promise to provide information about why guns are particularly lethal.

The Causes of Differential Lethality

Guns may cause increases in the death rate from assault in a variety of different ways. The use of guns as opposed to other weapons in assault may be associated with both mechanical and social changes in violent assault that can increase death rates. Among the mechanical or instrumentality aspects of gun use that can increase death rates are: the greater injurious impact of bullets, the longer range of firearms; and the greater capacity of firearms for executing multiple attacks. Among the features in social setting related to gun use are: the need to use more lethal instruments of assault in situations where an attacker fears that his adversary may have a gun, the need to sustain or intensify a deadly assault because an opponent possesses or is using firearms, and the increased willingness to use guns and other lethal weapons in personal conflict because such weapons are used generally. All of these aspects may increase the lethality of assaults committed with guns, but by no means to the same degree. There are also two social impacts of gun possession and use that can lower death rates: the deterrence of assaults because of fear of gun-owning victims and the prevention of attempted assaults by an armed victim.

Instrumentality Effects

Of all the possible ways that gun use increases the deadliness of attacks, the theory that gunshot wounds inflict more damage than other methods of personal attacks is considered the most important and has been the subject of the most research.

The early debate about the influence of guns on deaths from assault involved different theories of the types of intention that produced assaults that lead to death. Marvin Wolfgang in his landmark study of homicide doubted that the weapon used in an attack made much difference in the chance that a death would result since so many different weapons could produce death if an attacker tried hard enough. Zimring responded to this assertion with a study of knife and gun assaults and killings in Chicago.

Zimring's data suggested that many homicides were the result of attacks apparently conducted with less than a single-minded intent to kill. Unlike the Wolfgang study where only fatal attacks were examined, the first Zimring study compared fatal and nonfatal gun and knife assaults in Chicago over four police periods. The study found that 70 percent of all gun killings in Chicago were the result of attacks that resulted in only one wound to the victim, and most attacks with guns or knives that killed a victim looked quite similar to the knife and gun attacks that did not kill. From this data, Zimring argued that most homicides were the result of ambiguously motivated assaults, so that the offender would risk his victim's death, but usually did not press on until death was assured.

Under such circumstances, the capacity of a weapon to inflict life-threatening injury would have an important influence on the death rate from assault. The 1968 Chicago study found that gun attacks were about five times as likely to kill as knife attacks, and this ratio held when the comparison was controlled for the number of wounds inflicted and the specific location of the most serious wound. Since knives were the next most deadly frequently used method of inflicting injury in attacks, the large difference in death rate suggested that substituting knives or other less dangerous instruments for guns would reduce the death rate from assault.

This weapon dangerousness comparison was first reported for Chicago in 1968 and has been replicated in other sites. Follow-up studies have shown that a difference in weapon as subtle as firearm caliber can double the death rate from gun assaults. The summary conclusion from this line of research can be simply stated: the objective dangerousness of a weapon used in violent assaults appears to be a major influence on the number of victims who will die from attacks. This "instrumentality effect" is the major documented influence of guns on death rate.

The use of guns in robbery is different from their use in wounding since the weapon is not necessarily used to inflict harm. Because robberies with guns frighten their victims into complying with the robbers' demands more than other robberies, a smaller number of gun robberies result in woundings than personal force robberies and robberies with knives. Still, the greater dangerousness of guns when fired more than compensates for the lower number of wounds. For street robberies and those that take place in commercial establishments, the death rate for every 1000 gun robberies is about three times that generated by robberies at knife point and about ten times the death rate from robberies involving personal force.

Another way of estimating the impact of gun use on the dangerousness of robbery is to focus on the prevalence of gun use in fatal and nonfatal robbery incidents. . . .

Firearms are responsible for 40 percent of robberies and 73 percent of all robbery killings in the United States, so that the apparent death rate from gun robbery nationwide is four times that of nongun robberies in the aggregate. . . .

The death rate comparison . . . is subject to at least two qualifications. In the first place, the difference in death rate noted in the figure already takes into account whatever savings of life results from the lower rate of resistance to gun-using robbers. So the difference in death rate from gun robbery as a result of the greater injury potential of bullet wounds may be larger than the 4-to-1 ratio. . . .

The second qualification cuts in the opposite direction. Many of the robberies committed with guns involve commercial entities and other relatively well-defended robbery targets. These robberies might involve a greater risk of injury or death that is to some degree independent of the weapon used by the robber. The switch to knives or blunt instruments in such cases might lead to a higher rate of victim injury or death than is generated by other types of knife and blunt instrument robbery. Of course, some of these difficult target robberies might not be committed if firearms were not available. So the calculus of comparison between gun robberies and other types of robbery is both multidimensional and complex.

There is one sense in which what we call global gun-versus-nongun comparisons in robbery are less problematic than global comparisons involving assault. Because persons committing assault intend to injure, the weapons they select may be probative of their intention to risk a lethal outcome. Since robbery involves only the threat of force, the choice of weapon may not directly reflect an intention to do harm and the choice of more dangerous weapons may not as closely reflect a more serious intention to injure. The robber may not intend any harm at the point of choosing weapons, and differences in total death rate may thus reflect only instrumentality effects.

Range
... In those circumstances where attacks are initiated or completed at long range, a firearm is a necessary weapon. Included in such attacks are sniper incidents, many assassination attempts, other assaults from a distance at a defined and frequently guarded target, as well as more common "drive-by" shootings where a target may or may not have been preselected, but where the defining characteristic of the attack is shooting at long range. The official records on such killings are not complete. The Federal Bureau of Investigation reported a total of ninety-seven sniper killing cases between 1990 and 1992, but did not have a code for drive-by shootings. The Los Angeles police estimated about thirty drive-by fatalities in 1991 out of about 1000 cases (no national-level estimates are available).

Capacity for Multiple Attack
Most firearms have the capacity to shoot many separate bullets in a relatively short period of time and with a minimum of physical effort on the part of the shooter. A revolver typically has a six-shot capacity and is easy to reload. Pistols typically carry six to nine rounds and can carry many more. Rifles vary from single-shot weapons to some with very large capacity clips and magazines.

There are two ways in which the capacity for multiple-wound infliction can produce a higher death rate from assault than would occur if more time and effort were required to repeat or intensify an attack. In the first place, several shots can be fired at the same victim producing wounds where the first attempt missed or resulting in multiple wounds that involve a much higher probability of death. In the second place, the multiple-shot capacity of many firearms can mean that more than one victim can be wounded—and put at risk of death—during the same assault.

The assault studies conducted in the late 1960s and early 1970s did not show a high proportion of multiple-wound attacks. Indeed, the failure of most shooters to exhaust the capacity of their firearms is cited as strong evidence against the proposition that most gun fatalities were not the result of kill-at-any-cost intentions. The more specific study of whether firearms with multiple capacity are more often used to produce multiple wounds has not yet been attempted.

Crude empirical soundings regarding whether guns are more often used in multiple-victim killings are not difficult to conduct in the age of the computer, but an all-fatality sample may be biased. Using data from the Federal Bureau of Investigation's Supplementary Homicide Reports for the years 1976–1992, we tested the hypothesis that guns would more often be the instrument of attack in assaults that resulted in more than one fatality than in assaults in which only one victim died. We found a modest but consistent confirmation of the hypothesis. In all seventeen years covered by the data set, the proportion of gun use in multiple-victim killings was higher than in single-victim killings. When cases involving young children are deleted from the analysis, weapons other than guns are used in about one out of every four multiple-victim incidents, as compared with one out of three single-victim killings, as shown by Figure 1.

Figure 1

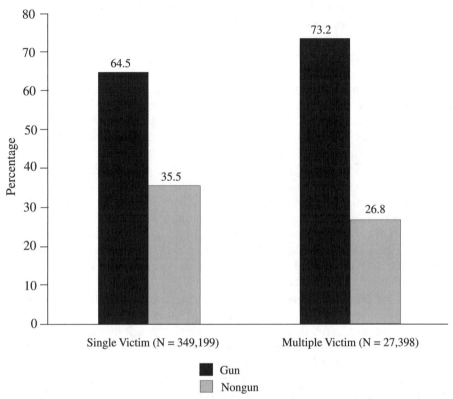

Firearms by Single or Multiple Victim (Excluding Child Cases), United States, 1976–1992

Source: U.S. Department of Justice, Federal Bureau of Investigation, 1994.

The larger proportion of multiple killings committed with guns probably represents an increase in death rate on top of the differential deadliness effects discussed earlier, but these two effects overlap in a study that considers only multiple killings. A larger proportion of attacks on multiple victims with knives or clubs may result in only one death because other victims survive a knife attack but are killed in a gun attack. The research question is whether gun attacks on multiple victims produces even higher differential deadliness over knife attacks than is found in single-victim assaults. A study of nonfatal as well as fatal attacks might decide this issue, but has not yet been undertaken.

Social Factors

The mechanical factors just discussed are characteristics of guns that may influence the death rate from attacks committed with firearms. What we call social factors are the many ways in which a social environment where many people possess and use firearms in interpersonal assault may have an influence on the extent to which assaults lead to fatal conclusions. There are at least three different theories as to how a social environment of high gun use can increase killings and at least two theories about how a social environment of extensive gun ownership and use might reduce violent deaths. But precise and specific empirical evaluation of theories about social and environmental effects is not easy.

One way in which a social environment of frequent gun assaults can increase the death rate from assault is by making those engaged in physical combat resort to more lethal instruments of assault and also to continue and intensify an assault because an opponent is armed. A social environment of frequent gun use multiplies the number of cases where both sides in a conflict possess lethal weapons. This should increase the death rate from both gun and knife attacks by motivating more sustained application of lethal force because of the counterforces risked if the attacker desists too soon.

One common feature of a two-way gun fight is that each combatant is unwilling to stop shooting until it seems clear that his opponent is incapable of shooting back. For this reason, it seems likely that the death rate from bilateral gun fights will be much higher than in situations where one party is armed with a gun and the other party has no deadly weapon. An attack where only one participant uses lethal force should be less likely to produce death because the combatant who controls the lethal force can stop pressing his attack without risking being shot or stabbed.

A second environmental influence closely related to the problem of bilateral lethal force is the way in which fear that others may have guns may motivate people to arm themselves with deadlier weapons than they might otherwise feel would be necessary for either self-defense or attack. When approaching a conflict in which guns are believed to be present, a potential combatant is more likely to feel it necessary to arm himself with a knife or a gun. The irony here is that one element that may increase the use of firearms in combat is a fear of guns in the hands of others. In this way increases in gun use can, in many social settings, become self-fulfilling prophecies.

A third effect of an environment where gun use is frequent that might increase mortality rates from assault is that a high frequency of gun use might lead citizens to expect that firearms are used in interpersonal conflict. On this theory, an increase in gun use would occur, not only out of fear, but out of social habit as the widespread practice of carrying and using guns generates a belief that gun use is a normal part of interpersonal conflicts. The use of a gun in many serious conflicts may no longer be regarded as deviant behavior. This could increase guns use over time substantially. We know of no way to directly measure the extent of this type of legitimation of the use of deadly force, but it is an influence that could be of considerable significance.

There are two current theories about how a social environment of frequent gun use might reduce the death toll from criminal violence: self-defense and deterrence. The self-defense theory argues that a larger number of firearms produces a larger proportion of gun ownership and self-defense gun use. Potential crime victims will use guns to prevent or thwart attack and thus reduce the death toll—at least among nonoffenders—from assault. The extent of this direct self-defense dividend from high gun ownership is the subject of a lively debate.

One major methodological problem with measuring self-defense is that asking persons in a survey whether they have used a gun to prevent a criminal act produces self-serving statements that cannot be verified. *Each* party to an argument that turned violent is likely to regard the other party as a criminal aggressor, and to think that his own use of force was permissible self-defense. When talking to only one of two combatants, the story one is likely to hear is that a crime was prevented by a gun even though the respondent's opponent would swear that in fact a crime was committed by the person representing himself as the victim. Official police statistics on assault involve an umpire's decision made by police about the culpability of the parties. But survey research cannot generate a valid test of the allegations of a self-serving respondent.

A final theory of social influence argues that widespread gun ownership and use deters criminal assault because would-be offenders recognize the high probability that a criminal attack will be met with lethal force. The probability of substantial across-the broad crime reduction from this kind of armed citizen deterrence is emphasized frequently by opponents of gun control legislation in the United States. And it has been associated with legislative proposals to loosen restrictions on carrying concealed guns. Indeed one small city in Georgia passed an ordinance requiring citizen possession of firearms for which the stated rationale was deterrence.

The measurement of the types of social impact that have been outlined in this section is difficult and some of the most important social influences are the most difficult to assess empirically. The degree to which widespread ownership and use of guns leads to the expectation that they will be used in personal assaults could have a substantial impact on the amount of lethal violence experienced in a society incrementally over a long period of time. But the rigorous empirical assessment of this would be practically impossible to execute because it would be a process taking place gradually over decades without any specific landmarks to be the focus of evaluation. Yet the potential importance of this factor in determining a society's rate of lethal interpersonal violence is not smaller merely because it is not susceptible to rigorous measurement.

Some of the theories of social influence outlined above can be tested in relatively straightforward ways. The quantity and quality of self-defense uses of firearms can be assessed using police statistics and, to a lesser extent, surveys. Police statistics can provide a minimum estimate of incidents of citizen self-defense where a neutral factfinder affirms that the person using the force was not to blame for the event. Survey reports of self-defense can be useful in defining issues even if the factual accounts in the survey cannot be verified. When surveys show that 70 percent of all claimed incidents of crime prevention concern the offense of aggravated assault, the criminologist can pay specific attention to assault and homicide statistics in studying the influence of gun ownership and use on crime.

Another opportunity for straightforward evaluation is the comparison of multiple-wounding and case-fatality rates in one- and two-way gun battles.

That sort of specific assessment would be a logical next step in the epidemio-logical research into intentional injury that is in progress in the United States.

There are a number of hypotheses that cannot be isolated and separately measured. If high gun ownership environments are associated with higher-than-average proportionate use of guns in assault, is this because would-be attackers are afraid their opponents may be armed or is it another manifesta-tion of a general social expectation that it is permissible to use guns in certain types of social conflict? If the widespread availability of handguns prevents some lethal attacks but also increases the death rate from attacks, how can these two countervailing tendencies be isolated and measured?

To some extent, the difficulties of isolating each element of gun influ-ence for individual assessment are intractable, but the precise measure of indi-vidual influences on death rates may also be relatively unimportant. From a social policy standpoint, the sort of global assessment that was discussed ear-lier may tell us all that we have to know because it provides an estimate of the magnitude of the net effect of variations in gun use over time and cross-nationally.

The major problem with many such global estimates by themselves, however, is the issue of causal ordering. But once the mechanical ways in which gun use increases the death rate from assault have been identified and measured, it may be possible to approach the sort of global estimates discussed earlier with more confidence that variations in gun use are, for the most part, independent variables in the equation and that variations in homicide rates are, again for the most part, the dependent variables. If so, a large positive cor-relation between percentage firearms use in homicide and rates of homicide over time tells us that mechanical and social elements that accompany increases in gun use have a much greater elevating influence on death rates than any restraining influence that may be concurrent. If lethal violence is the focus of social concern, such an aggregate conclusion may be more important than the precise assessment of the impact of specific aspects of firearms use.

Firearms Use As Contributing Cause

The use of firearms in assault and robbery is the single environment feature of American society that is most clearly linked to the extraordinary death rate from interpersonal violence in the United States. But the strength of this rela-tionship does not mean that firearms ownership and use has a simple, invari-able, or independent influence on homicide rates. In this section, we consider the question of the causal connection between gun use and lethality. We do this not only because it is an important issue in relation to firearms and lethal violence, but also because reflecting on the questions of causation that arise in connection with firearms teaches us an important lesson about the role of many other environmental influences on the incidence of lethal violence.

The American debate about guns has produced one of the few causal cri-tiques ever to appear on a bumper sticker: the famous "Guns don't kill people, people kill people." Behind the strong sentiment that inspired this and a multi-tude of related appeals lies an important logical point. Firearms ownership and use is neither a necessary nor a sufficient cause of violent death in the United States. Firearms are not a necessary cause of killings because of the wide array of alternative methods of killing that are available ranging from the strangler's hands to car bombs. Even in the United States in 1996, nearly 30 percent of all killings did not involve guns. Moreover, the widespread availability of firearms is not a sufficient condition for intentional homicide by a wide margin. One-half of all American households own guns and it is estimated that one-quarter of all households own a handgun—the weapon used in three-quarters of all gun homicides. Yet only a small fraction of all gun owners become gun attackers. The logical point here is that guns do not become dangerous instruments of attack if they are not used in an attack.

If gun use is neither a necessary nor a sufficient cause of violent death, what is the proper descriptive label for the role gun use plays in deaths due to intentional injury? The most accurate label for the role of firearms in those cases of death and injury from intentional attacks in which they are used is *contributing cause*. Even where the availability of a gun plays no important role in the decision to commit an assault, the use of a gun can be an important contributing cause in the death and injury that results for gun attacks. When guns are used in a high proportion of such attacks, the death rate from violent attack will be high. Current evidence suggests that a combination of the ready availability of guns and the willingness to use maximum force in interpersonal conflict is the most important single contribution to the high U.S. death rate from violence. Our rate of assault is not exceptional; our death rate from assault is exceptional.

The role of gun use as a contributing cause means that the net effect of firearms on violence will depend on the interaction of gun availability with other factors that influence the rate of violent assaults in a society and the willingness of people to use guns in such assaults. So the precise contribution of firearms to the death toll from violence is contingent on many other factors that may influence the number and character of violent attacks.

Some implications of this contingency deserve emphasis. Introducing 10,000 loaded handguns into a social environment where violent assault is a rare occurrence will not produce a large number of additional homicide deaths unless it also increases the rate of assault. The percentage increase in homicide might be considerable if guns become substitutes for less lethal weapons. But the additional number of killings would be small because of the low rate of attack. Introducing 10,000 handguns into an environment where rates of attack and willingness to use handguns in attack are both high is a change that would produce many more additional deaths. The net effect of guns depends on how they are likely to be used.

One corollary of viewing guns as an interactive and contributing cause to intentional homicide is that societies with low rates of violent assault will pay a lower price if they allow guns to be widely available than will societies with higher rates of violence. The sanguine sound bite encountered in American debates about guns is: "An armed society is a polite society." This does not seem particularly plausible to us, but it seems likely that only a very polite society can be heavily armed without paying a high price.

The United States of the 1990s is far from that polite society. Our considerable propensity for violent conflict would be a serious societal problem even if gun availability and use were low. But the very fact that the United States is a high-violence environment makes the contribution of gun use to the death toll from violence very much greater. When viewed in the light of the concept of contributing causation, the United States has both a violence problem and a gun problem, and each makes the other more deadly.

POSTSCRIPT

Do More Guns Lead to Less Crime?

As a growing number of scholars question the alleged connection between guns and violence, America is clearly becoming anti-gun, particularly handguns and tactical weapons, as well as averse to allowing citizens to legally carry concealed weapons. Tragedies involving guns, both on school yards and in inner cities, are routinely reported on by the media.

Lott not only says that guns reduce crime, but he also dismisses several policies of those purporting to have a rational approach to gun control. He contends that research shows that mandatory waiting periods, background checks, weapons buybacks, training sessions, and even gun locks have little effect on reducing gun homicides. He cites statistics that indicate that almost no citizens who have permits to carry concealed weapons actually commit gun-related crimes.

Meanwhile, Zimring and Hawkins present much data to show that guns directly contribute to America's out-of-sight homicide rate. They argue that although carrying guns can make a society polite, that is true only if society is already polite. When guns are allowed in a violent society, they insist, then violence is bound to follow.

Can the two sides of this issue be synthesized? For example, should policymakers allow handguns but make the legal response to abuse even more severe? Also, what can be done to get illegal weapons out of the hands of criminals? Neither side considers the contention that since there will always be thousands of illegal guns floating around, a rational policy would be to regulate and carefully control the production and distribution of bullets.

An overview of this issue plus an extensive debate on stricter controls at gun shows can be found in the November 1999 issue of *Congressional Digest,* a special issue on "Firearms in America." Among the many attacks on Lott and the question of defensive gun uses is O. Duncan's "Gun Use Surveys: In Numbers We Trust?" *The Criminologist* (January/February 2000) and "The Effect of Concealed Weapons Laws: An Extreme Bound Analysis," by W. Bartley and M. Cohen, *Economic Inquiry* (April 1998).

An excellent book by a prominent scholar who persistently questions key aspects of gun control research is G. Kleck's *Targeting Guns: Firearms and Their Control* (Aldine de Gruyter, 1997). Two other critical evaluations of current policies is D. D. Polsby's "From the Hip," *National Review* (March 24, 1997) and G. L. Carter's *The Gun Control Movement* (Macmillan, 1997). A witty discussion of scholars who disagree over the issue is "Showdown," by C. Mooney, *Lingua Franca* (February 2000).

ISSUE 15

Should the Police Enforce Zero-Tolerance Laws?

YES: George L. Kelling and William J. Bratton, from "Declining Crime Rates: Insiders' Views of the New York City Story," *The Journal of Criminal Law & Criminology* (Summer 1998)

NO: Judith A. Greene, from "Zero Tolerance: A Case Study of Police Policies and Practices in New York City," *Crime & Delinquency* (April 1999)

ISSUE SUMMARY

YES: George L. Kelling, a professor in the School of Criminal Justice at Rutgers University, and William J. Bratton, former New York City Police Department commissioner, strongly defend Kelling's formulation of zero tolerance/broken windows theory and Bratton's implementation of Kelling's ideas. They assert that crime, especially homicides, has rapidly declined in New York City as a result of this policing mode.

NO: Judith A. Greene, senior fellow of the Institute on Criminal Justice of the University of Minnesota Law School, examines many alternative explanations for New York's crime decline and concludes that zero tolerance is only partially responsible at best. She compares New York's policing model with San Diego's community policing model, and she argues that the later is just as effective and less costly in terms of both community relations and needed personnel.

$\mathbf{M}$any ironies, paradoxes, and contradictions permeate this issue in terms of both criminal justice and policing. First, the theory of crime control put forth in March 1982 by George L. Kelling and James Q. Wilson in their article "Broken Windows," *Atlantic Monthly,* is one of the few examples of specific ideas clearly formulated by scholars that have been directly drawn from to guide crime control practices in the real world. Part of the reason for its application is that Kelling was on hand as a consultant to encourage its development.

Second, it is rare to see immediate results from any criminal justice policy shift. Although critics contend that former police commissioner William

J. Bratton or current commissioner Howard Safir's zero-tolerance mode of policing did not cause New York's rapid crime drop, there is little doubt that a miracle somehow occurred in New York City.

Third, while any innovations or program changes in criminal justice (especially in agencies as close-knit as the police) will generate misunderstanding and strains, this is a calculated part of the costs. The trade-off for an improved technology or mode of police interaction is often hurt feelings, bruised egos for those whose old way of doing things are modified or discarded, and diffuse resentments fueled at times by overt envy. In addition, with virtually any new crime control practice mistakes will happen. These also should be factored into the costs for improvements. However, the incredible backlash from the New York City model of policing was unexpected. Moreover, unlike the vast majority of new police innovations, the backlash is not internal. Instead, the backlash has been primarily external. First, many scholars indignantly attacked zero tolerance as racist, retrograde, and a violation of the narrowly framed "depolicing" perception since the 1960s of what police work is supposed to be about (the less policing the better). Next came the predictable bitterness of political and community interest groups who sometimes feel threatened by any neighborhood success that they do not control or can claim for their own. The tragic mistakes that may or may not have been a result of zero tolerance—such as the killing of minority citizens mistakenly thought to be threatening criminals—more than provide proof for skeptics of zero tolerance that the experiment is racist, misguided, and contemptible. In some states, political candidates have leaped into office or been thrown out based on their positions on zero-tolerance policing.

A last irony is that while the definition of many criminal justice and criminological terms are ambiguous (including crime itself!), the meaning of *zero tolerance* is highly problematic. Many scholars and politicians have distanced themselves from the term, substituting phrases that sound more politically correct. As you read the following selections, consider the different components of zero tolerance/broken windows policing. What is the role of the cop on the beat? The administrators? Technologies? Compare and contrast community policing with Kelling and Bratton's approach. Notice that most consider zero tolerance a polar opposite of community policing. Yet defenders such as Kelling and Bratton seem to suggest that community policing can be subsumed under zero tolerance. How can that be?

In her selection, Judith A. Greene cites several criticisms of the New York approach, then compares and contrasts its crime reduction statistics with that of San Diego, California. That city has the allegedly opposite policing style, community policing, to New York's. As you read Greene's selection, consider the basis for her comparison and the importance and value of doing comparative analysis in criminology. Note also the many favorable aspects of Bratton's administration as commissioner that she identifies. How would you separate the alleged good from the alleged bad in zero tolerance? Should this style of policing be encouraged?

George L. Kelling and
William J. Bratton

 **YES**

Declining Crime Rates

Introduction

Something dramatic happened in New York City in 1994: a lot of people stopped committing crimes, especially violent ones. The reduction in the number of persons committing murders, for example, while not unprecedented, was extraordinary. Since 1994, a debate has raged about why this happened. Putting our position up front, we believe the police played an important, even central, role in getting people to stop committing crime in New York City. Despite arguments to the contrary,[1] no evidence exists that the substantial drops in crime in New York City, especially the initial ones when one of the authors of this paper, William Bratton, was commissioner, were the result of economic change, changes in drug use patterns, or demographic changes. Arguably, New York City's economy, drug use patterns, and demography might be different now in 1998. Unemployment was at 10% the month Bratton took over the New York City Police Department (NYPD) (January 1994) and at 8.7% when he resigned (April 1996)—hardly a booming economy. And remember as well, the initial reductions in crime were so steep that by August of 1995—three years ago, but only twenty months after Bratton took office—*New York* magazine declared in a cover story, "The End of Crime As We Know It."

Readers should understand that this debate about the origins of crime reductions in the United States, especially in New York City, are not just academic in the sense that detached scholars are searching objectively for some "truth" lurking out there somewhere in the data. In fact, criminological and political ideologies have shaped a good portion of this debate and are barely beneath the surface of even the most "detached" presentations. We do not pretend to be free from strong points of view about what happened in New York City. We were there and our presence belies any "detached objectivity." Yet, we are not alone in having important vested interests in the outcome of the debate. Aside from the lack of any competing explanations, our confidence that the police played an important role in New York City has three origins:

1. We had a guiding "idea" about how to prevent crime; put another way, we had a theory of action;

2. We applied this idea in New York City's subway and, without anticipating it, the subway experiences became the "pretest" for what was
to happen later citywide;
3. Bratton, most importantly, but Kelling as well, had been struggling
with issues of how to improve policing through police leadership,
management, and administration for over two decades—principles
developed in the context of organizational and policy literature and
experience.

In the three sections that follow, we will be brief. We have written elsewhere about these issues and will not repeat our arguments here in detail.

The "Idea"—Broken Windows

The "broken windows" metaphor had its origin in an *Atlantic Monthly* article
by James Q. Wilson and Kelling. It argued that, just as a broken window left
untended was a sign that nobody cares and leads to more and severe property
damage, so disorderly conditions and behaviors left untended send a signal
that nobody cares and results in citizen fear of crime, serious crime, and the
"downward spiral of urban decay." The article also argued that whenever
crime and communities verged on being out of control in the past, residents
and authorities in neighborhoods moved to reassert controls over youth and
over disorderly behavior.

The implications of this point of view are that minor offenses have serious consequences for the life of neighborhoods and communities. Citizens,
city officials, and police ignore them at their peril. This point of view is at odds
with the reigning crime control policy view that had been developing
throughout the 1950s and 1960s and made explicit by President Johnson's
Crime Control Commission. Police, in this view, are "law enforcement officers," the front end of the criminal justice system whose business is serious
crime—arresting offenders. For a variety of reasons police got out of the business of minor offenses. These reasons went beyond the utilitarian view that
scarce police resources should best be concentrated on "serious" crimes. They
included an understanding of how police abused loitering and vagrancy ordi-
nances in the past; a desire for less intrusive policing and a more judicious use
of police authority in a democracy; and, a view that many of the offenses, like
prostitution, are victimless.

Nonetheless, we argued that the links between disorder, fear, and crime
went something like the following:

Disorder → Citizen Fear → Withdrawal (Physical & Social) →
Increased Predatory Behavior → Increased Crime → Spiral of Decline

According to this model, waiting until serious crimes occur to intervene
is too late: dealing with disorderly behavior early, like successful communities
have in the past, prevented the cycle from accelerating and perpetuating itself.

Moreover, experiences in the subway taught us that many chronic, serious offenders also behave in a disorderly fashion and commit minor offenses

like farebeating. Police order maintenance activities also give police the opportunity to make contact with and arrest serious offenders for minor offenses.

We never claimed that order maintenance alone is the sole means of preventing crime. Solving crimes, incarceration, social change, deterrence by other means, police presence and persuasion, citizen vigilance, reduction of opportunities, environmental design, and other factors play a role as well. In New York City's subway, however, we argue that order maintenance was an especially significant part of reclaiming the subway and reducing crime.

The Subway

In April of 1989, Robert Kiley, Chairman of New York State's Metropolitan Transportation Authority (MTA) asked Kelling to assist the MTA in solving a problem in the New York City Transit Authority's subway (NYCTA). Kiley believed that the subway was in deep trouble—passenger usage of the subway was in rapid decline. New York City's late 1980s economic slump partially explained this decline. But marketing surveys suggested a more complicated problem: "homelessness" was frightening passengers and causing them to abandon the subway in droves. This was after $8 billion dollars had been poured into the subway to upgrade trains and tracks during the early and mid-1980s.

The NYCTA had already largely solved the problem of subway graffiti–a problem considered so intractable that its eradication was considered by some to be one of the most successful urban policy "wins" on record. Yet, despite this achievement, the frightening and intimidating behavior of a large group of miscreants overmatched whatever advantages accrued from graffiti elimination.

For those who have not experienced New York's subway during the late 1980s, its nightmarish circumstances are hard to describe. "In your face" panhandlers confronted riders throughout the system, from station entrances to trains. A quarter of a million passengers a day were "farebeaters," going over, under, and around turnstiles. Youths deliberately blocked turnstiles, held open emergency gates, and extorted fares from passengers. Platforms, trains, and passageways reeked from public urination and defecation. Young men stalked tollbooths planning to rob them if by any chance their doors were opened. These same tollbooths–literally under siege–had already been firmly secured, including being equipped with special automatic fire extinguishers that would be activated if youths poured gasoline into the money window and lit it to force toll-takers to open booth doors Drug and alcohol abusers and the emotionally disturbed, often one and the same, sprawled throughout the entire system–at times taking over entire cars on a train. Robberies of passengers were increasing.

For the Transit Police Department (TPD), at this time an independent police department of some 4,000 officers, it was business as usual. They shared the common view held by everyone from homeless advocates, to the New York City Civil Liberties Union, to the *New York Times*. The problem was "homelessness" and homelessness was not the TPD's problem. Robberies consumed its attention. For example, the TPD was eager to restart an earlier discredited decoy unit. When confronted by Kiley about the subway's "home-lessness" problems, TPD's administration at first balked. Later, under pressure, it proposed massive cleaning crews armed with high-powered hoses sup-ported by a special police unit that would eject the "homeless" as they "inter-fered" with or got in the way of cleaning.

The story of reclaiming the subway by the police has been told elsewhere and need not be repeated here. Summarizing, a large scale problem-solving exercise was conducted, the problem in the subway was properly understood as illegal disorderly behavior, policies were developed and officers trained to deal with disorder. The legal battles over police activities to rein in panhan-dling were fought and ultimately won; TPD leadership, however, was recalci-trant and the effort flagged. Bratton was recruited as Chief of the TPD in April of 1990; he provided leadership and implemented a large-scale effort to restore order. Following these actions, serious crime began an immediate and steep decline.

Disorder and crime are no longer serious problems in New York's subway—it is among the safest in the world. It feels, smells, and "tastes" differ-ent. Indeed, the culture was so different that by the mid-1990s the Transit Authority initiated a civility campaign, encouraging citizens to queue before boarding trains—a campaign that would have been a joke in the late 1980s. Returning ex-New Yorkers are stunned by the changes.

We highlight the subway experience because it has been lost in the big-ger New York City disorder and crime story, especially since the TPD was absorbed by the New York City Police Department (NYPD) in 1995. Yet, it is an important story. It is probably one of the largest problem-solving exercises on record. The police tactics, organizational change, and administrative pro-cesses implemented in the TPD foreshadowed changes in the New York City Police Department. Still and all the reclamation of the subway stands as a major event in public policy—certainly on a par with graffiti eradication—that raised and managed complex policy, constitutional, legal, and moral issues.

From our point of view and within the context of this discussion, it is especially important because it is hard to attribute the changes in the subway to anything other than police action. To be sure, the NYCTA implemented major efforts to deal with the genuinely homeless who were attempting to use the subway as a surrogate shelter. Graffiti had been eliminated and trains and tracks upgraded. Attempts had been made to target-harden the tollbooths and token-boxes (youths had been able to "spring" their doors with large screwdriv-ers and steal hundreds of tokens at a time), and some areas had been blocked off to the public. Moreover, subway officials were implementing a "station manager" program that focused on restoring a sense of station "ownership" and concern for passengers. But the subway environment was spinning out of control despite subway improvements and attempts at target hardening. More-over, post-hoc explanations used to explain the later citywide reductions in crime—changes in drug use patterns, improved economy, declines in the num-ber of youths, etc.—simply do not apply. Drug selling was not a major issue in the subway; unemployment was increasing during the time in question; and there was no evidence of a decline in the youth population.

The question is raised, "But isn't the subway a simpler system and easier to reclaim than city streets and public spaces?" This is the point of the subway story. It is a simpler system. People pay to enter it. There are few private spaces–only trains, platforms, passageways, and entrances and exits. One would expect that if police action, in this case to restore order, were to have an impact in any setting, it would be in such a restricted environment. From our standpoint it was an ideal place to test the broken windows hypothesis: that is, one way to reduce fear of crime and prevent serious crime is to restore order. The subway is a system in which the potentially confounding variables cited by social scientists are controlled.

Certainly, we cannot aver with scientific certainty that the crime reductions in the subway are the result of the police intervention. We put forward the following, however:

1. In response to a growing problem, the TPD developed a specific set of interventions that included police tactics and changes in organizational structure and administrative processes;
2. The TPD "called its shots," predicting that order could be restored and that crime would be reduced;[2]
3. Immediately following the intervention, crime began a steep decline.

The "after, therefore because of" fallacy? Perhaps. We doubt it. No other explanation seems plausible. Did graffiti elimination play a role? Target hardening? Social services for the genuinely homeless? Other factors? Of course. But action by the TPD achieved a "tipping point." We will return to the idea of "tipping point."

A final point in this introduction: no explanation of what happened in New York City can ignore the subway experience. While originally not conceived of as such, it became the pretest to what happened in the city.

Leadership and Management

The New York *City* story is more complicated than the subway story. New York City is an intricate political, social, economic, and cultural entity in its own right. It has elaborate linkages to state, national, and international institutions and forces. Crime is more complicated in the city than in the subway. For example, the serious crime problem in the subway is largely robbery, with most of them being "grab and run"—crimes that, while not trivial, are less ominous than many of the confrontational robberies on city streets. Crime varies in other respects as well.

Moreover, more complex control systems operate in the city—from the "small change" of neighborhood life, to schools, churches, family, workplace, business improvement districts, community groups, and others. Potentially confounding influences are not naturally controlled.

The NYPD is more complicated than the TPD was, and, frankly, it was in deep trouble when Bratton assumed control in 1994. Its troubles with abuse and corruption during the early 1990s were well known, largely as a result of newspaper revelations and the subsequent work of the Mollen Commission.

But there was another story in the NYPD, as least as dark as the abuse and corruption accounts, but far less well known—the lack of quality policing. Since the 1970s Knapp Commission, the NYPD has been preoccupied with corruption. So much so that it was widely understood, but only partially true, that the "business" of the NYPD had become "staying out of trouble." And, of course, the most certain way to stay out of trouble was "to do nothing." Surely this is an overstatement, but nonetheless, it had considerable basis in fact. Most symptomatic of this "stay out of trouble by doing nothing" orientation was that line patrol officers were restrained by policy from making drug arrests, even if dealing was conducted right in front of their noses. In respects it was the worst of all possible scenarios: too much abuse and corruption, too much corruption control, and not enough quality policing. Bratton described the NYPD administrative world in *Turnaround:*

> [T]he New York City Police department was dysfunctional.
> First, it was divided into little fiefdoms, and some bureau chiefs didn't even talk to each other. OCCP didn't talk to patrol, patrol didn't get along with the Detective Bureau, and nobody talked to internal affairs. . . .
> . . . Each bureau was like a silo: Information entered at the bottom and had to be delivered up the chain of command from one level to another until it reached the chief's office. . .
> . . . .
> When Maple [a key Bratton advisor who had been a lieutenant in the TPD and who was a deputy commissioner under Bratton] analyzed the bureaus, the news got worse. How was the NYPD deployed? The Narcotics Bureau, he discovered, worked largely nine to five or five to one, Monday through Friday. The warrant squad was off weekends. Auto-crimes squad, off weekends. Robbery squads? Off weekends. The community-policing officers—those six thousand baby-faced twenty-two-year-olds who were going to solve all the neighborhoods' problems—off weekends. Essentially, except for the detectives, patrol officers, and some other operations going round the clock, the whole place took Saturdays and Sundays off.

Leading and managing such troubled organizations had become Bratton's stock-in-trade. The NYPD had been the fifth police organization he had headed that was in organizational trouble. His conviction that leading, inspiring, and directing middle-management was the key to improving police organizations was evident in a paper he published with Kelling and was apparent in his work with the TPD. His closest organizational advisors, Robert Wasserman (a police leader and consultant for over 30 years) and Robert Johnson (President of First Security—a Boston-based private security firm) had struggled with management issues for decades. Wasserman, who had been an advisor to previous NYPD Commissioner Lee Brown, knew where the strengths of the NYPD were buried. Johnson had struggled to find leadership and management methods in the private sector to maintain core values and technologies in highly decentralized and geographically dispersed organizations. Other key advisors included John Linder, who had developed methods to do quick scans on organizational problems and opportunities, and Jack Maple, who is perhaps one of the savviest, street wise, and creative cops around. The ideas for

Compstat—an organizational method both for holding precinct commanders accountable and for developing anti-crime tactics—grew directly out of the private sector management experiences of Johnson and the street sense of Maples.

This, too has all been discussed previously. We summarize it here to make the following point: Bratton approached his commissionership in New York City with a clear plan. He had an idea about how to prevent crime; he had an organizational strategy he wanted to implement; and he had pre-tested both with great success in New York City's subways. Again as in the subway, he called his shots—both by demanding that mid-level managers be held accountable for crime reduction and by producing plans for dealing with specific problems such as guns, youth violence, domestic violence, quality of life, auto crimes, and others. One of the hallmarks in social science is that research should be guided by theory. Bratton's strategy was, in effect, management guided by theory. Innovations were implemented and crime dropped. A lot.

Conclusion

What happened in New York City? We, of course, will never know with scientific certainty. No credible alternatives, however, have been put forward to contradict our belief that police action played a pivotal role. In the final analysis, we believe that we have seen New York City do what cities and communities have traditionally done when confronted by disorder, crime, and mayhem: it has moved to reassert control over disorderly behavior, fear, and crime.

The move to reassert control has been discernible in New York City since the late 1970s. Communities organized, business improvement districts organized, graffiti was eliminated from the subway, additional police were recruited and hired, prosecutors turned to communities for guidance (especially in Brooklyn), order was restored in the subway, and Mayor Rudolph Giuliani was given a political mandate to restore order and help bring crime under control. But, there were limits to what could be accomplished without an active police presence. Things had been allowed to deteriorate for so long, aggressive youths had been so emboldened—indeed in the absence of an active police presence, they virtually dominated public spaces in many communities—that traditional control measures were simply not robust enough to restrain their predatory behavior. And, in the midst of the "crack" epidemic, their violence spun out of control. Thus, the pattern described in Fagan et al.'s "Tale of Two Trends" comes as no surprise to us. They compare non-gun homicides with gun homicides. That non-gun homicides should be declining over an extended period of time is consistent with our view of how New Yorkers have been reclaiming their city over the long haul. Fagan et al.'s assertion that "The rate of lethal violence broke important new ground only after 1995 or 1996" is consistent with our interpretation as well. This was the *exact* period during which police were reinvigorated and their impact started to be felt. Likewise, we have no quarrel with Curtis' basic thesis,[3] that poor people are capable of helping themselves. We have never asserted otherwise: it has been basic to

Bratton's practice and it is explicit in both the original "Broken Windows" and "Fixing Broken Windows."

Our basic premise is this: the restoration of assertive policing in 1994 and 1995 interacted with community forces to achieve an unprecedented "tipping point" in violent and other forms of crime. Community forces, although formidable, could not do it alone. History and research gives us evidence that police cannot do it alone. To assert that both the community and police played significant roles demeans neither. Can we ever be more specific in attributing causality? We doubt it.

The interesting question is, however, why things got so out of control. What happened that communities throughout the country either lacked the will or capacity to maintain order and keep its miscreants under control during the past three decades? Certainly macroeconomic and demographic forces were at play. More specifically the forces that have been aligned against neighborhoods and communities over the last three decades have been staggering. As Kelling wrote elsewhere:

> Aside from the seemingly inevitable growth of the suburbs, consider what was done to our cities during the 1950s, 1960s, and 1970s. In the name of urban renewal, entire inner-city neighborhoods were torn apart. No provisions were made for displaced residents, so naturally they moved into adjacent neighborhoods. Because many of those displaced were African Americans, real estate blockbusters followed them, undercutting property values and scaring other residents into moving. In the renewal areas, concrete blocks of multistory public housing was built, often, as in Chicago with external unsecured elevators. This was the housing of the last resort for the most troubled and troublesome families. Expanded tenant "rights," however, made it virtually impossible to evict troublemakers regardless of their behavior or capacity for mayhem. Expressway construction followed and cut wide swaths through communities, displacing entire neighborhoods and dividing others. Neighborhood schools were abandoned and students were bussed throughout the city. Mental hospitals emptied patients onto city streets and drunkenness was decriminalized. The mentally ill and alcohol and drug abusers drifted into urban centers. In the name of their "liberty interests" and to forestall family and governmental abuse, parental and governmental authority over youths was reduced. To ensure that . . . children would not be stigmatized, we abandoned the idea of early identification of predelinquents.[4]

Intermingling with these urban policies, were equally disastrous police and criminal justice policies that grew out of the 1960's Presidential Commission on Law Enforcement and the Administration of Justice. Its position was explicit: poverty, racism, and economic injustices caused crime. To prevent crime one had to eliminate these "root causes." The business of the police and other criminal justice agencies became arresting and processing offenders. This view became so pervasive that many early defenders of community policing asserted that because police could not deal with poverty, racism, etc., they could do little about crime. Thus the crime problem was "de-policed" for many police leaders—a view that most line officers found absolutely unacceptable, complicating the implementation of community policing. Police tactics grew out of these assumptions and police became "law enforcement officers" responding to serious crimes and calls for service—their isolation in cars virtually "de-policing" city streets. The political far right came in with their variation: crime was caused by breakdown of family values associated with welfare. Consequently, crime prevention was held hostage by both the ideologies of the far left and right: economic redistribution or elimination of welfare. Aside from community policing, criminal justice innovations were limited to more certain and longer incarceration.

Happily, police, criminal justice practitioners, and urban officials are breaking new ground. Most criminal justice professionals have no quarrel with the idea that disorder and crime are somehow linked to poverty, racism, and breakdown of values. But, they also understand that these linkages interact in an extraordinarily complex way. Meantime, they have rediscovered policing, as opposed to law enforcement, and prevention, as opposed to case processing. The changes that are taking place in the basic modalities of many public housing agencies, schools, zoning agencies, city attorneys' offices, and other agencies are equally as impressive. The interesting thing, as both of us travel around the country, is that different cities are doing it in different ways. The starting points are different. Powerful collaborations are forming among citizen groups, business, city agencies, prosecutors, correctional officials, and others. They take different configurations in different cities and deal with different problems in different ways. But this, of course, is the lesson. Each city is singular. Within cities, communities are unique. They are asserting control over themselves in unique ways as well.

In sum, neither of us would back away from a concluding statement in Bratton's *Turnaround:*

> In terms of importance and potential and commitment, police in America are probably the most misunderstood entity in public life today. Old images exist, and, in truth, old-guard departments exist as well. But, as we approach the millenium, there is a new breed of police leader and a new breed of police officer. We need more of them.
>
> I was privileged during my last half-dozen years in policing to work on the national and international stage, and I feel there is still more the police can do. The turnaround of the NYPD was the catalyst for the turnaround of New York City itself and offers a potential blueprint for the turnaround of the crime situation in the entire country. We clearly showed that when properly led, properly managed, and in effective partnership with the neighborhoods and the political leaders, police can effect great change. We have clearly shown that police can take back streets that were given up as lost for decades. The continuing challenge for American police leaders is to take them back in a lawful and respectful manner so that the behavior of the police reflects the civil behavior society expects of its citizens.

Notes

1. *See generally,* Alfred Blumstein & Richard Rosenfeld, *Explaining Recent Trends in U.S. Homicide Rates,* 88 J. CRIM. L. & CRIMINOLOGY 1175 (1998).

2. The TPD's slogan under Bratton was "Disorder, farebeating, and robbery are one problem—deal with one and you deal with all."

3. Richard Curtis, *The Improbable Transformation of Inner-City Neighborhoods: Crime, Violence, Drugs and Youth in the 1990s*, 88 J. CRIM. L. & CRIMINOLOGY 1233, 1263 (1998).

4. George L. Kelling, National Institute of Justice, *Crime Control, The Police, and Culture Wars: Broken Windows and Cultural Pluralism, in* II PERSPECTIVES ON CRIME & JUSTICE: 1997–1998 LECTURE SERIES 1, 13–14 (1998).

Judith A. Greene  **NO**

Zero Tolerance

The police reforms introduced in New York City by William Bratton are now hailed by Mayor Rudy Giuliani as the epitome of "zero-tolerance" policing, and he credits them for winning dramatic reductions in the city's crime rate. But the number of citizen complaints filed before the Civilian Complaint Review Board has jumped skyward, as has the number of lawsuits alleging police misconduct and abuse of force. Comparison of crime rates, arrest statistics, and citizen complaints in New York with those in San Diego— where a more problem-oriented community policing strategy has been implemented—gives strong evidence that effective crime control can be achieved while producing fewer negative impacts on urban neighborhoods.

The 1998 New York City Mayor's Management Report lists many concrete improvements in the quality of life in New York City, which Mayor Rudy Giuliani believes have been won directly through the New York Police Department's targeted approach to crime control—now held up by many observers as the epitome of "zero-tolerance" policing. . . .

The Mayor's office reports that from 1993 to 1997 the number of felony complaints in New York City dropped by 44.3 percent: a 60.2 percent drop in murders and nonnegligent homicides, a 12.4 percent drop in forcible rape, a 48.4 percent drop in robbery, and a 45.7 drop in burglary. Mayor Giuliani points out that New York City is responsible for a large share of the overall crime reduction for the country as a whole. Comparing data from cities of more than 100,000 population for the first half of 1997 with data from these cities in the first half of 1993, the mayor's management report asserts that New York City accounted for 32 percent of the overall drop in FBI Index Crimes, 29 percent of the drop in murders, and 44 percent of the drop in larceny/thefts.

The Mayor's office credits the New York Police Department's (NYPD's) "Compstat" system for much of the progress made in reducing crime. Compstat was introduced by Police Commissioner William Bratton, who had served as commissioner for the first 27 months (from January 1994 to April 1996) of Giuliani's first term as mayor. The Compstat system puts up-to-date crime data into the hands of NYPD managers at all levels and bolsters a department-wide process for precinct-level accountability in meeting the department's crime-reduction goals.

From Judith A. Greene, "Zero Tolerance: A Case Study of Police Policies and Practices in New York City," *Crime & Delinquency,* vol. 45, no. 2 (April 1999). Copyright © 1999 by Sage Publications, Inc. Reprinted by permission. Some notes and references omitted.

As described in Bratton's recent book, *Turnaround: How America's Top Cop Reversed the Crime Epidemic,* the Compstat system is built on four concepts: (1) accurate and timely intelligence, (2) rapid deployment of personnel and resources, (3) effective tactics, and (4) relentless follow-up and assessment. Compstat is the engine that drives "zero-tolerance" policing in New York City, and it is at the heart of the strategic organizational changes that Bratton introduced when he took command of the NYPD in 1994.

Bratton moved vigorously to transform the police department from top to bottom and to transfuse the department with a new mindset about what the police could and should do to attack the problem of crime and reduce its impact on the residents of the city. He directly confronted the common wisdom of many experts—and, perhaps, most New Yorkers—that the NYPD was too large, too rigid, too bureaucratic, and too parochial to be able to embrace the kinds of radical changes in policies and practices that would be required in a serious effort to win measurable reductions of the city's high crime rates. And he proved that they were wrong.

Zero-tolerance policing puts major emphasis on the kinds of "quality-of-life" issues that set the drumbeat rhythm for Giuliani's 1993 mayoral campaign. The "Squeegee Men" (beggars who accosted drivers in their cars to scrub their windshields and panhandle for cash), the petty drug dealers, the graffiti scribblers, and the prostitutes who ruled the sidewalks in certain high-crime neighborhoods all were targeted in candidate Giuliani's campaign promise to reclaim the streets of New York for law-abiding citizens.

Prior to his election, Giuliani's professional career had been spent in law enforcement. It is no coincidence that these types of disorderly persons and small-time criminals exactly fit the flesh-and-blood profile of the "broken windows" theory of policing. . . . The broken windows theory holds that if not firmly suppressed, disorderly behavior in public will frighten citizens and attract predatory criminals, thus leading to more serious crime problems.

Although "reclaiming the open spaces of New York" was but one of six specific crime strategies that Bratton designed and introduced to reshape the goals of the NYPD, it was moved quickly to the front of the line when city officials began to make the claim that the Giuliani administration's police reforms were *causing* the decreases in crime. Cracking down hard on the most visible symbols of urban disorder proved to be a powerful political tool for bolstering Giuliani's image as a highly effective mayor. The speed with which the city's crime statistics have fallen has been taken by many to prove that Wilson and Kelling are correct and that serious crime problems can be quelled by mounting a large-scale attack on petty crime and disorderly behavior through a broken windows, zero-tolerance strategy.

To at least some extent, rhetorical emphasis on the broken windows theory has served to obscure the truly phenomenal record that William Bratton set in managing organizational change within the NYPD. As chief executive officer of one of the world's largest police agencies, he introduced new management tools, techniques, and technology at lightning speed and moved quickly to decentralize authority. . . .

But Bratton's concept and style of police management has driven the NYPD a distinct and substantial distance apart from the community policing concepts that have been used to reshape and redirect police services in many other American cities. Moreover, some of these cities are closely rivaling the crime-reduction record set in New York City.

Ironically, Bratton has broad knowledge of and deep experience with community policing. He was a leading innovator in the development of the neighborhood policing concept while serving as a young officer in the Boston Police Department. He has often publicly expressed solid confidence in the basic tenets of the community policing movement—forging close working partnerships with the community, problem solving to address the causes of crime, and a fundamental commitment to crime prevention. . . .

An ambitious gun interdiction program was initiated during the [David] Dinkins administration [which preceded Giuliani] by Assistant Police Commissioner Jeremy Travis, who now heads the National Institute of Justice. This effort was spurred forward in 1993 by the Bureau of Alcohol, Tobacco, and Firearms—then under the leadership of Ronald Noble at the Department of Justice. The well-publicized 1993 interdiction campaign pre-dated the Bratton/Giuliani gun strategy and involved capture of several large stores of weapons before they reached the hands of teenagers on New York City streets.

The early foundation for community policing in New York had been laid in the mid 1980s—during the [Ed] Koch administration—through a joint NYPD/Vera Institute of Justice pilot effort. Once the Safe Streets program was in place, Commissioner [Lee] Brown was able to design and build a citywide community policing program. Yet, in his book, *Turnaround*, Bratton abruptly dismissed this community-policing effort (already in place when he was named Police Commissioner) in three brief paragraphs.

In *Turnaround*, Bratton maintained that the program—although focused on the beat cop—had no real focus on crime, and he complained that the young officers assigned to community-policing beats were unprepared and ill equipped to handle the complex issues that underlie the crime problem in New York City. Moreover, he charged, even those few capable of winning significant results were never given the necessary authority to follow through under the NYPD's system of centralized decision making.

In a 1996 lecture sponsored by the Heritage Foundation, Bratton discussed the flaws that he perceives in the community policing initiatives of the early 1990s. He argued that community policing in New York was hampered by a lack of attention to those quality-of-life issues that cause widespread fear of crime among the public and by an unwieldy and highly centralized, over-specialized police bureaucracy. . . .

Once recruited by Mayor-elect Giuliani to serve as commissioner of the NYPD, Bratton used his prior experience combating subway crime as a springboard into a citywide campaign to aggressively apprehend the perpetrators of quality-of-life crimes on the streets. Bratton's managerial reforms were brilliantly innovative, using up-to-the-minute technology. But at the neighborhood level, his crime-fighting strategies were grounded in traditional law enforcement methods and in relentless crackdown campaigns to arrest and jail low-level drug offenders and other petty perpetrators. . . .

Bratton's crime-prevention concepts are more often cloaked in military campaign metaphors—" in New York City, we now know where the enemy is" —than in the public-health/epidemiological images now more common in community-focused prevention efforts elsewhere. And his quality-of-life law-enforcement style was hyperaggressive. In *Turnaround,* Bratton describes how his school truancy program grabbed so many school-age kids off the streets that "we had to set up 'catchment' areas in school auditoriums and gymnasiums." He retooled New York City's drug enforcement effort to target more muscle toward low- and middle-level dealers, and he lifted a longstanding police policy that discouraged drug enforcement arrests by patrol officers—freeing them to seek warrants, make narcotics arrests, and go after those they suspected of drug dealing for quality-of-life violations to sweep them off the streets and into the jails (Bratton 1998, p. 227).

Bratton attacked the legal restrictions that had impeded aggressive enforcement against those deemed disorderly. He "took the handcuffs off" the police department and unleashed patrol officers to stop and search citizens who were violating the most minor laws on the books (e.g., drinking a beer or urinating in public), to run warrant checks on them, or just to pull them in for questioning about criminal activity in their neighborhood. If, in the course of such an incident, a weapon was found and confiscated, Bratton asserts that it was lawful prevention of crime "before it happened."

If, as its keystone crime-prevention strategy, New York City has turned away from community policing and chosen instead a zero-tolerance campaign that is heavily reliant on traditional methods of law enforcement to eradicate quality-of-life problems, what negative consequences have resulted from this choice? And which New Yorkers have borne the brunt of these negative consequences?

Joel Berger—a prominent New York City civil rights attorney who represents alleged victims of police misconduct and abuse in New York City—reports that legal filings of new civil rights claims against the police for abusive conduct have increased by 75 percent in the city over the last four years. Berger says that the largest increase in new claims of this type occurred during the most recent fiscal year, indicating that the problem of police brutality is getting worse, not better.

Amnesty International has reported that police brutality and unjustifiable use of force is a widespread problem in New York City. There is a wealth of documentation to support the charge that police misconduct and abuse have increased under the Giuliani administration's zero-tolerance regime. The total number of citizen complaints filed annually with the Civilian Complaint Review Board (CCRB) increased more than 60 percent between 1992 and 1996, and Mark Green—the elected New York City public advocate—has charged that the police torture of Abner Louima in a precinct station house in the Borough of Brooklyn in the summer of 1997 was part of a larger "pattern of police abuse, brutality, and misconduct" in New York City that the Giuliani administration has failed to address. . . .

Complaints by citizens in New York City about police misconduct and abuse, and the response to these complaints by the New York City CCRB and the NYPD, have been the subject of hot debate between some resistant city officials and those who advocate for a more effective process to increase police accountability for abuse of citizens. From the start, Mayor Giuliani resisted the effort to establish an independent CCRB. By the time it was set up, its budget had been slashed by 17 percent (about a million dollars) as compared with the police department-based civilian complaint unit it had replaced.

According to New York City Public Advocate Mark Green, recent CCRB complaint data suggest that the problem of police misconduct is disproportionately concentrated in New York City's high-crime minority neighborhoods. Nine out of 76 precincts account for more than 50 percent of the increase in CCRB complaints since 1992; 21 precincts account for more than 80 percent. Mark Green charges that those precincts with the highest incidence of misconduct "appear to have disproportionately higher percentages of African American and Latino residents." Norman Siegel—director of the New York Civil Liberties Union (NYCLU) and a harsh critic of the mayor on these issues—has presented data showing that three quarters of all CCRB complaints are filed by African Americans and Latinos. He reports that African Americans (who make up 29 percent of the city's population) filed 53 percent of all complaints in 1996.

Moreover, the vast majority of complaints filed with the CCRB are never substantiated, and the small portion that are substantiated usually do not result in proper disciplinary actions. In the first eight months of last year, only 8 percent of the 3,991 cases filed with the CCRB were substantiated. Furthermore, Public Advocate Mark Green has complained that so few substantiated cases ever result in charges brought or disciplinary actions taken by the police department that the civilian complaint process is a sham.

This brief review of the downside *costs* that many New Yorkers argue have been incurred through the city's reliance on a highly aggressive, traditional law-enforcement style of policing begs the *benefits* question: Is there hard evidence that this strategy has been truly effective in reducing crime? How valid are the claims made by Mayor Giuliani that his police policies are responsible for the city's remarkable crime reduction record? . . .

Serious violent crime rates have been falling for the nation as a whole. The National Crime Victimization Survey crime-trends data (1973–1996) published by the Bureau of Justice Statistics indicate that rapes declined 60 percent from 1991 to 1996, whereas robberies began to decline more recently; Robberies were down 17 percent from 1994 to 1996. Aggravated assaults declined by 27 percent from 1993 to 1996. The victimization data show that total violent crime was down 19 percent from 1994 to 1996. Data from the National Center for Health Statistics indicate that the nation's homicide rate fell by 10 percent from 1991 to 1995. Property crimes are also on the decline for the nation as a whole, according to the National Crime Victimization Survey. The rates reported for total property crime show a 25 percent decline from 1991 to 1996.

It has been argued by many that widespread innovations in police practices have made a major contribution to reducing crime—from the zero-tolerance campaign in New York City to community-policing strategies involving problem solving and police/community partnerships elsewhere. Yet, crime has fallen substantially in some locales where these reforms have not been embraced.

The huge increase in the incarceration rate resulting from mandatory minimum drug laws, "three strikes, you're out" laws, and other policy shifts producing longer prison terms are claimed by almost all proponents of these "get tough" approaches to be the force driving crime rates downward. But increased incarceration doesn't seem to explain many of the differences found when states are compared. New York City has experienced one of the sharpest declines in violent crime, but its jail population is down, and the New York state prison population growth rate slowed to less than one percent in 1997. The state's prison population growth rate has been relatively modest during the 1990s compared to states such as Texas and California. Crime rates were already beginning to fall before the state of Washington became the first to pass three-strikes legislation in 1993. Most states are enjoying declining crime rates regardless of whether they have such laws. . . .

If there is an ascendant theory among American criminologists, it may be simply stated: No single factor, cause, policy, or strategy has reduced the drop in crime rates.

A variety of structural changes in high-crime urban neighborhoods are cited by many experts as plausibly combining to produce declining crime rates. Many academic experts have long held that demographic factors are the most significant contributors to crime rates. Overall crime rates (as distinct from violent street crime) have been drifting downward for many years, as has alcohol consumption—a factor strongly associated with a broad range of criminal activity. America's healthy economy has produced low unemployment rates, another factor generally associated with lower crime rates.

Overall shifts in public attitudes regarding the problem of crime and increased public intolerance for various types of disorderly conduct that are believed to be criminogenic have stimulated moves toward the policing reforms and the "get tough" measures cited above, but they have also led to a raft of community organizing activities that may be paying off in reduced levels of crime. . . .

The binge of drug and/or gang-related violence in the 1980s left many dead, disabled, or in prison. Some argue that these causalities are now shaping marked shifts in values and attitudes among urban youth. Demand for crack cocaine has waned and—stimulated by tougher police enforcement against handguns—minor confrontations are said to be less likely to erupt into deadly shootouts. . . .

Recently, much social science research attention has turned to the declining homicide rates in many cities across the country. A team of researchers led by Pamela Lattimore (Lattimore, Trudeau, Riley, Leiter, and Edwards 1997) at the National Institute of Justice has discovered a strong correlation between cocaine use levels within the urban criminal population and changes in homicide rates. Alfred Blumstein has studied handgun murders involving urban street youth. He has pointed out that the surge in this type of gun violence in the late 1980s has drawn attention away from the more long-term and steady trend of declining homicides for adults age 25 and older since 1980. The surprising decline in homicides since 1991 is driven largely by the falling incidence of gun homicides among the younger group.

The decline in homicides among *older* Americans cited by Blumstein includes a steady decline in national rates of intimate-partner homicide over the past two decades. Laura Dugan has traced the effects of three significant social developments on this type of homicide: changes in patterns of domesticity (exposure reduction), in the status of women, and in increased provision of domestic violence resources. Her research highlights the importance of legal advocacy efforts to expand the effective use and enforcement of restraining orders, although these measures are shown to favorably affect homicide rates solely from married male victims. Susan Wilt (1998; Wilt, Illman, and Brody-Field 1997) has been tracking homicides in New York City using data from the public health system. She has found that homicides of female victims have fallen far more slowly since 1990 than the decline for male victims (a 20 percent decline for females compared to a 51 percent decline for males). Wilt was able to obtain data to classify homicides by type, and she found that over this period, intimate partner homicides of women have not declined in New York City.

Jeffrey Fagan is conducting an important study of homicides in New York City geared specifically to documenting the effects of criminal justice policies on this problem. Fagan, along with Franklin Zimring and June Kim, has just completed a report that examines homicide patterns in the city back to the 1950s and compares the recent decline with homicide patterns in other American cities. By tracking homicide trends by type since 1985, they have determined that patterns in New York City for gun and non-gun killings differ sharply. The trend data for non-gun homicides show a fairly steady decline through the whole period, whereas gun homicides doubled between 1985 and 1991, returning to the 1985 level by 1995.

Examining trends in drug use and demographics, Fagan et at. believed them to be important factors but could not say to what extent they have influenced the decline. . . . They posited that the NYPD gun strategy may be the most salient factor. At the same time, they cautioned that it is not possible to unequivocally establish the strength of these policing strategies relative to the other factors that are interacting with the shifts in police practices. Moreover, they warned that simple regression (i.e., the tendency of crime problems to shift continuously, up and down, drawing cyclical patterns over time) cannot yet be ruled out as the cause of the recent decline in gun homicides.

. . . Malcolm Gladwell, a writer for *The New Yorker* magazine, has carefully considered the phenomenon of dropping crime rates in New York City. He offers an interesting theory—drawn from the annals of public health—that provides some clues about how distinctly divergent factors in disparate locales might result in similar patterns of falling crime.

In his 1996 *The New Yorker* article, "The Tipping-Point," Gladwell defines this public health expression as "the point at which an ordinary and stable phenomenon—a low-level flu outbreak—can turn into a public health crisis." Applied to the phenomenon of crime, this epidemiological argument means that once crime reaches a certain level or critical point, it spreads in a "non-linear" fashion—that is, at some point in time a small incremental increase in criminal activity can fuel a dramatic upturn in crime rates. One example that Gladwell gives involves drive-by shootings in Los Angeles, which, after seven years of fluctuating up and down between 22 and 51, rose steadily from 57 in 1987 to 211 in 1992.

Happily, the tipping-point phenomenon may .also apply in reverse. When the level of crime in a community reaches a tipping point, any strategy that can effect even a small decrease may be able to trigger dramatic drops in crime rates. But the tipping-point theory also implies layers of subtle complexity that must be carefully assessed in the development of crime control policies because when the level of crime is not at or near the tipping point, large investments in crime-fighting activities may yield very small effects if any.

. . . Expert opinion notwithstanding, suppose it is true that a new policing strategy can turn the tide of crime and produce a dramatic ebb in its volume? Is a New York City zero-tolerance campaign the only possible approach? Is it the best approach? What other options should be considered? Are there other theories about effective crime control that can help us answer these questions?

Tracey Meares (1998), a law professor at the University of Chicago, has been studying the role of community social organization in reducing crime. She points out that certain critical mediating factors can produce differential crime rates in communities with similar socioeconomic conditions. If stronger elements of social organization—cohesive friendship networks, shared cultural values, supervision of teens, participation in church groups, parent-teacher associations, community policing organizations, and so forth—are present in a given neighborhood, crime will be less common than in neighborhoods where these elements have eroded.

Meares has applied this framework to critique the efficacy of various law enforcement strategies—especially drug enforcement efforts—to enhance or hinder crime control in communities. She argues that whereas "get tough" measures that lead to lengthy incarceration of a large number of young drug offenders may offer a measure of short-term relief for law-abiding residents of a drug-ravaged community, in the long run, the negative consequences may wash out the short-term positives. This is because the deterrent effects of such a strategy are weak at best, whereas its damaging effects—disruption of family ties, stigmatizing barriers to labor market participation, increased levels of alienation and distrust—may prove criminogenic in themselves.

This may be especially true in African American communities, where the asymmetry of current drug-enforcement policies has exacerbated longstanding attitudes of distrust between residents and police that are grounded in both negative stereotypes and historical events. . . .

San Diego and New York City have enjoyed virtually equal reductions in rates of serious crime over the first half of the 1990s. From 1990 to 1995, a period when the NYPD gained a 39.5 percent increase in the number of sworn officers, New York City's reduction in crime was 37.4 percent, whereas San Diego's was 36.8 percent, but during this same period the increase in sworn officers on the San Diego police force *was only 6.2 percent.* According to San Diego police officials, this is a far more favorable "yield" in terms of crimes reduced per each additional officer.

San Diego's police executives began to experiment with a form of community policing—the Neighborhood Policing Philosophy as they term it—in the late 1980s. In 1993, they laid the groundwork for a department-wide restructuring process coupled with an effort to retrain the entire force in problem-oriented (as opposed to incident-based) policing methods. Two key concepts of neighborhood policing in San Diego—as described by San Diego Police Department (SDPD) officials—are that police and citizens share responsibility for identifying and solving crime problems and that law enforcement is one important tool for addressing crime, but it is not an end in itself.

The emphasis of the San Diego neighborhood-policing approach is on creating problem-solving partnerships and fostering connections between police and community for sharing information, working with citizens to address crime and disorder problems, and tapping other public and private agencies for resources to help solve them. The types of activities fostered by the neighborhood policing strategy in San Diego resemble many that are common elements of community policing elsewhere, such as the following:

- support for "neighborhood watch" and citizen patrol groups that look for suspicious activity, identify community problems, and work on crime prevention projects;
- use of civil remedies and strict building code enforcement to abate nuisance properties and close down "drug houses"; and
- collaboration with community organizations and local business groups to clean up, close down, or redesign specific locations and properties that repeatedly attract prostitution, drug, and gang problems.

The role of organized neighborhood volunteers in efforts to impact local crime problems—and thus national crime patterns—is too often overlooked or misunderstood. There are important differences between community *policing* and community *participation,* yet San Diego seems to be striving to integrate these distinct, semiautonomous crime prevention tools. The SDPD has recruited and trained a pool of more than 1,000 citizen volunteers who perform a broad array of crime prevention and victim assistance services.

The restructuring of police services in San Diego has involved a geographic consolidation of 68 existing patrol sectors and a reconfiguration of their boundaries to correspond to 99 distinct neighborhoods defined by community residents. Laptop computers equipped with mapping software are now being introduced to automate field reporting and to put up-to-date crime and calls-for-service data into the hands of patrol officers. . . .

Table 1

Adult Arrests in New York City

	1993	1994	1995	1996
Total arrests	255,087	307,802	316,690	314,292
Total felony arrests	125,684	138,043	135,141	132,601
Felony drug arrests	39,298	44,442	43,698	45,312
Total misdemeanor arrests	129,403	169,759	181,549	181,691
Misdemeanor drug arrests	27,446	42,546	52,891	54,133
Misdemeanor DWI arrests	5,621	5,628	5,763	4,624
Other misdemeanor arrests	96,335	121,585	122,895	122,934

Note: DWI = driving while intoxicated.

Table 2

Adult Arrests in San Diego

	1993	1994	1995	1996
Total arrests	56,631	55,887	55,909	48,264
Total felony arrests	17,007	17,135	16,854	13,825
Felony drug arrests	5,808	6,432	6,685	5,034
Total misdemeanor arrests	39,624	38,752	39,055	34,439
Misdemeanor drug arrests	7,099	8,313	7,965	6,352
Misdemeanor DWI arrests	3,782	3,649	3,749	3,545
Other misdemeanor arrests	28,743	26,790	27,341	24,542

Note: DWI = driving while intoxicated.

Data from the New York State Department of Criminal Justice Services from 1993 through 1996 show that arrests in New York City rose by 23 percent across the board, Reflecting the broken windows, zero-tolerance policing strategy introduced by Bratton, misdemeanor arrests rose by 40 percent—led by drug arrests, which were increased by 97 percent over this period.

Arrest statistics provided by the SDPD for this same period show a marked contrast, reflecting the contrasting philosophy of neighborhood policing adopted in that city.

Across the board, arrests have fallen in San Diego by 15 percent, whereas reductions for key indicators of crime (homicides and FBI Index Crimes) closely rival the crime reductions in New York City. Total complaints filed during this period with the SDPD regarding police misconduct fell from 522 in 1993 to 508 in 1996.

San Diego police executives are understandably pleased with the recent dramatic drop in crime in their city. However, they have been less inclined than their counterparts in New York City to estimate the extent to which these trends may be directly attributed to the department's neighborhood policing and community-involvement efforts.

. . . Zero-tolerance policing in New York City uses the Compstat system to direct hyperaggressive crime-control tactics toward high-crime "hot spots," and city officials have been quick to claim credit for a dramatic drop in crime. Yet, the sharp contrast in arrest patterns and citizen complaints between New York City and San Diego offers compelling evidence that cooperative police-community problem solving can provide effective crime control through more efficient and humane methods. Moreover, the San Diego strategy seems better designed to support and sustain vital elements of community social organization that can inhibit criminality and build safer neighborhoods over the long run.

Note

1. Whereas community policing engages neighborhood residents in identification of crime problems and in planning crime-control strategies, community participation entails residents becoming directly involved in crime prevention activities and in effecting structural solutions to the neighborhood problems that give rise to crime.

References

William Bratton. 1998. *Turnaround: How America's Top Cop Reversed the Crime Epidemic*. New York: Random House.

Lattimore, Pamela K., James Trudeau, K. Jack Riley, Jordan Leiter, and Steven Edwards. 1997. *Homicide in Eight U.S. Cities: Trends, Context, and Policy Implications*. Washington, DC: Department of Justice, National Institute of Justice.

Meares, Tracey. 1998. "Place and Crime." *Chicago-Kent Law Review* 73: 669.

Wilt, Susan. A. 1998. *Changes in Assault Injuries and Death Rates in New York City 1990–1995*. New York: Department of Public Health, Injury Prevention Program.

Wilt, Susan A., Susan M. Illman, and Maia BrodyField. 1997. *Female Homicide Victims in New York City 1990–1994*. New York: Department of Public Health, Injury Prevention Program.

POSTSCRIPT

Should the Police Enforce Zero-Tolerance Laws?

Implicit in the broken windows theory is the community's abandonment of the people's civic responsibility to maintain their neighborhoods. The role of police then becomes one of restoring order by driving out the newly ensconced criminal elements. Certainly this approach takes as central the importance of community (including the lack of community, which results in crime). Greene does not consider synthesizing the two perspectives. How might that be done?

Is it possible that zero tolerance/broken windows policing is functional in extremely high crime areas but only for a short amount of time (e.g., less than a year)? If so, would this help to reduce the likelihood of "hyperaggressive" policing's becoming routinized so that citizens' rights are increasingly ignored?

Some suggest that even if terrible abuse of police power is the price to be paid for aggressive policing, the trade-off is more than worth it. Dozens of police officers' lives and hundreds of citizens' lives are saved in a few short years. If such reductions in violent crimes could be achieved only if they were accompanied by a relatively small number of blatant police abuses, would the trade-off be worth it? Is it possible, as Greene and many others say, to achieve a reduction in crime through other policing tactics? Also, is a comparison of New York and San Diego on the basis that they both have populations over 100,000 a fair one?

A helpful report by Kelling is *"Broken Windows" and Police Discretion* (October 1999), published by the National Institute of Justice. Bratton's most comprehensive discussion and defense of his position is *Turnaround: How America's Top Cop Reversed the Crime Epidemic*, coauthored by P. Knobler (Random House, 1998). For a trenchant criticism of zero-tolerance polices, see S. Henry et al., "Broken Windows: Prevention Strategy or Cracked Policy?" *Critical Criminologist* (Fall 1997).

Another attack on Kelling is *Shattering "Broken Windows": An Analysis of San Francisco's Alternative Crime Policies* by D. Macallair and K. Taqi-Eddin (October 1999), published by the Justice Policy Institute. More neutral research is presented in "Problem-Oriented Policing in Public Housing," by L. Maerolle et al., *Justice Quarterly* (March 2000). For additional attacks on zero tolerance, see the articles other than Kelling and Bratton's in the summer 1998 edition of *The Journal of Criminal Law & Criminology*. An early debate between P. Ruffins, in "How the Big Apple Cut to the Core of Its Crime Problem," and former New York City mayor David N. Dinkins, in "Does Quality-of-Life Policing Diminish Quality of Life for People of Color?" can be found in the July 1997 issue of Crisis.

Crime-Free America

Crime-Free America is a grassroots, nonprofit group dedicated to ending the crime epidemic that it feels has gripped the United States during the last four decades. This site links to the Bureau of Justice Statistics, crime forums, and crime watch profiles.

`http://crime-free.org`

Violent Criminal Apprehension Program

The Violent Criminal Apprehension Program (VICAP) is a nationwide data information center that collects, collates, and analyzes crimes of violence—specifically murder. A program of the FBI's National Center for the Analysis of Violent Crime, its mission is to aid cooperation, communication, and coordination among law enforcement agencies and to provide support for their efforts.

`http://www.fbi.gov/programs/vicap/vicap.htm`

The Fully-Informed Jury and Jury Nullification

This site reprints a handful of articles on jury nullification, allows users to take a poll on the practice, and offers links to other sites related to juries and jury nullification.

`http://www.freeandrea.org/jurynull.htm`

Drug War/Death Squad Links Worldwide

The many annotated links at this site purport to expose the worldwide abuses of the CIA, FBI, DEA, etc., in fighting the international drug war and in other arenas.

`http://homepages.go.com/~marthag1/newdex.htm`

PART 5

Future Trends in Criminology and Criminal Justice

*I*n the field of criminal justice, forecasting is an important device that entails extrapolating from present trends and projecting solutions to organizational problems. Criminologists supply the needed data, including the rates, frequencies, and distributions of crime. Yet even if we indeed know who commits what crimes, where, when, how, and why with any real certainty, there is no guarantee that this knowledge will hold true a few years from now. Moreover, as debatable as current policy proposals are, what we should do in the future is even more so. Might one way to make a better future be for juries to help to reduce inequities? Will locking up repeat offenders for life prove to be the best public policy? Finally, over 50 years after the Holocaust and 25 years after the victories of the civil rights movement, widespread violations of human rights are once again assuming a prominent place both on the world scene and within criminal justice. The past becomes the future as crime control is once again debated, this time on an international scale and with human rights as the focus.

- Should Marijuana Be Legalized?

- Do Three Strikes Sentencing Laws and Other "Get Tough" Approaches Really Work?

- Should Juries Be Able to Disregard the Law and Free "Guilty" Persons in Racially Charged Cases?

- Should Behavior Modification Techniques Be Used to Brainwash Criminals?

ISSUE 16

Should Marijuana Be Legalized?

YES: Ethan A. Nadelmann, from "An End to Marijuana Prohibition—The Drive to Legalize Picks Up," *National Review* (July 12, 2004)

NO: John P. Walters, from "No Surrender," *National Review* (September 27, 2004)

ISSUE SUMMARY

YES: Ethan A. Nadelmann, the founder and director of the Drug Policy Alliance, contends that contemporary marijuana laws are unique among American criminal laws because no other law is both enforced so widely and yet deemed unnecessary by such a substantial portion of the public. Enforcing marijuana laws also wastes tens of billions of taxpayer dollars annually.

NO: John P. Walters, director of the Office of National Drug Control Policy, argues that marijuana does the most social harm of any illegal drug. Moreover, Walters asserts that the ultimate goal of those who advocate marijuana legalization is tolerated addiction.

Should people be free to smoke marijuana without fear of criminal sanctions? Or, does smoking marijuana harm society as a whole as well as the drug user? A recent study by the Sentencing Project, a Washington-based think tank, has concluded that the drug war in the United States has shifted significantly in the past decade from a focus on hard drugs to marijuana law enforcement. Is this focus on marijuana suppression an effective or efficient way to spend our tax dollars? Moreover, is it good social policy to use criminal punishment to try to prevent people from using marijuana? The answers to these questions defy an easy resolution; however, some things are very clear about marijuana usage in the United States.

First, large numbers of people are affected by the stringent enforcement of our nation's marijuana laws. A recent study found that approximately 700,000 people are arrested on marijuana charges each year, and 60,000 are confined to jails and prisons. Moreover, approximately 87 percent of marijuana arrests are for nothing more than simple possession of small quantities. (Drug Policy Alliance, "Warning: Marijuana Causes Drug Czar to Behave Irrationally, Act Paranoid and

Waste Billions of Dollars," May 4, 2005, http://drugpolicy.org.) Second, the costs to taxpayers to enforce marijuana laws are considerable. The annual price tag for enforcing marijuana laws is approximately $10–15 billion.

Moreover, recent studies suggest that a large number of Americans appear to favor decriminalization of marijuana. One poll suggests that 72 percent of Americans believe that fines, not imprisonment, are appropriate sanctions for violating marijuana laws. Moreover, approximately 80 percent of the people surveyed supported medical marijuana use.

In his classic essay "On Liberty," nineteenth century philosopher John Stuart Mill discussed the nature and limits of power that can be legitimately exercised by society over an individual. Stated Mill:

> [T]he sole end for which mankind are warranted, individually or collectively, in interfering with the liberty of action of any of their number is self-protection. That the only purpose for which power can rightfully be exercised over any member of a civilized community, against his will, is to prevent harm to others. His own good, either physical or moral, is not a sufficient warrant. He cannot rightfully be compelled to so or forebear because it will be better for him to do so, because it will make him happier, because, in the opinions of others, to do so would be wise or even right.

Is the decision to use marijuana properly left to the realm of individual conscience? Or, is society merely trying to protect itself? The authors of the articles in this section have very different viewpoints on this issue.

Ethan A. Nadelmann, the founder and director of the Drug Policy Alliance, believes that "the criminalization of marijuana is costly, foolish, and destructive." For example, Alabama currently imprisons people convicted three times of simple marijuana possession for 15 years to life. Moreover, foreign-born residents can be deported, and a parent's marijuana use may be the basis for taking away his or her children or placing them in foster care. Observes Nadelmann: "No one has ever died from a marijuana overdose, which cannot be said of most other drugs."

John P. Walters, director of the Office of National Drug Control Policy, disputes Nadelmann's contentions and believes that our marijuana laws are an effective "safeguard." Moreover, he asserts that legalization would increase drug use, health care costs, and "further burden our education system." Walters contends as well that those who advocate for drug legalization will never be satisfied with a limited distribution of medical marijuana, or its sale in convenience stores. Rather, asserts Walters, "[t]heir goal is clearly identifiable: tolerated addiction."

So, which position is the correct one? Would the legalization of marijuana have dire consequences for society? Should society interfere with an individual's decision to smoke a joint in his or her living room at 10:00 PM on a Saturday night while eating a pepperoni pizza and watching a movie on television? What about persons undergoing medical treatment who believe that their conditions are somehow improved by smoking marijuana: Should they have access to legal marijuana without any fear of criminal prosecution?

Ethan A. Nadelmann  **YES**

An End to Marijuana Prohibition: The Drive to Legalize Picks Up

Never before have so many Americans supported decriminalizing and even legalizing marijuana. Seventy-two percent say that for simple marijuana possession, people should not be incarcerated but fined: the generally accepted definition of "decriminalization." Even more Americans support making marijuana legal for medical purposes. Support for broader legalization ranges between 25 and 42 percent, depending on how one asks the question. Two of every five Americans—according to a 2003 Zogby poll—say "the government should treat marijuana more or less the same way it treats alcohol: It should regulate it, control it, tax it, and only make it illegal for children."

Close to 100 million Americans—including more than half of those between the ages of 18 and 50—have tried marijuana at least once. Military and police recruiters often have no choice but to ignore past marijuana use by job seekers. The public apparently feels the same way about presidential and other political candidates. Al Gore, Bill Bradley, and John Kerry all say they smoked pot in days past. So did Bill Clinton, with his notorious caveat. George W. Bush won't deny he did. And ever more political, business, religious, intellectual, and other leaders plead guilty as well.

The debate over ending marijuana prohibition simmers just below the surface of mainstream politics, crossing ideological and partisan boundaries. Marijuana is no longer the symbol of Sixties rebellion and Seventies permissiveness, and it's not just liberals and libertarians who say it should be legal, as William F. Buckley Jr. has demonstrated better than anyone. As director of the country's leading drug-policy-reform organization. I've had countless conversations with police and prosecutors, judges and politicians, and hundreds of others who quietly agree that the criminalization of marijuana is costly, foolish, and destructive. What's most needed now is principled conservative leadership. Buckley has led the way, and New Mexico's former governor, Gary Johnson, spoke out courageously while in office. How about others?

From *National Review*, July 12, 2004, pp. 28–33. Copyright © 2004 by Ethan Nadelmann. Reprinted by permission of the author. www.drugpolicy.org

A Systemic Overreaction

Marijuana prohibition is unique among American criminal laws. No other law is both enforced so widely and harshly and yet deemed unnecessary by such a substantial portion of the populace.

Police make about 700,000 arrests per year for marijuana offenses. That's almost the same number as are arrested each year for cocaine, heroin, methamphetamine, Ecstasy, and all other illicit drugs combined. Roughly 600,000, or 87 percent, of marijuana arrests are for nothing more than possession of small amounts. Millions of Americans have never been arrested or convicted of any criminal offense except this. Enforcing marijuana laws costs an estimated $10–15 billion in direct costs alone.

Punishments range widely across the country, from modest fines to a few days in jail to many years in prison. Prosecutors often contend that no one goes to prison for simple possession—but tens, perhaps hundreds, of thousands of people on probation and parole are locked up each year because their urine tested positive for marijuana or because they were picked up in possession of a joint. Alabama currently locks up people convicted three times of marijuana *possession* for 15 years to life. There are probably—no firm estimates exist—100,000 Americans behind bars tonight for one marijuana offense or another. And even for those who don't lose their freedom, simply being arrested can be traumatic and costly. A parent's marijuana use can be the basis for taking away her children and putting them in foster care. Foreign-born residents of the U.S. can be deported for a marijuana offense no matter how long they have lived in this country, no matter if their children are U.S. citizens, and no matter how long they have been legally employed. More than half the states revoke or suspend driver's licenses of people arrested for marijuana possession even though they were not driving at the time of arrest. The federal Higher Education Act prohibits student loans to young people convicted of any drug offense; all other criminal offenders remain eligible.

This is clearly an overreaction on the part of government. No drug is perfectly safe, and every psychoactive drug can be used in ways that are problematic. The federal government has spent billions of dollars on advertisements and anti-drug programs that preach the dangers of marijuana—that it's a gateway drug, and addictive in its own right, and dramatically more potent than it used to be, and responsible for all sorts of physical and social diseases as well as international terrorism. But the government has yet to repudiate the 1988 finding of the Drug Enforcement Administration's own administrative law judge, Francis Young, who concluded after extensive testimony that "marijuana in its natural form is one of the safest therapeutically active substances known to man."

Is marijuana a gateway drug? Yes, insofar as most Americans try marijuana before they try other illicit drugs. But no, insofar as the vast majority of Americans who have tried marijuana have never gone on to try other illegal drugs, much less get in trouble with them, and most have never even gone on to become regular or problem marijuana users. Trying to reduce heroin addiction by preventing marijuana use, it's been said, is like trying to reduce motorcycle fatalities by cracking down on bicycle riding. If marijuana did not exist, there's little reason to believe that there would be less drug abuse in the U.S.; indeed, its role would most likely be filled by a more dangerous substance.

Is marijuana dramatically more potent today? There's certainly a greater variety of high-quality marijuana available today than 30 years ago. But anyone who smoked marijuana in the 1970s and 1980s can recall smoking pot that was just as strong as anything available today. What's more, one needs to take only a few puffs of higher-potency pot to get the desired effect, so there's less wear and tear on the lungs.

Is marijuana addictive? Yes, it can be, in that some people use it to excess, in ways that are problematic for themselves and those around them, and find it hard to stop. But marijuana may well be the least addictive and least damaging of all commonly used psychoactive drugs, including many that are now legal. Most people who smoke marijuana never become dependent. Withdrawal symptoms pale compared with those from other drugs. No one has ever died from a marijuana overdose, which cannot be said of most other drugs. Marijuana is not associated with violent behavior and only minimally with reckless sexual behavior. And even heavy marijuana smokers smoke only a fraction of what cigarette addicts smoke. Lung cancers involving only marijuana are rare.

The government's most recent claim is that marijuana abuse accounts for more people entering treatment than any other illegal drug. That shouldn't be surprising, given that tens of millions of Americans smoke marijuana while only a few million use all other illicit drugs. But the claim is spurious nonetheless. Few Americans who enter "treatment" for marijuana are addicted. Fewer than one in five people entering drug treatment for marijuana do so voluntarily. More than half were referred by the criminal-justice system. They go because they got caught with a joint or failed a drug test at school or work (typically for having smoked marijuana days ago, not for being impaired). or because they were caught by a law-enforcement officer—and attending a marijuana "treatment" program is what's required to avoid expulsion, dismissal, or incarceration. Many traditional drug-treatment programs shamelessly participate in this charade to preserve a profitable and captive client stream.

Even those who recoil at the "nanny state" telling adults what they can or cannot sell to one another often make an exception when it comes to marijuana—to "protect the kids." This is a bad joke, as any teenager will attest. The criminalization of marijuana for adults has not prevented young people from having better access to marijuana than anyone else. Even as marijuana's popularity has waxed and waned since the 1970s, one statistic has remained constant: More than 80 percent of high-school students report it's easy to get. Meanwhile, the government's exaggerations and outright dishonesty easily backfire. For every teen who refrains from trying marijuana because it's illegal (for adults), another is tempted by its status as "forbidden fruit." Many respond to the lies about marijuana by disbelieving warnings about more dangerous drugs. So much for protecting the kids by criminalizing the adults.

The Medical Dimension

The debate over medical marijuana obviously colors the broader debate over marijuana prohibition. Marijuana's medical efficacy is no longer in serious dispute. Its use as a medicine dates back thousands of years. Pharmaceuticals products containing marijuana's central ingredient, THC, are legally sold in the U.S., and more are emerging. Some people find the pill form satisfactory, and others consume it in teas or baked products. Most find smoking the easiest and most effective way to consume this unusual medicine, but non-smoking consumption methods, notably vaporizers, are emerging.

Federal law still prohibits medical marijuana. But every state ballot initiative to legalize medical marijuana has been approved, often by wide margins—in California, Washington, Oregon, Alaska, Colorado, Nevada, Maine, and Washington, D.C. State legislatures in Vermont, Hawaii, and Maryland have followed suit, and many others are now considering their own medical-marijuana bills—including New York, Connecticut, Rhode Island, and Illinois. Support is often bipartisan, with Republican governors like Gary Johnson and Maryland's Bob Ehrlich taking the lead. In New York's 2002 gubernatorial campaign, the conservative candidate of the Independence party, Tom Golisano, surprised everyone by campaigning heavily on this issue. The medical-marijuana bill now before the New York legislature is backed not just by leading Republicans but even by some Conservative party leaders.

The political battleground increasingly pits the White House—first under Clinton and now Bush—against everyone else. Majorities in virtually every state in the country would vote, if given the chance, to legalize medical marijuana. Even Congress is beginning to turn; last summer about two-thirds of House Democrats and a dozen Republicans voted in favor of an amendment co-sponsored by Republican Dana Rohrabacher to prohibit federal funding of any Justice Department crackdowns on medical marijuana in the states that had legalized it. (Many more Republicans privately expressed support, but were directed to vote against.) And federal courts have imposed limits on federal aggression: first in *Conant* v. *Walters*, which now protects the First Amendment rights of doctors and patients to discuss medical marijuana, and more recently in *Raich* v. *Ashcroft* and *Santa Cruz* v. *Ashcroft*, which determined that the federal government's power to regulate interstate commerce does not provide a basis for prohibiting medical-marijuana operations that are entirely local and non-commercial. (The Supreme Court let the *Conant* decision stand, but has yet to consider the others.)

State and local governments are increasingly involved in trying to regulate medical marijuana, notwithstanding the federal prohibition. California, Oregon, Hawaii, Alaska, Colorado, and Nevada have created confidential medical-marijuana patient registries, which protect bona fide patients and caregivers from arrest or prosecution. Some municipal governments are now trying to figure out how to regulate production and distribution. In California, where dozens of medical-marijuana programs now operate openly, with tacit approval by local authorities, some program directors are asking to be licensed and regulated. Many state and local authorities, including law enforcement, favor this but are intimidated by federal threats to arrest and prosecute them for violating federal law.

The drug czar and DEA spokespersons recite the mantra that "there is no such thing as medical marijuana," but the claim is so specious on its face that it clearly undermines federal credibility. The federal government currently provides marijuana—from its own production site in Mississippi—to a few patients who years ago were recognized by the courts as bona fide patients. No one wants to debate those who have used marijuana for medical purposes, be it Santa Cruz medical-marijuana hospice founder Valerie Corral or National Review's Richard Brookhiser. Even many federal officials quietly regret the assault on medical marijuana. When the DEA raided Corral's hospice in September 2002, one agent was heard to say, "Maybe I'm going to think about getting another job sometime soon."

The Broader Movement

The bigger battle, of course, concerns whether marijuana prohibition will ultimately go the way of alcohol Prohibition, replaced by a variety of state and local tax and regulatory policies with modest federal involvement. Dedicated prohibitionists see medical marijuana as the first step down a slippery slope to full legalization. The voters who approved the medical-marijuana ballot initiatives (as well as the wealthy men who helped fund the campaigns) were roughly divided between those who support broader legalization and those who don't, but united in seeing the criminalization and persecution of medical-marijuana patients as the most distasteful aspect of the war on marijuana. (This was a point that Buckley male forcefully in his columns about the plight of Peter McWilliams, who likely died because federal authorities effectively forbade him to use marijuana as medicine.)

The medical-marijuana effort has probably aided the broader anti-prohibitionist campaign in three ways. It helped transform the face of marijuana in the media, from the stereotypical rebel with long hair and tie-dyed shirt to an ordinary middle-aged American struggling with MS or cancer or AIDS. By winning first Proposition 215, the 1996 medical-marijuana ballot initiative in California, and then a string of similar victories in other states, the nascent drug-policy-reform movement demonstrated that it could win in the big leagues of American politics. And the emergence of successful models of medical-marijuana control is likely to boost public confidence in the possibilities and virtue of regulating non-medical use as well.

In this regard, the history of Dutch policy on cannabis (i.e., marijuana and hashish) is instructive. The "coffee shop" model in the Netherlands, where retail (but not wholesale) sale of cannabis is defacto legal, was not legislated into existence. It evolved in fits and starts following the decriminalization of cannabis by Parliament in 1976, as consumers, growers, and entrepreneurs negotiated and collaborated with local police, prosecutors, and other authorities to find an acceptable middle-ground policy. "Coffee shops" now operate throughout the country, subject to local regulations. Troublesome shops are shut down, and most are well integrated into local city cultures. Cannabis is no more popular than in the U.S. and other Western countries, notwithstanding the effective absence of criminal sanctions and controls. Parallel developments are now underway in other countries.

Like the Dutch decriminalization law in 1976, California's Prop 215 in 1996 initiated a dialogue over how best to implement the new law. The variety of outlets that have emerged—ranging from pharmacy-like stores to medical "coffee shops" to hospices, all of which provide marijuana only to people with a patient ID card or doctor's recommendation—play a key role as the most public symbol and manifestation of this dialogue. More such outlets will likely pop up around the country as other states legalize marijuana for medical purposes and then seek ways to regulate distribution and access. And the question will inevitably arise: If the emerging system is successful in controlling production and distribution of marijuana for those with a medical need, can it not also expand to provide for those without medical need?

Millions of Americans use marijuana not just "for fun" but because they find it useful for many of the same reasons that people drink alcohol or take pharmaceutical drugs. It's akin to the beer, glass of wine, or cocktail at the end of the workday, or the prescribed drug to alleviate depression or anxiety, or the sleeping pill, or the aid to sexual function and pleasure. More and more Americans are apt to describe some or all of their marijuana use as "medical" as the definition of that term evolves and broadens. Their anecdotal experiences are increasingly backed by new scientific research into marijuana's essential ingredients, the cannabinoids. Last year a subsidiary of *The Lancet*, Britain's leading medical journal, speculated whether marijuana might soon emerge as the "aspirin of the 21st century," providing a wide array of medical benefits at low cost to diverse populations.

Perhaps the expansion of the medical-control model provides the best answer—at least in the U.S.—to the question of how best to reduce the substantial costs and harms of marijuana prohibition without inviting significant increases in real drug abuse. It's analogous to the evolution of many pharmaceutical drugs from prescription to over-the-counter, but with stricter controls still in place. It's also an incrementalist approach to reform that can provide both the control and the reassurance that cautious politicians and voters desire.

In 1931, with public support for alcohol Prohibition rapidly waning. President Hoover released the report of the Wickersham Commission. The report included a devastating critique of Prohibition's failures and costly consequences, but the commissioners, apparently fearful of getting out too far ahead of public opinion, opposed repeal. Franklin P. Adams of the *New World* neatly summed up their findings:

Prohibition is an awful flop.
　　We like it.
It can't stop what it's meant to stop.
　　We like it.
It's left a trail of graft and slime
It don't prohibit worth a dime
It's filled our land with vice and crime.
　　Nevertheless, we're for it.

Two years later, federal alcohol Prohibition was history.

What support there is for marijuana prohibition would likely end quickly absent the billions of dollars spent annually by federal and other governments to prop it up. All those anti-marijuana ads pretend to be about reducing drug abuse, but in fact their basic purpose is sustaining popular support for the war on marijuana. What's needed now are conservative politicians willing to say enough is enough: Tens of billions of taxpayer dollars down the drain each year. People losing their jobs, their property, and their freedom for nothing more than possessing a joint or growing a few marijuana plants. And all for what? To send a message? To keep pretending that we're protecting our children? Alcohol Prohibition made a lot more sense than marijuana prohibition does today—and it, too, was a disaster.

NO

John P. Walters

No Surrender: The Drug War Saves Lives

The prospect of a drug-control policy that includes regulated legalization has enticed intelligent commentators for years, no doubt because it offers, on the surface, a simple solution to a complex problem. Reasoned debate about the real consequences usually dampens enthusiasm, leaving many erstwhile proponents feeling mugged by reality; not so Ethan Nadelmann, whose version of marijuana legalization ("An End to Marijuana Prohibition," NR, July 12) fronts for a worldwide political movement, funded by billionaire George Soros, to embed the use of all drugs as acceptable policy. Unfortunately for Nadelmann, his is not a serious argument. Nor is it attached to the facts.

To take but one example, Nadelmann's article alleges the therapeutic value of smoked marijuana by claiming: "Marijuana's medical efficacy is no longer in serious dispute." But he never substantiates his sweeping claim. In fact, smoked marijuana, a Schedule I controlled substance (Schedule I is the government's most restrictive category), has no medical value and a high risk of abuse. The Food and Drug Administration notes that marijuana has not been approved for any indication, that scientific studies do not support claims of marijuana's usefulness as a medication, and that there is a lack of accepted safety standards for the use of smoked marijuana.

The FDA has also expressed concern that marijuana use may worsen the condition of those for whom it is prescribed. Legalization advocates such as Nadelmann simply ignore these facts and continue their promotion, the outcome of which will undermine drug-prevention and treatment efforts, and put genuinely sick patients at risk.

The legalization scheme is also unworkable. A government-sanctioned program to produce, distribute, and tax an addictive intoxicant creates more problems than it solves.

First, drug use would increase. No student of supply-and-demand curves can doubt that marijuana would become cheaper, more readily available, and more widespread than it currently is when all legal risk is removed and demand is increased by marketing.

From *National Review*, vol. 56, no. 18, September 1997, pp. 41–42. Copyright © 1997 by John P. Walters. Reprinted by permission.

Second, legalization will not eliminate marijuana use among young people any more than legalizing alcohol eliminated underage drinking. If you think we can tax marijuana to where it costs more than the average teenager can afford, think again. Marijuana is a plant that can be readily grown by anyone. If law enforcement is unable to distinguish "legal" marijuana from illegal, growing marijuana at home becomes a low-cost (and low-risk) way to supply your neighborhood and friends. "Official marijuana" will not drive out the black market, nor will it eliminate the need for tough law enforcement. It will only make the task more difficult.

In debating legalization, the burden is to consider the costs and benefits both of keeping strict control over dangerous substances and of making them more accessible. The Soros position consistently overstates the benefits of legalizing marijuana and understates the risks. At the same time, drug promoters ignore the current benefits of criminalization while dramatically overstating the costs.

Government-sanctioned marijuana would be a bonanza for trial lawyers (the government may wake up to find that it has a liability for the stoned trucker who plows into a school bus). Health-care and employment-benefits costs will increase (there is plenty of evidence that drug-using employees are less productive, and less healthy), while more marijuana use will further burden out education system.

The truth is, there are laws against marijuana because marijuana is harmful. With every year that passes, medical research discovers greater dangers from smoking it, from links to serious mental illness to the risk of cancer, and even dangers from in utero exposure.

In fact, given the new levels of potency and the sheer prevalence of marijuana (the number of users contrasted with the number of those using cocaine or heroin), a case can be made that marijuana does the most social harm of any illegal drug. Marijuana is currently the leading cause of treatment need: Nearly two-thirds of those who meet the psychiatric criteria for needing substance-abuse treatment do so because of marijuana use. For youth, the harmful effects of marijuana use now exceed those of all other drugs combined. Remarkably, over 40 percent of youths who are current marijuana smokers meet the criteria for abuse or dependency. In several states, marijuana smoking exceeds tobacco smoking among young people, while marijuana has become more important than alcohol as a factor in treatment for teenagers.

Legalizers assert that the justice system arrests 700,000 marijuana users a year, suggesting that an oppressive system is persecuting the innocent. This charge is a fraud. Less than 1 percent of those in prison for drug violations are low-level marijuana offenders, and many of these have "pled down" to the marijuana violation in the face of other crimes. The vast majority of those in prison on drug convictions are true criminals involved in drug trafficking, repeat offenses, or violent crime.

The value of legal control is that it enables judicial discretion over offenders, diverting minor offenders who need it into treatment while retaining the authority to guard against the violent and incorrigible. Further, where the sanction and supervision of a court are present, the likelihood of recovery is greatly increased. Removing legal sanction endangers the public and fails to help the offender.

Proponents of legalization argue that because approximately half of the referrals for treatment are from the criminal-justice system, it is the law and not marijuana that is the problem. Yet nearly half of all referrals for alcohol treatment likewise derive from judicial intervention, and nobody argues that drunk drivers do not really have a substance-abuse problem, or that it is the courts that are creating the perception of alcoholism. Marijuana's role in emergency-room cases has tripled in the past decade. Yet no judge is sending people to emergency rooms. They are there because of the dangers of the drug, which have greatly increased because of soaring potency.

Legalization advocates suggest that youth will reduce their smoking because of this new potency. But when tobacco companies were accused of deliberately "spiking" their product with nicotine, no one saw this as a public-health gesture intended to reduce cigarette consumption. The deliberate effort to increase marijuana potency (and market it to younger initiates) should be seen for what it is—a steeply increased threat of addiction.

Proponents of legalization argue that the fact that 100 million Americans admit on surveys that they have tried marijuana in their lifetime demonstrates the public's acceptance of the drug. But the pertinent number tells a different story. There are approximately 15 million Americans, mostly young people, who report using marijuana on a monthly basis. That is, only about 6 percent of the population age twelve and over use marijuana on a regular basis.

To grasp the impact of legal control, contrast that figure with the number of current alcohol users (approximately 120 million). Regular alcohol use is eight times that of marijuana, and a large part of the difference is a function of laws against marijuana use. Under legalization, which would decrease the cost (now a little-noticed impediment to the young) and eliminate the legal risk, it is certain that the number of users would increase. Can anyone seriously argue that American democracy would be strengthened by more marijuana smoking?

The law itself is our safeguard, and it works. Far from being a hopeless battle, the drug-control tide is turning against marijuana. We have witnessed an 11 percent reduction in youth marijuana use over the last two years, while perceptions of risk have soared.

Make no mistake about what is going on here: Drug legalization is a worldwide movement, the goal of which is to make drug consumption—including heroin, cocaine, and methamphetamine—an acceptable practice. Using the discourse of rights without responsibilities, the effort strives to establish an entitlement to addictive substances. The impact will be devastating.

Drug legalizers will not be satisfied with a limited distribution of medical marijuana, nor will they stop at legal marijuana for sale in convenience stores. Their goal is clearly identifiable: tolerated addiction. It is a travesty to suggest,

as Ethan Nadelmann has done, that it is consistent with conservative principles to abandon those who could be treated for their addiction, to create a
situation in which government both condones and is the agent of drug distribution, and to place in the hands of the state the power to grant or not grant
access to an addictive substance. This is not a conservative vision. But it is the
goal of George Soros.

POSTSCRIPT

Should Marijuana Be Legalized?

Marijuana has been around for a long time. It was not until 1937 that the Marijuana Tax Act banned most recreational and medicinal uses of this popular drug in the United States. Since that time, there has been significant controversy about whether our marijuana laws are effective, or whether they are a bad social policy that should be abandoned in favor of a more enlightened approach to drug abuse.

According to a 1998 study by the Harvard School of Public Health, 78 percent of Americans believe that U.S. anti-drug efforts have failed. In addition, 94 percent believe that the United States has lost control of the illegal drug problem, and 58 percent maintain that the problem is getting worse. At the same time, only 14 percent favored drug legalization, while a majority favored more severe prison sentences. (See Robert J. Blendon and John T. Young, "The Public and the War on Illicit Drugs," *Journal of the American Medical Association* (March 18, 1998, p. 827). Please note that a more recent survey has found that 34 percent of Americans support making "the use of marijuana legal." See Colleen McMurray, "Medicinal Marijuana: Is It What the Doctor Ordered?" *The Gallup Poll Tuesday Briefing* (December 2003. p. 89).) These statistics are interesting for a number of reasons.

At first glance, the percentages seem somewhat schizophrenic—even though the vast majority of Americans believe that U.S. drug control policies have failed and that the problem of drug abuse is getting worse, only a small minority of respondents believe that drugs should be legalized. One source asserts that this apparent contradiction may suggest that:

> [P]ublic support for the 'drug war' is more about moral values or fears than rational public safety measures. The bureaucracies and businesses engaged in the 'drug war' have been successful in creating support that is independent of failure to achieve objectives and rational analysis and evaluation. (PUBLIC OPINION, "News Briefs," March–April 1998, http://www.ndsn.org/marapr98/opinion.html.)

Could the statement above actually be true? Is it possible that bureaucracies, such as U.S. law enforcement agencies, and businesses with ties to drug law enforcement may have an interest in continuing the war on drugs regardless of whether it is good for society? For a classic discussion of these issues, see: Howard S. Becker, *Outsiders: Studies in the Sociology of Deviance* (The Free Press, 1963); for a more recent treatment of these issues, see Jeffrey Reiman, *The Rich Get Richer and the Poor Get Prison: Ideology, Class and Criminal Justice*, 7th ed. (Allyn & Bacon, 2004); Robert J. MacCoun and Peter Reuter, Jr., *Drug War Heresies: Learning from Other Vices, Times and Places* (Cambridge University Press, 2001).

Additional informative resources include: Clare Wilson, "Miracle Weed," *New Scientist* (February 5–11, 2005); David T. Courtwright, "Drug Wars: Policy Hots and Historical Cools," *Bulletin of the History of Medicine* (Johns Hopkins University Press, Summer 2004); Bruce Bullington, "Drug Policy Reform and Its Detractors: The United States as the Elephant in the Closet," *Journal of Drug Issues* (Summer 2004); Michael M. O'Hear, "Federalism and Drug Control," *Vanderbilt Law Review* (April 2004); Sasha Abramsky, "The Drug War Goes Up in Smoke," *The Nation* (August 18–25, 2003); David Boyum and Mark A. R. Kleiman, "Breaking the Drug-Crime Link," *Public Interest* (Summer 2003); Alex Kreit, "The Future of Medical Marijuana: Should the States Grow Their Own?" *University of Pennsylvania Law Review* (May 2003); Vanessa Grigoriadis, "The Most Stoned Kids on the Most Stoned Day on the Most Stoned Campus on Earth," *Rolling Stone* (September 16, 2004).

ISSUE 17

Do Three Strikes Sentencing Laws and Other "Get Tough" Approaches Really Work?

YES: Eugene H. Methvin, from "Mugged by Reality," *Policy Review* (July/August 1997)

NO: David Shichor, from "Three Strikes As a Public Policy: The Convergence of the New Penology and the McDonaldization of Punishment," *Crime & Delinquency* (September 1997)

ISSUE SUMMARY

YES: Eugene H. Methvin, senior editor for *Reader's Digest*, contends that a very small number of juveniles and adults commit the majority of serious crimes. The main solution to the crime problem, then, is to identify them as early as possible and increase the punishments each time they offend, eventually incarcerating the repeat offenders.

NO: Professor of criminal justice David Shichor argues that the "three strikes" policy is permeated with negative unanticipated consequences; it is costly; inefficient, and unfair; and it does little to reduce crime.

The traditional approaches to crime are retribution (sometimes conceptually couched as vengeance or justice), deterrence, and incapacitation. Many criminologists and liberal politicians called for rehabilitation during the twentieth century. For a variety of reasons, including increasing fear of crime, significant increases in violent crimes in many areas, a shrinking economy, and the election in 1980 of a conservative president, there has been a decisive paradigmatic shift. Current constructions of the crime problem and responses to crime policies seem to ignore rehabilitation as a goal of incarceration.

"Criminals need to be locked up," many say these days, because they deserve to be punished, to deter others from doing the same thing, and to get bad people off the streets. Structural or environmental factors, with their concomitant theoretical response modalities, are forgotten by many. That is, racism, blocked opportunities, lack of education, poverty, and the like as theorized causes of crime implying a need for rehabilitation (such as job training, education, and improved opportunities) are seemingly receding rapidly into distant criminological memory.

Initially framed as federal law, now being replicated in different variants in 24 states, three-strikes criminal justice ideologically "makes sense" within the current weltanschauungen (world view). If an individual has already committed two serious felonies and now commits a third one, defenders argue, what can be more rational than making sure that he gets a very long sentence for his third crime? Studies show that a hard core of offenders, if taken off the streets, would save taxpayers hundreds of thousands of dollars a year. A life prison sentence would clearly incapacitate them. Individuals, then, would be deterred from committing their third crime, and general deterrence would result from others being afraid of being imprisoned for the remainder of their lives.

Supporters of tough sentencing laws also say, if criminals have already done terrible things and are obviously still doing them, justice would be served better by separating them from you and me. After all, what good has "rehabilitation" done them if they are still committing crimes?

In the second selection, David Shichor attempts to counter much of this by applying to penology four key concepts—efficiency, calculability, prediction, and control—derived from social theorist George Ritzer's "McDonaldization of society" theory. What distinguishes modern, industrial societies from all others is the bureaucratization of social and economic life. According to classic theorist Max Weber (1864–1920), whom both Shichor and Ritzer draw from, modernity necessitates increased rational behavior that is oriented to economic values over family and personal ones. Both market and social life are increasingly routinized, controlled, planned, and calculated. This enables increased productivity and industrial survival. However, as Weber warned with his prophecy of the "iron cage of the future" consequence, there is a tremendous cost: Life becomes more routinized and regimented. People and policies run the risk of becoming robot-like. Ritzer extends this argument to suggest that with increased technological efficiency comes a curvilinear relationship (a U-shaped curve). That is, after certain points, the "efficiency" and "savings" backfire, or become counterproductive and irrational.

As you wrestle with this important debate, notice Eugene H. Methvin's classifications of the types of offenders in the first selection. Which does he seem to be addressing? What does he see as the causes of crime? Are they sometimes contradictory? How often does Shichor actually prove that three strikes does not work as opposed to speculating that it *could* be a problem?

YES

Eugene H. Methvin

Mugged by Reality

The most serious offenders against people and property in this country generally hit their criminal peak between 16 and 18 years of age. The hardcore young thug-to-be starts stealing from mama's purse before he's 10. By the fourth and fifth grades, he is skipping school. As he enters his teens, he's gangbanging—and on the track to prison or an early violent death. Typically he is committing burglaries at about 15, armed robberies at 16, and often killing by 18—and sometimes much younger. After years of effort to contain the crime committed by these hoodlums, we know what works and what doesn't. At long last, we have all the knowledge we need to design an effective strategy for the prevention of crime.

> *1. Most serious crime is committed by a violent minority of predatory recidivists.*

Criminologist Marvin Wolfgang compiled records of all of the 9,945 males born in 1945 and attending school in Philadelphia between the ages of 10 and 18. A mere 627—just under 7 percent—were chronic offenders, with five or more arrests by age 18. These so-called Dirty Seven Percenters committed more than half of all offenses and two-thirds of the violent crimes, including all the murders, that were committed by the entire cohort.

Wolfgang followed his "Class of '45" through its 30th year in 1975. Shockingly few offenders were incarcerated. Even the 14 murderers among them spent an average of only four years behind bars for these crimes. Worse, these hardcore criminals admitted in interviews that, for each arrest, they typically got away with 8 to 11 other serious crimes. Wolfgang found that 70 percent of juveniles arrested three times committed a fourth offense; of those, 80 percent not only committed a fifth offense, but kept at it through 20 or more. If the city's judges had sent each Dirty Seven Percenter to prison for just a year after his *third* offense, Wolfgang calculated, Philadelphians would have suffered 7,200 fewer serious crimes while they [were] off the streets.

Wolfgang's findings electrified the law-enforcement world. At the request of U.S. Attorney General Edward Levi, Wolfgang repeated the study on the 13,160 Philadelphian males born in 1958. The proportion of chronic offenders was virtually the same: 982 young men (7.5 percent) collected five or more arrests before age 18. But the crimes committed by the "Class of '58" were bloodier and far more frequent. Compared with the Class of '45, these youths were twice as likely to commit rape and aggravated assault, three times more likely to murder, and five times more likely to commit robbery. They were, concluded Wolfgang, "a very violent criminal population of a small number of nasty, brutal offenders. They begin early in life and should be controlled equally early."

Other studies with different methodologies corroborated Wolfgang's approximate finding of 7 percent in places as different as London; Copenhagen; Orange County, California; Racine, Wisconsin; Columbus, Ohio; Phoenix, Arizona; and Salt Lake City, Utah.

2. *A minority of this minority is extraordinarily violent, persistent, or both.*

They are "Super Predators," far more dangerous than the rest. Researchers for Rand questioned 2,190 prisoners convicted of robbery in California, Texas, and Michigan. Nearly all admitted to many more crimes than those for which they were jailed. But a tiny fraction of these career criminals proved to be *extraordinarily* frequent offenders. The least active 50 percent of burglars averaged a little under six burglaries a year, while the most prolific 10 percent averaged more than 230. The least active 50 percent of the robbers committed five robberies a year on average, but the top 10 percent averaged 87. The distribution of drug-dealing offenses was even more skewed: Half of these convicts did 100 deals a year on average, while the highest tenth averaged 3,251.

Sociologist Delbert S. Elliott of the University of Colorado has tracked a nationally representative sample of 1,725 boys and girls who were between 11 and 17 years old in 1976. By 1989, 369 of them had committed one or more serious, violent offenses. But only 32 were high-rate offenders. Year after year, those in this small group committed an average of 30 violent crimes each and hundreds of lesser crimes. Just under 2 percent of the whole, they accounted for half the serious crimes committed by the entire group. These Super Predators distinguish themselves by their arrest records, by the early age at which they first tangle with the law, and by the seriousness of their early offenses. Nationally, we can crudely estimate the current crop of young "super felons" at about 500,000 of our 26.7 million 11- to 17-year-olds.

3. *Most of these persistent predators are criminal psychopaths, and we now have a scientifically valid instrument to identify them with reasonable accuracy.*

Psychopaths are responsible for more than half of all serious crimes. The normal criminal has an internalized set of values, however warped, and he feels guilt whenever he violates his standards. The psychopath doesn't even know what guilt is, because he has never experienced it. But he is good at *faking* it.

Even within prison populations, psychopaths stand out because their antisocial and illegal behavior is more varied and frequent than that of ordinary criminals. In prisons and mental hospitals, they are generally the nastiest inmates. They are more resistant to treatment, more likely to try to escape, and more violent with other inmates and the staff. After they are released, they re-offend at four to five times the rate of other criminals. Psychopaths constitute an estimated 1 to 2 percent of the population—and 20 to 25 percent of our prison population. This means the United States has at least *2 million* psychopaths.

After 25 years of research, psychologist Robert D. Hare of the University of British Columbia developed a reliable instrument for diagnosing psychopathy: the Hare Psychopathy Check List [PCL]. After interviewing relatives and associates and studying criminal and other records, a trained clinician interviews the subject and scores him on 20 personality traits and behaviors characteristic of this personality disorder. Is the person glib, manipulative, a liar, sexually promiscuous, grandiose in his sense of self-worth, impulsive, averse to boredom, incapable of remorse? Was he trouble from an early age? Does he have a juvenile and adult arrest record? Has he had many short-term marital relationships? And so on.

Hare, in his 1993 book *Without Conscience: The Disturbing World of Psychopaths Among Us,* says: "Psychopaths are social predators who charm, manipulate, and ruthlessly plow their way through life, leaving a broad trail of broken hearts, shattered expectations, and empty wallets. Completely lacking in conscience and feelings for others, they selfishly take what they want and do as they please, violating social norms and expectations without the slightest sense of guilt or regret."

Studies of Canadian and American convicts released from prison show that only about 20 percent of the low scorers on the PCL are re-arrested within three years, but 80 percent of the high scorers end up back behind bars.

The PCL can be a powerful tool for prison administrators, parole boards, judges, and others who must cope with this extraordinarily destructive population. High scorers are poor risks for probation or parole and good candidates for maximum sentences in higher security institutions. Maryland prison officials have used the PCL to assess some 10,000 inmates. It has enabled them to divert low scorers from costly maximum-security facilities into lower-cost units or parole, freeing up 1,100 prison beds a day, which yields $19.8 million in savings a year. Moreover, the state has avoided an estimated $55 million in new prison construction. Canada, New Zealand, the United Kingdom, and most American states are now using the PCL in their prison systems.

> 4. *Savvy police, prosecutors, and judges can identify and isolate high-rate violent predators.*

In Miami, sociologist James A. Inciardi used a "snowballing" interview technique to find them. He sent researchers into high-crime neighborhoods to talk to youngsters about "who's doing drugs" and "who's into crime." They found 611 youngsters ages 12 to 17 who admitted to multiple crimes and repeated drug use. Ninety percent of them had been arrested, an equal proportion had been thrown out of school, and almost half had been incarcerated. Typically they began to use alcohol at age seven and turned to crime and drugs at 11; almost two-thirds had participated in a robbery by the age of 13. The interviewees confessed to a total of 429,136 criminal acts during the year prior to their interviews—more than 700 each, or nearly two a day. Of these acts, 18,477, or 30 apiece, were major felonies, including 6,269 robberies and 721 assaults. Nearly 18 percent had committed armed robberies, as young as 14, and 90 percent carried weapons most of the time. Among this violent crowd, 361 committed the 6,269 robberies—an average of 17 each—and two-thirds of them robbed before the age of 13.

If sociologists can find the Super Predators, police can, too. William Bratton proved it, first in New York City's subway system in 1990, then city-wide after Mayor Rudolph Giuliani named him police commissioner in 1994. By 1990, the New York subway had become a lawless jungle. Riders were deserting by the tens of thousands. An estimated 180,000 fare evaders jumped the turnstiles every day, costing the system $65 million a year. Vandals jammed coin slots and opened exit doors; aggressive panhandlers threatened riders on the cars; muggers stole their tokens and money. Violent teenagers prowled the subways in "wolfpacks."

As the chief of New York's 4,000 transit police offices, Bratton created strategies for winnowing out the criminal minority. He ordered uniformed officers to enforce all subway rules. He planted plainclothes teams to arrest fare evaders. Each of them was searched; one in 14 was arrested for packing illegal guns, and one out of seven was wanted on previous criminal warrants. Whenever detectives caught one mugger, they extracted information about other wolfpack members. They also tracked down a group of about 75 hard-core graffiti vandals. Bratton insisted that his officers act on bench warrants for subway crimes within 24 hours. Their apprehension rate rose sharply to more than 60 percent. The hunters became the hunted. Bratton's strategies cut subway crime by two-thirds—and robberies by three-fourths. Fare evaders were reduced by two-thirds, too. Riders returned by the ten of thousands. By 1994 New York's subways were the scene of fewer than 20 felonies a day, down 64 percent in five years.

Named in 1994 to head the whole police department, Bratton and his deputy commissioner, Jack Maple, implemented a strategy of "relentless pursuit." Bratton personally urged officers to cite citizens for "quality of life" offenses such as drinking beer in pubic, smoking marijuana, or urinating in the street, and to frisk offenders for illegal weapons at the slightest suspicion. Maple launched a campaign to remind officers to interrogate every arrestee. Talented interrogators created a three-day "verbal judo" course at the police academy to teach officers how to extract information from suspects. New York's cops responded enthusiastically, and with dramatic results. A topless dancer arrested for prostitution fingered the bouncer at her Brooklyn club in an unsolved murder. A car thief turned in a fence, who then turned in a father-son gun-dealing team. A parolee arrested for failing to report turned out to have been the only eyewitness to a drug-related murder.

This campaign produced "a miracle happening before our eyes," says Jeffrey Fagan, the director of Columbia University's Center for Violence Research and Prevention. From 1994 to 1996, New York City's murders declined by 49 percent, robberies 43 percent, burglaries 39 percent, and grand larcenies 32 percent. In 1995, the city accounted for 70 percent of the heralded national decline in serious crimes.

5. *The rehabilitation ideal of the juvenile-court system leads to costly coddling of serious and persistent offenders.*

Studies show that youths who land in juvenile court a second time will likely become chronic offenders. Howard N. Snyder, a researcher with the National Council of Family and Juvenile Court Judges, analyzed the records of 48,311 boys who went through juvenile courts in Utah and Arizona. More than half never returned after the first trip. But most of those who landed in court a second time before their 16th birthdays became persistent repeaters, and the earlier their first prosecution, the more likely they were to be violent chronics.

It is important to note that a troublesome youngster typically has 10 to 12 contacts with the criminal-justice system and many more undiscovered offenses before he ever receives any formal "adjudication," or finding of guilt, from a judge. He quickly concludes that he will never face any serious consequences for his delinquency. For each young chronic offender who comes before him, a juvenile-court judge typically moves toward more severe punishments and costly interventions in five or more small steps. Snyder recommends that judges impose upon second-time convicts stiffer penalties and the more intense (and costly) rehabilitation programs. Waiting until the fourth or fifth offense to do so only wastes court time and money—and looses serious crime upon the public.

In Richmond, Virginia, a juvenile-court psychologist estimated that court costs, rehabilitation efforts, and incarceration for just 14 defendants who cycled through her court regularly totaled more than $2 million. Welfare, food stamps, court-appointed lawyers, and other services over the years swelled their cost to taxpayers to more than $5 million. She tracked 56 young men locked in the youth-detention center over one five-day period. On average, they were 15 years old and had compiled 12 arrests apiece for crimes of escalating severity. Social-service agencies had intervened in their lives at an average age of nine, and their criminal activity began four years later, on average, though some started as early as age seven. Their offenses ranged from curfew violation to rape and murder. A year later, one-third had graduated to adult prisons. Three-fourths were still incarcerated or faced new charges or warrants. Almost all those older than 15 who had been released faced new charges.

6. *Punishment works—and the United States has barely tried it.*

Psychologist Sarnoff A. Mednick of the University of Southern California studied the records of thousands of Danish criminals and discovered that punishment is very effective in deterring crime. He compared the criminal histories of thousands of offenders in Copenhagen and Philadelphia who had exactly four or five arrests. Those who received four punishments in a row for

their crimes were unlikely to have a fifth arrest. But those who had been punished irregularly after the earlier arrests were more likely to be arrested again.

Mednick studied 28,879 males born in Copenhagen between 1944 and
1947 who lived there through age 26. He found that 6,579 had at least one
arrest. The third of arrestees who were not punished went on to commit far
more crimes. Mednick found 3,809 offenders were punished after every single
arrest, while 2,793 were not. Those who escaped punishment committed
three times as many crimes as those consistently punished. Punishment delivered after every offense significantly reduced later offenses. But an offender
who was punished for early crimes and received none for later offenses
resumed criminal activity at the higher rates.

It made little difference whether the punishment was fines, probation,
or incarceration. Consistent delivery of sanctions was more effective than
intermittent sanctions, and criminal recidivism recovered when punishment
was discontinued. Severity of sanction also made little difference: Longer jail
terms, higher fines, and longer probations did not decrease subsequent
offenses more than lighter sanctions did.

"Punishment is very effective in suppressing crime, and it does not have
to be severe if you get on them early enough," says Mednick. "The way to
reduce prison populations is to punish offenders from their first offense with
graduated, increasingly severe and certain sanctions. But the records show we
do not do that in America." Mednick compared the Danish criminals to those
in Marvin Wolfgang's Philadelphia cohort studies. The Philadelphia figures
confirmed the effectiveness of punishment, but he also found that only
14 percent of the four- and five-time offenders in the Philadelphia cohorts
were punished, compared with 60 percent of those in Denmark.

"The big problem with our handling of criminals in America is that
they're not punished," he wrote. "People are usually surprised to hear that,
because of all our prisons. But the fact is by the time a guy makes his way to
jail, that's very often his first punishment. And he usually has committed 15
offenses by then. He might have been arrested 10 times. In Philadelphia, the
kids committed huge numbers of offenses, and serious ones, and nothing
happened. They just laughed. Our laws provide severe punishments,
but . . . they deter not the criminals but the judges. They don't want to throw
a kid who's done some little thing in jail, so they just let him go."

7. Prisons work, and they are a relative bargain.

Critics of incarceration claim it has failed because about two-thirds of
those released soon land back behind bars. But these studies begin with a
batch of released convicts, and each batch contains a high proportion of
repeaters who cycle through the revolving doors of justice. Moreover, criminologists have found that these hard-core repeaters get away with a dozen or
more serious crimes for every arrest. But two-thirds to three-fourths of criminals sent to prison for the first time never return.

One study that tracked the careers of 6,310 California prisoners released in
1962–63 revealed a shocking picture. These were hard-core criminals: 56 percent

had been in prison before, and 44 percent served time for violent crimes, burglary, or robbery. Over the next 26 years, these convicts were arrested 30,464 times, and were probably responsible for more than a quarter-million unsolved crimes. More than half the arrests were nuisance offenses such as parole violations, drunk driving, and disorderly conduct. But the ex-cons were also arrested for about 10,000 serious crimes, including 184 homicides, 2,084 assaults, 126 kidnappings, 144 rapes, 2,756 burglaries, 655 auto thefts, and 1,193 robberies. California could have kept all 5,192 second-termers locked away for an estimated cost of only $2.1 billion—a real bargain in public safety.

Patrick A. Langan, a statistician at the U.S. Department of Justice, calculates that, by doubling the number of criminals in prison from 1973 to 1982, the United States reduced reported crime by 10 to 20 percent. This amounted to 66,000 to 190,000 fewer robberies and 350,000 to 900,000 fewer burglaries in 1982 alone. By tripling the prison population from 1975 to 1989, Langan estimates, we prevented 390,000 murders, rapes, robberies, and aggravated assaults just in 1989.

California tripled its prison population in the decade after 1984—and achieved a significant drop in the rates of reported crime from its peak in 1980–81. Bucking nationwide trends, by 1993 California had reduced murders by 10.4 percent, rapes by 36 percent, and burglaries by a whopping 43 percent. By the 1990s, that meant nearly 1,000 fewer murders, 16,000 fewer robberies, and a quarter of a million fewer burglaries yearly. The overall serious crime rate fell 14 percent.

The American public is catching on. In 1990, Oregon voters passed, by a margin of three to one, an anti-crime initiative that requires a criminal convicted of a second violent offense to serve his entire sentence with no parole. In November 1993, voters in Washington state passed by a similar margin a "three strikes and you're out" law, which imposes automatic life sentences for three-time felony convicts. Within two years, 14 states altogether and Congress had adopted such laws.

California has been a leader in the "three strikes" movement. The state automatically doubles the sentence for a felon with a prior conviction for a serious or violent felony. A third felony of any sort can trigger a life sentence, with eligibility for parole after 25 years. Philip J. Romero, Governor Pete Wilson's chief economist, estimates that the new law will add an extra 8,300 convicts a year to the state's prison population and will cost $6.5 billion for new prisons in the first five years—but will save society $23 billion net in crime prevented. A Rand study concluded that the new California law, if fully implemented, will cut serious felonies committed by adults between 22 and 34 percent.

In 1994, the American Legislative Exchange Council, the largest bipartisan association of state legislators, published a stunning analysis of prison populations and crime rates in all 50 states. The 10 states that increased their prison populations the most in relation to serious crimes between 1980 and 1992 cut their crime rates by an average of 19 percent. Meanwhile, the 10 states with the smallest increases in incarceration rates saw their crime rates go up by 9 percent on average.

In the 1980s, New Hampshire's legislature executed one of the sharpest policy reversals in the nation. For 20 years, legislators had added little new prison capacity, and the imprisonment rate—the number of prisoners per 1,000 crimes—declined by more than 80 percent, the third sharpest decline of any state. Meanwhile crime had soared by 579 percent, the highest increase in the nation.

All that changed after convicted killer Edward Coolidge, while serving a prison sentence of 25 to 40 years, was released after 18 years with "time off for good behavior." Coolidge had murdered Pamela Mason, a teenaged baby-sitter, and left her abused body in a snow bank. Outraged at his early release, Mason's family started a statewide petition drive for a "truth in sentencing" law to require convicts to serve their minimum sentences in full. Legislators passed the law in 1984 and appropriated $65 million for new prison construction. As a result, New Hampshire increased its incarceration rate between 1980 and 1992 more than any state. In the meantime, crime declined by 34 percent, the steepest drop in the nation.

> 8. *Families are the first line of defense, and we now know how to target and help children raised in our "cradles of crime."*

Experts agree that criminal behavior patterns crystallize by the age of eight, and sometimes much sooner. After age eight, youngsters are less likely to respond to correctional treatment as they gravitate toward truancy, street gangs, violent crime, and prison or early death. In Bellingham, Washington, Detective Steve Lance, who directs a police unit that targets serious habitual offenders who are juveniles, echoes: "If we wait until they're eight, it's too late. We've got to get them when they're *two.*"

Dozens of scientific studies back up the cop's street wisdom. For 60 years, criminologists and psychologists have tracked thousands of youngsters from early childhood into their adult years, identifying the risk factors and early warning signs of delinquency and persistent crime. In recent decades, they have carefully evaluated various early interventions and correctional treatments, comparing treated youngsters to matched groups of untreated ones, winnowing what works and what doesn't. Today we know that the typical "cradles of crime" are households headed by poor unwed mothers who bore their first children as teenagers and live on welfare, usually in public housing with others like them, with few law-abiding, employed male role models among them. Seventy percent of the juvenile offenders in our state reform institutions grew up in a household with only one parent or no parent at all. Children whose mothers are teenagers when they are born have a 10.3 percent chance of landing in jail as juveniles, triple that of children whose mothers bore them between the ages of 20 and 23.

A number of early-childhood intervention programs have been shown to knock many high-risk youngsters off the track to crime, prison, and possible early violent death:

New York   Syracuse University's Family Development Research Program experimented with a concentrated five-year child-care program for the group at highest risk for child-abuse and neglect complaints: poor, mostly single, pregnant teenagers who had not completed high school. Sixty-five of the women received prenatal health care and two years of weekly home visits by specialists who taught parenting skills, provided counseling in employ-ment and education, and encouraged friends and family to help. Until their children entered public school, they received free day care at the University Children's Center, which aims to develop children's intellectual abilities.

At age 15, the delinquency rate of these kids was 89 percent lower than that of a control group. Moreover, the few who had tangled with the law committed less serious and fewer offenses than their counterparts. The untreated youngsters had cost the criminal-justice system alone—excluding injuries or property losses to victims—$1,985 apiece, compared with $186 per treated child.

Michigan   David Weikart, a University of Michigan doctoral candidate, ran-domly chose for a two-year enrichment program 58 three- and four-year-old black children from a poor Ypsilanti neighborhood with a terrible school fail-ure rate. The program kids attended daily two-hour classes in small groups with a specialist in the teaching of language through play. Counselors visited their homes weekly to reinforce class activities and to teach the mothers parenting skills.

By the time they turned 27, the pre-schooled group earned higher grades and were more likely to have graduated, found well-paying jobs, and formed stable families than those in a control group. Even more sensational, the pre-schooled group averaged half the arrests of the control group, and only a fifth as many had been arrested five or more times. For every $1 spent on early enrichment, taxpayers realized $7.16 in benefits, mostly in savings from crimes prevented.

Quebec   Richard Trembley, a psychologist from the University of Montreal, tracked 104 of the most disruptive boys from 53 kindergartens. He gave 46 of the boys and their families two years of special training. Parents on average took part in 20 one-hour sessions in how to monitor their chil-dren's behavior, praise and punish effectively, and handle family crises. Their boys got 19 sessions in how to make friends, invite others to play, handle anger, respond to rejection and teasing, and follow rules. Five years later, when the boys were 12, the proportion of those who had been involved in gang mischief, a precursor of serious delinquency, was one-tenth that of the untreated youths.

The popular "Head Start" program was also modeled on the Ypsilanti experiment's successes. But, says James Q. Wilson, a political scientist at UCLA, bureaucrats and policymakers "stripped it down to the part that was the most popular, least expensive, and easiest to run, namely, pre-school education. Absent from much of Head Start are the high teacher-to-child caseloads, the extensive home visits, and the elaborate parent training—the very things that probably account for much of the success of these programs."

A National Strategy

In outline, a strategy for reducing crime through prevention and punishment would look like this: We should identify the families—mostly households started by unwed teenage mothers—that are likely to be "cradles of crime." For a modest investment, we can sharply reduce the likelihood that their children will engage in persistent criminality by providing educational enrichment, parenting advice, and training in disciplined behavior. In pre-school or first or second grades, we can apply screening techniques at school to find those youngsters with a high risk of troubled futures. At the first contact with police, we should begin keeping permanent records. At the second offense, at the latest, we should bring to bear our best efforts at intensive supervision and family intervention, and impose the first of a series of unequivocal and escalating sanctions. Jailing serious three-time offenders would be a prudent alternative to suffering the millions of crimes habitual criminals perpetrate each year. We should insist that police and prosecutors learn to identify and pursue repeat offenders aggressively. We should hold judges and parole boards accountable for sentencing and incarcerating those felons for whom intervention has come too late, and we should not shrink from investing in the prison space needed to keep recidivists off the streets for good.

It is both humane and smart to turn delinquent youngsters away from a path of crime early, but in cases where all these efforts ultimately fail, in the words of the late sociologist Robert Martinson, "Lock 'em up and weld the door shut!" Our crime rates will plummet.

NO

David Shichor

Three Strikes As a Public Policy

This article analyzes the theoretical principles of the recently legislated "three strikes and you're out" laws. In many respects, these are related to the "new penology" that shifted the focus of criminological and penological interest from the individual offender toward the control of aggregates. Furthermore, the analysis relates the three-strikes measures to the cultural model of the "McDonaldization" of society in which the principles of the fast-food restaurant dominate many aspects of American society. These principles include efficiency, calculability, predictability, and control mainly by nonhuman technology. The analysis in this article, which focuses especially on the three-strikes law in California, suggests that three-strikes laws can be viewed as a part of the McDonaldization trend.

Introduction

Street crime has become one of the major public concerns in the United States during the past two decades. In response to it, several "war on crime" campaigns have been waged since the 1970s, and there is a growing public demand to get "tough on crime" and to get even tougher on violent and repeating criminals. . . . In the spring of 1994, the U.S. prison population passed the 1 million mark and the nation gained the dubious honor of having the highest incarceration rate in the world. By 1996, the U.S. jail and prison population was around the 1.5 million mark.

. . . [T]he Violent Crime Control and Law Enforcement Act, also known as the Federal Crime Bill, was enacted by Congress [in 1994]. Among other things, this law "mandates life in prison for criminals convicted of three violent felonies or drug offenses if the third conviction is a federal crime." It became labeled, using the popular baseball lingo, as the "three strikes and you're out" law. Several states followed suit and enacted similar measures. One of those mentioned most often was the California mandatory sentencing law, which came into effect in March 1994 and prescribes that "felons found guilty of a third serious crime be locked up for 25 years to life." . . .

This article focuses on the "three-strikes" laws in general with particular emphasis on the California measure because that law has been the most

From David Shichor, "Three Strikes As a Public Policy: The Convergence of the New Penology and the McDonaldization of Punishment," *Crime & Delinquency*, vol. 43, no. 4 (September 1997). Copyright © 1997 by Sage Publications, Inc. Reprinted by permission. Notes and some references omitted.

scrutinized and quoted in the professional literature so far. Although there are differences in some of details among the various three-strikes laws, their main aims and principles are similar.

Several scholars maintain that recent penal thinking and the ensuing policies have gone through a major paradigm change. According to them, a "new penology" has emerged shifting the traditional penological concern that focused on the individual offender to an actuarial model focusing on the management of aggregates. . . .

The analysis to follow examines three-strikes laws in relation to the new penology and in relation to their connections to a more general socio-cultural orientation, identified by Ritzer (1993) as the "McDonaldization" of society, based on the rationalization process suggested by Max Weber (one of the pioneers of sociological thought), that is embodied in the model of fast-food restaurants. . . .

Three Strikes and the New Penology

. . . The change from penal policies aimed at punishment and rehabilitation of individuals to the management and control of certain categories of people has followed the pessimism expressed about the criminal justice system's ability to change offenders, making them into law-abiding citizens. In this vein, Bottoms noted that "the abandonment of the rehabilitative ethic has led to a widespread abandonment of hope" because the idea of rehabilitation was an expression of optimism about human nature and about the ability of social organizations to bring out the positive in people. The new penology takes for granted that a high level of criminal behavior will continue to occur, and its concern is how to manage the criminal justice system efficiently rather than to effect major changes in crime rates or to bring about rehabilitation of a significant number of offenders.

The new penology has rekindled the historical notion of "dangerous classes" that traditionally has been linked to the urban poor. Feeley and Simon (1992) claimed that the new penology is oriented toward the management of a "permanently dangerous population." Their description of this population parallels Wilson's (1987) depiction of the "underclass," which, because of the social realities of capitalist industrial societies in which production is based on a high level of technology and a reduction of manual labor, became a marginal population, unemployable, lacking in adequate education and marketable skills, and without any real prospects or hope to change its situation. . . .

The new penal approach, focusing on the control and management of specific aggregates, has made increasing use of actuarial methods that rely heavily on statistical decision theory, operations research techniques, and system analysis to devise and implement penal policies. These reflect the positivist orientation in criminology that concentrates on "methods, techniques, or rules of procedure" rather than on "substantive theory or perspectives." . . .

Three-strikes laws have historical roots in American penology. . . . They are based on the penal principle of incapacitation. . . . In theory, three-strikes laws were meant to target repeating violent and dangerous felons, similar to "selective incapacitation" strategies. . . .

Simon and Feeley (1994) criticized the three-strikes measures, stating, "This spate of three-strikes laws as well as other types of mandatory sentences can easily be characterized as mindless 'spending sprees' or 'throwing money at a problem' without likelihood of benefit." . . .

The McDonaldization of Punishment

In a recent book, Ritzer (1993) used the analogy of fast-food establishments to characterize and analyze the social and cultural ethos of modern technological societies, particularly that of the United States. He defined McDonaldization as "the process by which the principles of the fast-food restaurant are coming to dominate more and more sectors of American society as well as the rest of the world." This process also has a major impact on the social control policies of these societies. The theoretical underpinnings of the three-strikes measures, their definitions of strikeable offenses, and the wide-scale public support of these types of legislation are closely related to, and are influenced by, McDonaldazation.

In this model, which is based on the Weberian concept of "formal rationality" (Weber 1968), there are four basic dimensions of the fast-food industry: efficiency, calculability, predictability, and control. Efficiency refers to the tendency to choose the optimum means to a given end, calculability is identified as the tendency to quantify and calculate every product and to use quantity as a measure of quality, predictability has to do with the preference to know what to expect in all situations at all times, and control involves the replacement of human technology with nonhuman technology in a way that goods, services, products, and workers are better controlled. Ritzer (1993) suggested that there are various degrees of McDonaldization and that some phenomena are more McDonaldized than others. As mentioned previously, the contention of this article is that three-strikes laws are promoting punishment policies in accordance with this model. . . .

The Irrational Consequences of McDonaldization in Penology

Three-strikes laws and McDonaldization are phenomena of modernization that put a high value on rationality. However, although McDonaldization represents rationalism (i.e., scientific approach, positivism, modernity), it also leads to irrational consequences. Borrowing from Weber's concept of the "iron cage of rationality," Ritzer referred to these consequences as the "irrationality of rationality." In the case of McDonaldization, irrationalities may result in inefficiency, incalculability, unpredictability, and lack of control, which may have serious effects on penal policies and practices.

Inefficiency

One of the inefficiencies of fast-food sites is that although they are meant to be "fast," often long lines of people have to wait to be served (Ritzer 1993). In the criminal justice system, three-strikes laws contribute to the clogging up of courts and the overcrowding of confinement facilities. The measure also seems to have had a major impact on the number of cases that go to trial. In California before the new law came into effect in March 1994, about 90% to 94% of all criminal cases were settled through plea bargaining. But in the summer of that year, Santa Clara County projected a 160% increase in the number of criminal trials. In an assessment of the preliminary impacts of the three-strikes implementation for the first eight months, the California Legislative Analyst's Office (1995b) found a 144% increase in jury trials in Los Angeles County. In San Diego County, it is expected that there will be a 300% increase in jury trials. The decline in plea bargaining is the result of the mandatory aspect of the three-strikes law. Many offenders feel that they cannot gain much from a negotiated settlement under the new law and that it is preferable to exercise their constitutional right to jury trials without increasing their risks of substantially more severe sentences. The increase in the number of trials not only has affected the three-strikes cases but also has caused delays in non-strike criminal and civil cases. For example, Los Angeles district attorney transferred a large number of attorneys who previously were handling white-collar cases to work on three-strikes offenses.

The growing backlog in the courts also has had an impact on county jails because more suspects are detained for longer periods of time prior to their trials. . . .

Another efficiency issue is concerned with the type of offenders handled by the three-strikes law. This law was enacted to curb violent crime, or at least "serious" crime, through the incapacitation of "dangerous" and violent criminals. However, early findings in California indicate that most offenders prosecuted and convicted under this measure have been brought into the system for nonviolent offenses. Furthermore, this measure inevitably will increase the numbers of elderly inmates in prisons because of the long terms mandated in this legislation. In 1994, inmates age 50 years or older represented about 4% of the California prison population, but it was estimated that by 2005 they will constitute around 12% of the inmates. . . .

According to all indications, the three-strikes law will increase considerably the cost of criminal justice operations because (a) more people will be detained in jails, (b) the increase in the number of trials will necessitate the building of more courts and the hiring of more judges and other court personnel, (c) the number of long-term prisoners will grow and so more prisons will have to be built, (d) the growing number of elderly prisoners will need additional (and more expensive) health care than prisons usually provide, and (e) welfare agencies will have to support a larger number of dependents of incarcerated felons for longer periods of time than ever before.

. . . Greenwood et al. (1994) projected that, in California, "to support the implementation of the law, total spending for higher education and other services would have to fall by more than 40 percent over the next 8 years."

Incalculability

The outcomes of three-strikes cases, which were supposedly easily calculable, often are not so. . . .

For example, because of overcrowding of jails by detainees who were reluctant to plea bargain, many minor offenders have been released early from jail, and a large number of misdemeanants have not even been prosecuted. Thus, the calculability of punishment for minor offenders has been neglected and even sacrificed for that of three-strikes offenders. In other instances, some arrests that could have been qualified as three-strikes cases have been processed as parole violations rather than new offenses and, thus, were not considered as felonies. In other cases, prosecutors and judges have ignored some previous felonies or redefined them as nonstrike offenses. . . .

[L]ittle concern has been paid to the concept of justice that requires a balance between the seriousness of the crime and the severity of punishment. In 1994, a California offender was sentenced to prison for 25 years to life for grabbing a slice of pepperoni pizza from a youngster (this sentence was reduced in January 1997, and he will be released by 1999). Another offender received 30 years to life for stealing a video recorder and a coin collection. Still another three-striker got 25 years to life for stealing a package of meat worth $5.62, apparently to feed his family. More recently, a heroin addict with a record of previous theft-related offenses was sentenced to 25 years to life for stealing two pair of jeans worth $80 from a store. . . . Similarly, another aspect of justice, equal treatment, is being neglected because three-strikes measures focus almost exclusively on street crimes that usually are committed by poor offenders. Meanwhile, crimes of the middle and upper classes either are not affected or will be handled even more leniently than before because the criminal justice system that is overoccupied by predatory street crimes will have diminishing resources to deal with them. . . . Thus, the implementation of this measure will increase perceptions, which already are pervasive among many, that the criminal justice system is biased, discriminatory, and unjust.

Another factor that adds to the incalculability of this measure is that it is not applied uniformly. Data pertaining to the first six months of implementation compiled by the Los Angeles Public Defender's Office indicate that minorities with criminal histories comparable to those of White offenders were being charged under the three-strikes law at 17 times the rate of Whites. . . .

Unpredictability

Several of the issues concerning predictability resemble those that emerged in relation to efficiency and calculability. For various reasons, the outcomes of three-strikes cases are not as clearly predictable as they were intended to be, based on this law's mandatory and determinate nature. For example, in some instances victims refuse to testify when the convictions would carry sentences of long-term incarceration under the three-strikes law. In other cases, juries may fail to convict for the same reason. . . .

[B]ecause of jail overcrowding caused by the growing numbers of detainees waiting for trials, many sheriff departments release minor offenders early to ease the situation. Sometimes this is done because of court orders that limit facility crowding. According to court sources, in Los Angeles County, misdemeanor offenders sentenced to one year in jail are serving on the average only 19 days. Thus, the implementation of the three-strikes law, instead of increasing the predictability of punishment, may have an opposite impact in non-strike cases. Moreover, . . . the outcome of a case under this law may be entirely different from what was foreseen because juries may refuse to convict, authorities may refuse to press a felony charge, or the courts may not count previous felonies. Also, by decreasing considerably the number of plea bargains and by increasing the number of jury trials, a larger number of outcomes may become unpredictable. Although plea bargaining should not be considered as the best method of dispensing justice, it does provide a certain level of predictability. . . .

[T]hree-strikes laws cannot predict, and are not interested in predicting, the effects of the punishment on individual convicts, and they may waste a great deal of money, time, and effort on false positives by keeping those who would not cause further harm to society incarcerated for long periods of time. . . . Three-strikes legislation was based on the assumption that the high rate of criminal behavior of "dangerous" offenders already has been proven; however, many times it is dependent on how the offenders' criminal records are being used by the prosecution and the courts. . . .

Lack of Control

Rational systems often can spin out of the control of those who devise and use them (Ritzer 1993). Sentencing based on an almost automatic decision-making system drastically reduces the court's authority to consider particular circumstances of offenses and individual differences among offenders. However, there are experts who maintain that to render a high quality of justice, a certain degree of judicial discretion is essential. . . .

There also is the issue of "hidden discretion"; that is, whereas the court's decision-making power in the imposition of punishment is severely curtailed, the discretion of law enforcement, and especially that of the prosecution, increases greatly. The charges brought against a suspect will be determined by these agencies. The major discretionary decision in many instances will be whether a case should be filed as a misdemeanor or a felony, which bears directly on the application of three-strikes laws. . . . [T]he ability of the judicial system to control the imposition and administration of the law will be affected. In many instances, the lack of control will stem not from the latitude in sentencing but rather from the growing discretionary powers given to agencies in the pretrial stages of the criminal justice process. Because of the reduced visibility of decision making in the determination of charges, in many cases sentencing disparities among jurisdictions may become even greater in spite of the promise of increased control over such differences under three-strikes laws.

. . . Many three-strikes cases involve property offenders and drug abusers rather than vicious, violent criminals. . . .

Conclusion

The three-strikes laws that have spread recently in the United States are a reaction to a moral panic that has swept the country since the late 1970s. On the public policy level, these measures can be viewed as being related to the new penology trend. They are based on the concern for managing aggregates of "dangerous" people rather than being concerned with rendering justice, protecting the community, or attempting to rehabilitate individual offenders. The emphasis is on rational criminal justice operations that apply management methods based on statistical estimates of patterns of crimes and future inmate populations, risk indicators of future criminal behavior, operations research, and system analysis.

Three-strikes laws also are in line with the modern sociocultural ethos of McDonaldization (Ritzer 1993), a model built on the principles of rationality embodying an attitude that "it is possible to calculate and purposively manipulate the environment." However, the quest for extreme rationality can lead to irrationalities in the practical workings of this model. Often, the application of three-strikes laws results in inefficiency of the criminal justice process, punishments are not always clearly calculable, predictability of outcomes may be negatively affected by rational procedures, and the system may lose control over the nature of punishment. In short, as is the case with many other public policies, three-strikes laws could lead to a host of unintended consequences that may defeat the purposes for which they were intended. Probably, the greatest irrationality of the penal policy represented by three-strikes laws is their tremendous economic cost. . . . In sum, it seems that, as Ritzer claimed, modern contemporary society is locked into the "iron cage of rationality," which is characterized by policies made on a rational basis that lead to irrational consequences. This is demonstrated in current penal policies.

References

Greenwood, Peter W., C. Peter Rydell, Allan F. Abrahamse, Jonathan P. Caulkins, James Chiesa, Karyn E. Model, and Stephen P. Klein. 1994 *Three Strikes and You re Out: Estimated Benefits and Costs of California s New Mandatory Sentencing Law.* Santa Monica, CA: RAND.

Irwin, John and James Austin. 1994. *It Is About Time: America s Imprisonment Binge.* Belmont, CA: Wadsworth.

Kramer, John H. and Jeffery T. Ulmer. 1996. "Sentencing Disparity and Departures From Guidelines." *Justice Quarterly* 13:81–105.

McCarthy, Nancy. 1995. "A Year Later, '3 Strikes' Clogs Jails, Slows Trials." *California Bar Journal,* March: 1, 6–7.

Ritzer, George. 1993. *The McDonaldization of Society.* Newbury Park, CA: Pine Forge.

Saint-Germain, Michelle A. and Robert A. Calamia. 1996. "Three Strikes and You're In: A Streams and Windows Model Incremental Policy Change." *Journal of Criminal Justice* 24:57–70.

Shichor, David and Dale K. Sechrest. 1996. "Three Strikes as Public Policy: Future Implications." Pp. 265–77 in *Three Strikes and You're Out: Vengeance as Public Policy*, edited by D. Shichor and D. K. Sechrest. Thousand Oaks, CA: Sage.

Turner, Michael G., Jody L. Sundt, Brandon K. Applegate, and Francis T. Cullen. 1995. "'Three Strikes and You're Out' Legislation: A National Assessment." *Federal Probation* 59 (3): 16–35.

Weber, Max. 1968. *Economy and Society*. Totowa, NJ: Bedminster.

POSTSCRIPT

Do Three Strikes Sentencing Laws and Other "Get Tough" Approaches Really Work?

Before three strikes, most states already had provisions for enhancing sentences for those with prior serious convictions. However, with the passage of three strikes, life or lengthy sentences after a third violent felony conviction became mandatory. However, exactly which felonies are "third strikeable"; the number of inmates incarcerated under this mandate; negative consequences such as jail overcrowding due to offenders opting to go to trial instead of plea bargaining, which would automatically result in life or lengthy sentences with no hope of parole; and the reluctance of prosecutors to charge offenders who might face life after committing a relatively minor felony are remarkably inconsistent from state to state.

The two states that initially passed three strikes, Washington and California, have had radically different experiences. For example, Washington has had only 86 inmates incarcerated under this provision, while California has had over 26,000. The issue of fairness of law is self-evident from these statistics as well as racial, economic, and other disparities identified by Shichor. Yet defenders of three strikes point out that in a democracy, citizens have a right to pass legislation that they feel will protect them. Even if there are extreme cases, such as receiving a life sentence for stealing a slice of pizza, people still have that right.

Some suggest that criminologists who ridicule the severity of assaults are being arrogant by trivializing possible harms experienced by those whose personal space was invaded. Moreover, the examples that Methvin cites of horrible crimes committed by individuals with several prior, equally terrible felonies—who, if three strikes had been applied, could not have done additional harm—can easily be multiplied. They would probably far exceed the examples that Shichor gives of life sentences resulting from "minor" acts of violence.

Two striking cases involving repeat offenders include the 1994 murder of 7-year-old Megan Kanga by two-time convicted offender Jesse Timmendequas and the 1978 case in which violent felon Lawrence Singleton chopped off a 15-year-old California girl's arms after raping her. He served less than 10 years and was recently convicted of first-degree murder in Florida. These cases are troubling. What may be equally troubling, however, as Shichor illustrates, is that a significant number of "striked" criminals (at least in California) were not convicted on their third offense of *violent* felonies. Moreover, thus far it is unclear whether or not the policy has resulted in a net lowering of crime rates. Most studies indicate that the law, its applications, and its consequences are uneven.

Recent studies by Shichor include "Private Prisons, Criminological Research, and Conflict of Interest: A Case Study," coauthored by G. Geis and A. Mobley, *Crime and Delinquency* (July 1999) and *Privatization in Criminal Justice: Past, Present, and Future* coedited by M. J. Gilbert (Anderson, 2000). For a current debate on the effectiveness of incarceration and the allegation that nonviolent offenders are being sentenced to longer terms than violent ones, see "Alternative Sanctions: Diverting Nonviolent Prisoners to Intermediate Sanctions," by J. Petersilia, as well as comments by J. J. DiIulio, Jr., and N. Morris, in E. L. Rubin, ed., *Minimizing Harm: A New Crime Policy for Modern America* (Westview Press, 1999). In an apparent modification of his support of three strikes and other get-tough approaches, DiIulio has commented that locking offenders up is reaching a point of "diminishing returns." See W. Raspberry, "Conveyor-Belt Justice," *The Washington Post* (April 5, 1999).

An outstanding book that is already being widely discussed and that supports the view that getting tough on criminals has backfired is J. May, ed., *Building Violence: How America's Rush to Incarcerate Creates More Violence* (Sage Publications, 2000). An excellent work that examines the unanticipated negative consequences of current crime policies for women and children is S. L. Miller, ed., *Crime Control and Women: Feminist Implications of Criminal Justice Policy* (Sage Publications, 1998).

Excellent overviews of three-strikes laws are "Three Strikes and You're Out: A Review of State Legislation," by J. Clark et al., *National Institute of Justice* (September 1997); "Striking Out: The Crime Control Impact of 'Three-Strikes' Laws," by V. Schiraldi and T. Ambrosio, *The Justice Policy Institute* (March 1997); *Three Strikes and You're Out: Vengeance as Public Policy* edited by D. Shichor and E. K. Sechrest (Sage Publications, 1996); and *The Tough-On-Crime Myth* by P. Elikann (Plenum, 1996).

Another helpful study is "Assessing Public Support for Three-Strikes-and-You're-Out Laws," by F. Cullen et al., *Crime and Delinquency* (October 1996). Sources agreeing with Methvin are B. Jones, "California's Three-Strikes Law Has Made Big Cuts in Crime," *The New York Times* (April 20, 1995) and *Body Count* by J. J. DiIulio, Jr., et al. (Simon & Schuster, 1996). For a critique of the get-tough movement, see "Science and the Punishment/Control Movement," by T. Clear, *Social Pathology* (Spring 1996). For an update of his thesis, see G. Ritzer's *The McDonaldization Thesis: Explorations and Extensions* (Sage Publications, 1998). For charges that the National Institute of Justice (NIJ) censored a critical study of the three-strikes policy, see S. Glass, "Anatomy of a Policy Fraud," *The New Republic* (November 17, 1997).

Should Juries Be Able to Disregard the Law and Free "Guilty" Persons in Racially Charged Cases?

YES: Paul Butler, from "Racially Based Jury Nullification: Black Power in the Criminal Justice System," *Yale Law Journal* (December 1995)

NO: Randall Kennedy, from "After the Cheers," *The New Republic* (October 23, 1995)

ISSUE SUMMARY

YES: Paul Butler, an associate professor at the George Washington University Law School, notes that a vastly disproportionate number of blacks in America are under the auspices of the criminal justice system. In order to balance the scales of justice, he argues, black jurors should acquit black defendants of certain crimes, regardless of whether or not they perceive the defendant to be guilty.

NO: Randall Kennedy, a professor at the Harvard Law School, in examining the acquittal of O. J. Simpson, finds it tragic that black jurors would pronounce a murderer "not guilty" just to send a message to white people. He maintains that, although racism among the police and others is deplorable, allowing black criminals to go free does not help minorities, particularly since their victims are likely to be other blacks.

The man that is not prejudiced against a horse thief is not fit to sit on a jury in this town.
—George Bernard Shaw (1856–1950)

The jury system of justice in the United States is considered by many to be sacred. Some 200,000 criminal and civil trials are decided by approximately 2 million jurors each year. Although the vast majority of cases do not go to trial, the symbolic importance of jury trials is great.

In theory, during a trial, the judge decides on correct legal procedures and matters of legal interpretation, while juries decide, based on the evidence, the guilt or innocence of the defendant. Generally, a person accused of a felony (a serious crime) or a misdemeanor in which a sentence of six months or more is possible, could request a jury trial. In all but six states and in the federal courts, juries consist of 12 jurors. In most states, a conviction must be by unanimous decision. Judges can sometimes set aside guilty verdicts that they feel are unfair, but verdicts of not guilty can never be changed.

The jury system is not without its critics. Many have expressed concern that juries do not always consist of the defendant's peers. In many states, for example, women were not allowed to serve on juries until relatively recently. Blacks and other minorities were either directly blocked from serving or were kept off juries by the jury selection process itself. Furthermore, in most states jurors were drawn from voter registrations, which meant that the poor—for whom political elections are frequently not of great concern—were disproportionately underrepresented. In many states, attorneys could exclude blacks from serving on juries. But in *Batson v. Kentucky* (1986), the U.S. Supreme Court ruled that jurors could not be challenged solely on the basis of their race.

Jury nullification—in which a jury acquits a criminal defendant even though guilt has been proven—can be seen throughout U.S. history. Before the Revolutionary War, for example, some juries acquitted men who they felt were being treated unfairly by the British. Many northern juries refused to convict people accused of aiding runaway slaves. And juries have acquitted defendants because they felt that the police or prosecutors were bullying or unfairly treating them. Note that in these examples, the justification for nullification seems to be based on the juries' sense of justice, not on the guilt or innocence of the defendant.

However, not all historical instances of jury nullification are what would likely be considered noble reasons. For instance, until not long ago, very few whites accused of killing blacks were ever found guilty in many parts of the United States. None until the 1960s were ever sentenced to death for killing a black person. Few who participated in black lynchings were even charged with a crime, and the few who were always got off.

In the following selections, Paul Butler—despite jury nullification's checkered past—encourages jurors to acquit black defendants in many cases to remedy past and current discrimination in the criminal justice system. Randall Kennedy argues that the "need to convict a murderer" and the "need to protest the intolerability of official racism" must remain separate if either need is to be met. He maintains that promoting jury nullification as a legitimate way to right racial wrongs will only worsen the crime situation in black communities. As you read this debate consider what unanticipated consequences, both positive and negative, might arise if jury nullification is widely accepted.

YES

Paul Butler

Racially Based Jury Nullification: Black Power in the Criminal Justice System

In 1990 I was a Special Assistant United States Attorney in the District of Columbia. I prosecuted people accused of misdemeanor crimes, mainly the drug and gun cases that overwhelm the local courts of most American cities. As a federal prosecutor, I represented the United States of America and used that power to put people, mainly African-American men, in prison. I am also an African-American man. During that time, I made two discoveries that profoundly changed the way I viewed my work as a prosecutor and my responsibilities as a black person.

The first discovery occurred during a training session for new assistants conducted by experienced prosecutors. We rookies were informed that we would lose many of our cases, despite having persuaded a jury beyond a reasonable doubt that the defendant was guilty. We would lose because some black jurors would refuse to convict black defendants who they knew were guilty.

The second discovery was related to the first but was even more unsettling. It occurred during the trial of Marion Barry, then the second-term mayor of the District of Columbia. Barry was being prosecuted by my office for drug possession and perjury. I learned, to my surprise, that some of my fellow African-American prosecutors hoped that the mayor would be acquitted, despite the fact that he was obviously guilty of at least one of the charges—an FBI videotape plainly showed him smoking crack cocaine. These black prosecutors wanted their office to lose its case because they believed that the prosecution of Barry was racist.

There is an increasing perception that some African-American jurors vote to acquit black defendants for racial reasons, sometimes explained as the juror's desire not to send another black man to jail. There is considerable disagreement over whether it is appropriate for a black juror to do so. I now believe that, for pragmatic and political reasons, the black community is better off when some non-violent lawbreakers remain in the community rather than go to prison. The decision as to what kind of conduct by African Americans ought to be punished is better made by African Americans, based on their understanding of the costs and benefits to their community, than by the traditional criminal justice process, which is controlled by white lawmakers and white law enforcers. Legally, African-American jurors who sit in judgment of African-American accused persons have the power to make that decision. Considering the costs of law enforcement to the black community, and the failure of white lawmakers to come up with any solutions to black antisocial conduct other than incarceration, it is, in fact, the moral responsibility of black jurors to emancipate some guilty black outlaws.

⋆◈⋆

Why would a black juror vote to let a guilty person go free? Assuming the juror is a rational, self-interested actor, she must believe that she is better off with the defendant out of prison than in prison. But how could any rational person believe that about a criminal?

Imagine a country in which a third of the young male citizens are under the supervision of the criminal justice system—either awaiting trial, in prison, or on probation or parole. Imagine a country in which two-thirds of the men can anticipate being arrested before they reach age thirty. Imagine a country in which there are more young men in prison than in college.

The country imagined above is a police state. When we think of a police state, we think of a society whose fundamental problem lies not with the citizens of the state but rather with the form of government, and with the powerful elites in whose interest the state exists. Similarly, racial critics of American criminal justice locate the problem not with the black prisoners but with the state and its actors and beneficiaries.

The black community also bears very real costs by having so many African Americans, particularly males, incarcerated or otherwise involved in the criminal justice system. These costs are both social and economic, and they include the large percentage of black children who live in female-headed, single-parent households; a perceived dearth of men "eligible" for marriage; the lack of male role models for black children, especially boys; the absence of wealth in the black community; and the large unemployment rate among black men.

According to a recent *USA Today/CNN/Gallup* poll, 66 percent of blacks believe that the criminal justice system is racist and only 32 percent believe it is not racist. Interestingly, other polls suggest that blacks also tend to be more worried about crime than whites; this seems logical when one considers that blacks are more likely to be victims of crime. This enhanced concern, however, does not appear to translate to black support for tougher enforcement of criminal law. For example, substantially fewer blacks than whites support the death penalty, and many more blacks than whites were concerned with the potential racial consequences of the strict provisions of last year's crime bill. Along with significant evidence from popular culture, these polls suggest that a substantial portion of the African-American community sympathizes with racial critiques of the criminal justice system.

African-American jurors who endorse these critiques are in a unique position to act on their beliefs when they sit in judgment of a black defendant. As jurors, they have the power to convict the accused person or to set him free. May the responsible exercise of that power include voting to free a black defendant who the juror believes is guilty? The answer is "yes," based on the legal doctrine known as jury nullification.

Jury nullification occurs when a jury acquits a defendant who it believes is guilty of the crime with which he is charged. In finding the defendant not guilty, the jury ignores the facts of the case and/or the judge's instructions regarding the law. Instead, the jury votes its conscience.

The prerogative of juries to nullify has been part of English and American law for centuries. There are well-known cases from the Revolutionary War era when American patriots were charged with political crimes by the British crown and acquitted by American juries. Black slaves who escaped to the North and were prosecuted for violation of the Fugitive Slave Law were freed by Northern juries with abolitionist sentiments. Some Southern juries refused to punish white violence against African Americans, especially black men accused of crimes against white women.

The Supreme Court has officially disapproved of jury nullification but has conceded that it has no power to prohibit jurors from engaging in it; the Bill of Rights does not allow verdicts of acquittal to be reversed, regardless of the reason for the acquittal. Criticism of nullification has centered on its potential for abuse. The criticism suggests that when twelve members of a jury vote their conscience instead of the law, they corrupt the rule of law and undermine the democratic principles that made the law.

There is no question that jury nullification is subversive of the rule of law. Nonetheless, most legal historians agree that it was morally appropriate in the cases of the white American revolutionaries and the runaway slaves. The issue, then, is whether African Americans today have the moral right to engage in this same subversion.

Most moral justifications of the obligation to obey the law are based on theories of "fair play." Citizens benefit from the rule of law; that is why it is just that they are burdened with the requirement to follow it. Yet most blacks are aware of countless historical examples in which African Americans were not afforded the benefit of the rule of law: think, for example, of the existence of slavery in a republic purportedly dedicated to the proposition that all men are created equal, or the law's support of state-sponsored segregation even after the Fourteenth Amendment guaranteed blacks equal protection. That the rule of law ultimately corrected some of the large holes in the American fabric is evidence more of its malleability than its goodness; the rule of law previously had justified the holes.

If the rule of law is a myth, or at least not valid for African Americans, the argument that jury nullification undermines it loses force. The black juror is simply another actor in the system, using her power to fashion a particular outcome. The juror's act of nullification—like the act of the citizen who dials 911 to report Ricky but not Bob, or the police officer who arrests Lisa but not Mary, or the prosecutor who charges Kwame but not Brad, or the judge who finds that Nancy was illegally entrapped but Verna was not—exposes the indeterminacy of law but does not in itself create it.

A similar argument can be made regarding the criticism that jury nullification is anti-democratic. This is precisely why many African Americans endorse it; it is perhaps the only legal power black people have to escape the tyranny of the majority. Black people have had to beg white decision makers for most of the rights they have: the right not to be slaves, the right to vote, the right to attend an integrated school. Now black people are begging white people to preserve programs that help black children to eat and black businesses to survive. Jury nullification affords African Americans the power to determine justice for themselves in individual cases, regardless of whether white people agree or even understand.

❧

At this point, African Americans should ask themselves whether the operation of the criminal law system in the United States advances the interests of black people. If it does not, the doctrine of jury nullification affords African-American jurors the opportunity to exercise the authority of the law over some African-American criminal defendants. In essence, black people can "opt out" of American criminal law.

How far should they go—completely to anarchy, or is there someplace between here and there that is safer than both? I propose the following: African-American jurors should approach their work cognizant of its political nature and of their prerogative to exercise their power in the best interests of the black community. In every case, the juror should be guided by her view of what is "just." (I have more faith, I should add, in the average black juror's idea of justice than I do in the idea that is embodied in the "rule of law.")

In cases involving violent *malum in se* (inherently bad) crimes, such as murder, rape, and assault, jurors should consider the case strictly on the evidence presented, and if they believe the accused person is guilty, they should so vote. In cases involving non-violent, *malum prohibitum* (legally proscribed) offenses, including "victimless" crimes such as narcotics possession, there should be a presumption in favor of nullification. Finally, for non-violent, *malum in se* crimes, such as theft or perjury, there need be no presumption in favor of nullification, but it ought to be an option the juror considers. A juror might vote for acquittal, for example, when a poor woman steals from Tiffany's but not when the same woman steals from her next-door neighbor.

How would a juror decide individual cases under my proposal? Easy cases would include a defendant who has possessed crack cocaine and an abusive husband who kills his wife. The former should be acquitted and the latter should go to prison.

Difficult scenarios would include the drug dealer who operates in the ghetto and the thief who burglarizes the home of a rich white family. Under my proposal, nullification is presumed in the first case because drug distribution is a non-violent *malum prohibitum* offense. Is nullification morally justifiable here? It depends. There is no question that encouraging people to engage in self-destructive behavior is evil; the question the juror should ask herself is whether the remedy is less evil. (The juror should also remember that the criminal law does not punish those ghetto drug dealers who cause the most injury: liquor store owners.)

As for the burglar who steals from the rich white family, the case is troubling, first of all, because the conduct is so clearly "wrong." Since it is a non-violent *malum in se* crime, there is no presumption in favor of nullification, but it is an option for consideration. Here again, the facts of the case are relevant. For example, if the offense was committed to support a drug habit, I think there is a moral case to be made for nullification, at least until such time as access to drug-rehabilitation services are available to all.

Why would a juror be inclined to follow my proposal? There is no guarantee that she would. But when we perceive that black jurors are already nullifying on the basis of racial critiques (i.e., refusing to send another black man to jail), we recognize that these jurors are willing to use their power in a politically conscious manner. Further, it appears that some black jurors now excuse some conduct—like murder—that they should not excuse. My proposal provides a principled structure of the exercise of the black juror's vote. I am not encouraging anarchy; rather I am reminding black jurors of their privilege to serve a calling higher than law: justice.

I concede that the justice my proposal achieves is rough. It is as susceptible to human foibles as the jury system. But I am sufficiently optimistic that my proposal will be only an intermediate plan, a stopping point between the status quo and real justice. To get to that better, middle ground, I hope that this [selection] will encourage African Americans to use responsibly the power they already have.

Randall Kennedy

NO

After the Cheers

The acquittal of O. J. Simpson brings to an end an extraordinary criminal trial that attracted, like a magnet, anxieties over crime, sex, race and the possibility of reaching truth and dispensing justice in an American courtroom. The verdict is difficult to interpret since juries are not required to give reasons for the conclusions they reach and since, even if jurors do articulate their reasons, there remains the problem of deciphering them and distinguishing expressed views from real bases of decision.

My own view is that the verdict represents a combination of three beliefs. One is that the prosecution simply failed to prove that O. J. Simpson was guilty beyond a reasonable doubt. Reasonable people could come to this conclusion. After all, police investigators displayed remarkable incompetence, the prosecution erred mightily—remember the gloves that did not fit!—and, of course, there was the despicable [police officer] Mark Fuhrman. Even with help given by several questionable judicial rulings before the trial and near the end, the prosecution did permit a reasonable juror to vote to acquit on the basis of the evidence presented. I disagree with that conclusion. But I do concede that it could be reached reasonably and in good faith.

If this belief is what prompted the decision of all twelve of the jurors who acquitted Simpson, their decision has little broader cultural significance than that reasonable jurors sometimes come to different conclusions than those which many observers favor. I doubt, though, that this belief was the only or even the dominant predicate for the acquittal. I say this based on what I have heard many people say and write about the evidence presented at the trial and also on the remarkably short time that the jury deliberated. If the jury was at all representative of the American public, particularly that sector of the public which leaned toward acquittal, it was probably influenced considerably by two other beliefs.

The first is characterized by an unreasonable suspicion of law enforcement authorities. This is the thinking of people who would have voted to acquit O. J. Simpson even in the absence of Mark Fuhrman's racism and the L.A. police department's incompetence and even in the face of evidence that was more incriminating than that which was produced at trial. There is a paranoid, conspiracy-minded sector of the population that would honestly though irrationally have rejected the state's argument virtually without

From Randall Kennedy, "After the Cheers," *The New Republic* (October 23, 1995). Copyright © 1995 by The New Republic, Inc. Reprinted by permission.

regard to the evidence. One of the things that nourishes much of this community, particularly that part comprised of African Americans, is a vivid and bitter memory of wrongful convictions of innocent black men and wrongful acquittals of guilty white men. A key example of the former were the convictions of the Scottsboro Boys in the 1930s for allegedly raping two white women. Now it is widely believed that these young men were framed. A key example of the latter was the acquittal of the murderers of Emmett Till forty years ago. In the face of over-whelming evidence of guilt, an all-white jury in Summer, Mississippi, took an hour and seven minutes to acquit two white men who later acknowledged that they had killed Till for having whistled at the wife of one of them. Asked why the jury had taken an hour to deliberate, one of the jurors declared that it would not have taken so long if they hadn't paused for a drink of soda pop. Some readers may find it hard to believe that these despicable events of sixty and forty years ago influence the way that people now evaluate people and events. But just as some in the Balkans remember battles fought 600 years ago as if they happened yesterday, so too do many blacks recall with pained disgust the racially motivated miscarriages of justice that they have helplessly witnessed or been told about. That recollection, refreshed occasionally by more recent outrages, prompts them to regard prosecutions against black men—especially black men accused of attacking white women—with such an intense level of skepticism that they demand more than that which should convince most reasonable people of guilt beyond a reasonable doubt.

A third belief is that to which [defense lawyer] Johnnie Cochran appealed directly in his summation when he pleaded with jurors to help "police the police." This belief animates jury nullification. By nullification, I mean the act of voting for acquittal even though you know that, in terms of the rules laid down by the judge, the evidence warrants conviction. A nullifier votes to acquit not because of dissatisfaction with the evidence but because, in the phrase of choice nowadays, he wants "to send a message." In many locales, black people in particular want to send a message that they are way past tolerating anti-black racism practiced by police and that they are willing to voice their protest in a wide variety of ways, including jury nullification. Frustrated, angry and politically self-aware, some black citizens have decided to take their protest against racism in the criminal justice system to the vital and vulnerable innards of that system: the jury box.

In a certain way, the specter of this sort of jury nullification represents an advance in American race relations. Not too long ago, blacks' dissatisfactions with the criminal justice system could often be largely ignored without significant immediate consequence because whites, on a racial basis, excluded them from decisionmaking. Invisible in courthouses, except as defendants, blacks could safely be permitted to stew in their own resentments. Now, however, because of salutary reforms, blacks are much more active in the administration of criminal justice and thus much more able to influence it.

Notwithstanding this advance, however, the current state of affairs as revealed by the Simpson case is marked by several large and tragic failures. The first and most important is the failure on the part of responsible officials to clearly, publicly and wholeheartedly abjure racism of the sort that Mark Fuhrman displayed during his hateful career as a police officer. Fuhrman's prejudice and his ability to act on it likely had much to do with O. J. Simpson's acquittal. His bigotry provided a vivid basis for the argument that the police framed Simpson. His bigotry also provided an emotionally satisfying basis upon which to follow Cochran's invitation to "send a message" by voting to acquit. In other words, the state inflicted upon itself a grievous wound when its representatives failed to establish a rigorous, anti-racist personnel policy that might have obviated the problem that ultimately crippled the prosecution most. Perhaps more headway on this front will now be made; practicality and morality dictate a more vigorous push against racism in law enforcement circles.

A second failure has occurred within the ranks of those who cheered the acquittal. I have no objection to cheers based on the assumption that the jury system worked properly, that is, cheers based on an honest and reasonable perception that the acquittal has freed a man against whom there existed too little evidence for a conviction. I get the impression, though, that there are other sentiments being voiced in the celebrations of some observers, including feelings of racial solidarity, yearnings to engage in racial muscle-flexing and a peculiar urge to protect the hero status of a man whose standing within the black community rose precipitously by dint of being charged with murder.

The failure of those moved by these sentiments is two-fold. First, such feelings can only predominate by minimizing the stark fact that two people were brutally murdered and by resisting the claim that *whoever* committed that dastardly deed ought to be legally punished, regardless of his color and regardless of the racism of Mark Fuhrman and company. To subordinate the need to convict a murderer to the need to protest the intolerability of official racism is a moral mistake. Both could have been done and should have been done. Contrary to the logic of Johnnie Cochran's summation, neither jurors nor onlookers were trapped in a situation in which they had to choose one imperative over the other. Second, as a practical matter, it cannot be emphasized too frequently the extent to which the black community in particular needs vigorous, efficient, enthusiastic law enforcement. As bad as racist police misconduct is, it pales in comparison to the misery that criminals (most of whom are black) inflict upon black communities. After all, blacks are four times as likely as whites to be raped, three times as likely to be robbed, twice as likely to be assaulted and seven times as likely to be murdered.

The problem of criminality perpetrated by blacks is the one that many black political leaders appear to have trouble discussing thoroughly. A good many prefer condemning white racist police to focusing on ways to render life in black communities more secure against ordinary criminals. That Simpson allegedly killed two white people makes him in some eyes far easier to rally around than had he allegedly killed two black people. This difference in sympathy based on the race of victims is itself a profoundly destructive racialist impulse, one deeply rooted in our political culture. But there is yet another difficulty with this particular racialist response. Like so much else about the Simpson case, the racial demographics of those who were killed was atypical. Because the more typical scenario features black victims of murder, those who claim to speak on behalf of blacks' interests should be extremely wary of supporting anything that further depresses law enforcement's ability to apprehend and convict those who prey upon their neighbors.

The O. J. Simpson trial is obviously a complicated event that will take years to understand more fully and place into proper perspective. At this point, however, the result, like so much of the trial itself, leaves me—normally an optimist—overcome by a sense of profound gloom.

POSTSCRIPT

Should Juries Be Able to Disregard the Law and Free "Guilty" Persons in Racially Charged Cases?

Should jury nullification be used to reduce inequities? Can a jury's decision to acquit a guilty person be considered a form of discretion, comparable to a person's decision to dial or not to dial 911 in an emergency or a police officer's deciding whether or not to arrest a potential suspect? Butler says, "Jury nullification affords African Americans the power to determine justice . . . regardless of whether white people agree or even understand." Is this statement blatantly racist? One critic has suggested that Butler's discussion is actually a satire. Could this be true?

An interesting concept that neither Butler nor Kennedy consider is the possibility of victim, community, or police "nullification." In other words, if many felt that criminals who were minority members would be allowed to go free by sympathetic juries, the probability would be high that even fewer cases would get to trial than currently do: the police, victims' families, or even vigilantes might be driven to administer "neighborhood justice" in order to ensure that criminals are punished.

The acquittal of murder suspect O. J. Simpson on October 3, 1995, revived debate on jury nullification. A thoughtful discussion is J. Q. Wilson, "Reading Jurors' Minds," *Commentary* (February 1996). A radically different analysis is T. Morrison and C. Lacour, eds., *Birth of a Nation'Hood: Gaze, Script, and Spectacle in the O. J. Simpson Case* (Pantheon Books, 1997). For another example of Kennedy's thinking, see his *Race, Crime and the Law* (Vintage Books, 1998).

Among the many attackers of Butler's thinking is J. Rosen, in "The Bloods and the Crits," *The New Republic* (December 9, 1996); E. M. Brown, in "The Tower of Babel: Bridging the Divide Between Critical Race Theory and 'Mainstream' Civil Rights Scholarship," *Yale Law Journal* (November 1995); and A. Leipold, in "The Dangers of Race-Based Jury Nullification: A Response to Professor Butler," *UCLA Law Review* (October 1, 1996). Outstanding current sources include B. R. Boxill, *Blacks and Social Justice*, 3rd ed. (Rowman & Littlefield, 2000); *The Color of Justice: Race, Ethnicity, and Crime in America*, 2d ed., by S. Walker, C. Spohn, and M. DeLone (Wadsworth Thomson Learning, 2000); *No Equal Justice: Race and Class in the American Criminal Justice System* by D. Cole (New Press, 2000); *"Law Never Here": A Social History of African American Responses to Issues of Crime and Justice* by F. Y. Bailey (Praeger, 1999); *The Color of Crime* by K. K. Russell (New York University Press, 1998); and *African-American Males and the Law: Cases and Materials* by F. D. Weatherspoon (University Press of America, 1998).

ISSUE 19

Should Behavior Modification Techniques Be Used to Brainwash Criminals?

YES: James V. McConnell, from "Criminals Can Be Brainwashed—Now," *Psychology Today* (April 1970)

NO: Jessica Mitford, from "The Torture Cure: In Some American Prisons It Is Already 1984," *Harper's Magazine* (1973)

ISSUE SUMMARY

YES: The late University of Michigan psychologist James V. McConnell argues that society has the technology to brainwash criminals and turn them into productive citizens.

NO: Celebrated author the late Jessica Mitford contends, however, that sensory deprivation and other forms of behavior modification are immoral and constitute the legally sanctioned use of torture.

The issue of whether to brainwash criminals may well be one of the most compelling controversies in this book. Suppose for a minute that we have the solution to crime—we can turn any criminal, no matter how violent or seemingly incorrigible, into a decent law-abiding citizen in a matter of weeks. The person receiving the "treatment" would no longer even have the urge to commit crimes. He or she would become a model citizen in every way. Should we use it? What moral problems would such a solution present?

Moral choice is the defining characteristic of humanity. Anything that eliminates the element of moral choice from behavior will negate human nature. Behavioral psychologists believe that human conduct results from a conditioning process that begins at birth. It assumes that all behavior is the result of past conditioning, which includes whether past conduct has been rewarded or punished. Therefore, if a person commits criminal behavior, he or she must be effectively reconditioned.

Although the principles of behavioral psychology have great potential for changing human behavior, their implications for moral choice must be considered carefully. Should we use it to turn criminals into productive members of society? The authors to the articles in this section would respond to this question in very different ways.

Psychologist James V. McConnell argues that no person owns his or her own personality. He believes that it is forced on you by your genetic constitution and by your environment. Because you had no say about the personality you acquired, there is no reason to believe you should have the right to refuse to acquire a new personality if your old one is antisocial. He also observes that the techniques of behavioral psychology "make even the hydrogen bomb look like a child's toy, and of course they can be used for good or for evil."

This observation is an interesting one indeed. If the principles of behavioral psychology could be used to turn a criminal into a productive, law-abiding citizen, the converse must be true as well: A law-abiding citizen could be turned into a criminal if the behavioral technology were to be abused.

In addition, we must consider the issue of the definition of crimes and who creates them. Most of us would agree that intentional actions that harm others should be considered crimes. Laws against murder, rape, assault, theft, property destruction, arson, and similar crimes have virtually universal support. What about marginal behaviors that generate less social consensus, however? For example, if a police officer lets a traffic violator go and accepts a $100 bribe, he or she has committed a felony in most jurisdictions. Why then isn't it bribery when a politician accepts a campaign contribution from an environmental polluter who then gets favorable legislative treatment? Or a drug company that contributes to golfing junkets for a politician who then sponsors a bill to give such corporations favorable tax treatment? These are difficult questions that point to a controversial answer: Persons with power make the law in order to enhance and protect their own interests.

Jessica Mitford, who titled her book chapter "Clockwork Orange," would agree that behavior modification techniques may be abused. In her most famous work, *Kind and Usual Punishment: The Prison Business*, Mitford asks: "Do prison experiments in behavior modification and ubiquitous surveillance foreshadow a Clockwork Orange society to come? . . . The questions are chilling because empirical data, as well as the prophecies of artistic perception, suggest such a direction."

As you read the articles in this section, think about the use of behavior modification and brainwashing techniques. Is Anthony Burgess correct when he asserts that there is no moral component to human behavior unless there is free will? If we do, in fact, have the technology to change criminals into law-abiding citizens through the use of behavioral modification and brainwashing, should we do it? Likewise, imagine for a moment, that you now hold the solution to crime in a small vial in the palm of your hand. What would you do with it? The answer to this question may not be as easy as it seems.

YES

James V. McConnell

Criminals Can Be Brainwashed—Now

The purpose of a law is to regulate human behavior—to get people to do what we want them to do. If it doesn't, it's a failure, and we might as well admit it and try something else. Laws should be goal-oriented; they must be judged by their results, or we're just kidding ourselves. Any time we pass a law that more than a handful of people violate, the law is probably a bad one. Man is the only animal capable of shaping his own society, of changing his own destiny. We must use this capability to build a society in which laws become guidelines rather than threats, guidelines so strong that no one would want to do anything other than follow them.

Liberal doctrine assumes that crime is society's fault, not the fault of the individual who happens to commit the crime.* So you shouldn't punish the individual, you should try to change the sick society that spawned the crime in the first place.

The conservative tends to see mankind as basically evil, born with genetically determined instincts that force man to behave wickedly whenever possible. The only way to stop this innate immorality is to stamp it out. Stomp on it. Catch the criminal and beat the living hell out of him; that will make him a much better person. We've molly-coddled the bastards long enough.

Both positions are terribly, terribly naive and ineffective. Somehow we've got to learn how to *force* people to love one another, to *force* them to want to behave properly. I speak of psychological force. Punishment must be used as precisely and as dispassionately as a surgeon's scalpel if it is to be effective.

I've spent a good many years training flatworms in my laboratory, which is why I'm so knowledgeable about *human* behavior, of course. We can train flatworms to do a great many things because we've learned the proper techniques and because we follow instructions exactly. For example, suppose we want to train a worm to run through a maze. The worm must learn that the white alley is always safe, but the black alley will lead to punishment—painful electric shock. There is our worm wandering contentedly when it comes to a

---

* But the doctrine is changing, as Psychology Today *readers indicated by their responses* [November] *to our Law & Society opinion study.*

choice point. The worm heads into the black alley, for worms tend to prefer black before they're trained. So we give the beast a bit of a shock, just to teach it a lesson. It took us years to learn that we have to control the polarity of the shock very carefully, otherwise the shock itself will propel the animal into the wrong alley. The next thing we had to learn was *when* to give the shock. If you shock the worm too soon, it never learns to connect the punishment with the black alley. If you delay the shock even a couple of seconds after it has stuck its head in the black alley, the worm doesn't come to associate *entering* the black alley with the punishment, so it goes right on entering the black alley time after time after time.

The amount of punishment you give is important, too. We learned that if we gave our worms more than one or two very quick shocks when they entered the wrong alley, they became so disturbed that they would stop and refuse to move at all.

It took years, but we now know enough that we can train the animals very quickly. We have no trouble training worms, but we have one hell of a time trying to train new laboratory assistants. We explain our findings to them, and they nod their heads, but they don't really believe us and they don't really understand.

I have a friend, a distinguished scientist, who visited my lab one day. He was so fascinated by the worms that he wanted to train one himself. I explained everything to him and he nodded his head and insisted that he understood—after all, he had raised three kids, hadn't he, and he had taught several thousand medical students over the years. Reluctantly I put a fresh worm in the maze and handed this man the apparatus controlling the shock.

The flatworm crawled along the maze quite nicely, came to the first choice point, and headed into the black alley. Of course, my friend pressed on the wrong button, gave shock of the wrong polarity and propelled the poor worm into the black alley. "Silly animal," the man muttered; he pressed the wrong button again. The worm went further into the wrong alley. "Get out of there, you idiot," he shouted at the worm, and held the shock button down for several seconds.

The worm, I regret to say, went into convulsions about this time and simply lay on its back writhing. My friend thrust the control apparatus back into my hands, advised me that the damned worm was obviously too stupid to learn even the simplest task, and stalked out of the lab.

The more that I think about it, the more convinced I am that the mistake was all mine. Why should I let him try to train a worm . . . or a rat . . . or a human being . . . unless he had been given the proper education first?

Of course you see the trouble here. Each of us considers himself an unqualified expert on behavior, particularly on human behavior. It's utter nonsense, of course. We won't let a lawyer plead a case or a physician remove an appendix or a teacher conduct a class unless he's had extensive training and passed tests to prove his qualifications. Yet the only test a prospective parent has to pass is the Wasserman, and the only license he needs to practice the upbringing of children is obtainable for five dollars or so at the local marriage bureau.

But I digress. When you're training animals—be they humans or flat-worms—there are times when you absolutely have to use punishment, for there are situations in which no other form of behavioral control works. But we use pain only when we wish to remove one very specific type of behavior from an organism's response-repertoire, and we use it very, very carefully.

In contrast to this scientific approach, the conservative insists that punishment be used not to control behavior—that is, to prevent crime—but rather as a kind of divine retribution to be enacted on those poor, miserable sinners who break the law. If the worm doesn't behave properly, shock the hell out of him. That'll learn 'im. Worms ought to be bright enough to know better. The conservative's viewpoint is utterly predictable to anyone who understands the relationship between frustration and aggression. It's very easy for a psychologist to devise a situation in which a laboratory animal is intensely frustrated. Under such conditions, the frustrated beast quite predictably turns on and attacks any scapegoat that happens to be handy. When humans are frustrated, they typically become aggressive. That's a natural law, not just an opinion of mine. When lawmakers don't understand some aspect of the world around them, and when they are frustrated by something the people do or the President does or the Supreme Court rules, the lawmakers typically respond by passing a highly punitive and aggressive law. Yet these are the very situations in which punishment has little or no effect on the behavior of the people the lawmakers want to influence or control. And so bad laws get written, not because they're effective but because they make the lawmakers feel good.

In effect, we have but two means of educating people or rats or flat-worms—we can either reward them for doing the right thing or punish them for doing the wrong thing. Most people believe it's more humane to use reward. Surely we would all agree that rewards are usually more pleasant than punishments, and that love seems a nicer way of influencing people than hate. But blind love is even more dangerous than blind hate, for we can all identify hate and reject it, but love is something we've been told is good, good, good.

In Los Angeles there's a psychologist named Ivar Lovaas who is helping revolutionize the fields of clinical psychology and psychiatry. Dr. Lovaas works chiefly with autistic children, so socially retarded that they are little more than animals. They do not speak any known language, they seem to refuse all contact with other human beings. Until were recently they were considered almost hopeless; none of the usual forms of psychotherapy seemed to help them at all. And then along came behavioral psychologists like Ivar Lovaas who took a startling new viewpoint toward helping these kids.

The usual autistic child is lost in passivity, but a few of these very disturbed children go beyond passivity into self-destruction. The self-mutilating autistic child will tear at his flesh with both hands, bite off his own fingers, chew off his own shoulder. As you might guess, it's terrifying to watch these children.

Lovaas believes that autistic children cannot be brought back into the fold of humanity unless they can be taught to speak English or some other language. But how can you go about teaching a child to speak when he prefers to use his mouth to bite his own flesh rather than to speak words? Obviously, the first thing you have to do is to stamp out the self-destructive behavior and then worry about teaching the child how to talk.

Greg was about 11 years old when he was first brought to Dr. Lovaas' laboratory at UCLA. Greg had spent seven of his 11 years in a children's mental hospital. He was violently self-destructive; the nurses at the hospital were convinced that he would kill himself unless he were physically restrained 24 hours a day. None of the usual psychotherapy had worked with Greg. So, for seven years, Greg had been tied to a hospital bed, so tightly that he could barely move. When Greg first came to Lovaas' laboratory, his little body was so twisted from this confinement that he could barely walk.

It took Dr. Lovaas about 30 seconds to stamp out Greg's self-destructive behavior. Lovaas got a cattle prod—a long stick with electrodes at one end that deliver a very painful shock when they touch bovine—or human—flesh. He then turned Greg loose. As soon as Greg made his first self-destructive movement, Lovaas reached over and gave him a good jolt of electricity. Greg stopped moving and what might have been a puzzled look flashed across his face. He seemed to decide that the shock was a mistake, an accident, for a few seconds later he began to tear at his flesh again. Immediately Lovaas reached out with the cattle prod again and shocked the boy. Greg didn't like that at all, not one little bit. He looked up at Lovaas in disbelief and sat there for a few seconds more, then made one last attempt to hurt himself. One more jolt of electricity did the trick. Greg almost never again tried to harm himself when Lovaas was around. What standard therapy had been unable to do in seven years Lovaas did in 30 seconds. And then, once the self-destructiveness was gone, Lovaas could put the cattle prod aside and go on to the more important and difficult task of teaching Greg to speak by rewarding him whenever he made the proper sounds.

The behavior of children like Greg had been a great puzzle until people like Lovaas began analyzing it. Why would kids want to mutilate themselves? It didn't seem that any sensible goal could be achieved by such behavior, so the psychiatric world decided that these kids were hopelessly insane and they were locked up in hospitals and strapped down to beds all their short, miserable lives. But when Lovaas went to watch these kids in a hospital he noticed something rather strange. As soon as a child began self-destructive behavior, one of the nurses would run to his bed, wrap her arms around him and fuss gently that he mustn't do that sort of thing. Of course, the child couldn't understand much English, so the words were probably wasted on him. But the love and affection weren't. As soon as the nurse turned loose, the child began hurting himself again, and the nurse would return with more hugs and kisses, and the cycle repeated itself. The nurses genuinely loved the kids and wanted to help them. When Lovaas pointed out that they were killing the children with the wrong kind of love administered at the wrong times they refused to believe him. And they undoubtedly thought Lovaas was a terrible, cold-hearted and cruel scientist because he used punishment on kids when everybody knew that kids ought to be loved.

If you take an autistic child out of that hospital and bring him to Lovaas' laboratory, the chances are very good that he can be helped enormously. Leave him in the hospital with the loving nurses and he will probably stay sick the rest of his brief, unhappy life.

When you look at prisons you find much the same situation, I fear. Very few criminals are cured of antisocial behavior while they're in prison, just as very few patients are cured of sick behavior in today's mental hospitals. And in both cases, most of the blame can be placed squarely on staff. A psychologist at an Eastern university told me a most interesting story about a project that the university had undertaken at a large Federal penitentiary. It seems that someone had a great idea that group therapy with a mixed population of guards and prisoners might be productive. So a few therapy groups were formed and the guards and the prisoners had at each other—verbally, that is. After a few weeks, the project collapsed like a punctured balloon—the *guards* couldn't take it any longer. It seems that the therapy was working too well— for the first time the guards began to gain some insight into their own behavior patterns, and they just couldn't face up to what they were really like inside.

As far as most behavioral psychologists are concerned, sick behavior has to be learned. Autistic kids have to learn self-mutilating behavior—it doesn't come built into their genes. We help autistic kids get well by re-educating them, by retraining them, by undoing the bad things they learned so early in life and by teaching them healthy behavior instead. And most behavioral psychologists would insist that criminal behavior has to be learned too, and that whatever is learned can be unlearned.

Back in the early 1950s, the Canadian and U.S. Governments set up the Distant Early Warning (DEW) line of radar stations dotted in the ice and snow far above the Arctic Circle. There's not much up there for entertainment— those rumors about hospitality prostitution among the Eskimos are somewhat exaggerated. So the soldiers listened to radio; Radio Moscow came in much more clearly than most Canadian and American stations and beamed English-language broadcasts at DEW-line personnel. So the Canadian government called in Canada's greatest psychologist, Donald Hebb of McGill University, to determine whether soldiers isolated in boring environments are more than ordinarily susceptible to propaganda. And thus began a set of studies called experiments in sensory deprivation.

Hebb hired college students at $20 a day to do absolutely nothing. Each was confined to a tiny cubicle. An air conditioner obscured all outside noises. A mask over his eyes blocked out all visual stimulation. His arms were encased in long cardboard mailing tubes to prevent touching. He was fed and watered as necessary, but otherwise he was required to lie on a comfortable bed as quietly as he could.

Hebb expected the students to last at least six weeks. None of them lasted more than a few days. During the first 24 hours they caught up on their sleep, but after that the experience became progressively more painful for all of them. They reported long stretches in which they seemed to be awake, but their minds were turned off entirely—they simply didn't "think" at all. They were tested while they were in the cubicles, and most of them showed marked deterioration in intellectual functioning. Many experienced vivid hallucinations—one student in particular insisted that a tiny space ship had got into the chamber and was buzzing around shooting pellets at him. Most of all, though, the students were bored. They tried to trick the experimenter into talking with them. In a subsequent experiment, Hebb let them listen to dull recorded speeches which they could start by pressing a button. The experimenters, who had to listen too, almost went out of their minds, but the students seemed to enjoy thoroughly hearing the same stock-market report a hundred or more times a day. And when Hebb provided propaganda messages instead of stock-market reports, he found that whatever the message was, no matter how poorly it was presented or how illogical it sounded, the propaganda had a marked effect on the students' attitudes—an effect that lasted for at least a year after the students came out of the deprivation chambers.

Hebb's findings led many other investigators to begin work on sensory deprivation.

It is axiomatic in the behavioral sciences that the more you control an organism's environment, the more you can control its behavior. It goes without saying that the only way you can gain complete control over a person's behavior is to gain complete control over his environment. The sensory-deprivation experiments suggest that we should be able to do exactly that.

I believe that the day has come when we can combine sensory deprivation with drugs, hypnosis and astute manipulation of reward and punishment to gain almost absolute control over an individual's behavior. It should be possible then to achieve a very rapid and highly effective type of positive brainwashing that would allow us to make dramatic changes in a person's behavior and personality. I foresee the day when we could convert the worst criminal into a decent, respectable citizen in a matter of a few months—or perhaps even less time than that. The danger is, of course, that we could also do the opposite: we could change any decent, respectable citizen into a criminal.

We must begin by drafting new laws that will be as consonant as possible with all the human-behavior data that scientists have gathered. We should try to regulate human conduct by offering rewards for good behavior whenever possible instead of threatening punishment for breaches of the law. We should reshape our society so that we all would be trained from birth to want to do what society wants us to do. We have the techniques now to do it. Only by using them can we hope to maximize human potentiality. Of course, we cannot give up punishment entirely, but we can use it sparingly, intelligently, as a means of shaping people's behavior rather than as a means of releasing our own aggressive tendencies. For misdemeanors or minor offenses we would administer brief, painless punishment, sufficient to stamp out the antisocial behavior. We'd assume that a felony was clear evidence that the criminal had somehow acquired full-blown social neurosis and needed to be cured, not punished. We'd send him to a rehabilitation center where he'd undergo positive brainwashing until we were quite sure he had become a law-abiding citizen who would not again commit an antisocial act. We'd probably have to restructure his entire personality. The legal and moral issues raised by such procedures are frighteningly complex, of course, but surely we know by now that there are no simple solutions.

Many cling to the old-fashioned belief that each of us builds up his personality logically and by free will. This is as patently incorrect as the belief that the world is flat. No one owns his own personality. Your ego, or individuality, was forced on you by your genetic constitution and by the society into which you were born. You had no say about what kind of personality you acquired, and there's no reason to believe you should have the right to refuse to acquire a new personality if your old one is antisocial. I don't believe the Constitution of the United States gives you the *right* to commit a crime if you want to; therefore, the Constitution does not guarantee you the right to maintain inviolable the personality it forced on you in the first place—if and when the personality manifests strongly antisocial behavior.

The techniques of behavioral control make even the hydrogen bomb look like a child's toy, and, of course, they can be used for good or evil. But we can no more prevent the development of this new psychological methodology than we could have prevented the development of atomic energy. By knowing what is scientifically possible and by taking a revolutionary viewpoint toward society and its problems, we can surely shape the future more sanely than we can if we hide our collective heads in the sand and pretend that it can't happen here. Today's behavioral psychologists are the architects and engineers of the Brave New World.

Jessica Mitford

 NO

The Torture Cure

. . . Some disconcerting conclusions about the efficacy of [prison] treatment [programs] are set forth in a report to the State Assembly titled "The California Prison, Parole, and Probation System." It cites an exhaustive study conducted for the Department of Corrections in which the researchers observed gloomily, "Thousands of inmates and hundreds of staff members were participating in this program at a substantial cost to the Department of Corrections in time, effort, and money. Contrary to the expectations of the treatment theory, there were no significant differences in outcome for those in the various treatment programs or between the treatment groups and the control group." They further reported that group counseling did not lessen adherence to the inmate code, nor did it reduce the frequency of discipline problems.

James O. Robison, author of the report and longtime researcher for the Department of Corrections, traced the course of disillusionment. "The high mystique of treatment peaked at the end of the Fifties," he told me. "The idea took hold in Corrections that at last, through sophisticated techniques of psychotherapy, we have it in our power to transform the deviant and to predict with accuracy his future behavior. But in the early Sixties the high priests of Corrections began a sifting of the entrails. After that, disenchantment and embarrassment set in—the reason was the evident empirical failure of the treatment programs, as demonstrated by the recidivism rate remaining constant over the years.

"The rationale for failure was always, 'We haven't carried treatment far enough, there isn't enough of it, it isn't professional enough'—in other words, we need more and better of same, in spite of the fact we've seen it doesn't work. Even this reasoning began to break down in the middle Sixties, when there was more attention paid to the fact nothing was happening and more talk of '*Why?*'

"What you are likely to see now is the end of the liberal treatment era—the notion that you can make convicts into converts of the dominant culture 'religion,' the missionary fervor—that's being replaced with 'behavior modification' experiments. The latest reasoning is that it's costly and inappropriate to go the psychotherapy route with these people, to pay high-priced psychiatrists to *talk* them into recognizing the truth of our 'religion'; instead, we'll focus on their deviant behavior and force them to shape up. Of course, this flies in the face of the earlier rhetoric. The Behaviorists say they are bad; not mad, and we can stop them being bad by utilizing new techniques. This fits in with the law-and-order, no-nonsense conservative viewpoint: henceforth the slogan will be, 'They must be *made* to behave.'"

This new trend in Corrections must be highly inspiriting for the behavioral scientists, who have long been eyeing the prisons as convenient reservoirs of human material on which to try out new theories. The shape of things to come was forecast a decade ago at a seminar of prison wardens and psychologists chaired by James V. Bennett, then director of the U.S. Bureau of Prisons. As described in *Corrective Psychiatry & Journal of Social Change*, Second Quarter, 1962, the seminar provided "provocative, fruitful interaction between social scientists and correctional administrators."

Addressing himself to the topic "Man Against Man: Brainwashing," Dr. Edgar H. Schein, associate professor of psychology at MIT, told the assembled wardens: "My basic argument is this: in order to produce marked change of behavior and/or attitude, it is necessary to weaken, undermine, or remove the supports to the old patterns of behavior and the old attitudes"; this can be done "either by removing the individual physically and preventing any communication with those whom he cares about, or by proving to him that those whom he respects are not worthy of it and, indeed, should be actively mistrusted."

Dr. Schein, who said he got most of his ideas from studying brainwashing techniques used by North Korean and Chinese Communists on GI prisoners of war, cautioned has audience not to be put off by this fact: "These same techniques in the service of different goals may be quite acceptable to us. . . . I would like to have you think of brainwashing not in terms of politics, ethics, and morals, but in terms of the deliberate changing of human behavior and attitudes by a group of men who have relatively complete control over the environment in which the captive population lives."

Some of the techniques which could usefully be applied in the U.S. prisons: "Social disorganization and the creation of mutual mistrust" achieved by "spying on the men and reporting back private material"; "tricking men into written statements" that are then shown to others, the objective being "to convince most men they could trust no one," "undermining ties to home by the systematic withholding of mail." The key factor is change of attitude: "Supports for old attitudes have to be undermined and destroyed if change is to take place. . . . Do we not feel it to be legitimate to destroy the emotional ties of one criminal to another, or of a criminal to a sick community?" How to bring about the desired change was explained by Dr. Schein: "If one wants to produce behavior inconsistent with the person's standards of conduct, first disorganize the group which supports those standards, then undermine his other emotional supports, then put him into a new and ambiguous situation for which the standards are unclear, and then put pressure on him. I leave it to you to judge whether there is any similarity between these events and those which occur in prisons when we teach prisoners 'to serve their own time' by moving them around and punishing clandestine group activity not sanctioned by the prison authorities." . . .

Summarizing the discussion, Dr. Bennett pointed out that the federal prison system, with some 24,000 men in it, presents "a tremendous opportunity to carry on some of the experimenting to which the various panelists have alluded." He added, "What I am hoping is that the audience here will believe that we here in Washington are anxious to have you undertake some of these things: do things perhaps on your own—undertake a little experiment of what you can do with the Muslims, what you can do with some of the sociopath individuals."

❧

That Dr. Bennett's counsel was taken to heart by his subordinates in the federal prison system can be inferred from a report addressed to the United Nations Economic and Social Council, prepared and smuggled out of Marion Federal Penitentiary in July 1972, by the Federal Prisoners' Coalition, a group of convicts housed in the segregation unit for refusing to participate in the behavioral research programs. "In the latter part of 1968 some changes in the U.S. Department of Justice enabled the U.S. Bureau of Prisons to make a quiet beginning at implementing an experimental program at Marion Federal Prison to determine at first hand how effective a weapon brainwashing might be for the U.S. Department of Justice's future use," says the report. It describes how Dr. Martin Groder, prison psychiatrist, applies the proposals outlined in Dr. Schein's paper to "agitators," suspected militants, writ-writers, and other troublemakers. The first step, according to the report, is to sever the inmate's ties with his family by transferring him to some remote prison where they will be unable to visit him. There he is put in isolation, deprived of mail and, other privileges, until he agrees to participate in Dr. Groder's Transactional Analysis program. If he succumbs, he will be moved to new living quarters where he will be surrounded by members of Dr. Groder's "prisoner thought-reform team," and subjected to intense group pressure. "His emotional, behavioral, and psychic characteristics are studied by the staff and demiprofessional prisoners to detect vulnerable points of entry to stage attack-sessions around. During these sessions, on a progressively intensified basis, he is shouted at, his fears played on, his sensitivities ridiculed, and concentrated efforts made to make him feel guilty for real or imagined characteristics or conduct. . . . Every effort is made to heighten his suggestibility and weaken his character structure so that his emotional responses and thought-flow will be brought under group and staff control as totally as possible.

". . . It is also driven in to him that society, in the guise of its authorities, is looking out for his best interests and will help if he will only permit it to do so. Help him be 'reborn' as a highly probable 'winner in the game of life,' is the way this comes across in the group's jargon." Once reborn as a winner, he will be moved into a plush living area equipped with stereo, tape recorders, typewriters, books. He is now ready to indoctrinate newcomers into the mysteries of the group "and like a good attack dog, he is graded and evaluated on his demonstrated capacity to go for the vulnerable points of any victim put before him." The entire program is made self-perpetuating and economically feasible by the participants doing the work themselves, says the report: "They are taught to police not only themselves but others, to inform on one another in acceptable fashion—as, bringing out misconduct of another in a truth-session is not considered informing even if a staff member is present.". . .

◦◦◦◦

A further elaboration on the brainwashing theme is furnished by James V. McConnell, professor of psychology at the University of Michigan, in an article in the May 1970 issue of *Psychology Today* titled "Criminals Can Be Brainwashed—Now." It reads like science fiction, the fantasy of a deranged scientist. Yet much of what Dr. McConnell proposes as appropriate therapy for tomorrow's lawbreaker is either already here or in the planning stages in many of the better financed prison systems.

Dr. McConnell, who spent many years successfully training flatworms to go in and out of mazes at his bidding by administering a series of painful electric shocks, now proposes to apply similar techniques to convicts: "I believe the day has come when we can combine sensory deprivation with drugs, hypnosis, and astute manipulation of reward and punishment to gain almost absolute control over an individual's behavior . . . We'd assume that a felony was clear evidence that the criminal had somehow acquired full-blown social neurosis and needed to be cured, not punished . . . We'd probably have to restructure his entire personality.". . .

Noting that "the legal and moral issues raised by such procedures are frighteningly complex," Dr. McConnell nevertheless handily disposes of them: "I don't believe the Constitution of the United States gives you the *right* to commit a crime if you want to; therefore, the Constitution does not guarantee you the right to maintain inviolable the personality forced on you in the first place—if and when the personality manifests strongly antisocial behavior."

The new behavioral control techniques, says Dr. McConnell, "make even the hydrogen bomb look like a child's toy, and, of course, they can be used for good or evil." But it will avail us nothing to "hide our collective heads in the sand and pretend that it can't happen here. Today's behavioral psychologists are the architects and engineers of the Brave New World."

For some convicts in California, those perceived as "dangerous," "revolutionary," or "uncooperative" by the authorities, it *has* happened here, and Dr. McConnell's Brave New World is their reality. Signposts in this bizarre terrain may need translation for the auslander:

Sensory Deprivation: Confinement (often for months or years) in the Adjustment Center, a prison-within-a-prison.

Stress Assessment: The prisoner lives in an open dormitory where it is expected he will suffer maximum irritation from the lack of privacy. He is assigned to the worst and most menial jobs. In compulsory group therapy sessions staff members deliberately bait the men and try to provoke conflicts among them. The idea is to see how much of this a person can stand without losing his temper.

Chemotherapy: The use of drugs (some still in the experimental stage) as "behavior modifiers," including antitestosterone hormones, which have the effect of chemically castrating the subject, and Prolixin, a form of tranquilizer with unpleasant and often dangerous side effects.

Aversion Therapy: The use of medical procedures that cause pain and fear to bring about the desired "behavior modification."

Neurosurgery: Cutting or burning out those portions of the brain believed to cause "aggressive behavior."

⋅◈⋅

The "Behavior Modification" programs are for the most part carried out in secret. They are not part of the guided tour for journalists and visitors, nor are outside physicians permitted to witness them. Occasionally word of these procedures leaks out, as in the autumn of 1970, when *Medical World News* ran an article titled "Scaring the Devil Out" about the use of the drug Anectine in "aversion therapy" in the California prisons.

Anectine, a derivative of the South American arrow-tip poison curare, is used medically in small doses as a muscle relaxant, but behavioral researchers discovered that when administered to unruly prisoners in massive amounts—from twenty to forty milligrams—it causes them to lose all control or voluntary muscles.

An unpublished account of the Anectine therapy program at Vacaville, California, by two of the staff researchers there, Arthur L. Mattocks, supervisor of the research unit, and Charles Jew, social research analyst, states that "the conceptual scheme was to develop a strong association between any violent or acting-out behavior and the drug Anectine and its frightful consequences," among which were "cessation of respiration for a period of approximately two minutes' duration." Of those selected to endure these consequences, "nearly all could be characterized as angry young men," say the authors. Some seem to have been made a good deal angrier by the experience, for the report notes that of sixty-four prisoners in the program "nine persons not only did not decrease but actually exhibited an increase in their overall number of disciplinary infractions."

According to Dr. Arthur Nugent, chief psychiatrist at Vacaville and an enthusiast for the drug, it induces "sensations of suffocation and drowning." The subject experiences feelings of deep horror and terror, "as though he were on the brink of death." While he is in this condition a therapist scolds him for his misdeeds and tells him to shape up or expect more of the same. Candidates for Anectine treatment were selected for a range of offenses: "frequent fights, verbal threatening, deviant sexual behavior, stealing, unresponsiveness to the group therapy programs." Dr. Nugent told the *San Francisco Chronicle*, "Even the toughest inmates have come to fear and hate the drug. I don't blame them, I wouldn't have one treatment myself for the world." Declaring he was anxious to continue the experiment, he added, "I'm at a loss as to why everybody's upset over this."

More upset was to follow a year later, when the press got wind of a letter from Director Raymond Procunier to the California Council on Criminal Justice requesting funding estimated at $18,000 for "neurosurgical treatment of violent inmates." The letter read, in part: "The problem of treating the aggressive, destructive inmate has long been a problem in all correctional systems. During recent years this problem has become particularly acute in the California Department of Corrections institutions . . . This letter of intent is to alert you to the development of a proposal to seek funding for a program involving a complex neurosurgical evaluation and treatment program for the violent inmate . . . surgical and diagnostic procedures would be performed to locate centers in the brain which may have been previously damaged and which could serve as the focus for episodes of violent behavior. If these areas were located and verified that they were indeed the source of aggressive behavior, neurosurgery would be performed . . ." Confronted by reporters with this letter, Laurence Bennett, head of the Department of Corrections Research Division, explained: "It is not a proposal, it's just an idea-concept." He added wistfully, "It's quite likely that we will not proceed with this, but if we had unlimited funds we would explore every opportunity to help anyone who wants such assistance."

Although the plan for psychosurgery was halted—at least temporarily—by the newspaper uproar that ensued, the authorities have other methods at hand for controlling the unruly, principal among which is forced drugging of prisoners. In widespread use throughout the nation's prisons is the drug Prolixin, a powerful tranquilizer derived from phenothiazine, which, if given in large doses, produces dangerous and often irreversible side effects. A petition addressed to the California Senate Committee on Penal Institutions by La Raza Unida, a Chicano organization of prisoners confined in the California Men's Colony, describes these: "The simple fact that a number of prisoners are walking the yard in this institution like somnambulists, robots, and vegetables as a result of this drug should be reason enough to make people apprehensive as to the effect it is having. That no prisoner feels safe because he never knows when he will become a candidate for said drug is another factor in producing tension in this institution."

According to its manufacturer, E. R. Squibb, Prolixin is "a highly potent behavior modifier with a markedly extended duration of effect." Possible adverse side effects listed by Squibb include: the induction of a "catatonic-like state," nausea, loss of appetite, headache, constipation, blurred vision, glaucoma, bladder paralysis, impotency, liver damage, hypotension severe enough to cause fatal cardiac arrest, and cerebral edema. Furthermore, Squibb cautions that "a persistent pseudo-parkinsonian [palsy-like] syndrome may develop . . . characterized by rhythmic, stereotyped dyskinetic involuntary movements . . . resembling the facial grimaces of encephalitis . . . The symptoms persist after drug withdrawal, and in some patients appear to be irreversible."

⚜

The Theme of Prison as a happy hunting ground for the researcher is very big in current penological literature. In *I Chose Prison,* James V. Bennett poses the question, What will the prisons of 2000 A.D. be like? And answers it: "In my judgment the prison system will increasingly be valued, and used, as a laboratory and workshop of social change." Dr. Karl Menninger echoes this thought in *The Crime of Punishment:* "About all this [causes of crime], we need more information, more research, more experimental data. That research is the basis for scientific progress, no one any more disputes . . . Even our present prisons, bad as many of them are, could be extensively used as laboratories for the study of many of the unsolved problems."

Taking these injunctions to heart, researchers are descending in droves upon the prisons with their prediction tables, expectancy scales, data analysis charts. With all the new money available under federal crime control programs, and the ingenuity of grant-happy researchers, the scope of the investigations seems limitless. . . .

✤

Details of [an experimental and] highly specialized [service] to be rendered to eighty-four chosen from [Folsom prison], and the nature of the needed intervention, were discussed at a "think session' called in November 1971 at the University of California at Davis by Laurence Bennett, head of the Department of Corrections Research Division. Participants were some twenty-five representatives of the healing professions—medicine, psychology, psychiatry—many of them faculty members from nearby universities and medical schools.

The new unit, said Max May, program administrator, would be closely modeled after Patuxent Institution in Maryland, with four twenty-one-man cellblocks, "single five-by-seven-foot cells with bars, only we call them barriers." Construction costs would be kept to a minimum since the prisoners were to build their own cages, the work, according to the grant application, consisting "primarily of pouring two concrete floors, erecting wire screen partitions, also a gun tower."

The objective, said Bennett, is "to develop a basic knowledge of the causes of aggressive, violent behavior. Our aim is to learn how to identify small groups, how to deal with them more adequately. We hope through psychological management to learn how to lessen their violence potential."

Discussion from the floor, and at the pleasant luncheon gathering in the faculty club dining room, centered on methods by which this might be accomplished: "We need to find the stimulus to which the subject responds. We also need to find out how he thinks *covertly* and to change how he thinks." "We need to dope up many of these men in order to calm them down to the point that they are accessible to treatment." "Those who can't be controlled by drugs are candidates for the implantation of subcortical electrodes [electrodes plunged deep into the brain]."

Dr. Keith Brody of Stanford University, who said he runs a "unit for mood disorders," stressed the importance of "intensive data collection" via spinal taps and other tests: "These tests can lead to therapy decisions. We need to segregate out and dissect out these sub-groups." Other proposals for therapy were to burn out electrically those areas of the brain believed to be the "source or aggressive behavior"—one speaker said he reckoned about 10 percent of the inmates might be candidates for this treatment; the administration of antitestosterone hormones, which have the effect of emasculating the subject; the use of pneumo-encephalograms (injecting air into the brain cavities).

Asked whether the Anectine torture "therapy" would be resumed in the new unit, Bennett did not answer directly but declared with some exasperation, "If it could be shown empirically that hitting an inmate on the head with a hammer would cure him, I'd do it. You talk about his civil rights—civil rights for what? To continue to disrupt society?" Nor would be answer the further questions: "Does not the prison system itself, and particularly the Adjustment Center, generate violence?" and "Would the researchers be directing any part of their inquiry to violence by guards against prisoners?"

As for the compliant participation of the distinguished group of faculty members in this bizarre discussion, one possible explanation was suggested by the lone black psychiatrist present, Dr. Wendell Lipscomb, who had stormed out of the meeting half-way through, declaring he "couldn't take any more of this crap." Later, he told me, "What you were seeing at that meeting were the grant hunters, hungry for money, willing to eat any shit that's put before them."

POSTSCRIPT

Should Behavior Modification Techniques Be Used to Brainwash Criminals?

Criminal behavior is a complex problem. The solution that Dr. McConnell proposes is fairly simple and attractive: recondition those who have demonstrated a criminal propensity and return them to society as productive citizens. There are significant problems with this approach, however.

First, behavioral psychology proceeds from a deterministic model—human behavior is the product of the experience and prior learning. Behaviors that have been rewarded in the past will be repeated; those that have been punished will be extinguished. There is little room for free will in this paradigm. All behavior, including criminality, is the result of prior learning.

How does this deterministic model fit into the concept of individual responsibility emphasized in the U.S. justice system? At first glance, it does not appear to fit well. Our penal philosophy asserts that punishment is justified because an individual has freely chosen to commit a criminal act. To punish someone for actions that are not freely chosen seems contrary to our philosophy of punishment, and perhaps even immoral.

Second, Dr. McConnell states: "[y]ou had no say about what kind of personality you acquired, and there's no reason to believe you should have the right to refuse to acquire a new personality if your old one is antisocial." U.S. courts may well disagree with this proposition. In recent years, the courts have recognized a wide variety of non-traditional property rights, such as intellectual property. It would not be much of a stretch to hold that psychological reconditioning programs violate a fundamental right to maintain inviolable his or her personality. Recently, in *Walker v. Montana*, 68 P.3d 872 (2003), the Montana supreme court held that a behavior modification plan used at its state prison violated the Montana constitution's guarantee of human dignity. Moreover, the Court held if the specific conditions of confinement "cause serious mental illness to be greatly exacerbated or if it deprives inmates of their sanity, then prison officials have deprived inmates of the basic necessity for human existence and have crossed into the realm of psychological torture."

Third, as Jessica Mitford points out, behavior modification and brainwashing of institutionalized populations may be immoral. If correctional authorities give a prison inmate a choice between spending the next 20 years in prison, or undergoing behavioral treatment and being released in a relatively short period of time, is there any real choice?

The questions in this section are compelling ones indeed. As you might imagine, there are very strong sentiments on both sides of this issue. For additional resources, see: Donald A. Dripps, "Fundamental Retribution Error: Criminal Justice and the Social Psychology of Blame," *Vanderbilt Law Review* (October 2003); Israel Goldiamond, "Toward a Constructional Approach to Social Problems: Ethical and Constitutional Issues Raised by Applied Behavior Analysis," *Behavior and Social Issues* (Spring 2002); Brian M. Maletzky and Cynthia Steinhauser, "A 25-Year Follow-Up of Cognitive/Behavioral Therapy with 7.275 Sexual Offenders," *Behavior Modification* (April 2002); Michael L. Prendergast, David Farabee, Jerome Cartier, and Susan Henkin, "Involuntary Treatment within a Prison Setting," *Criminal Justice and Behavior* (February 2002); Kathryn J. Fox, "Changing Violent Minds: Discursive Correction and Resistance in the Cognitive Treatment of Violent Offenders in Prison," *Social Problems* (February 1999); Bob Remington and Marina Remington, "Behavior Modification in Probation Work: A Review and Evaluation," *Criminal Justice and Behavior* (June 1987); Reid H. Montgomery, Jr., and Ellis C. MacDougall, "Curing Criminals: The High-Tech Prisons of Tomorrow," *The Futurist* (January/February 1986); Hugo Adam Bedau, "Physical Interventions to Alter Behavior in a Punitive Environment: Some Moral Reflections on New Technology," *The American Behavioral Scientist* (May/June 1975).

Additional resources include: Anthony Burgess, *A Clockwork Orange* (W.W. Norton, 1962, republished in 1986); Jessica Mitford, *Kind & Usual Punishment: The Prison Business* (Alfred A. Knopf, 1973); Robert Adams, *Abuses of Punishment* (St. Martin's Press, 1997); B.F. Skinner, *Beyond Freedom and Dignity* (Hackett, 1971); and George Orwell, *1984* (Signet Books, 1949, republished in 1990).

Contributors to This Volume

EDITOR

THOMAS J. HICKEY is a professor of criminology at the University of Tampa. He received his bachelor's degree from Providence College, masters and Ph.D. degrees from Sam Houston State University, and a law degree from the University of Oregon, School of Law. His areas of expertise include criminology and law, and he is the author of two books, *Criminal Procedure* (McGraw-Hill, 1998, 2001) and *Stand: Legal Issues* (Coursewise, 1999), as well as many journal articles. He is also a licensed attorney who specializes in the areas of labor law and tort litigation. Professor Hickey may be reached by e-mail at `thickey@ut.edu`.

AUTHORS

WILLIAM J. BRATTON, currently president of Carco Group, Inc., began his career as a police officer in Boston, Massachusetts, in 1970 and rose to superintendent of police by 1980. He was appointed Boston police commissioner in 1993 and police commissioner of New York City in 1994.

PAUL BUTLER is an associate professor of law at the George Washington University Law School. He also served in the Justice Department's Public Integrity Section for several years.

FRANCIS T. CULLEN is the Distinguished Research Professor of Criminal Justice at the University of Cincinnati in Cincinnati, Ohio.

EMILE DURKHEIM (1858–1917) was a French sociologist and one of the founders and leading figures of modern sociology. He was a professor of philosophy at the University of Bordeaux.

BARRY C. FELD is the Centennial Professor of Law at the University of Minnesota Law School, where he has been teaching since 1972, and the author of *Readings in Juvenile Justice Administration* (Oxford University Press, 1999).

JILL GORDON is on the faculty of the Virginia Commonwealth University Department of Criminal Justice. Her most resent research has focused on a prison devoted exclusively to treating juvenile substance abusers in Virginia and on diversion programs for juveniles.

JUDITH A. GREENE is a senior fellow of the Institute on Criminal Justice at the University of Minnesota Law School.

GORDON HAWKINS is senior fellow of the Earl Warren Legal Institute at the University of California at Berkeley.

RICHARD J. HERRNSTEIN (d. 1994) was the Edgar Pierce Professor of Psychology at Harvard University in Cambridge, Massachusetts, and a trustee for the Cambridge Center for Behavioral Studies.

GEORGE L. KELLING is a professor in the School of Criminal Justice at Rutgers University and a professor emeritus in the College of Criminal Justice at Northeastern University. He is coauthor, with Catherine M. Coles, of *Fixing Broken Windows: Restoring Order in American Cities* (Free Press, 1996).

RANDALL KENNEDY is a professor of law at Harvard Law School and the author of *Race, Crime and the Law* (Vintage Books, 1998).

BILLY LONG is an assistant professor of criminal justice at Kentucky Wesleyan College.

JOHN R. LOTT, JR., teaches criminal deterrence and law and economics at the University of Chicago Law School, where he is the John M. Olin Visiting Law and Economics Fellow.

MICHAEL J. LYNCH is a professor in the department of criminology at the University of South Florida. He has published extensively in the area of environmental crime, race and justice, and criminological theory. His most recent book, coauthored with Ronald G. Burns, is titled *The Sourcebook on Environmental Crime* (LFB, 2004). Professor Lynch has also served as division chair for the critical criminology section of the American Society of Criminology.

ELIZABETH H. McCONNELL is an associate professor in and chair of the department of criminal justice at Charleston Southern University in Charleston, South Carolina. She is coauthor, with Laura J. Moriarity, of *American Prisons: An Annotated Bibliography* (Greenwood, 1998).

JAMES V. McCONNELL, the late biologist and animal psychologist, was a professor who taught for many years at the University of Michigan. He founded the *Journal of Biological Psychology*, and was known for his research on planarians. McConnell was targeted by the Unibomber, Theodore Kaczynski, and suffered a hearing loss when a bomb, disguised as a manuscript, was opened at his home.

ROBERT K. MERTON, the late preeminent American sociologist, received his Ph.D. from Harvard University in 1936. He served as a professor at Harvard and at Columbia University. His prolific work focused not only on criminology and deviant behavior, but also on the effects of mass media on society. Merton wrote as well about the dysfunctional consequences of bureaucracy. He is widely regarded as one of the more influential social scientists of the twentieth century. Merton's works include *Social Theory and Social Structure* (Free Press, 1949, 1968) and *On Theoretical Sociology* (Free Press, 1967).

EUGENE H. METHVIN is the senior editor for *Reader's Digest.* He has reported on the American criminal justice system for more than 40 years.

JESSICA MITFORD, who immigrated to the United States after a privileged childhood in England, was a committed communist and a prolific writer. Her works included: *The American Way of Death* (1963), *The Trial of Dr. Spock* (1970), *Kind and Usual Punishment: The Prison Business* (1973), and *The Making of a Muckraker* (1979). She died in 1996.

DANIEL PATRICK MOYNIHAN is the former senior U.S. senator (D) from New York (1976–2001). He has held academic appointments at Cornell University, Syracuse University, and Harvard University.

CHARLES MURRAY is the Bradley Fellow at the American Enterprise Institute and the author of *Losing Ground* (Basic Books, 1986).

ETHAN A. NADELMANN is a highly respected critic of U.S. and international drug control policies. He received his B.A., J.D., and Ph.D. degrees in political science from Harvard University as well as a masters degree in international relations from the London School of Economics. In 1994, with the support of George Soros, he founded the Lindesmith Center, a leading drug policy institute. He currently serves as director of the Lindesmith Center-Drug Policy Foundation. Nadelmann's works have been published in *Science, Rolling Stone, National Review, The Public Interest, Daedalus,* and various other publications.

FRANK M. OCHBERG, a psychiatrist, is an adjunct professor of criminal justice and journalism and a clinical professor of psychiatry at Michigan State University. He is the author of *Post-Traumatic Therapy and Victims of Violence* (Brunner/Mazel, 1988).

ADRIAN RAINE is the Robert Grandford Wright Professor in the department of psychology, University of Southern California. He received his bachelor's degree in experimental psychology from Oxford University in 1977, and his D. Phil. in psychology from York University in England in 1982. After working as a prison psychologist, he became a university professor and in 1999, was named the Robert Grandford Wright Professor of Psychology at the University of Southern California. Dr. Raine's research has focused on the biosocial bases of violent behavior. He is a prolific writer, who has published numerous books and over 100 professional journal articles.

JEFFREY REIMAN is the William Fraser McDowell Professor of Philosophy at American University in Washington, D.C., and the author of *Justice and Modern Moral Philosophy* (Yale University Press, 1992).

PENNY A. ROBINETTE is an administrator at the Presbyterian Child Welfare Agency in Richmond, Kentucky.

VINCENT SCHIRALDI is founder and executive director of the Center on Juvenile and Criminal Justice and director of the Justice Policy Institute, a think tank in San Francisco and Washington, D.C., that analyzes crime policy.

JANELL D. SCHMIDT, supervisor of the Milwaukee County Child Protective Services, has worked with Lawrence W. Sherman on criminal justice research projects for the Crime Control Institute in Washington, D.C.

LAWRENCE W. SHERMAN is a professor of criminology in the Institute of Criminal Justice at the University of Maryland in College Park, Maryland, and president of the Crime Control Institute in Washington, D.C.

DAVID SHICHOR is a professor in the department of criminal justice at California State University, San Bernardino.

EVAN STARK is an associate professor of public administration and social work at Rutgers University in Newark, New Jersey.

JARED TAYLOR, president of the New Century Foundation, is an author and commentator on race in U.S. politics. He is also the editor of *American Renaissance* magazine. His works include *Paved with Good Intentions: The Failure of Race Relations in Contemporary America* (Carol & Graf, 1992).

BOB TREBILCOCK writes frequently for *Redbook* magazine on news and social issues.

KARI A. VANDERZYL is a graduate of the Northern Illinois University School of Law and is a licensed attorney in the state of Illinois.

ERNEST VAN DEN HAAG is a retired professor of jurisprudence and public policy. He has contributed more than 200 articles to magazines and sociology journals in the United States, England, France, and Italy, and he is the author of *Punishing Criminals: Concerning a Very Old and Painful Question* (Basic Books, 1978).

DAVID VON DREHLE is an art editor for *The Washington Post*. His publications include *Among the Lowest of the Dead* (Times Books, 1995).

JOHN P. WALTERS, the nation's "drug czar," became the director of the Office of National Drug Control Policy (ONDCP) in 2001. He controls all aspects of federal drug initiatives. Walters was formerly chief of staff for William Bennett, the former drug czar and conservative commentator, and has been responsible for the government's various anti-drug programs and has presided over a dramatic increase in federal spending for drug-control programs. His drug-control strategy has emphasized demand reduction and market disruption. Walters, who holds a B.A. from Michigan State University and an M.A. from the University of Toronto, has taught political science at Michigan State University and at Boston College.

GLAYDE WHITNEY, the late professor of psychology and neuroscience at Florida State University, taught behavior genetics and the history of science. He was also past-president of the Behavior Genetics Association.

JULIA WILKINS is a special education teacher and a freelance writer based in Buffalo, New York. She is the author of *Group Activities to Include Students With Special Needs: Developing Social Interactive Skills* (Corwin Press, 2000).

JAMES Q. WILSON is the James Collins Professor of Management and Public Policy at the University of California, Los Angeles, and chair of the board of directors of the Police Foundation. He is the author of *Bureaucracy: What Government Agencies Do and Why They Do It* (Basic Books, 1989).

LAWRENCE WRIGHT is a graduate of Tulane University and the American University in Cairo, where he taught English and received an M.A. in applied linguistics in 1969. He has worked for *Texas Monthly* and *Rolling Stone*. He has written several books and is currently writing a history of al-Queda, which is scheduled to be published in Fall 2006. Wright is co-author of *The Seige*, which starred Denzel Washington, Bruce Willis, and Annette Benning. He has won the New York University Olive Branch Award for international reporting as well as the Overseas Press Club's Ed Cunningham Award for best magazine reporting.

JASON ZIEDENBERG is a policy analyst with the Justice Policy Institute.

FRANKLIN E. ZIMRING is the William F. Simon Professor of Law and director of the Earl Warren Legal Institute at the University of California at Berkeley. His many publications include *American Youth Violence* (Oxford University Press, 2000).

HOWARD ZONANA is a professor of psychiatry in the School of Medicine at Yale University and director of the Law and Psychiatry Division of the Connecticut Mental Health Center. He is also the medical director of the American Academy of Psychiatry and the Law.

Index

Note: *Italic* page numbers indicate figures and tables.